Burt

In the Beginning

Decked out for the hunt, King Assurbanipal of Assyria pursues his quarry, as depicted in a bas-relief from the seventh century B.C.

In the Beginning
An Introduction to Archaeology

BRIAN M. FAGAN

University of California, Santa Barbara

Little, Brown and Company   Boston

Library of Congress Catalog Card No. 74–183044

First Printing

Published simultaneously in Canada
by Little, Brown & Company (Canada) Limited

Printed in the United States of America

Credits for Illustrations

Cover photo: Altamira prehistoric cave painting from Editorial Photocolor Archives

The sources for the text figures appear below, except for those given with the illustrations. The artwork has, for the most part, been redrawn; the artists are Richard H. Sanderson and New England Illustrators, Inc. The author wishes to thank the publishers, authors, photographers, and illustrators involved for their courtesy in granting permission to use their material. The figures without specified credits have been drawn specially for this book.

FRONTISPIECE: Hirmer Fotoarchiv, Munich, Germany. Courtesy of the Trustees of the British Museum, London. Used in *Crade of Civilization,* p. 63, © 1967 Time Inc.
CHAPTER 2: *2.2* (after Oakley) and *2.3* Redrawn from John Alexander, *The Directing of Archaeological Excavations,* Figs. 16a and 36; London: John Baker Publishers Limited, 1970. New York: Humanities Press, Inc. *2.4* and *2.10* After J. G. D. Clark, *Starr Carr,* Figs. 78 and 27b; London: Cambridge University Press, 1954. *2.6* After F. Clark Howell. Redrawn by permission of the American Anthropological Association from *American Anthropologist,* "Observations on the Earlier Phases of the European Lower Paleolithic," Vol. 68, No. 2, Pt. 2, 1966, Fig. 16. *2.7* After I. W. Cornwall, *Bones for the Archaeologist,* Fig. 22; London: Phoenix House, 1956. Redrawn by permission of Winant Towers, Ltd., London. *2.8* and *2.9* Adapted from Kenneth P. Oakley, *Frameworks for Dating Fossil Man* (Chicago: Aldine Publishing Company: London: Weidenfeld and Nicolson, 1964), Figs. 22 and 7; copyright © 1964 by Kenneth P. Oakley. *2.11* Redrawn from *Prehistoric Europe: The Economic Basis* by J. G. D. Clark, Fig. 145, with the permission of the publishers, Stanford University Press. Copyright © 1952 by J. G. D. Clark; London: Methuen and Company, Ltd. *2.12* Redrawn from F. E. Zeuner, *Dating the Past,* Fig. 3; London: Methuen and Company, Ltd., 1958. *2.13* After Hans E. Suess, "Secular Variations of the Cosmic-Ray-Produced Carbon 14 in the Atmosphere and Their Interpretations," *Journal of Geophysical Research,* 70:23, 1965, Fig. 4.
CHAPTER 3: *3.1* Sir Mortimer Wheeler and the Society of Antiquaries of London.
CHAPTER 4: *4.1* From *Gentleman's Magazine,* 1852, p. 569. *4.2, 4.3,* and *4.10* Sir Mortimer Wheeler and the Society of Antiquaries of London. *4.6* and *4.8* After Ivor Noël Hume, *Historical Archaeology,* Figs. 10 and 23; New York: Alfred A. Knopf, Inc., 1968. Redrawn by permission of the author, the publisher, and Curtis Brown, Ltd. Copyright © 1968 by Ivor Noël Hume. *4.9* Brian M. Fagan.
CHAPTER 5: *5.1* J. Desmond Clark. *5.2* After Richard G. Klein, *Man and Culture in the Late Pleistocene,* Fig. 50; San Francisco: Chandler Publishing Co., 1969. *5.3* J. Desmond Clark. Used in *Early Man,* p. 70, © 1965 Time, Inc. *5.4* After J. G. D. Clark, *Star Carr,* Fig. 4; London: Cambridge University Press, 1954. *5.5* and *5.6* After Charles B. M. McBurney, *The Haua Fteah (Cyrenaica),* Pl. I.2(a), and Fig. I.3; London: Cambridge University Press, 1967, *5.7* From *Early Man,* p. 165, photograph by Robert Morton, © 1965 Time Inc. *5.10, 5.20, 5.21,* and *5.32* Redrawn from John Alexander, *The Directing of Archaeological Excavations,* Figs. 33, 25, 34, 58; London: John Baker Publishers Limited, 1970; New York: Humanities Press, Inc. *5.11* and *5.23* Copyright reserved: Winchester Excavations Committee. *5.12* Redrawn from *Prehistoric Europe: The Economic Basis* by J. G. D. Clark, Fig. 66, with the permission of the publishers, Stanford University Press. Copyright © 1952 by J. G. D. Clark; London: Methuen and Company Ltd. *5.14, 5.15,* and *5.30* Brian M. Fagan. *5.16* After Sir Mortimer Wheeler, *Archaeology from the Earth,* Fig. 16;

Oxford: Clarendon Press, 1954. *5.17* and *5.18* Adapted from Stuart Piggott, *Ancient Europe* (Chicago: Aldine Publishing Company, 1965), Figs. 21 and 67; copyright © Stuart Piggott, 1965. Edinburgh: Edinburgh University Press. *5.19* Sir Mortimer Wheeler and the Society of Antiquaries of London. *5.22* and *5.33* After Sir Mortimer Wheeler in John Alexander, *The Directing of Archaeological Excavations*, Figs. 50 and 60; London: John Baker Publishers Limited, 1970; New York: Humanities Press, Inc. *5.25, 5.26, 5.29,* and *5.31* Sir Mortimer Wheeler (*5.29* and *5.31* copyright Society of Antiquaries of London). *5.27* Patricia M. Christie. *5.34* After Ivor Noël Hume, *Historical Archaeology*, Fig. 15; New York: Alfred A. Knopf, Inc., 1968. Redrawn by permission of the author, the publisher, and Curtis Brown, Ltd. Copyright © 1968 by Ivor Noël Hume. 5.35 Wilfred Shawcross.

CHAPTER 6: *6.1* After Charles B. M. McBurney, *The Haua Fteah (Cyrenaica)*, Fig. II.6; London: Cambridge University Press, 1967. *6.2* and *6.5* After J. G. D. Clark, *Star Carr*, Figs. 8 and 73; London: Cambridge University Press, 1954. *6.3* and *6.17* After Sonia Cole, *The Neolithic Revolution*, Figs. 25 and 6; London, 1959. By permission of the Trustees of the British Museum (Natural History). *6.8* Redrawn from M. L. Ryder, *Animal Bones in Archaeology*, 1969, Figs. 5 and 6; Oxford: Blackwell Scientific Publications Ltd. *6.9* and *6.18* Copyright reserved: University Museum of Archaeology and Ethnology, Cambridge, England. *6.10* After S. von Heberstain, *Rerum Moscoviti carum commentarii*, Berlin (1549). *6.11* After Sir Arthur Evans, *The Palace of Minos at Knossos*, London, 1921, by permission of Agathon Press Inc., New York. *6.12* Courtesy of The Oriental Institute of the University of Chicago. Used in *Cradle of Civilization*, p. 89, © 1967 Time Inc. *6.13* After N. de G. Davies, *The Rock Tombs of El Armarna*—V, London, 1908. *6.16* and *6.26* After J. G. D. Clark, *Aspects of Prehistory*, Figs. 12 and 9, Berkeley, 1970. Originally published by the University of California Press; redrawn by permission of The Regents of the University of California. *6.19, 6.21,* and *6.25* Redrawn from *Prehistoric Europe: The Economic Basis* by J. G. D. Clark, Figs. 44, 17, and 11, with the permission of the publishers, Stanford University Press. Copyright © 1952 by J. G. D. Clark. London: Methuen and Company Ltd. *6.20* and *6.22* Brian M. Fagan. *6.23* South African Archaeological Bulletin, Vol. V, No. 18, June 1950, cover design. *6.24* Patricia Vinnecombe, "A Fishing Scene from the Tsoelike River, South-Eastern Basutoland," *South African Archaeological Bulletin*, Vol. 15, No. 57, March 1960, p. 15, Fig. 1.

CHAPTER 7: *7.1* From *Early Man*, p. 163, drawing by Jay H. Matternes, © 1965 Time Inc. *7.2, 7.4, 7.5,* and *7.12* Redrawn from *Early Man*, pp. 105, 110, and 111, drawings by Lowell Hess, © 1965 Time Inc. *7.6* After Derek Roe, *Prehistory*, Figs. 10 and 11, © 1970 by Derek Roe. Originally published by the University of California Press; redrawn by permission of The Regents of the University of California and Macmillan London and Basingstoke. Based on Fig. 7, No. 9, and Fig. 26, No. 3, in *The Swanscombe Skull, A Survey of Research on a Pleistocene Site*, Royal Anthropological Institute, *Occasional Paper, No. 20. 7.7* Derek Roe. Copyright Pitt Rivers Museum, University of Oxford. *7.8* After J. M. Coles and E. S. Higgs, *The Archaeology of Early Man*, Fig. 81; London: Faber and Faber Ltd., 1968; New York: Praeger Publishers, Inc. *7.9, 7.10* and *7.11* After F. Bordes, *The Old Stone Age*, Figs. 34, 54, and 55; London: Weidenfeld & Nicolson Ltd., 1968. *7.13* After G. H. S. Bushnell, *The First Americans*, Fig. 2; copyright © 1968 Thames and Hudson Ltd., London. *7.14* After J. G. D. Clark, *Star Carr*, Fig. 35; London: Cambridge University Press, 1954. *7.15* Olmec jade ceremonial axe, 9th–4th c. B.C., courtesy of the Trustees of the British Museum, London, photograph by Derek Bayes. From *Ancient America*, p. 32, © 1967 Time Inc. *7.16* After J. G. D. Clark, *Aspects of Prehistory*, Fig. 6, Berkeley, 1970. Originally published by the University of California Press; redrawn by permission of The Regents of the University of California. *7.17, 7.23, 7.26, 7.27,* and *7.30* Brian M. Fagan. *7.18* Kenneth MacLeish. Used in *Early Man*, p. 59, © 1965 Time Inc. *7.19* J. Vertut. *7.20* and *7.24* Redrawn from Gordon R. Willey, *An Introduction to Archaeology*, Volume One: *North and Middle America*, © 1966, Figs. 7–11, 7–12, and 3–98, by permission of Prentice-Hall, Inc., Englewood Cliffs, N.J. *7.29* Adapted from Stuart Piggott, *Ancient Europe* (Chicago: Aldine Publishing Company, 1965), Fig. 66; copyright © Stuart Piggott, 1965. Edinburgh: Edinburgh University Press. *7.31* After Kenneth P. Oakley, *Man the Toolmaker*, Fig. 12; London, 1949. By permission of the Trustees of the British Museum (Natural History). *7.32* From *Invitation to Archaeology* by James Deetz, Fig. 9. Copyright © 1967 by James Deetz. Redrawn by permission of the author and Doubleday & Company, Inc.

CHAPTER 8: *8.1* After Sir John Evans from J. G. D. Clark, *Archaeology and Society*, Fig. 18; London: Methuen and Company Ltd., 1939; reprinted by Barnes and Noble, New York. *8.2* After Derek Roe, *Prehistory*, Fig. 99, © 1970 by Derek Roe. Originally published by the University of California Press; redrawn by permission of The Regents of the University of California and Macmillan London and Basingstoke. Also originally published in the *Proceedings of the Prehistoric Society*, 1963, 29:258–325, and the *Guide Catalogue of the Neolithic and Bronze Age Collections in Devizes Museum*, p. 130. *8.3* After James A. Ford, technical manual 1, *A Quantitative Method for Deriving Cultural Chronology*, Fig. 8, Pan American Union, published by the Organization of American States, Washington, D.C., 1962. *8.4, 8.5,* and *8.6* From *Invitation to Archaeology* by James Deetz, Figs. 5, 7, and 10. Copyright © 1967 by James Deetz. Redrawn by permission of the author and Doubleday and Company, Inc. *8.7* After Richard G. Klein, *Man and Culture in the Late Pleistocene,* Fig. 60; San Francisco: Chandler Publishing Co., 1969.

CHAPTER 9: *9.1* Photograph by Roloff Beny. Used in *Ancient America,* p. 47, © 1967 Time Inc.

CHAPTER 10: *10.1* Woodcut by Hans Burgkmaier the Elder (1508). *10.2* From F. Péron, *Voyage de découvertes aux terres australes,* Paris, 1807–1816. *10.3* From Robert Fitzroy, *Narrative of the Surveying Voyages of H.M.S. "Adventure" and "Beagle" between 1826 and 1836,* London, 1839. *10.4* Courtesy of Musée de l'Homme, Paris. Used in *Early Man,* p. 145, © 1965 Time Inc. *10.5* Ralph Morse, *Life* Magazine, © Time Inc.

CHAPTER 11: *11.1* Martin Chambi. Used in *Ancient America,* pp. 136–137, © 1967 Time Inc. *11.2* Derek Roe. Copyright Pitt Rivers Museum, University of Oxford.

CHAPTER 12: *12.1* Dmitri Kessel, *Life* Magazine, © Time Inc. *12.2* Rhodesia National Tourist Board.

For Judy
with love—and not least
because of Catticus

Preface

This introduction to archaeology approaches the subject both from the historical angle and from the perspective of the latest scientific methods. Its aim is to provide a comprehensive summary of the methods and techniques of archaeology for beginning students and interested persons who have not encountered the prehistoric past before.

In the Beginning summarizes the early development of archaeology, chronological methods, site survey and excavation, and analysis of prehistoric economies and artifacts. A major section of the book traces the history of archaeological theory from the Age of Romance to the 1970s, putting the latest advances in the subject into a wider perspective.

Archaeology has witnessed a knowledge explosion in the past decade and we face a major shift in research objectives in which both sophisticated systems models and quantitative methods will play an increasingly important part. Future archaeologists will undoubtedly need a grounding in scientific method and explanation,[1] as well as statistical techniques—these topics, while discussed, are not treated exhaustively here.

Included are a glossary of technical terms and a bibliography that

---

[1] For a brief synthesis of explanation in archaeology, see Patty Jo Watson, Steven A. LeBlanc, and Charles L. Redman, *Explanation in Archaeology,* New York, 1971.

Some reading in the works of philosophers of science belonging to the logical, positivist school is desirable for professionally oriented students. Two basic references are: Carl G. Hempel, *Philosophy of Natural Science* (New York, 1966), and Ernst Nagel, *The Structure of Science: Problems in the Logic of Scientific Explanation* (New York, 1966).

lists books covering the prehistoric archaeology of different areas of the world; these works could be read in conjunction with this volume. Each chapter is supplemented with notes at the back of the book, which can be used to base further discussion or to suggest more exhaustive reading on particular topics. The notes and bibliography offer greater flexibility in learning than serried rows of uncritically presented references.

This book has been written from predominantly English language sources for a number of reasons. The recent spate of archaeological literature has been enormous and my reading has been necessarily selective and predominantly in English. Readers are directed toward English language sources as much as possible as this is, in most cases, their mother tongue. Those interested in a more detailed knowledge of a particular topic are strongly advised to consult a specialist before wading into archaeological literature in other languages. Inevitably, this volume has some bias toward the achievements and writings of English-speaking archaeologists, an emphasis that evolved from linguistic abilities and time, rather than nationalistic propensities. The horsemen of Pazyryk and the Shang tombs are as much part of archaeology as Cahokia and medieval Winchester.

I am very grateful to all those colleagues and students who have commented on this book in draft form, especially Drs. Ralph M. Rowlett, Albert Spaulding, and Barbara Voorhies. I am deeply indebted to Dr. Elvin Hatch for his constant advice and criticism of Chapters 10 and 11. Valuable contributions were also made by Michael Bisson and my wife. Mrs. Linda Cordell was of the greatest assistance with Part Three, and her advice has been invaluable. Mrs. Phyllis Frezin shouldered the unenviable task of typing my complicated arabesques. Miss Freda Alexander was an able and efficient editor in Boston. This book would never have been written without Milton Johnson at the other end of the telephone—I have enjoyed both his encouragement and his lunches.

Contents

In the Beginning

Part One
Digging up the Past

A mere hole in the ground, which of all sights is perhaps the least vivid and dramatic, is enough to grip their attention for hours at a time.

P. G. Wodehouse, *A Damsel in Distress*

Chapter 1
Introduction

"And God said, 'Let us make man in our image, after our likeness: and let them have dominion over the fish of the sea, and over the fowl of the air, and over the cattle, and over all the earth, and over every creeping thing that creepeth upon the earth.'" Thus the first chapter of Genesis, a majestic panorama of the story of the Creation, gives an account of man's origins familiar to centuries of scholars and worshippers. Indeed, man has probably always been curious about his origins, and sought justification for his presence on this planet. This intellectual curiosity about his antecedents has led man to historical inquiry and to development of archaeology as a serious discipline for studying prehistoric culture, as well as to historiography which is a major concern of twentieth-century scholars. Lively speculation about the past reflects man's attempts to create theoretical models of his ancestry, either based on philosophical models or, more recently, on scientific fact.

To many people, the past is featureless, without any memorable events to partition it or bring it into focus. Their perspective covers only several generations of family history or, conceivably, a few centuries of written history dealing with the deeds of kings and politicians. To most Americans, the history of the American Indian involves them little emotionally, for their identification with the New World is a provincial one, bounded by the frontiers of their own society and its limited history. The written history of American Indians, on the other hand, hardly exists, but their ancestry extends many thousands of years back into a still imperfectly known past. Many

3

black Africans are conscious that their societies have existed for centuries, and retain a lively curiosity about tribal history, listening eagerly to the accounts which tribal historians have handed down orally from generation to generation. Only in recent years have oral historians and archaeologists begun to recover Africa's unwritten past, thus giving its new nations a longer perspective and greater national identity.

Studying archaeology is one of the primary ways in which mankind's featureless past can be put into correct philosophical perspective. Yet the researches of archaeologists remain surprisingly unfamiliar to the public, which pictures the archaeologist as a grey-bearded treasure hunter, perpetually digging around pyramids. Nothing could be further from the truth. Archaeological research has become meticulous, laborious, and complicated, with many startling achievements to its credit. Man's origins have been traced back over 5 million years. Human settlement in the New World has been dated to over 20,000 years ago, while farming villages in the Near East have been excavated and dated to nearly 8000 B.C. Major changes in human culture have been traced through millennia of prehistoric time, while increasingly accurate methods of dating the past have been developed and applied to archaeological sites all over the world. The archaeologist's work is transforming featureless prehistory into a fascinating landscape of hominid evolution, cultural change, and technological advance— reflecting man's increased control over his natural environment. The first steps toward a world prehistory have been taken, giving new perspectives of time and human history, as well as exciting theoretical models of man's past.

THE FIRST ARCHAEOLOGISTS

The intellectual curiosity of early scholars about their past was the first stage in developing archaeology as a serious scientific discipline. Although, in the sixth century B.C., the Babylonian king Nabonidus did engage in some antiquarian research and made excavations at Ur-of-the-Chaldees, he was hardly an archaeologist. Greek writers like Herodotus travelled widely, and came into contact with barbarian peoples living on the fringes of the Ancient World, who were still living in prehistory. Herodotus left valuable, if picturesque, descriptions of the Scythians and their material culture, confirmed by excavations in modern times, but no one set out to make a systematic study of European or Saharan tribes. Although neither the Greeks nor Romans excavated for the past, the former began to reach the stage of rational reflection about man's origins, a necessary stage before the impetus to study the past systematically. Their reflections probably arose from their concern with the relationship between primitive peoples and their own comfortable civilization. One philosophical model of early man was that of Hesiod,[1] * who wrote a book entitled *Works and Days* in the eighth century B.C. He visualized man's past as five distinct stages. An age of Gold and the Immortals was comprised of people who "dwelt in ease and peace upon their lands with many good things, rich in flocks and loved by the blessed gods." An age of Silver found man infinitely less respectable. An age of Bronze arrived when man originated from "a brazen race sprung from ash trees, who delighted in war." These men were the first to eat animal food and to use bronze for their armor and houses, as well as their implements—iron was not yet in use. The last two ages included that of the Epic Heroes, who were a distinct improvement on their predecessors, and the age of Iron, one of terrible sorrow when man never ceased laboring during the day and perished by night. Hesiod's speculations are typical of ancient scholars, who approached the unknown past with a philosophy tempered with inherited knowledge of recent prehistory, a familiarity with Homer, and a wide geographic background. A similar concept of ages, this time of stone, bronze, and iron, is that of a Chinese writer in A.D. 52, perhaps derived from a folk memory of prehistoric achievement.

Archaeology really developed in the last two hundred years, but has its roots in a heightened intellectual curiosity about the past some centuries earlier.[2] At the end of the Middle Ages and during the Renaissance there was a revival of interest in the Classical world. Renewed study of Greek and Roman literature revealed fascinating accounts of hitherto unknown peoples who were living in much of Central and Northern Europe during Classical times, so an additional chapter of man's past was suddenly added to the comfortable world of the Middle Ages. Sixteenth-century scholars and travelers began to study the archaeological remains of the Greek and Roman civilizations.

During succeeding centuries the discovery of Classical antiquities led to a dramatic increase in interest in the past. Men of leisure and wealth traveled widely in Italy and Greece studying antiquities and acquiring many examples of Classical sculpture and statuary. These visible remains of the past turned men's minds toward their own origins. Frustrated Classical antiquarians and other scholars who remained at home began to speculate about ancient British and European history, too; they acquired an active interest in the conspicuous ar-

* See pages 320–321 for notes to Chapter 1.

chaeological sites which dotted the European landscape. In England, monuments such as Stonehenge and Avebury were examined; burial mounds were found scattered throughout the rolling grasslands of Wessex. Taking the first steps in the rediscovery of prehistory, local antiquarians and topographers traveled widely throughout Europe examining antiquities and describing them; they speculated on their origins, liberally using legends and folklore. These gentlemen did not excavate the sites they discovered, they merely described them. (Figures 1.1–1.6 show the locations of most sites mentioned in the text.)

One famous antiquarian was William Camden (1551–1623),[3] who was successively a schoolmaster and then an authority on heraldry. Camden traveled extensively in Great Britain, studying its antiquities and describing archaeological sites. He was a meticulous observer and even recorded crop marks—a phenomenon widely used today in archaeological reconnaissance from the air—for he observed the streets of the Roman town of Silchester from the differential growth marks in the corn fields growing on the site. In 1586 Camden published a volume entitled *Britannia*, the first complete directory to the antiquities of Britain. His purpose was clearly set out: "to renew the memory of what was old, illustrate what was obscure, and settle what was doubtful, and recover some certainty in our affairs." The great geographer Abraham Ortelius begged him to "acquaint the world with Britain, that ancient island; that is to restore Britain to its Antiquities and its Antiquities to Britain."

Two other celebrated antiquarians were John Aubrey (1626–1697), a Wiltshire squire, and William Stukeley (1687–1765),[4] both of whom carried on the tradition so ably started by Camden. John Aubrey and his contemporaries were much influenced by the romantic accounts of primitive peoples described by explorers and voyagers to the New World, Africa, and Asia. The cartographer John Speed published vivid accounts of the strange customs of American Indians, who, with other strange peoples, were described as living in a vague kind of romantic savagery. The concept of the "Noble Savage" came into fashion, and inevitably affected antiquarian writing and interpretation (see Figure 10.1). Sober antiquarian observation combined with fanciful speculation and classical allusion to bring the past to life. John Aubrey writing at his best typifies such seventeenth-century expression:

> Let us imagine then what kind of countrie this was in the time of the
> Ancient Britons. By the nature of the soil, which is a sour woodsere land,
> very natural for the production of akes especially, one may conclude that

Fig. 1.1   *Archaeological sites in the United States and Mesoamerica. The Virú Valley in Peru does not appear on the map.*

this North Division was a shady dismal wood; and the inhabitants almost as savage as the Beasts whose skins were their only rayment. The language British, which for the honour of it was spoken from the Orcades to Italie and Spain. The Boats of the Avon (which signifies River) were basketts of twigges covered with an oxe skin; which the poore people in Wales use

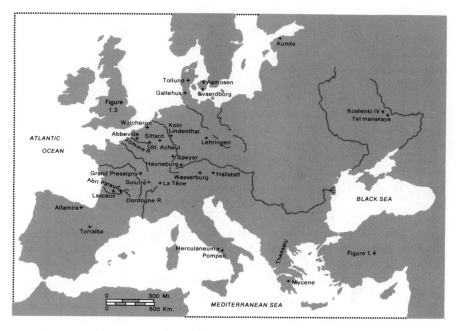

Fig. 1.2   Archaeological sites in Europe.

to this day. They call them curricles. Within this Shire I believe that there were several Reguli which often made war upon another; and the great ditches which run on the Plaines and elsewhere so many miles (not unlikely) their boundaries; and withal served for defense against the incursions of their enemies, as the Pict's wall, Offa's Ditch; and that in China, to compare things small to great. Their religion is at large described by Caesar. Their priests were Druids some of their temples I pretend to have restored, as Avebury, Stonehenge, etc. as also British sepulchres. Their way of fighting is lively sett down by Caesar. Their camps with their way of meeting I have sett down in another place. They knew the use of iron. . . . They were two or three degrees I suppose less savage than the Americans. . . . The Romans subdued and civilized them.[5]

Aubrey and Stukeley, the latter remembered above all for his preoccupation with the ancient British cult of the Druids, described by Caesar, were at a loss to interpret the numerous sites they described. In the end they were forced to interpret their finds in terms of their only available historical source, the Classical past. But the seventeenth-century antiquarian was beginning to recognize that there was a long period of prehistoric time preceding the Roman occupation of Europe. It began to seem that archaeology was the best prospect for uncovering earlier times.

Fig. 1.3   Archaeological sites in the United Kingdom.

THE ANTIQUITY OF MAN

One problem that antiquarians of the seventeenth and eighteenth centuries faced was a complete lack of information on how long man had been living on the earth. The prehistoric past was confusing, for archaeologists had no means of dating prehistory, nor had they any chronological depth for their finds. Until these two requirements

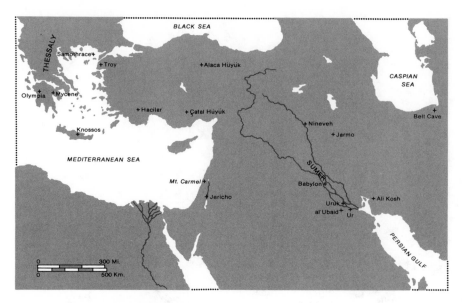

Fig. 1.4   Archaeological sites in the Near East.

were satisfied, archaeologists could not introduce order into the incredible jumble of antiquities beginning to crowd the collectors' cabinets and the pages of antiquarian topographies.

One problem was the dogma of the Christian church. The first chapter of Genesis stated that God created the world and man in six days. The story of Adam and Eve provided an entirely consistent explanation for the Creation of Man and the world's population. The Bible's early chapters are full of complicated genealogical tables for the early families who populated the earth. Men attempted to use the tables for calculating the date of the Flood and the Creation. In 1650 Archbishop James Ussher used the genealogies in the Old Testament to calculate that the world was created in 4004 B.C. This was refined by Dr. John Lightfoot of Cambridge who published a monograph in 1642 in which he declared that man was created at 9 A.M. on October 23, 4004 B.C.[6] These calculations and theories received almost universal acceptance and became a dogmatic canon defended with almost fanatical frenzy in the nineteenth century. It was a comfortable theory which allowed approximately 4,000 years for all prehistoric time. All kinds of romantic legends were concocted to fill these 4,000 years, in order to produce some explanation for the chaotic jumble of antiquities found both by surface discovery and, increasingly during the eighteenth century, by excavations.

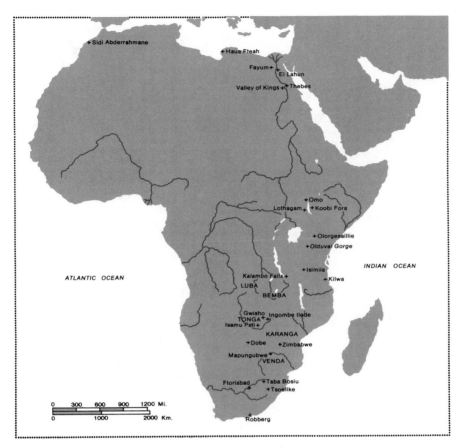

Fig. 1.5   *Archaeological sites in Africa.*

Excavation became popular with those unable to afford the expense of a grand tour to the Mediterranean. Local squires began to excavate the burial mounds and other antiquities on their property. One was English landowner Sir Richard Colt-Hoare, who dug no less than 379 burial mounds in the early nineteenth century, not only recording his observations with care, but also distinguishing between different types of burial, as well as original and later interments. He published his archaeological sites in detail, as part of a history of Wiltshire county, dealing specifically with the archaeological record as opposed to folklore and family histories. But, after ten years' work, he was forced to confess total ignorance as to the builders of these burial mounds: "We have evidence of the very high antiquity of our Wiltshire barrows but none respecting the tribes to whom they appertain, that

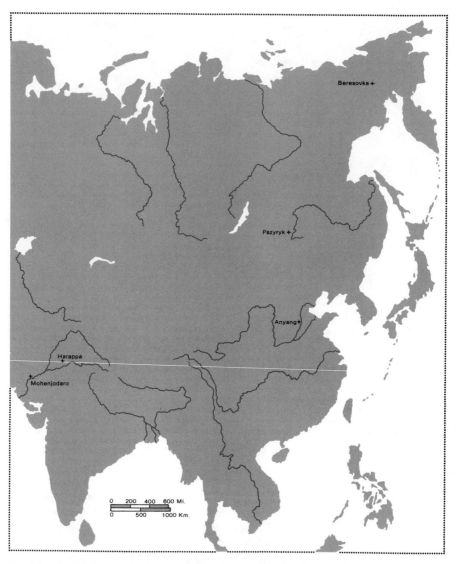

Fig. 1.6   Archaeological sites in Asia. Galatea Bay, Auckland, New Zealand, does not appear on the map.

can rest on solid foundations."[7] So he ascribed the prehistoric sites of Wiltshire to the Ancient Britons. No one had as yet found a way of putting in order the 4,000 years of prehistory alleged to exist by Biblical scholars.

Discoveries were beginning to come to light, however, which threw serious doubt on Ussher's dating. Ever since the sixteenth century, discoveries had been made both of extinct animals' bones and also of stone tools whose shapes differed so from natural rocks that it was difficult to explain them away. A number of authorities interpreted such rocks as thunderbolts, or meteorites. Others, however, such as the sixteenth-century scholar, Mercati, disagreed and called them weapons used by peoples ignorant of the use of iron.[8] Seventeenth-century antiquarians like Sir William Dugdale and Dr. Robert Plot believed that these stone tools were weapons used by the Ancient Britons before metallurgy was known. In the same century, Isaac de la Peyrère described the so-called thunderbolts as the tools of men who dated before the time of Adam; his book was burned in public. These finds, mainly of isolated tools, were attracting attention among scholars interested in the past, but no one as yet recognized them as evidence for man's high antiquity.

Then people began to find the bones of monstrous extinct animals such as the elephant and hippopotamus in European river gravel beds, in direct association with the very stones described by the antiquarians as the tools of ancient man. In 1715 John Bagford reported the discovery of a stone axe and elephant bones found in London gravel beds by a man called Conyers. The finder described the tool as that of an ancient Briton who did not know how to use metal, but Bagford said the elephant was Roman.

A far more significant discovery was made by a country squire in Suffolk named John Frere. On June 22, 1797, Frere wrote to the Secretary of the Society of Antiquaries describing and enclosing some stone implements found in a gravel pit at Hoxne. His letter and finds were published in the Society's journal. The tools consisted of a series of what are now known as Acheulian hand axes which were found 3.7 meters (12 feet) below the surface in direct association with the bones of extinct animals. Frere described them: "They are, I think, evidently weapons of war fabricated and used by a people who had not the use of metals. . . . The situation in which these weapons were found may tempt us to refer them to a very remote period indeed, even beyond that of the present world."[9]

John Frere's remarks were noted but forgotten. By this time people were familiar with stone implements but they were not ready to accept the idea that they came from a remote past beyond that of the comfortable world described by Sir Thomas Browne in 1635: "Time we may comprehend 'tis but five days elder than ourselves and hath the same Horoscope with the World." The Biblical story of the Creation still had a great hold on scientists of the time. In the early nineteenth century, people were still vociferously supporting Archbishop Ussher's chronology for the Creation. Typically, William Paley wrote his *Natural*

Theology in 1802, in which he endeavored to prove that man had inhabited the world for 6,000 years and that it "teemed with delighted existence"—a beautiful world inhabited by beautiful people.[10] By the late eighteenth century, a serious anomaly between the archaeological record and theological canon was increasingly apparent. The antiquarians were confused by a lack of time depth, and had no means of classifying the past, and were mystified by the increasing frequency with which stone tools were being found in contexts that, theologically speaking, were impossible. They lacked a chronology for the period between written history and 4004 B.C., and failed to realize that cultural reconstruction was possible in prehistory. Man's high antiquity had to be proven and a means of measuring prehistoric time devised before archaeology came into its own as a serious, scientific discipline.

The events which led up to the recognition of the antiquity of man resulted from a number of basic discoveries in biology, geology, and paleontology.[11] Vertebrate paleontology was not studied much until the eighteenth century, when a remarkable Frenchman, Jacques Cuvier (1769–1832) began a lifetime's work on fossil mammals. The first great paleontologist, Cuvier studied the fossil records of rocks and the geological history of the world by using his animals as type indicators for different strata, distinguishing periods when particular species such as dinosaurs had been dominant. In so doing he denied stoutly that man also existed in the fossil record. Instead, his interpretation of the earth's history was based on the theory that there had been a series of great catastrophes which had resulted in the destruction of one fauna and the creation of another. The Biblical Flood was the latest catastrophic event in a long series of cataclysms. But at the same time, William "Strata" Smith (1769–1839), a geologist, was beginning to study the stratification of the earth. He recognized that the geological processes of erosion, accumulation, weathering, and tectonic movement, which were still occurring in his time, were far more likely agents of geological change than successive catastrophes. Smith produced a complicated table of geological time in which he identified a large number of different fossil animal types. He stressed that the rocks of the earth had formed as a result of continuous natural geological processes without the catastrophic changes proposed by Cuvier and others. In 1785, James Hutton (1726–1797) published his *Theory of the Earth,* in which he supported Smith's findings and proposed that the earth was formed by natural processes. This theory became known as the doctrine of uniformitarianism, and caused immediate controversy, dividing geologists into two distinct camps: one accepted the new doctrine, but the other was made up of ardent catastrophists, the most famous of whom was Dean William Buckland (1784–1856). His *Geology and Mineralogy Considered in Relation to Natural Theology* appeared in 1836 and became a best-seller. It set out to prove that the geological record was confirmation of the "power, wisdom and goodness of God as manifested in creation." The issue came to a head in the 1830s as a result of the publication of Sir Charles Lyell's *Principles of Geology*, produced in three volumes between 1830–1833. Lyell synthesized the latest data from geological sources and accepted the new theories in general terms; his book reached a popular audience and, gradually, uniformitarianism achieved much wider acceptance.[12]

The theory of uniformitarianism suggested that there was no reason at all why man should not have been living on the earth for far longer than the six thousand years of Ussher's chronology. This meant that one could readily accept the contemporaneity of man and extinct animals, an association of which many scientists were now finding increasingly numerous examples in different localities. But not until nearly twenty years after the publication of Lyell's volumes was the antiquity of man finally accepted by the scientific world.

Lyell's work also had a profound effect on Charles Darwin who published *The Origin of Species* in 1859.[13] Charles Lyell used the philosophy of gradual change in his geological textbook when he described the different types of fossils found in the successive strata of the earth. His conclusions assisted Darwin in his formulation of the theories of evolution and natural selection. The latter was able to demonstrate that life and animal forms could change as the result of natural selection through the survival of the fittest. This was a far more logical explanation than that of the paleontological catastrophists.

In the 1820s some excavations in English caves led to further discoveries of man and extinct animals. Father J. MacEnery excavated at Kent's Cavern near Torquay in Devon in 1824–1829. He found the remains of extinct animals associated with stone implements; the layer in which they were found was sealed by a zone of stalagmite, a cave deposit having the consistency of cement, which takes a long time to form. MacEnery discussed his finds with Dean Buckland, who refused to accept the contemporaneity of the bones and stones and insisted that Ancient Britons had made ovens in the stalagmite, thereby introducing their implements into the older, lower levels.

While MacEnery did not publish his results for fear of ridicule, a Frenchman named Jacques Boucher de Perthes was not afraid to do so.[14] In 1837, de Perthes, who was a customs officer at Abbeville in northwestern France, began collecting stone implements and fossils from the gravels of the Somme River. Immediately, he began to find hand axes and the bones of extinct animals in the same sealed gravel beds in such numbers that he was convinced that he had found pre-Flood man. He insisted that human beings had lived before the last catastrophic cataclysm to overwhelm the world, before the start of Ussherian time. De Perthes's findings were ridiculed when he published them in 1847, but he persisted in his investigations until word of his discoveries came to the ears of two eminent English scientists John Evans and Joseph Prestwich, who decided to visit Boucher de Perthes at Abbeville in 1859. They examined his findings and his sites and published papers upon their return to England which fully supported de Perthes's findings. In June, 1859, Evans spoke to the Society of Antiquaries in London; his paper contained this statement: "This much appears established beyond doubt, that in a period of antiquity remote beyond any of which we have hitherto found traces, this portion of the globe was peopled by man."[15]

In 1858 and 1859 a schoolmaster, William Pengelly, excavated at Kent's Cavern again, this time on behalf of a committee of the British Association for the Advancement of Science. He dug in a cave near the neighboring town of Brixham and discovered flint tools in association with the bones of lion, cave bear, mammoth, rhinoceros, and reindeer. Pengelly's findings, supporting those of de Perthes, finally dispersed the remaining confusion. There followed a rapid and fairly general acceptance of the idea, as a scientific fact, that man had been living on this earth longer than 4004 b.c., the date compounded by Archbishop Ussher and his successors. The new, potentially long chronology for man was made easier by the publication of Darwin's theory of natural selection, itself widely accepted by his fellow scientists soon after publication. Darwin himself was cautious in *The Origin of Species:* "Light will be thrown on the origin of man and his history." But Thomas Huxley, Darwin's most ardent supporter, went even further. Acceptance of Darwin's views, he said, "will extend by long epochs the most liberal estimate that has yet been made of the Antiquity of Man."[16] Apart from the religious controversies, however, people began to realize that the past before the advent of written records was knowable, and that it was possible to measure the enormous time scales going back to when man lived at the same time as extinct animals.

ARCHAEOLOGY IN THE NEW WORLD

With the widespread acceptance of the antiquity of man, archaeology spread its frontiers rapidly. The history of New World archaeology is intimately bound up with the development of prehistoric research in

Europe.[17] Speculation about the inhabitants of the New World was rife from the days of the earliest European settlement, a time when the perspectives of Western civilization were being widened rapidly. The Americas were inhabited by strange races whose civilizations were in some respects similar to, yet in others very different from, those of the Old World. John Speed's romantic visions of the Red Indian were one reason for the flourishing antiquarian tradition of eighteenth-century Europe. Others speculated as to the origins of these remarkable people; Ethiopians, Canaanites, Celts, Chinese, and Phoenicians were some of the peoples thought to have been the American natives' ancestors. A theory with a particularly long life considered the American Indians the descendents of the Ten Lost Tribes of Israel.

By the early nineteenth century, field research and museum work began to replace the wild speculations of earlier scholars. Site descriptions and excavations became more common, having their roots in the surveys of important sites by Spanish authorities in Central America and culminating in John Lloyd Stephens's and Frederick Catherwood's outstanding reports on Maya sites published in 1841-1843.[18] Some sober accounts of Indian mounds in North America began to appear. Thomas Jefferson excavated an Indian mound in Virginia in 1784, and made careful notes on his observations, which included some interpretation of occupation layers.[19] Caleb Atwater studied mounds and earthworks in Ohio in the early nineteenth century,[20] while E. G. Squier and E. H. Davis surveyed and dug others in the Ohio and Mississippi valleys, described in their important monograph *Ancient Monuments of the Mississippi Valley* in 1848. By the mid-nineteenth century, an era of factual description was beginning, which had its roots in a number of events. One was a long synthesis of American archaeology, written by Samuel Haven, called *Archaeology of the United States* and published by the newly established Smithsonian Institution in 1856. Haven's comprehensive essay reviews all the published speculations about the origins of the pre-Columbian Indians, most of which he dismissed as pure fantasy. After a review of historical linguistics and a survey of the racial characteristics of the American Indian, Haven describes the archaeology of North America, largely that of the mounds and earthworks of the eastern states containing artifacts of known historic Indian origin. In contrast, Caleb Atwater and other pioneers had regarded the Ohio mounds as the work of civilized ancients who were quite distinct from the modern Indian population. Samuel Haven agreed with other physical anthropologists that the American Indians were a distinct race with some Mongolian affinities, designating the earliest inhabitants of the New World as northeastern Asiatics who migrated into North America at an unknown date. He was careful not to embroil himself in the theological controversies between the catastrophists and the newer uniformitarian school, merely seeking enough time for the physical and linguistic diversity of the different American Indian tribes to be established.

Yet Haven's essay did reflect the new and more systematic approach to archaeology both in Europe and the New World, a symptom of an era of tremendous scientific advance on many fronts. Darwin's researches, the new geology, and Boucher de Perthes's discoveries, as well as the development of the Three-Age system in Scandinavia (described in Chapter 2), gave a new lease on life to a scientific approach to the problem of man's origins in the New World, with a search for Paleolithic man in North America and for the ancestors of the Indian tribes, whose ethnography was a subject of absorbing interest to nineteenth-century scholars. Mexican and Central American archaeology flourished, many scholars being attracted by the richness of the archaeological records and the native literature.

More important than the overoptimistic searchers for Paleolithic Man in the New World were the late nineteenth-century demonstrations that the Ohio mound builders were the ancestors of modern Indian populations, whose ethnography had long and largely unknown roots in the cultures of the past. Cyrus Thomas worked back from the ethnographic present to the archaeological past to prove the ownership of the mounds, publishing his results in an article entitled "Who Were the Mound Builders?" in 1884.[21] This approach to the American past became known in a more refined form as the "direct-historical approach," and was developed to a fine art in an expedition to the southwestern United States, which sought the prehistoric forebears of the Zuñi tribe. F. H. Cushing described the pottery of the Pueblo Indians in 1890,[22] and carried out much primary research in which anthropology and archaeology were combined to produce an effective approach to Zuñi history. Thus, the close marriage between archaeology and anthropology in New World archaeology stemmed directly from the field problem in North America, that of relating an indigenous population to spectacular prehistoric sites. Unlike European prehistorians, New World archaeologists had little or no identity with those they studied; they were concerned with the Indian tribe as a living and prehistoric entity whose culture, society, and identity had evolved through an unknown period of time. In contrast, one senses in the nineteenth-century European archaeologist a greater identity with the more recent prehistoric past and an intense nationalism resulting in a distinct motivation to write the prehistoric past of Europe as background to the great racial movements of more recent times and to justify major philological theories of the day. Archaeology was regarded as one of a battery of techniques used to study the history of European mankind. This dichotomy between New and Old World archaeology occurs early in the development of the subject, and is due almost entirely to historical circumstances.

ARCHAEOLOGY

The preceding include some of the major events leading to the development of archaeology as a scientific discipline, even if the direction of the subject and research in it have diversified over the years. Originally, in the nineteenth century, *archaeology* embraced the study of ancient history, but the word was gradually narrowed in meaning: in today's sense, it is the study of history or ancient cultures by the use of archaeological techniques. The label *prehistory* was first employed by a French scholar named Tournal in 1833, but came into widespread use in the middle of the nineteenth century to refer to the archaeology of the periods before literate history—which is the meaning used herein. Archaeology straddles many well established areas of academic inquiry, including anthropology, history, philosophy, and the natural sciences.[23] We have talked of archaeology as a "discipline," a label deliberately chosen as it fits well. The methods of archaeological research imply discipline—accurate recording, precise excavation, use of scientific method, and detailed analysis in the laboratory. In the academic world, too, the term refers to a subject that requires disciplined observation, deduction, and testing if it is to be successfully pursued. Everyone agrees that prehistoric archaeology involves the systematic study of archaeological sites and the artifacts found in them as a means of reconstructing life in the past. One studies the material remains of man in the past, whether from within the framework of anthropology, history, or other disciplines, but archaeology itself is really a distinct discipline, a combination of a wide battery of field, laboratory, and quantitative research methods oriented toward the study of man in the past, using interpretative techniques and theoretical concepts specially designed for this task.

To understand what archaeology involves necessitates some comprehension of the nature of archaeological evidence.[24] Archaeologists study those material remains of prehistoric man that have survived the ravages of time. As shown in Chapter 3, some raw materials preserve much more readily than others. Stone and clay vessels are virtually indestructible while wood, skin, metals, and bone are much more friable. Thus, in most archaeological sites only the most durable remains of human material culture are preserved for the archaeologist to study. Any picture of the prehistoric past obtained from archaeological investigations is likely to give a very one-sided picture of that life. As a result, the unfortunate archaeologist is like a detective fitting together a complicated series of clues to give a generalized impression, and explanation, of prehistoric culture and society. Much effort has gone into developing sophisticated methods for studying the prehistoric past. Often it is somewhat like taking a handful of miscellaneous objects—say two spark plugs, a fragmentary china cup, a needle, a grindstone, and a candle holder—and trying to reconstruct the culture of the makers of these diverse objects on the basis of the collection alone. Archaeologists have begun to develop sophisticated theoretical approaches to the material remains they study, making increasing use of hypothesis-testing and other attributes of scientific method to build testable propositions about the prehistoric past. Man's artifacts are seen as part of a system of interrelated phenomena in which culture is only one element.[25]

Most archaeologists would agree that there are three basic objectives in archaeological research—reconstruction of culture history, reconstruction of past lifeways, and the study of cultural process.[26] The first two objectives have been the subject of inquiry for many years, and some methods used and results obtained are summarized in this volume. How were stone implements made? What smelting processes resulted in the production of early copper tools? What was the significance of ivory to the prehistoric Eskimo? How did early man make his living? These are examples of questions which may confront the excavator. The tendency until recently has been to concentrate on description of the past and on the classification of archaeological cultures and artifacts. But the third objective, that of explaining cultural process in the past, is assuming increasing importance and becoming a paramount concern of many scholars. New heuristic methods such as Systems Theory and the use of Scientific Method are becoming more commonplace in archaeology,[27] and are discussed in Chapter 11. More and more archaeologists are using new theoretical approaches to the past in order to overcome the serious limitations of archaeological evidence itself when considered in isolation from other aspects of cultural systems.

There is a great diversity of archaeologists. Some study the living floors of early man and have a pressing concern with stone technologies and Pleistocene geology. Many archaeologists study the prehistory of early food production in the New and Old Worlds, developing new techniques for the study of prehistoric food residues and early domestic animals. Others study the origins of urban civilization or Mesoamerican states. Archaeologists examine the material remains of Colonial American settlements, medieval cities, or even early factories of the Industrial Revolution. Many Classical archaeologists are predominantly art historians or experts on hieroglyphics, while others will play an active role in the writing of national histories for new nations, where archaeology is a primary source of historical information.

The diversity of approaches to archaeology and its problems, as well as to the differing historical perspectives of the subject result in contrasting definitions and attitudes toward archaeology. In the United States, we have noted that archaeology is regarded as the concern of a special type of anthropologist.[28] Anthropology in the American context is the study of man in a very broad sense. It includes his culture, his psychology, and his physical anthropology, as well as the interrelationships between various aspects of man's being. American scholars regard archaeologists as anthropologists who usually excavate the material remains of man in the past, giving anthropology a time dimension. Thus, many of their objectives go beyond the basic description of artifacts and archaeological cultures to the explanation of cultural change, process, and evolution in prehistory. An impressive array of methods and theoretical approaches has been developed to study prehistoric social organization, settlement patterns, and economy, but the ultimate aim of New World archaeologists is not only description of the past but also determination of the nature of cultural societies at different stages in man's evolution in all parts of the world. The American archaeologist is thus particularly concerned with the development of testable propositions relating to man's past which are supported, modified, or rejected on the basis of excavated and analyzed archaeological data.

While American archaeology owes its approaches to the close marriage between anthropology and the study of the past, European archaeologists are much more forthright in their definition of archaeology as a part of history.[29] In the Old World, the arts of excavation have been developed to a high pitch by a historical tradition which began with A. H. L. Fox Pitt Rivers and continued with Sir Mortimer Wheeler and many postwar archaeologists. Both British and Continental prehistorians have placed great emphasis on the recovery of data from the ground, on the tracing of settlement patterns and structures, on economic reconstruction, and on the detailed analysis of artifact types and complicated typologies. Many archaeologists have acquired international reputations on the basis of their skill as excavators or museum men. The archaeologist is seen as a craftsman with diverse skills, not the least of which is the effective writing of history, both to amplify the written record and also to create a historical story, albeit incomplete, for periods when no archives exist to throw light on the deeds of chiefs or the attitudes of individuals.

One can argue in circles forever as to the correct definition and disciplinary place of archaeology. The subject itself is basically a battery of methods and techniques for the study of man in the past. Whether the discipline is a science, an art, or a part of anthropology or history, is perhaps irrelevant, for its basic concern, like that of much anthropology or all of history, is the understanding of man in the past.

HISTORY AND ARCHAEOLOGY

Although both historians and archaeologists study man in the past, there is a sharp distinction between the types of evidence which they employ.[30] Historians rely on written records such as government archives, private papers, and other documentary sources for primary evidence for the reconstruction of man's history since the beginnings of writing. The historical record extends back to about 3000 B.C. in the Near East, even if the earlier portions of this 5,000-year period are illuminated but little by documentary history. Continuous written history in Britain, on the other hand, begins with the Roman conquest some 2,000 years ago, while written records in the New World commenced with Christopher Columbus, even if the Maya had a script and a form of calendar. Some parts of the world did not come into contact with literate peoples until much more recently. The pastoral Khoi Khoi of the Cape of Good Hope emerged from prehistory in 1652 and were first known to the outside world when Bartholomew Diaz met them in the late fifteenth century. The tribes of the Central African interior had their first contact with David Livingstone in 1855. Continuous government records of this area did not begin until the late nineteenth century, while parts of New Guinea and the Amazon basin are still emerging from their prehistoric past. But, according to the latest researches, man has been living on this planet for at least 5 million years. Written history describes less than one-tenth of one percent of that enormous time. So archaeology remains the primary source of information on most of man's enormously long history since he was an Australopithecine on the East African savannah.

There is a sharp contrast between documentary history and a view of man's past reconstructed from the archaeological record. In the first place, the historian works with accurate chronologies. He can date an event certainly to within a year, possibly even as closely as a minute or second. Secondly, his history is that of individuals, groups, governments, and even several nations interacting with each other, reacting to events and struggling for power. He is able to glimpse the subtle interplay of human intellects, for his principal players have often recorded their impressions or deeds on paper. But there tend to be gaps in the record. Details of political events are likely to be far more complete than those of day-to-day existence or the trivia of village life. These were often of little consequence to contemporary observers, perhaps because they had experienced such commonplace things in the same way as we are used to driving in a car. Such minor details of past human behavior absorb students of ancient society, especially archaeologists interested in broad patterns of human change and early cultures, and it is here that the archaeologist may be useful to the historian. More and more excavations are being conducted on historical sites. The redoubtable King Henry VIII built a great palace at Nonsuch, south of London, in 1538, which was demolished 149 years later.[31] The ground plan was lost, despite a wealth of documentary information about the palace's history, until archaeologists uncovered the foundations of what was once one of the greatest buildings of Tudor England. They found not only the Banqueting Hall but also the wine cellar, and many fragments of the elaborate carved stone and molded plaster stucco, decoration from the fronts and inner courtyard of the building, which had made Nonsuch the talk of European society. The vast scheme of ornamentation was completely lost when seventeenth-century demolition contractors razed the palace.

On prehistoric sites, however, the archaeologist can at best only obtain a generalized and blurred impression of the period when a particular site was occupied. He is dealing with periods of human development and with broad patterns of human cultural change and behavior. His chronologies are less precise and the dates of occupation and abandonment of prehistoric settlements can rarely be established within such precise limits as a decade, let alone a year. The artifacts found in the excavations of the archaeologist represent the results of human behavior. They are anonymous, and rarely reveal the names of their owners. Man's achievements have become anonymous and no longer reflect the deeds of known individuals who have recorded their feelings for later generations to assess and discuss. Human behavior is reflected in many different ways in the archaeological record. It may be represented by large structures such as long houses, or monumental structures in stone too massive to be moved or studied outside their natural environment. Portable objects are the result of human behavior, too: stone implements, clay vessels, stone bowls, iron swords, or an infinite variety of ornaments, all of which can be removed from their archaeological context and studied in the laboratory. Equally well, the results of human behavior are seen in the fragmentary animal bones found with the tools of man, such as those discovered on early living floors in Africa, or in the sea shells found in the middens of California Indians. Sometimes special finds will throw detailed light on life in the past. A burial found in a cave dating to 12,000 B.C. in southwestern France is the result of human behavior. So is the imported faience bead of Mediterranean origin discovered in a northern European farming site, carried there along well-established trading routes. The archaeological record is formed from multiple types of evidence which reflect the infinite variability of human behavior. The archaeologist is thrown back on material objects which give the anonymous past which he reconstructs an immediate technological bias. Much of archaeology is traditionally concerned with inference and with analogy from artifacts, leading to an imaginative reconstruction of prehistory within the limitations of the archaeological evidence available.[32]

Archaeology can acquire a new dimension when used in conjunction with oral tradition. In many parts of the world where documentary history began with colonial rule in the late nineteenth century, where there were strongly centralized political organizations and kingships in prehistoric times, long genealogies and oral records of important political events and personalities may survive as important unwritten historical archives. These have been handed down from generation to generation and may extend back as far as 400 to 500 years into the past when circumstances for their preservation are favorable. Oral histories have been particularly well studied in parts of sub-Saharan Africa where scholars such as Jan Vansina[33] and others have worked hard to recover the lost history of the Bantu-speaking peoples of the tropical savannah regions of Central Africa. This type of research is an important primary historical source for the study of later prehistoric times. Archaeologists are beginning to cooperate with oral historians, adding valuable information on daily life among such groups to the traditional histories. The actual settlements attributed to ancient chiefs mentioned in the oral histories can be excavated, making the historical account a fuller one. The combination of two distinct types of historical discipline results in a much more complete picture of recent prehistoric society.

So the archaeologist must be a man of many parts. Aside from being a careful student of technology and material culture, he must have a thorough grounding in the identification, classification, and statistical treatment of artifacts, as well as in the principles of anthropology. He must be a skillful excavator and be able to apply the scientific method to his subject rigorously. Above all, he must be able to recognize the limitations of his evidence and of archaeology as a whole, and to comprehend the aims of historians and others who have no concern with archaeology. The reconstruction of prehistoric societies depends on research in many other fields, especially the natural sciences. Botanists provide identification of plants, while zoologists study the changing paleontological record found in early prehistoric sites. Chemists will process radiocarbon dates; soil scientists may provide critical information on the formation of occupation levels in ancient villages. These and many other related disciplines are all important to the archaeologist who must employ many differing scientific techniques in order to research some of the major events of human history. More and more multidisciplinary research teams are going into the field, ensuring effective cooperation between several disciplines such as archaeology, geology, pedology, and paleontology on the excavation itself.

What was the settlement pattern and way of life of the earliest hominids? How did man first "come down from the trees"? When did man first begin to make tools? When, where, and how did man first cultivate crops or domesticate animals? What is the early history of, and how revolutionary were the effects of, metallurgy on the history of mankind? When was the New World first populated by hunter-gatherers? These—historical events which were in their time as earth-shaking as the atomic bomb—and many other questions rely on the spade of the archaeologist for resolution. An understanding of the cultural processes involved in these events gives us a better perspective of our own culture and society.

Chapter 2

Time

A sense of time depth and chronology is something which we all possess to some degree. Indeed, man's innate curiosity about his past stems in part from his sense of time perspective as regards his own life and experience. Early antiquarians and theologians wrestled with the enigma of the Biblical legend of the Creation and the finds of fossil animals and human artifacts. Since the establishment of a high antiquity for man in 1859, however, the measurement of time has become one of the principal preoccupations of those who study the prehistoric past. How does one classify the past and measure the age of the great events of prehistory? The time dimension of archaeology is a vital element in our description and interpretation of prehistory.

The boundaries of our world are infinite. At one end of the time scale, the paleontologist and archaeologist are finding traces of early humans, dated by radioactive techniques to over 5.5 million years old. Today, we are reaching out into space with its incredible distances and toward other worlds, where, perhaps, human experience has been paralleled. Yet, our own perspectives of time and philosophies of life have taken little account of these vast new chronological horizons.

Consider for a moment how you view time. What is the earliest date you can remember? Mine is my third birthday—I have a vague memory of balloons and lots of people. My continuous memory of people as individuals and of day-to-day events begins at age 8. Most adults have a somewhat similar span of recollection, and a chronological perspective on their lives which extends back into early childhood. But our sense of personal involvement in human history only extends over the period of our lifetimes. We have an indirect involvement with the lives of our parents, relatives, or other friends, some of whom may have been alive 50 to 70 years before we were born. Perhaps our profoundest involvement with time occurs toward the end of our lives, with a period covering the lives of our immediate family. But we also have a marginal sense of longer chronologies and a perspective on events within them—our family ancestry, the history of our community, of our nation—and in these days of ardent internationalism, with the world as well. Few people have a sense of perspective for the whole span of human experience. Some still believe the Ussherian legend. We must look for a moment at the ways in which the vast new time scales of prehistory were established.

THE THREE AGES

In Chapter 1, we saw how the classification of the past was a major problem for early excavators, confronted with a jumble of artifacts from burial mounds or settlements. They had no means of subdividing or measuring the past. Until the nineteenth century, the world had been comfortably secure. Man had speculated freely about his origins, but within the narrow horizons of the Biblical account of the Creation. What happened before the Creation was a blank. Christians had contemplated eternity, but it was the shadowless, changeless eternity of God. Ussher's 6,000 years sufficed for all prehistory, even if subdividing the six millennia presented a problem. The story of archaeology is that of classifying and measuring time, a process given impetus by the apparently limitless frontiers of the prehistoric past opened up by Boucher de Perthes and Charles Darwin.

Scandinavian archaeologists were the first to develop a framework into which the bewildering mixture of artifacts from their excavations could be fitted. At the end of the eighteenth century, they were writing about ages of stone, copper, and iron, which flourished in prehistoric times. But as late as 1806, Professor Rasmus Nyerup of the University of Copenhagen complained that "everything which has come down to us from heathendom is wrapped in a thick fog; it belongs to a space of time which we cannot measure."[1]* Nyerup and others were responsible for the setting up of a Danish National Museum which housed a confusing collection of artifacts from bogs, burial chambers, and shell middens. The first curator of the Museum, Christian Jurgensen Thomsen (1788–1865), was appointed in 1816. Thomsen put the

* See pages 321–323 for notes to Chapter 2.

Museum collections in order by classifying them into three groups, representing ages of Stone, Bronze, and Iron, using sealed finds in graves as a basis for his classification. He claimed that his Three Ages were chronologically ranked.[2] Thomsen's bold classification was taken up by another Dane, J. J. A. Worsaae, who proved the basic stratigraphic validity of the system, and by studying archaeological finds from all over Europe demonstrated the widespread validity of what became known as the Three-Age System. Worsaae was a remarkable man, the first professional archaeologist to publish an exposition on excavation and classification of the past; this work which formed the foundation of most European archaeology[3] was printed in 1843, fifteen years before *The Origin of Species* was on the presses.

The Three-Age System was a technological subdivision of the prehistoric past, which gave the archaeologist a broad context within which his own finds could be placed. Thomsen, Worsaae, and others not only developed a museum classification system but also proved it by excavation. Worsaae admitted that he had been influenced by ethnographic accounts of stone-using Australians and Pacific islanders in postulating a Stone Age in the past. The close relationship of archaeology and anthropology was already clear. Thomsen's Three Ages were a first attempt at a chronology of relationship for the prehistoric past and were widely adopted as a basis for classifying prehistoric sites in the Old World. The establishment of a chronology for world prehistory thus began with Thomsen and Worsaae; the Three-Age scheme's validity was confirmed by excavations both in river gravels where the early flaked axes of Boucher de Perthes were found, and also in caves such as those excavated by Lartet and Christy in the Dordogne area of France which yielded different implements.[4] These in turn differed from those found in excavations in Swiss lakes where record low levels in 1853–1854 had exposed remains of prehistoric farming villages.[5] By the 1900s, scientists thought in terms of a Paleolithic or Old Stone Age to which the implements found in river gravels and the French caves belonged, a Neolithic, or Later Stone Age, when polished (as opposed to flaked) stone implements were in fashion, and Bronze and Iron Ages.[6] This framework for Old World prehistory, in a modified form, survives today (Table 2.1).

The Three-Age System of the Scandinavians was not adopted in North America. Systematic archaeological research flourished in the New World after 1859, but early attempts to find Paleolithic man were unsuccessful. The complicated geological strata of the European rivers with their rich storehouses of hand axes did not exist, but the relationships between the Indian population and the finds of the archaeologist were soon established. Stratigraphic observations and

Table 2.1   Some Nomenclature of Old World Archaeology

Approximate age in years	Geological era	Three-Age terminology	Important events
3000 B.C.		Iron Age Bronze Age Neolithic	Writing in the Near East Origins of food production
7800 B.C.	Holocene	Mesolithic	
35,000 B.C.		Upper Paleolithic	Origins of blade technology
70,000 B.C.	Pleistocene	Middle Paleolithic	
400,000 B.C.	(Quaternary)		Hand axes in widespread use
1.75 million B.C.		Lower Paleolithic	
±5 million B.C.			
	Pliocene		Origins of toolmaking

local cultural sequences did not preoccupy American archaeologists, unlike the European, and few researchers bothered to apply meticulous excavation techniques to later New World archaeological sites, in which, in any case, almost no metals were found. Not until 1914 did chronology and detailed stratigraphic observations of the past become important in American archaeology, when N. C. Nelson[7] and later A. V. Kidder began to use potsherds in southwestern sites as stratigraphic indicators; Kidder's classic excavations at the Pecos Pueblo[8] brought about a conference there in 1927 which delineated eight sequential stages of Pueblo culture. The foundations of accurate stratigraphic and chronological studies in American archaeology were soundly laid in the classic archaeological laboratory of the Southwest. We summarize some salient features of American archaeology in Table 2.2 and of human evolution in Figure 2.1, but it should be emphasized that both diagrams are so simplified as to be almost theoretical in impact.

RELATIVE AND ABSOLUTE CHRONOLOGY

As already observed, we all have a sense of time, indeed our lives are governed by appointments, airline schedules, and tax deadlines. We unconsciously add a sense of historical time to our daily round. When a radio station plays a tune first popular in 1958, the announcer may mention associations of that year, and jumbled events contemporary with the song fill our minds. People's birthdays, dates of elections, or space shots are all part of our sense of history, which is most strongly developed around our own lifetimes. Learning history is part of our school experience, a process that considerably extends

Table 2.2   General Outline of New World Archaeology[a]

Dates	South America	Mesoamerica	North America — Southwest	North America — Plains	North America — East
A.D. 1500	Inca Empire	Aztecs and other Toltecs	← Pueblo I–IV	← Plains Village Period	← Temple Mound Period
A.D. 1000	Tiahuanaco-Huari expansion	Classic Period (Maya)	→ Basketmaker I and II	→ Woodland Period	→ Burial Mound Period
	Mochica, Nasca, Tiahuanaco	Teotihuacán			
500 B.C.	Chavín Paracas	Pre-Classic Period	←	←	←
1000 B.C.	First ceremonial centers Maize grown				
2000 B.C.	Incipient cultivation and food collecting	Incipient cultivation and food collecting	Cochise Period	Archaic Period	Archaic Period
3000 B.C.			→	→	→
5000 B.C.	Early hunters and gatherers	Paleo-Indian Period	Paleo-Indian Period	Paleo-Indian Period	Paleo-Indian Period
7000 B.C.					
10,000 B.C.					
20,000 B.C.		— — — —	— — — —	— — — —	— — — —
±40,000 B.C.	— — — —				

[a] This is a gross simplification for vocabulary purposes, and many major cultural areas are omitted.

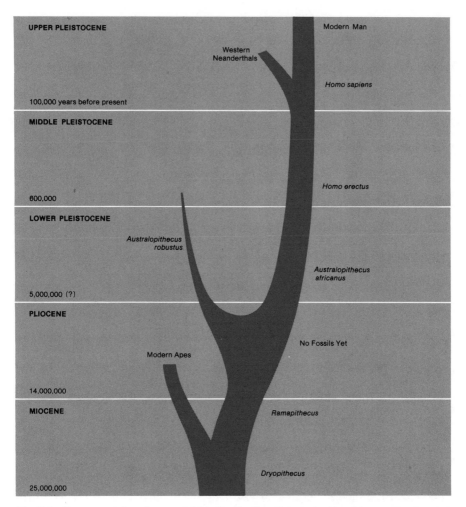

UPPER PLEISTOCENE

Modern Man

Western
Neanderthals

Homo sapiens

100,000 years before present

MIDDLE PLEISTOCENE

Homo erectus

600,000

LOWER PLEISTOCENE

*Australopithecus
robustus*

*Australopithecus
africanus*

5,000,000 (?)

PLIOCENE

No Fossils Yet

Modern Apes

14,000,000

MIOCENE

Ramapithecus

Dryopithecus

25,000,000

Fig. 2.1   Human evolution. (I am grateful to Dr. Geoffrey Gaherty for his advice on this diagram.)

our time perspective. Diverse histories are ordered into centuries, years, hours, and even minutes. George Washington's life story and his dates are known to most, because the events of his presidency are abundantly documented in school textbooks, archives, and historical records. Time is such an integral part of our lives that we tend to take it for granted, as well as the chronological subdivisions of our more recent history.

Studying documentary history revolves around people and events, political maneuvers and social change. A kaleidoscope of happenings threatens to engulf the person researching a rapidly deepening political crisis or field campaign. The exact chronological order of the contributing events has to be established as a preliminary to any serious research. At what exact moment on June 18, 1815, did Emperor Napoleon order his Imperial Guard to charge the British squares at Waterloo? At what point during the battle of Mobile Bay in 1864 did David Glasgow Farragut make his famous remark about torpedoes? These are details of consuming importance to the historian with his need for extreme accuracy.

Prehistoric chronologies cover far longer periods of time, millennia and centuries, as opposed to days or even minutes. Some idea of the scale of prehistoric time can be gained by piling up a hundred quarters. If the whole pile represents the time that man and his culture have been on earth, the length of time covered by historical records would equal considerably less than the thickness of one quarter. In fact, 99.9 per cent of man's history lies within prehistoric times. Prehistoric time scales are staggering and difficult to measure because cultural change has proceeded slowly for most of man's existence—the humdrum tempo of cultural evolution only accelerating in recent millennia. Without comparatively accurate chronologies, the landscape of prehistory is featureless, and we face the same problem as the early antiquarians.

Julius Caesar landed in Britain in 55 B.C.; Washington, D.C., was founded in A.D. 1800. These are dates in years, and immediately give us a sense of the *absolute date* of both events. The current absolute dates for the earliest hominids range around 5 million years ago—nothing like the preciseness of Caesar's—but are expressed in years and can be directly related to those of the Roman general who ended Britain's prehistoric isolation. In other words, the dating standards of the historian are being applied, albeit crudely, to the prehistoric past. Much experimental effort in archaeology during the last fifty years has attempted to devise accurate methods of absolute dating.[9] Archaeologists draw widely on the techniques used by geologists and invented by physicists and chemists, as well as in addition to inventing many ingenious devices for dating the past which enjoy momentary popularity before sinking into dignified obscurity. Absolute chronologies are so important that the enormous expenditure of time on devising methods of dating sites or objects is entirely justified.[10] Not only are dates important, but so are the interrelationships between one prehistoric society and another that are revealed by them. Are two neighboring prehistoric peoples within a limited area contemporary, or are they separated by a considerable time span? What effect did they have on one another? Is one derived from the other? What was the rate of cultural change or technological innovation? The solution of these problems depends upon accurate and reliable absolute chronologies, for neither technological advance nor cultural change proceeds at the same rate everywhere, even within limited geographic areas.

Relationships in time are simpler to establish. If I place a book on the table, and then pile another one on top of it, clearly the upper one of the two was placed on the table after, and at a later moment in time than, the original volume. The second book became part of the pile after the first, but how long afterward we have no means of telling. This example illustrates the principle of superposition, one of the cornerstones of archaeological research and *relative chronology*, that is, correlating prehistoric sites or cultures with one another by their relative age.

STRATIGRAPHY AND SUPERPOSITION

Stratigraphical observations and the principle of superposition are two foundations for effective study of man's past. The use of stratigraphy in archaeology came from the studies of geologists such as William Smith, Sir Charles Lyell, and others, in the late eighteenth and nineteenth centuries. The finding of stone implements in Pleistocene deposits like river gravels led to an intimate marriage between Stone Age archaeology and geology, and from there it was a logical step to the confines of an archaeological site. Relative chronology in archaeology has its basis in large- or small-scale stratigraphic observations in archaeological sites of all ages. As the eminent British archaeologist Sir Mortimer Wheeler has cogently argued, the basis of scientific excavation is the accurately observed and carefully recorded stratigraphic profile.[11]

The basic principle in most stratigraphic observation is a simple one: the geological layers of the earth are superimposed one upon another almost like the layers of a cake. Easily viewed examples are cliffs by the seashore or in quarries which show a series of geological levels. Obviously, any object found in the lowermost levels was deposited before the upper horizons were accumulated. In other words, the lower levels are *relatively earlier* than the upper strata. The superposition of a series of occupation levels or geological strata in order can be achieved by many different processes; wind erosion, water action, earthquakes, and glacial action have all played their part in the accumulation of the earth's strata. At times man's artifacts have been found in settlement sites contemporary with major geological events in situations where the stratigraphy of the geologist is in direct association with the prehistorian's findings.

Superposition is fundamental to studying archaeological sites, for many settlements, such as Near Eastern mounds, or Indian villages in the Ohio Valley, or cave sites, contain multilevel occupations whose decipherment is the key to their relative chronology. Sir Mortimer Wheeler has ably described the processes of human occupation as applied to stratigraphy:

> The human occupation of a site normally results in the accumulation of material of one kind or another on and about the area occupied. Objects are lost or discarded and become imbedded in the earth. Floors are renewed and old ones buried. Buildings crumble and new ones are built on the ruins. A flood may destroy a building or a town and deposit a layer of alluvium on its debris and later, when the flood has subsided, the level site may be reoccupied. Sometimes, the process is in the reverse direction. Evidences of occupation may be removed as in the deepening of an unsurfaced street by traffic, or the digging of a pit for the disposal of rubbish or for burial ... in one way or another the surface of an ancient town or village is constantly altering in response to human effort or neglect; and it is by interpreting rightly these evidences of alteration that we may hope to reconstruct something of the vicissitudes of the site and its occupants.[12]

Although we shall touch on the observation of stratigraphic profiles later on, Figures 2.2 and 2.3 present examples of sections illustrating the significance of stratigraphy in the archaeological record.[13]

Fig. 2.2   *An idealized section through an Upper and Middle Paleolithic cave in France. The four archaeological culture layers are separated by sterile layers, the Mousterian being earlier than the Aurignacian, and so on. Most stratigraphic sequences are, of course, much more complicated than this hypothetical example. (After Oakley.)*

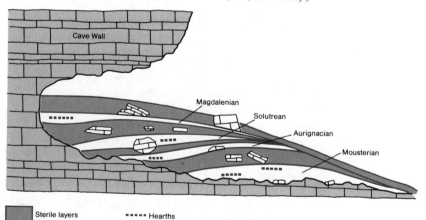

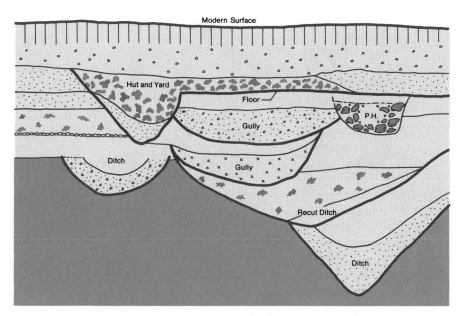

Fig. 2.3   A stratigraphic section through a town site in Cambridge, England, showing profiles of pre-historic and Roman enclosures and huts with a post hole (P.H.), gullies, and ditches. The complex stratigraphy is interpreted by correlating the various features with their horizontal layers. (One thirty-second actual size.)

Stratigraphy as applied to archaeological sites is on a much smaller scale than that of geology, but often correspondingly more complicated. Most archaeological relative chronology employs careful observations of sequences of occupation levels and the correlation of these with cultural sequences at other sites in the same area. Successive occupation levels can be found at the same spot, such as in a cave, fort, or mound site, where many generations of settlers lived within a circumscribed or restricted area. In other cases, however, the chronological sequence can be horizontal. Such a situation arises when economic or political conditions dictate a regular movement of villages when fields are exhausted or residence rules modified. In this case a cultural sequence may be scattered through a series of single-level occupation sites over a large area, and can only be put together by judicious survey work and careful analysis of the artifacts found in the different sites.

Occupation levels and other strata are useless if observed in isolation, for the artifacts, food bones, or other finds recovered from the layers of a site are as critical as the stratigraphy itself. Each level in a settlement, however massive or small, has its associated artifacts, the objects that the archaeologist uses as his indicators of cultural and economic change. Indeed, the finds in each layer and their associations often provide the basic material for relative chronology. Furthermore, the relative dating of many sites is complicated by other questions. Has the site been occupied continuously? Do stratigraphic profiles reflect a continuous occupation over a long period of time, or a sequence which has been interrupted several times by warfare, or simple abandonment of the site? Such problems can be resolved by careful examination of excavated profiles.

Another factor which may affect the interpretation of stratigraphy is the breaks or disruptions in the layering caused by human activity. Later occupants of a village may dig rubbish pits or graves into earlier strata. Cattle may be kept on the site, their hooves removing the soil and disturbing the upper levels of the underlying horizons; this process also may be caused by later people cultivating the rich soils of an abandoned village site. Building activities may cause foundation trenches and even stone walls to be sunk into earlier levels. The inhabitants' technological level has a direct bearing on their ability to destroy evidence of earlier and contemporary occupation. Obviously the inhabitants of a Near Eastern city are more likely to have destroyed evidence of earlier occupation with constant rebuilding than are a group of farmers without metal tools, who merely reoccupy earlier village sites with minimal disturbance of the underlying levels. Burrowing animals, too, enjoy archaeological sites, worming their way through the soft, organic soils of caves or village sites and disrupting stratigraphic observations over large areas of the settlement. Moles, gophers, and rabbits are foes of gardener and archaeologist alike.

PLEISTOCENE GEOCHRONOLOGY

For over 90 per cent of his existence on earth, man was a stone toolmaker. Most of his early history lies within the last major geological epoch, that of the Pleistocene, which began more than 2 million years ago and ended, by conventional definition, 8,000 years before Christ.[14] The Pleistocene was characterized by major fluctuations of climate, from extreme cold to tropical heat. Geologists consider the Pleistocene to be one of the most complicated of all field problems, for many of its deposits have local origin and incredible complexity. In extreme cases, the effects of glaciation and permafrost conditions might be combined with those of water action and extensive tectonic movement within the narrow confines of a single stratigraphic profile. From the archaeological point of view the attraction of the Pleistocene is in the direct association of human living sites with Quaternary deposits, because the major climatic events of the last two million years provide an admirable framework for a relative chronology of human culture. The science of geochronology, or geological dating, is a complex, multidisciplinary approach to dating early man, and involves the study of the Pleistocene geological record in many temperate and tropical areas.

Glaciations

Climatic changes during past millennia are preserved in numerous different types of deposit. Huge ice sheets covered much of northern Europe, North America, and the Alpine areas of France, Italy, and Switzerland. At least four times, arctic conditions prevailed over the Northern hemisphere, reflected in extensive deposits of glacial moraines and other related geological phenomena. These periods of extreme cold alternated with prolonged interglacial phases when the European climate was considerably warmer than today's. During the longest interglacial, tropical animals like the hippopotamus flourished in Western Europe. In the Old World, where man's prehistory extends back at least five million years, these glacial advances and retreats have been correlated with stages of human culture. European geologists have distinguished at least four glacial periods in the Alps, known as Gunz, Mindel, Riss, and Würm,[15] although there may have been other periods of intense cold (Table 2.3). Except in the closing millennia of the Pleistocene, there are few direct associations of human culture with deposits of the Ice Age glaciers. Numerous associated deposits, however, were laid down in periglacial areas which are associated directly with evidence of human occupation. These include river gravels affected by permafrost conditions and also extensive deposits of a windblown sand, called "loess," deposited over much of Central Europe by chilly Arctic winds blowing a detritus of fine dust from the ice sheets.[16]

High Sea Levels

High sea levels are another phenomenon extensively used to correlate archaeological remains with interglacial periods.[17] The study of sea levels is controversial, particularly in areas where extensive earth movement may have affected the elevation of ancient beach levels above the modern level. The study and correlation of raised beaches is based on the theory of Glacial Eustasy: during periods of intense cold when the Polar and Alpine ice sheets reached their maximum extent, a general fall in ocean levels resulted because moisture was incorporated into these ice sheets. With the shrinkage of ice sheets during the interglacials, the sea level rose and, in addition, the earth's

Table 2.3   Geological Events and Glaciations in Europe during the Pleistocene

Years	Alpine glaciation	Scandinavian glaciation	Loess	Sea level	Inter-glacial	Pollen species	Fossil animals	Key archaeological sites
8,000 B.C. to present	Postglacial		Weathering	Versilian		Temperate	Modern fauna	Mesolithic and later
8,000–70,000 (?) B.C.	Würm III, II, I	Weichsel	Younger Loess I–III				*Elephas primigenius*	Middle and Upper Paleolithic
		Weathering	Weathering	Monastirian 15–18 M	Eemian	No *Azolla*	*Elephas antiquus*	Levalloisian technology
	Riss II, I	Warthe Saale	Older Loess I–II					
270,000 (?) B.C.			Weathering	Tyrrhenian 30–45 M	Hoxnian	*Azolla filiculoides* (water fern)	*Elephas antiquus*	Hoxne, Swanscombe, Clacton
400,000 (?) (avg.)	Mindel II, I	Elster ?	Oldest Loess					Olduvai Gorge
(Climatic changes uncertain earlier than Mindel)				Sicilian I 100 M	Cromerian	*Azolla* a.ff. *filiculoides* (water fern)	*Archidiskodon* ? *Machairodus*	Olduvai Gorge
	Gunz	?	?					
				Calabrian 200 M	Tiglian	*Azolla tegelensis* (water fern)	Villafranchian[a]	
	Donau	?	?					

[a] Base of a Villafranchian faunal bed in Southern Europe dated to 3.0 million years; Upper Villafranchian faunal beds in East Africa dated to 1.75 million years.

crust gradually readjusted to compensate for the release of the extra weight of the glacial sheets. Major geographical changes resulted. For example, until 4000 or 5000 B.C., Britain was joined to the Continent by a strip of marsh; it covered what is now the North Sea and part of the English Channel. Similar, major sea-level changes have taken place in the New World, the Mediterranean area, and also Scandinavia (Figure 2.4).

Raised beaches are found in the geological record as a series of terraces along the fringes of modern coastal plains. They are widely distributed on the East Coast of the United States and especially in the Mediterranean, where they have been intensively studied by French and Italian geologists. In many parts of the world, modern beaches are dotted with shell middens which represent the occupations of recent prehistoric strandlooping peoples who lived on fish and shellfish. Many sites like this are found near Southern California beaches and on the southeastern and southwestern coasts of South Africa, yielding numerous fishbones and freshwater shells. Cave sites near the edge of the modern seashore were often occupied by prehistoric peoples with a similar dietary pattern. The cave at Robberg in the Cape Province of South Africa, which has been skillfully excavated by R. R. Inskeep,[18] furnished a wealth of information on ancient

Fig. 2.4   Great Britain and Scandinavia at the end of the Pleistocene, showing sea levels ca. 7000 B.C.

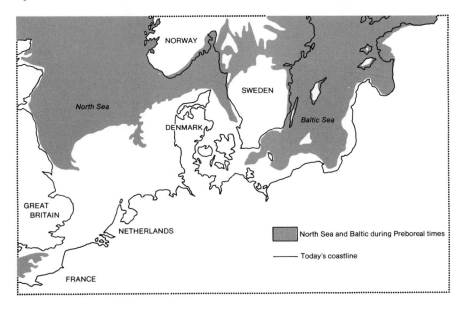

economic practices and fishing habits in a coastal region about the first millennium B.C., when the sea was slightly lower than it is now. The high-level beaches of the Mediterranean and Northwest Africa occasionally yield traces of earlier Stone Age occupation. One famous site is the raised beach at Sidi Abderrahmane[19] in Morocco. Here an early Pleistocene sea level was covered by a deposit of consolidated sand dune which not only sealed the beach but also a deposit of early stone artifacts. A subsequent higher sea level, belonging to the Mindel-Riss interglacial, cut a cave into this consolidated dune, in which man lived during the succeeding low sea level period, i.e., during the Riss glaciation. Hand axes, animal bones, and some fragments of the men who made the implements, *Homo erectus,* were found in the cave. The human fossil is securely relative-dated by its proximity to the high sea level of the preceding interglacial. Numerous other examples exist but, unfortunately, many archaeological sites found on high sea levels are extensively disturbed by later geological action and have, perhaps, a rather more marginal interest to the archaeologist than sites in less disturbed localities.

Lakes and Rivers

Lake beds and river gravels are some of the most important Pleistocene deposits used in relative dating. Small lakes and other permanent bodies of water were attractive habitats to early hunters. The Australopithecines at Olduvai Gorge were found on their living floors at the edge of a large shallow lake, their settlements subsequently buried by softly deposited water-lain sediments which did not disturb the abandoned artifacts and bones. Another famous example is John Frere's lake-bed site at Hoxne in England (Figure 2.5),[20] where the remains of a small interglacial lake are sealed between two glacial moraines of widely differing age.

The great river valleys of Europe and Africa have yielded a rich crop of stone tools dating from all Pleistocene periods. Early man favored the great floodplains of the Thames, Somme, Zambezi, and other large rivers,[21] for they furnished abundant game and vegetable foods as well as permanent water supplies and fish. Their hunting camps by the river banks were buried by alluvium or scattered by floodwater; the artifacts, and sometimes the bones of their quarry, became part of the Pleistocene gravels which form the sides of the modern river valley. The world's great rivers have become smaller since Pleistocene times, and have documented their history as a result of falling sea levels, crustal movement, or erosion. A series of stable periods or downcutting have formed terraces on the edge of the river valleys as the rivers became smaller. Quarries and natural exposures

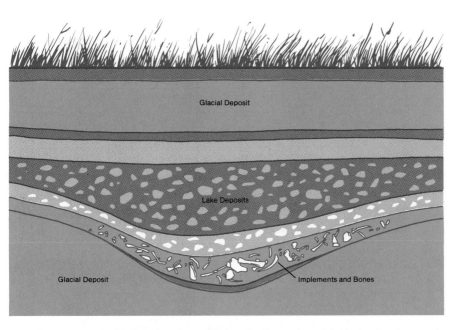

Glacial Deposit

Lake Deposits

Glacial Deposit   Implements and Bones

Fig. 2.5   A much simplified stratigraphic profile from the Hoxne site, England, showing the associa-
tion of implements and fossil bones with lake-bed deposits sealed by two layers of glacial
origin. (Not to scale.)

in the terraces yield stone tools to the archaeologist, which can be
relatively dated. A famous example is the Swanscombe skull site in
the Thames Valley where a human cranium was found in association
with stone hand axes; it was dated to the Mindel-Riss interglacial
(Figure 2.6).[22] River gravels are not, however, the most satisfactory
forms of archaeological deposit to analyze. Unlike lake beds, where
actual living floors are often preserved, the rough-and-tumble of water
action has often jumbled artifacts, transporting many some distance
from the living floor where they were used. The chances of finding
undisturbed living sites in river gravels is thus correspondingly lower.

Animal Bones

Another type of geochronology comes from the study of vertebrate
fauna found in Pleistocene sites. Stone Age man killed a wide range
of large and small mammals for food, whose broken bones are often
preserved in river gravels, living floors, and other sites. The animals
hunted often were species now extinct, such as the giant pigs and
buffalo found at Olduvai Gorge in Tanzania by Dr. Louis Leakey.[23]
Paleontologists have classified Pleistocene faunas from many localities,

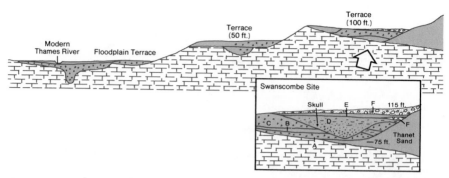

Fig. 2.6   A schematic diagram of the Thames terraces at Swanscombe, England, with a small inset of the Swanscombe site, showing the complex sequence of layers. Stone artifacts were found with the skull and were profuse in layers A, C, D, and F, with B and E sealing the culture layers. (North/south cross section; not to scale.)

often using the remains of animals hunted by man, and have tried to build up a very simple relative chronology of mammal types through the Pleistocene. The evolution of the large mammals proceeded rapidly during the Quaternary. Elephants, for example, changed radically during each European interglacial. The evolving species can be distinguished by the distinctive cusp patterns of their teeth (Figures 2.7 and 2.8).[24] In the Gunz-Mindel interglacial, an early form of *Palaeoloxodon antiquus* lived on the plains of Central Europe. During the Mindel-Riss or Great Interglacial, some quarter of a million years later, he was succeeded by a more developed form of the same species. Different elephants flourished during the colder spells. During the last glaciation, the mammoth, *Mammuthus primigenius*, a hairy elephant with large tusks, lived in Central Europe. A fairly reliable relative date can be assigned to a site where elephants occur merely by examining the teeth.

Unfortunately, however, the use of vertebrate fauna is severely limited by the difficulty of identifying different mammal species. Certain animals are more sensitive to climatic change than others. Some are tolerant of both cold and warm climates, although others prefer warm weather but can stand perversely low temperatures with remarkable resilience. Furthermore, so many environmental factors affect the distribution of mammals and the extinction of one species at the expense of another that it is very difficult to be sure that one is dealing with a chronological, as opposed to an environmental, difference. But, with Lower or Middle Pleistocene sites, the uses of animal bones as chronological indicators are magnified simply because enormous time scales are involved and minor details are obscured.

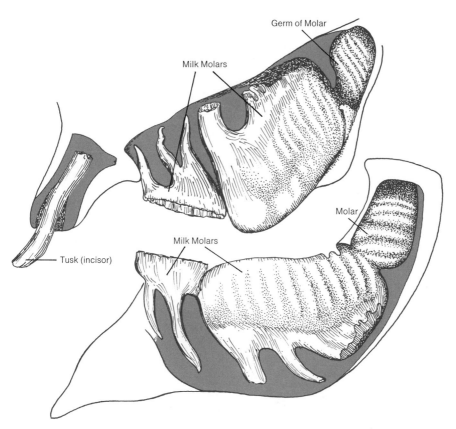

Fig. 2.7 *Elephant dentition in place in the skull, showing milk molar teeth and adult molars erupting.*
(After Cornwall.)

POLLEN ANALYSIS

Vegetation is one of the best indicators of ecological change, for it depends on climate and soil for survival and is a sensitive barometer of climatic alteration. Pollen analysis, or palynology, is a comprehensive way of studying ancient vegetation; it was developed in 1916 by a Swede, Lennart van Post, who used forest trees, and subsequently this analysis extended to all pollen-liberating vegetation. The principle of pollen analysis is simple.[25] Large numbers of pollen grains are suspended in the atmosphere and have remarkable preservative properties if deposited in an unaerated geological horizon. The pollen spores can be identified microscopically (Figure 2.9) with great accuracy and used to reconstruct the vegetation which grew near the spot

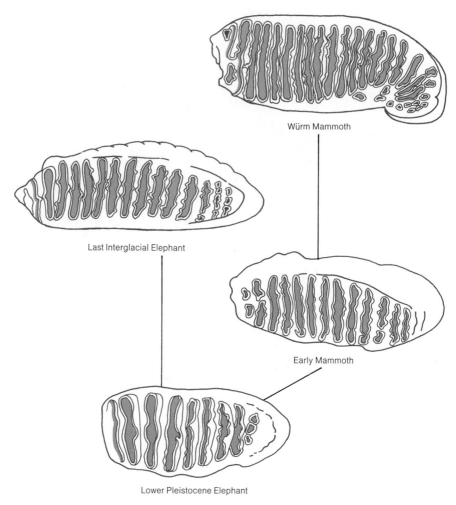

Würm Mammoth

Last Interglacial Elephant

Early Mammoth

Lower Pleistocene Elephant

Fig. 2.8   Grinding surfaces of third upper molars of four types of Pleistocene elephant, illustrating the differences in enamel patterns from earlier (bottom) to later (upper) types. (One-fifth actual size.) (After Oakley.)

where they are found. Palynology has been widely employed by botanists from many countries. Though the method has been especially used on peat-bog deposits and clays, it has also been applied to clay cores from Central African lakes, to samples obtained by dredging from the bed of the sea, and even to cave deposits and to lenses of organic material in the middle of river terraces.

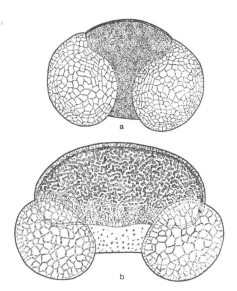

Fig. 2.9   Pollen spores. (a) Spruce. (b) Silver Fir. (Both 340 times actual size.) (After Oakley.)

Pollen spores are normally only identifiable under a very powerful microscope. Samples are taken through stratigraphic sections at close intervals and subjected to identification and statistical treatment. The grains of each genus or species present are counted, and the percentage of frequencies calculated. The counts are then correlated stratigraphically with one another to provide a sequence of vegetational change. When sufficient sections have been analyzed, the palynologist is able to zonate the vegetation according to distinct vegetational periods and to use such zones, and the characteristic pollen diagrams associated with them, as evidence for assigning a particular deposit to a place within a relative, chronological framework worked out at a series of type localities.

Palynology has obvious applications to prehistory, for sites are often found in swampy deposits where pollen is preserved, especially fishing or fowling camps and settlements near water. Isolated artifacts or even human corpses (such as that of Tollund man found in a Danish bog) are also discovered in these deposits; sometimes pollen is obtained from small peat lumps adhering to crevices in such finds. Thus the botanists can assign relative dates to even isolated finds which otherwise would remain undated. The palynologists have worked out a long sequence of vegetational history for Northern Europe, which begins about 13,000 B.C. with Arctic tundra covering much of Western Europe.[26] After a number of fluctuations, this gives way to birch and pine forest and later to mixed oak forest, characteristic of a temperate climate. A summary of the vegetational history of that area appears in Table 2.4. Pollen diagrams for earlier Pleistocene interglacials have also been obtained from many localities, sometimes in association with human artifacts. Obviously, an archaeological site with a pollen graph coinciding with that of a particular vegetational zone belongs within that period, an admirable method of relative chronology—an example appears in Figure 2.10.

Table 2.4   Postglacial Vegetational Zones in Northern Europe[a]

Approximate dates in years	Blytt and Sernander climatic periods	Zone numbers	Vegetation	Archaeology
600 B.C.	Sub-Atlantic (wetter and colder)	IX	Beech increase. Extensive clearance	Historic and Iron Age
3000 B.C.	Sub-Boreal (warm, dry, continental)	VIII	Decrease of mixed oak forest—more pine. Extensive forest clearance by man	Bronze Age "Neolithic"
5500 B.C.	Atlantic (warm maximum, moist and oceanic)	VII	Oak, elm, lime, alder (mixed oak forest)	"Neolithic" Mesolithic
7700 B.C.	Boreal (rising temperatures, dry, continental)	VI	Hazel, less pine, start of mixed oak forest	Mesolithic
8300 B.C.	Pre-Boreal (rising temperatures, cool)	V/IV	Birch, beech, pine	Mesolithic
8800 B.C.	Younger Dryas (cold)	III	Tundra	Late Glacial
10,000 B.C.	Allerod Oscillation (warmer interval)	II	Birch and oak, tundra	Hunting cultures
ca. 15,000 B.C.	Older Dryas (Arctic cold)	I	Arctic tundra	
	(end of Würm maximum)			

(handwritten left margin:) Valders — aligned with 8800 B.C. row
(handwritten left margin:) Two Creeks — aligned with 10,000 B.C. row

[a] Amended from Jane Gray and Watson Smith, "Fossil Pollen and Archaeology," *Archaeology*, 1962, 15 (1):16–26.

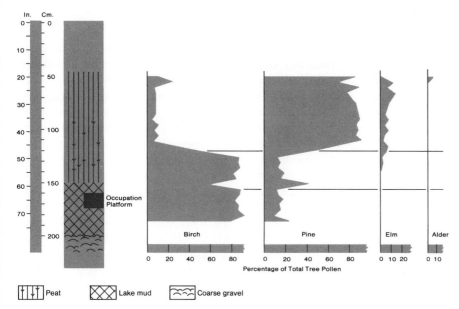

Fig. 2.10 *The pollen diagram from the hunting camp at Star Carr, England. The occupation platform was in use when birch was common near the site.*

Ordering of Artifacts

Another method of relative chronology uses artifacts found in sealed stratigraphic contexts. Fashions change, and the forms of artifacts do, too; particular styles enjoy fleeting popularity for varying periods of time before going out of favor. The celebrated Egyptologist Sir Flinders Petrie was among the first to use artifacts for chronological ordering, and developed a method of relative dating Pre-Dynastic Egyptian graves through stylistic changes in strap-handled vases.[27] Subsequently, many archaeologists have used pottery and other artifacts for similar research, basing their work on the assumption that "each type of artifact orginates at a given time at a given place, is made in gradually increasing numbers as time goes on, then decreases in popularity until it becomes forgotten, never to reoccur in an identical form."[28] Each chronological period has its own unique assemblage of artifacts and frequencies of different tool types. The presence or absence and relative abundance of artifacts are data which one can order through time, using the technique of seriation, described more fully in Chapter 8. But the principle of seriation is that of popularity, the basic assumption being that sites with the greatest agreement either in the occurrence of artifacts or in their frequencies will lie closest in time.

ABSOLUTE CHRONOLOGY

More effort has been devoted toward inventing methods of absolute dating in archaeology than to almost any other aspect of the subject. It is hardly surprising, for fundamental questions about the past are involved. How old is this tool? How long ago was that site occupied? Are these villages contemporary? These are probably the first questions asked by anyone curious about an artifact or a prehistoric village, as well as by the archaeologist himself. They remain some of the most difficult questions to answer.

An impressive array of chronological techniques has been developed to date the past. Some have become well established reliable methods of dating. Others, after a brief vogue, have been ejected into academic oblivion upon the discovery of some fatal flaw. In practice, the huge span of human cultural history is dated by a number of scientific methods; the chronological span is shown in Table 2.3. Potassium argon dating provides a somewhat generalized chronology for the first two-thirds of man's history, its recent limits reaching up to some 400,000 years ago. The other major radioactive technique, radiocarbon dating, covers a period from approximately 55,000 years ago up to as recently as A.D. 1500, when the standard errors are too large compared with the small time spans involved. (See Table 2.5.) No one has yet developed a dating method to cover the 350,000 years or so between the outer limits of radiocarbon dating and the beginnings of potassium argon chronology.[29]

Historical documents provide a fairly accurate chronology for kings and political events for over 5,000 years in the Near East and for shorter periods elsewhere in the world. Prehistoric chronology in the New World ends with white settlement of the Americas from the fifteenth century on. These more recent periods, frequently times when archaeology can be used in conjunction with historical documents or oral records, are covered by many other dating methods, including imported objects of known historical date and dendrochronology. Dates in years not only tell how old a site is, but also illuminate the relationships between different communities, cultures, or larger

Table 2.5   Radiocarbon Dates—Accuracy Shown by an Example

Sample radiocarbon date = 3,621 ± 180 years (plus or minus factor)
1 standard deviation = 3,441 or 3,801 years
With 1 deviation, it is 68% certain that the date span is correct.
2 standard deviations = 3,261 or 3,981 years
With 2 deviations, chances are 19/20 that the date span is correct.

geographic or social units. Were the inhabitants of a hill fort occupied in the first century B.C. in southern Britain contemporary with the people living on a similar site 150 miles away? Were two broadly similar prehistoric cultures, whose distributions overlap, contemporary, or was one earlier than the other? Did food production originate first in the Near East or in Southeast Asia? Was Patagonia settled by early man before Peru? Such questions, sometimes trivial, sometimes of major significance in the study of human history, can only be answered by absolute chronologies of acceptable accuracy and reliability.

OBJECTS OF KNOWN AGE

The most reliable dates are those derived from historical documentation of archaeological sites. We know, for example, the year when King Henry VIII began to build his palace at Nonsuch, England, as well as the chronology of Plimoth Plantation in Massachusetts, from contemporary records, and our primary interest lies in discovering details of settlement layout or day-to-day life. Many later sites yield easily dated artifacts, such as coins dropped by the inhabitants on the floors of buildings or elsewhere in the settlement's strata. Such objects can provide accurate dates for the earliest age of the archaeological sites being investigated.

Trade diffused similar, well dated objects from areas of advanced technological achievement to less fortunate regions of Europe, Africa, and Asia. Technological innovation flourished with the advent of urban civilization, with more advanced materials being used to create a wide range of luxury objects or ornaments. Chinese porcelain, Roman glass vessels, faience or glass beads, cotton and flax fabrics, bronze daggers, and Greek wine amphorae were luxuries diffused widely through the Ancient World, often to the barbarian tribes on the fringe of the unknown. The dates of styles of Chinese porcelain or Greek vases, changing according to the fashion's dictates, are firmly established in historical records. Such objects are found hundreds and even thousands of miles from the source of manufacture in undated prehistoric camps or trading centers. Since the date of the import is known at its source, the settlement in which it is found can be dated to a period at least as early as the exotic object of known age. This dating method is known as "cross-dating."[30]

Imports have proved of inestimable use in dating many sites far from the centers of ancient civilization. Chinese Nankin porcelain has been found in the far interior of southeast Africa, where the great trading confederacy of the hereditary chief Monomotapa flourished 500 years ago.[31] African minerals, ivory, and slaves were coveted by the Indian Ocean traders, who established well-trodden trade and barter routes into the African interior. They exchanged such exotic luxuries as seashells, Indian cloth and glass beads, and Chinese porcelain for copper, gold, iron, and ivory collected or mined by the chiefs of the African plateau. Zimbabwe was one of the greatest commercial and religious centers of the interior, a great complex of stone enclosures and spectacular walls, and for many centuries a headquarters of the Karanga kingdom. The nineteenth-century explorers who found Zimbabwe deep in the African savannah far from any known civilization were amazed and bemused; they described it as the lost kingdom of the Phoenicians and the Queen of Sheba. How else, they argued, could the great stone walls of Zimbabwe have been erected, for the local people had no knowledge of such activity. Theodore Bent, Richard Hall, and other investigators dated Zimbabwe to the pre-Christian era, and spoke of a lost civilization in the African bush. Then Randall MacIver came along, a pupil of the Egyptologist, Flinders Petrie, and trained in scientific excavation techniques. He realized the value of the Nankin china and Arab glass fragments found by diggers in the ruins, and sent them to experts in the British Museum in London. They reported that the imports dated to the thirteenth or fourteenth centuries A.D., so MacIver was able to demonstrate a medieval date for Zimbabwe and the southeast African gold trade, a dramatic example of how imports can date an archaeological site far from centers of literate civilization.

Imported luxuries are of considerable use for dating if their dates of manufacture in their homelands are known within fine limits, as well as their stratigraphic associations. Exotic imports were rare in most remoter areas, undoubtedly prized by their owners and sometimes kept as heirlooms. The Venda people of the Northern Transvaal, South Africa, still possess strings of ancestral glass beads which have been carefully preserved for generations.[32] Many originated as barter items in the prehistoric gold trade of earlier centuries. Similar cases are known from other parts of the world, complicating the dating of prehistoric settlements.

European prehistoric sites contain various small trade artifacts primarily of Mediterranean origin. The date, for example, of Egyptian faience beads in the Mediterranean basin has been established at about 1400 B.C.[33] Such ornaments are found in Europe as far north as Great Britain and Scandinavia, and provided a useful chronological horizon for sites containing them before the advent of radiocarbon dating (Figure 2.11). Although imports have a chronological range of several thousand years B.C., they are useless for dating the earlier millennia of prehistory.

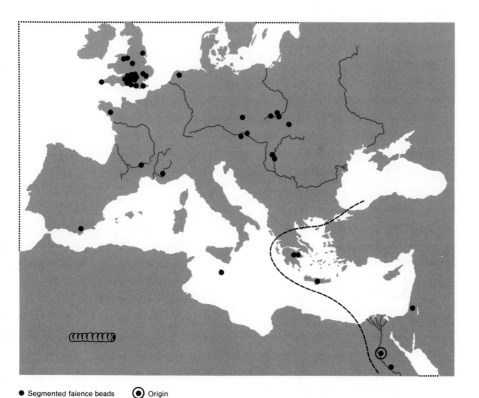

● Segmented faience beads   ⊙ Origin

Fig. 2.11 The distribution of segmented faience beads in Europe. Those within the broken line come from the Mycenaean, Cretan, and Egyptian distribution area. (After Clark.)

Cross-dating can, of course, be used with horizon markers of unknown absolute age, as well as with those of a known age in a historic context. Such relative dating horizon markers as particular forms of decorated potsherd or house types whose stratigraphic horizon is firmly and precisely established in one area can be used for the purpose of stratigraphic cross-correlations with other regions. This method is often employed in later European prehistory, but has been less frequently applied in the New World.

DENDROCHRONOLOGY

Dendrochronology, or tree-ring dating, was developed in Arizona by Dr. A. E. Douglass about 1913.[34] However, the idea of using tree rings as a method of dating archaeological sites is much older. As early as 1788, the Reverend Manasseh Cutler was counting the rings on trees growing on archaeological sites near Marietta, Ohio, and suggested that the site he was studying was about a thousand years old. But the prehistoric time scale established from tree rings goes back considerably further into the past, especially in the Southwest where it has been applied successfully to wooden beams in ancient Pueblos, preserved by the dry, desertic conditions. Both the slow-growing *Sequoia* and California bristlecone pine (*Pinus aristata*) provide long tree-ring sequences, the latter providing a continuous tree-ring chronology of 7,100 years. One pine tree 4,900 years old has been reported.

Everyone is familiar with tree rings, a concentric series of circles, each representing annual growth, visible on the cross section of a felled trunk. These rings are formed on most trees, but especially in areas where there is a marked seasonal weather change, either a wet and dry season, or marked alternation of summer and winter temperatures. As a rule, trees produce one growth ring a year, which is formed by the cambium lying between the wood and the bark. When the growing season starts, sets of large cells are added to the wood. These cells become thicker-walled and smaller as the growing season progresses—by the end of the growth season, cell production has ceased altogether. This process occurs every growing year; a distinct line is formed between the wood of the previous season and its small cells, and the wood of the following period and its new large cells. The thickness of each ring may vary according to the tree's age and annual climatic variations, thick rings being characteristic of good growth years.

Weather variations within a circumscribed area tend to run in cycles. A decade of wet years may be followed by five dry ones. One season may bring a forty-year rainfall record. These cycles of climate are reflected in patterns of thicker or thinner rings, which are repeated from tree to tree within a limited area. Dendrochronologists have developed sophisticated methods of correlating sets of rings from different trees so that they build up long sequences of rings from a number of trunks which may extend over many centuries (Figure 2.12). By using modern trees whose date of felling is known, they are able to reconstruct accurate dating as far back as 4,000 years ago. Actual applications to archaeological wood are much harder, but archaeological chronology for the American Southwest now goes back to the first century B.C.

The disadvantage of the method is the limited number of areas where it can be applied. In a climate which is generally humid or cold, or in an area where trees enjoy a constant water supply, the

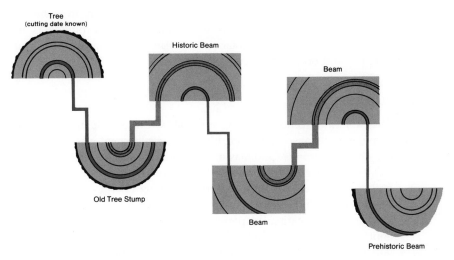

Fig. 2.12 Schematic drawings of a series of timbers, showing how a chronological sequence is built up.

difference in annual growth rings is either blurred or insignificant. Dendrochronology cannot be used under these circumstances. In addition to the Southwest, however, the method has been applied in the Missouri Valley, Canada, Scandinavia, England, and Germany. The results of such work are still experimental but a beginning has been made in establishing chronological sequences for such buildings as medieval churches, ancient town halls, and other structures.

The extremely accurate chronology for Southwestern sites has been achieved by correlating a master tree-ring sequence from felled trees and dated structures with beams from Indian pueblos. The beams in many such structures have been used again and again, so some are very much older than the houses which they were used to support. Such beams were found to link prehistoric dwelling sites and modern times. The earliest tree rings obtained from such settlements date to the first century B.C., but most timbers were in use between A.D. 1000 and historic times. There are some disadvantages to tree-ring dates, for readings from archaeological sites are affected by numerous factors. Many house beams are trimmed or reused several times, the outside surface of the log being removed in the process. The felling date cannot be established accurately without carefully observing the context and archaeological association of the beam.

Dendrochronology has a limited time span, but its accuracy is precise; its application has great importance, especially in semi-arid areas like the Southwest where the archaeologists' chronologies are envied by less fortunate scholars who wrestle with radiocarbon dating, imports, and other less accurate methods.

THERMOLUMINESCENCE

Thermoluminescence, a dating method with a formidable sounding name, is used on pottery, and is in the development stage.[35] It holds considerable promise and may one day provide absolute dating of even isolated potsherds. The principle is simple. The materials from which pottery is made have the property of storing energy by trapping of electrons as atomic defects or impurity sites. This stored energy can be released by heating the pottery, at which time visible light rays are emitted, known as thermoluminescence. All pottery and ceramics contain some radioactive impurities to a concentration of several parts per million. These materials emit alpha particles at a known rate, depending how densely concentrated they are in the sample. When an alpha particle is absorbed by the pottery minerals around the radioactive impurities, it causes mineral atoms to ionize. Electrons are then released from their binding to the nuclei and settle later at a metastable state of higher energy. This energy is stored unless the parent material is heated—for example, during the firing of a pot—when the trapped electrons are released and thermoluminescence occurs. Since the pot was fired, alpha particles are again absorbed by the material, and the thermoluminescence increases with time if the pot is heated again. Thus, to date a clay vessel involves measuring the thermoluminescence of the sample, as well as its alpha-radioactivity and its potential susceptibility to the production of thermoluminescence. In the laboratory, the trapped electrons are released from a powdered pottery fragment by sudden and violent heating under controlled conditions.

The method is still being developed, and there are numerous factors that affect its accuracy. Like other dating methods, results have been obtained initially from vessels of known age; because of these results, several investigators claim accuracies of plus or minus 5 per cent for prehistoric dates. Other proponents of the method are more cautious, however, and the potential of thermoluminescence will not fully be assessed for some time. But its future use could be unlimited for later prehistory, for pottery is one of the commonest archaeological finds.

At this point, though not described here, several other potential dating methods should be mentioned; these include archaeomagnetism, obsidian dating, and the Fission Track technique.[36]

RADIOCARBON DATING

Until recently no one had been able to date most archaeological sites at all precisely. Then, in 1949, J. R. Arnold and W. F. Libby published a paper in *Science* describing the dating of samples from objects of known age by their radiocarbon content.[37] The paper caused an archaeological furore, and once checked out was soon applied to organic materials from prehistoric sites, hitherto undated by any reliable chronometric method. Over twenty years have elapsed since the radiocarbon dating method became a regular part of the archaeologist's tool kit. For the first time a world chronology for prehistory has begun to emerge, based almost entirely on dates obtained from Libby's great discovery.

The radiocarbon dating method is based on the fact that cosmic radiation produces neutron particles in the upper atmosphere of the earth. Some particles hit atoms of ordinary nitrogen with an atomic weight of 14. These are captured by a nucleus which gives off a proton of atomic weight 1 thereby changing to carbon 14. Carbon 14, which is radioactive and by losing an electron reverts to nitrogen, is an isotope of ordinary carbon, which has an atomic weight of 12. It is believed to behave exactly like ordinary carbon from a chemical standpoint, and enters, together with ordinary carbon, into the carbon dioxide of the atmosphere, in which a constant amount of carbon 14 is to be found. The tempo of the process corresponds to the rates of supply and disintegration. Since living vegetation builds up its own organic matter by photosynthesis and by using atmospheric carbon dioxide, the proportion of radiocarbon present in it equals that in the atmosphere, neglecting the very short lifetime of individual plants compared with the half life of radiocarbon. As soon as an organism dies, no further radiocarbon is incorporated. The radiocarbon present in the dead organism will immediately begin to disintegrate slowly so that after 5,568 years[38] only half the original amount will be left, after about 11,400 years only a quarter, and so on. Thus, if you measure the ratio of carbon 14 to carbon 12, you can obtain an idea of the age of the specimen being measured. The initial amount of radiocarbon in a particular sample is low, so the limit of detectability is soon reached. Samples earlier than 50,000–60,000 years old contain insufficient quantities of carbon 14—the method is most effective on more recent sites.

Radiocarbon dates can be taken from samples of a wide range of organic material. About a handful of charcoal, burnt bone, shell, hair, skin, wood, or other organic substance is needed for the laboratory. The samples themselves are collected with meticulous care during excavation from impeccable stratigraphical contexts so that an exact location, specific structure, or even hearth is dated. Several dates should be taken from each level, as one sample may have been contaminated by a variety of causes. Modern rootlets, disturbances in the stratigraphy, and even packing with cotton wool or in newspapers can introduce younger carbon into an ancient sample, although some more obvious contaminations are eliminated by careful laboratory treatment.

The date arrives from the laboratory with a plus-or-minus factor attached to it, which is explained in Table 2.5. Thus a radiocarbon date is never the exact age of a sample, merely the statistically most likely *radiocarbon age.*[39] No one has yet been able to establish the exact relationship between a radiocarbon age and the true age of a sample, although calibrations with tree-ring dates will eventually provide an accurate true chronology for the past 4,000 years (Figure 2.13). Earlier dates will remain "radiocarbon ages" and, as such, are of unknown accuracy as there is as yet no means of extending dendrochronology further back into the past. "Before present," a term used with radiocarbon dates, means "before A.D. 1950"—by international agreement.

POTASSIUM ARGON DATING

The earliest sites dated by the radiocarbon method are about 55,000 years old, leaving an enormous span of human history still to be dated. Until recently, only relative dates were available for the earlier periods of the Stone Age, despite attempts to use solar radiation fluctuations as a basis for dating the recent geological past. But the geologists have recently developed a battery of radioactive and other counting techniques for dating the earth's age, one of which, the potassium argon method can be used to date geological strata as recent as 400,000 years old.[40] This method measures the ratio of potassium 40 (K40) to gas argon (A40), both elements which occur in many minerals. Radioactive K40 decays at a fixed rate to form A40. By measuring the ratio of K40 to A40 in a spectrometer, one can calculate the age of volcanic rocks like lava. Fortunately, many early human settlements in the Old World are found in volcanic areas, where such deposits as lava flows and tuffs are found in profusion.

The first and one of the most dramatic archaeological dates to be obtained from this method came from Olduvai Gorge, Tanzania, where Dr. and Mrs. Louis Leakey have found a long sequence of human culture extending over much of the Lower and Middle Pleistocene, associated with human fossils. Olduvai, a jagged slash in the

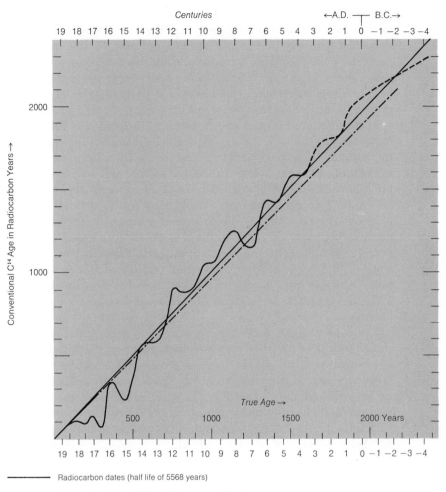

Fig. 2.13 This diagram was compiled by the La Jolla Radiocarbon Laboratory to show the approximate empirical relationship between radiocarbon dates and dendochronologically determined wood ages.

Serengeti Plains, was formed by earth movement which has exposed the beds of a long-forgotten Pleistocene lake overlying a layer of volcanic tuff. Early man camped around the shores of the lake; his living floors are preserved in the sides of the gorge, and his implements and broken animal bones lie on them where they were dropped by their owners, and were preserved under layers of fine lake silt. The remains of Australopithecines have been found on the living floors, associated with the tools and bones, together with lumps of lava either deposited naturally by the lake or brought to the site by early man. Some lava on the floors have been dated by the potassium argon technique, and samples from a living floor where the first cranium of *Australopithecus robustus* was discovered were dated to about 1.75 million years.[41] At the time, these and other nearly contemporary dates were a sensation, for most people had imagined that the Pleistocene began about a million years ago. At one step, man had almost doubled his antiquity. Even earlier dates have come from the Omo Valley in southern Ethiopia, where American, French, and Kenyan expeditions have investigated extensive Lower Pleistocene deposits long-known for their rich fossil beds. Fragmentary Australopithecines were found at several localities, but no traces of tools, potassium argon dates giving readings between 2 and 4 million for deposits yielding hominid fossils. Tools were found in levels between two dates of 2 and 2.5 million years. Chopper tools of undoubted human manufacture have come from Koobi Fora in Northern Kenya, dated to about 2.61 million years, at the time of writing the earliest known date for human artifacts.[42]

Unfortunately, the potassium argon method is comparatively inaccurate, with large statistical margins, amounting to as much as a quarter of a million years on Olduvai dates, and can only be used on a limited range of rocks, so that only those sites in volcanic areas can be dated by this method. This and other absolute dating methods have expanded the time scale of human evolution dramatically and revolutionized our ideas about the tempo of human evolution—gradual at first, with the pace of physical and cultural development accelerating rapidly from about 50,000 years ago to the present almost frenetic quest for change in human culture. Archaeological chronologies primarily aim to set up the time framework for our perception of the magnitude of human achievement.

Chapter 3
Preservation and Discovery

PRESERVATION

"After the exertion of entering into such a place, through a passage of . . . perhaps six hundred yards, nearly overcome, I sought a resting place, found one, and continued to sit; but when my weight bore on the body of an Egyptian, it crushed it like a band-box."[1]* Tomb robber Giovanni Belzoni wrote this in 1820 as he pillaged the mausolea of Egypt. How many times have we read that such and such a find was "crumbled to dust" upon discovery, or that exposure to the open air caused the finds to "dissolve before our very eyes." Modern archaeologists have developed a battery of methods to recover fragile objects from the soil, for preservation is a key factor both in the discovery of archaeological sites and in our reconstruction of the past. Whatever the theoretical approach one uses, a serious limiting factor to scientific investigation in archaeology is the degree to which sites and the artifacts preserved in them have survived many centuries in the inhospitable soil.

Preservation conditions depend largely on the soil and the general climatic regimen in the area of a site. Under favorable conditions, a wide range of artifactual materials are preserved, including such perishable items as leather containers, basketry, wooden arrowheads, or furniture. But under normal circumstances, usually only the most durable artifacts survive.

In general terms, the objects found in archaeological sites can be

* See pages 323–325 for notes to Chapter 3.

divided into two broad categories: inorganic finds and organic materials. Inorganic objects include stone implements made from a variety of rocks including flint, quartzite, and quartz, although these can weather quite severely, resulting in surface coating or patination. Gold, silver, bronze, copper, and lead, also inorganic substances, preserve well, but iron rusts easily and frequently only survives as a discoloration in the soil. Clay pots are among the most durable of human artifacts, especially if they are well fired, although the clay surfaces may be somewhat altered. Masonry and bricks fired in kilns survive well but have a rather limited role in the interpretation of the past, being confined to those prehistoric sites where substantial brick or stone structures are found. Sun-dried bricks or mud hut floors or walls have less durable characteristics, for they tend to become constituent elements of the archaeological deposits as a result of wind and weather. But they are often of critical use to stratigraphers or students of architectural styles in Near Eastern mounds or African villages.

An enormous range of organic substances were used by prehistoric man, whether a hunter or agriculturalist. Bones and antlers were vital raw materials to the Upper Paleolithic hunters of southwestern France 12,000 years before Christ; the Pueblo dwellers of the American Southwest used several types of fiber to make sophisticated baskets. Prehistoric Bushmen at the Gwisho hunting camps in central Zambia were making wooden digging sticks and fine arrowheads 4,000 years ago, which are perfectly preserved in the deposits of a hot spring.[2] The Acheulian hunter-gatherers of the Kalambo Falls lake basin in Central Africa were using wooden implements, including possibly a club, as early as 55,000 years ago,[3] and a yew spearpoint was found in the Middle Pleistocene deposits of the Clacton Channel in eastern England, a relic of a Pleistocene hunt (see Figure 7.16). Bone, ivory, hair, skin, and vegetal remains are other examples of organic materials utilized by prehistoric man. Alas, they only rarely survive in the archaeological record.

Waterlogged or peat-bog conditions are particularly favorable for preserving wood or vegetal remains, whether the climate is subtropical or temperate. While tropical rain forests such as those of the Amazon basin or the Congo are far from kind to wooden artifacts, many archaeological sites are found near springs or in marshes where the water table is high, and where perennial waterlogging of occupation layers has occurred since they were abandoned. Danish bogs have yielded a rich harvest of wooden hafted weapons, clothing, ornaments, traps, and even complete corpses, such as that of Tollund man.[4] This unfortunate individual's body was found by two peat cutters in 1950, lying on its side in a brown peat bed in a crouched position, a severe expression on the face and eyes lightly closed. Tollund man wore a pointed skin cap and a hide belt—nothing else. He had been hanged, the cord which was the cause of his death knotted tightly around his neck. The Tollund corpse has been shown to be about 2,000 years old and to belong to the Danish Iron Age. So perfect were preservation conditions that much of his skin still survived, and his peaceful portrait has been included in many archaeological volumes. A formidable team of medical experts examined his cadaver, among them a paleobotanist who established that Tollund man's last meal consisted of a gruel made from barley, linseed, and several wild grasses and weeds, eaten some twelve to twenty-four hours before his death. He is thought to have been a sacrificial victim of a fertility cult, hanged to ensure the success of crops and the continuation of life.

Most finds in waterlogged contexts are less spectacular, but often highly revealing, like Star Carr in northeast England (see Figure 2.10). Waterlogged deposits there preserved a wide range of organic materials, including a platform of birch saplings through which the reeds had grown later. Rolls of birch bark, a canoe paddle, numerous barbed spearheads, and a series of stag antler frontlets made into headdresses came from the platform area; chipping debris from the manufacture of numerous stone arrow barbs and scrapers littered the settlement. The excellent conditions preserved much organic material of the hunters' culture. As a result, Grahame Clark could paint vividly that the hunters' life style was oriented toward the red deer whose antlers provided so much of their tool kit, as well as other forest animals like the elk.

Before Star Carr was discovered, the only finds of this period in England had been some isolated bone or antler spearheads and scatters of the small stone tools used by hunters. Such limited discoveries are typical of unfavorable preservation conditions in temperate climates—the contrast with Star Carr is dramatic. Yet most archaeological sites are located in areas where soil or climatic conditions destroy all inorganic materials. Our total knowledge of the Middle Stone Age of Central Africa, for example, is confined to drawer after drawer of stone tools which, at best, can only tell us something about their makers' technological abilities.

Very arid environments, like those of the American Southwest or the Nile Valley, are even better than waterlogged localities. Undoubtedly one of the most famous of all archaeological discoveries is the amazing tomb of Tutankhamen (*ca.* 1345 B.C.), unearthed by Lord Carnarvon and Howard Carter in 1922,[5] where dry conditions were still damp enough to cause some deterioration of organic finds. The undisturbed burial chamber was opened, revealing the grave furniture exactly in the state in which it had been laid out by the king's mourners. Gilded wood chests, cloth, ivory caskets, models of chariots and boats, and mummies were all perfectly preserved, together with a bewildering array of jewelry and wall frescoes shining as brightly as the day they were painted, even showing the somewhat hasty execution accorded them by the artist. Tutankhamen's sepulchre provides as vivid a glimpse of the past as we are ever likely to obtain. Papyrus texts have been preserved by the dry Egyptian conditions in many Nile Valley cemeteries, too, giving an unrivalled picture of the Ancient Egyptian world.[6]

The American West is rich in organic finds. Arid levels at Danger Cave in Utah contained wooden arrows, knife handles, trap springs, and other wood tools,[7] and fiber sandals, string aprons, and baskets have come from Anasazi culture Basketmaker II sites, dating to between A.D. 46 and 330. As important as these artifacts are the caches of domesticated plant remains. Caves near the Talus Slope Village site in the northern San Juan region, near Durango, Colorado,[8] contained maize cobs and traces of squashes; wild foods included sunflower seeds, amaranth, and tansy mustard seeds. Other sites contained feathered ornaments, textiles, and netting. A series of burials from Coastal Peruvian Inca and pre-Inca sites have been recovered in a desiccated state, too, so much so that traces of tattooing and feathered headdresses have been recovered by the archaeologists.[9]

The dry conditions of Southwestern sites are highly conducive to the survival of vegetal remains, and archaeologists and botanists have been able to describe the evolution of maize and other domestic crops. The maize from the Durango sites is genetically more advanced than the earliest Mogollan maize from Bat Cave and Tularosa Cave.[10] MacNeish and others have similarly traced the history of domestic crops in Central America where dry conditions have also preserved cobs of early corn.[11] In contrast, the development of prehistoric agriculture in the Near East is less well known, owing to less favorable site conditions.

Arctic sites, too, are excellent for the preservation of man's past. The circumpolar regions of Siberia and the New World have acted like a giant refrigerator, where the processes of decay have been held in check for thousands of years. Close to the Arctic Sea, the carcasses of mammoths have survived thousands of winters in a state of perennial refrigeration. The Beresovka mammoth from Siberia was studied in 1901 by a Soviet expedition whose dogs ate the flesh of the Pleistocene beast as it was being dismembered.[12] The hair was perfectly preserved, and the remains of its last meal were found on its tongue and in its stomach.

Russian archaeologist Sergei Rudenko was responsible for some remarkable excavations at the Pazyryk burial mounds in Siberia, not far from the Chinese and Mongolian borders. The Pazyryk mounds lie in an area where summers are short and winters intensely cold, and have been dated by radiocarbon and cross-dating techniques to around 400 B.C. They are thought to be associated with the Yue-Chi peoples of southern Siberia. Although the mounds are south of the permafrost zones of Siberia, the sites themselves are permanently refrigerated, a special microclimate being formed inside them by the heat conducting properties of the stone cairn forming each mound's core. The mounds themselves covered burial shafts filled with logs and rocks; log chambers containing the burials lay under this filling. The roofs of the chambers were covered with birchbark strips and the flooring was often planked. The bodies were deposited in log coffins, invariably lying in an extended position with their heads facing east. They were usually partly clothed and accompanied by wooden pillows and tables with dishes of food—cheese and fluid residues in them. A wealth of small objects came from the burials, including a Chinese mirror, beads, seashells, lacquer, gold pins, and the remains of clothing. Horses were buried with their masters, having been dispatched with a pole axe and placed in the burial shafts. Seven to nine or more horses were usually thrust into the shafts, their heads often facing east. Bridles, saddles, and head decorations accompanied the horses. Solid-wheeled wooden trolleys were found in each barrow; one contained a four-wheeled carriage with draught pole. The horse carcasses were so well preserved in the refrigerated conditions that their hides could be studied: none had their winter coats. The horses were rather emaciated, as if they had survived a hard winter and had been slaughtered in early summer. Furthermore, the flowers of white-yellow scabious, which blooms between the end of June and early July, were found in the moss-packing of one burial chamber. Thus it was deduced that Pazyryk burials were interred in the early summer months.

The refrigerated conditions of the mounds preserved not only an array of wooden artifacts, horse harnesses, carpets, and even felt wall-coverings and canopies with elaborate naturalistic motifs, but also the clothes and flesh of the individuals buried there. Linen shirts adorned with braid, caftans decorated with leather and gold discs, and headdresses of felt and leather came from the coffins, as did women's bootees, aprons, and stockings. Much of the clothing was elaborately decorated, whereas the individuals' hair was shaved. In addition to small ornaments, several bodies bore remarkable and elaborate tattooing. One chief's body showed a lively picture of a monster like a lion-griffin or some other imaginary creature. Deer, birds, and carnivores also adorned his body, with tattooing over the heart and arms and also on the legs. Presumably the figures had some magical significance as well as a decorative intent.

The Pazyryk finds are so extensive that describing even a small proportion of them is impossible here.[13] Among the fascinating details is the fact that the horses bore ownership marks, their elaborate harnesses having analogy with Scythian practice; a lively and unusual animal art tradition is associated with the harness, art that is both exuberant and distorted to fit the twisted shapes of bridle and saddle fittings. The remarkable discoveries at Pazyryk have a local importance because they show the long cultural ancestry of the modern pastoral tribes of south Siberia. But to archaeology as a whole they reveal the potential richness of archaeological sites under the preservation conditions sometimes found in the Arctic.

Eskimo archaeology has benefitted enormously from the Arctic cold, where permafrost, especially in Greenland and the more northern parts of Arctic territory, has refrigerated wooden objects, bone and ivory artifacts, and the remains of animals hunted by the artifact makers. Sometimes summer thaws have softened the upper layers of Eskimo middens which resulted in some destruction of material, so only the lower horizons with their better refrigeration furnish a complete range of prehistoric artifacts. The Bering Straits area of Alaska is famous for some remarkable Eskimo settlements which have provided rich archaeological treasures. Miyowagh on St. Lawrence Island is a midden site belonging within the Northern Maritime subtradition, as much as two meters deep in some places; a seaside settlement, it is now over one-half mile from the ocean because of successive building of beach lines since the camp was occupied about 2,000 years ago. The earliest houses at Miyowagh were built on the shore, and covered by a rich, black midden of animal bones, baleen, and artifact waste. The houses were rectangular and had been floored with stone slabs; driftwood and whalebone walls were laid horizontally and held in place by upright posts and boulders; the roofs were probably made of timbers and whalebones. The entries to the huts were large passages. So many sea mammal bones were used in Miyo-wagh home construction that the pursuit of such beasts must have been a primary activity of the inhabitants. The ivory, wood, and bone components of the harpoons used in the chase are some of the most frequent finds in Arctic sites. Thanks to excellent preservation conditions, archaeologists can use the minor technical and stylistic changes in the harpoon to delineate landmarks in the Arctic cultural sequence. Ivory is so well preserved in Northern Maritime sites that Collins and other scholars have been able to describe the distinctive art of the Old Bering Sea phase with its characteristic linear and circle and dot motifs, used to adorn harpoon heads, needle cases, and other prosaic domestic objects.[14]

Another remarkable site is the Ipiutak settlement near Point Hope on the Chukchi Sea, dated to the first few centuries A.D.[15] Over 60 semi-subterranean dwellings were excavated out of an estimated 600–700 on the site. The floor level of the Ipiutak houses was about 50 centimeters (19 inches) below the ground, with the squarish floor between 3 and 7 meters (10 and 23 feet) in diameter. A central fireplace lay on the floor of packed gravel or logs, while sleeping benches of gravel and earth lined three walls. Vertical logs or poles, caulked with finer timbers, formed the walls; the whole structure, including the wooden roof, was covered with arctic moss. In a nearby cemetery, wooden coffins containing a single burial were built in small pits, most of them at least a half-meter (19 inches) deep. Few grave goods were associated with these burials in contrast to a series of skeletons deposited only a few centimeters below the surface. The bodies when discovered were partially disarticulated, lying in a deposit of wood fragments, which included some flamboyant ivory carvings, and midden soil. The excavators inferred that the dead had been deposited on the ground, enclosed in a wooden frame or a pile of logs. Elaborate ivory carvings were invariably associated with the surface burials at Ipiutak, preserved by the cold conditions which have pertained at the site since its abandonment. Ipiutak art is dominated by small sculptures of bears, walruses, and other animals, while composite masks and delicate spiral ornaments were probably fastened to the grave coverings. It is sobering to realize that under temperate conditions only stone artifacts and the outlines of the Ipiutak houses and bed platforms would have survived the 2,000 years since the settlement was occupied.

The deposit in which antiquities are found has an important bearing on their preservation, just as the association of one artifact with another within the soil has. Classic examples are the Roman cities of Herculaneum and Pompeii, overwhelmed by a sea of ash or lava in A.D. 79 by an eruption of Vesuvius graphically described by the elder Pliny. Pompeii has been excavated from the lava to reveal a Roman town in which life stopped at an instant in time. Bodies of people fleeing from the molten lava, dog corpses, and complete buildings came to light, giving a clear but pathetic picture of the doomed city in its last moments.

Geological deposits, such as oil-bearing layers in Poland or tar beds in the New World, have supplied many fossil remains of large mammals trapped in the treacherous deposits thousands of years ago. A dog corpse from a Basketmaker site in the Southwest survived so well in dry soil that the flies which fed on the putrefying corpse were found with the skeleton. Viking ships are preserved in the acid soils of temperate climates by the stones, clay, and peat packed around them by their owners. Even the wine of Roman times has come down to us. In 1867 a bottle of wine dating from the third century A.D. was found in a Roman sarcophagus at Speyer; the bottle was still full, and the liquid was analyzed to be wine mixed with honey. A thick layer of olive oil covered the wine, poured into the bottle by the original bottler to preserve the contents; this had become resinated, preventing the wine from evaporating.[16]

In spite of these exceptional instances, most soils tend to be destructive. Acid soils destroy inorganic objects rapidly, but the dark discolorations of postholes and hut foundations often remain, and challenge the archaeologist to reconstruct structures whose actual substance has vanished. The granitic soils of subtropical regions tend to be highly destructive, while the chalk deposits of Europe preserve animal bones, burials, and metals moderately well. The great loess belts of Central Europe have mantled many Upper Paleolithic settlements, preserving the floor plans of the mammoth hunters' camps, some of the earliest human structures ever recovered.[17]

The archaeologist who chances on a site where the conditions of preservation allow him a glance at the more perishable aspects of prehistoric man's material culture and economy is lucky. Small wonder that the most famous archaeological sites are those where climate, soil, or geology have been kind to the artifacts of prehistoric man.

FINDING ARCHAEOLOGICAL SITES

For the early antiquarians, sites were discovered by locating burial mounds, stone structures, hillforts, and other conspicuous traces of prehistoric man's impact on the European landscape. The "tells" of the Near East, occupied by generation after generation of city dwellers, were easily recognized by early travelers, and the temples and monuments of Ancient Egypt have attracted antiquarian and plunderer alike for many centuries. New World archaeological sites were described by some of the first conquistadores—later, Copán, the ruined Maya city, was studied by Garcia de Palacio in 1576. Maya sites were vividly cataloged by John Lloyd Stephens and Frederick Catherwood in the mid-nineteenth century, and the wonders of Mesoamerican civilization laboriously recovered from the rain forest that engulfed them.

But many prehistoric settlements are inconspicuous or even invisible to the naked eye, forgotten by the present inhabitants of the area where they are found. It is safe to say that many of the world's most conspicuous and spectacular archaeological sites are known, even if they have not been excavated. Today's archaeologist is often concerned with the location of large numbers of small sites within a well-circumscribed region as part of prehistoric settlement pattern study. His techniques of site location are many and ingenious, but still stem from perceptive observation in the field. Field archaeology, in the sense of site surveys conducted without recourse to excavation, has a respectable ancestry in the travels of William Camden and the generations of antiquarians who followed him. Camden himself was a perceptive field observer, who spoke with peasants and squires and observed the ways in which natural phenomena could be used to help the archaeologist. He visited the former Roman town at Richborough in Kent: "But now age has erased the very tracks of it; and to teach us that cities dye as well as men, it is at this day a cornfield, wherein when the corn is grown up, one may observe the draughts of the streets crossing one another (for where they have gone the corn is thinner)."[18]

Site survey became a serious part of archaeology when field archaeologists began to realize that man had enacted his life against the background of a contemporary landscape, and that all they would find would be what Francis Bacon defined as "some remnants of history which have casually escaped the shipwreck of time." The early twentieth century was a great time for field archaeology in Europe. J. P. Williams Freeman and O. G. S. Crawford, among others, traced Roman roads and ancient field systems, walking and bicycling over the countryside in search of known and unknown sites, while in Bolivia and Peru, Max Uhle, a German, was among those who pioneered systematic field survey in the New World. The techniques developed by these scholars form the basis for much archaeological fieldwork today.[19]

Before we examine some ways in which archaeological sites are located, we should define "field archaeology." Field survey is concerned with archaeological sites in space: prehistoric settlements are located, their surface features plotted and carefully reported, and their relationship to other sites recorded on detailed maps. Extensive surface collections are an important part of the survey process, for the artifacts found on a site, either exposed by natural factors or in animal burrows, give a general impression of its inhabitants. In the classical sense field archaeology involves no excavations, no studies of stratigraphic profiles from trenches, and no radiocarbon dating from excavated samples of charcoal; it is merely surface survey. Beyond the actual mechanics of site location, the information obtained from a field survey is concerned with the relationship—in space—of one site to another, and of coherent groups of sites with each other. Each settlement had an individual ecological niche, and a group of sites as a whole may have a complex relationship with a variety of soil types, water supplies, and vegetational covers, all of which may have varied in importance through time. Iron Age villages in southern Britain, for example, were often associated with complex agricultural systems, surviving in the archaeological record as field boundaries. The relationship between homesteads and fields was a critical factor in the residential stability, land-tenure systems, and society of the inhabitants of the area. Relationship in space is such an important part of prehistory that field archaeology has become an important handmaiden of those who study man's complex and ever-changing relationship with his environment.

AERIAL PHOTOGRAPHY

O. G. S. Crawford, best known as the founder of the celebrated archaeological journal *Antiquity*, was a brilliant exponent of field archaeology. A perceptive countryman, he soon became aware of the value of an overhead view of the countryside. Crawford had read Camden's accounts of Richborough and Roman Silchester, where the street plans were exposed in the growing corn, and had observed the rolling landscape of rural Britain from church towers and hills, a low sun or snow emphasizing the relief of prehistoric earthworks or field systems. Then, during World War I, Crawford flew as an observer on the Western Front, taking aerial photographs for reconnaissance purposes, and immediately realized the potential of air photography for the location and planning of all types of archaeological sites, even those invisible to the surface observer. The Germans even photographed deserted cities in the northern Sinai Desert during the war. Fields, streets, buildings, and other features showed up with astonishing clarity; Dr. Theodore Wiegand, who published the photographs, hailed a new era in archaeological reconnaissance. Thanks to these pioneer war surveys and the vigorous efforts of Crawford and other former airmen, aerial survey has become a formidable tool.[20] Thousands of hitherto unknown sites have been plotted on maps for the first time, whole field systems and roadways have been incorporated into panoramas of prehistoric or Roman landscapes in Italy and North Africa, and well-known sites like Stonehenge or Mesoamerican temples have been photographed in the context of their landscapes (Figure 3.1).

Aerial photography gives an unrivalled overhead view of the past.

Fig. 3.1   An aerial photograph of the earthworks at Maiden Castle, Dorset, England.

Sites can be photographed from oblique or vertical angles, at different seasons or times of day, and from many directions. Numerous sites which have left almost no surface traces on the ground have come to light through the all-embracing eye of the air photograph. Many earthworks or other complex structures have been levelled by plough or erosion, but their reduced topography clearly shows up from the air. The rising or setting sun can set off long shadows which emphasize the relief of almost vanished banks or ditches, so the features of the site stand out in the oblique light. Such phenomena are sometimes called "shadow sites." More important are crop and soil marks, found in areas where the subsoil is suitable to detect differences in soil color and in the richness of crop growth on a particular soil. Such marks cannot be detected easily on the surface, but can be clearly seen under favorable circumstances from the air. The principle upon which the crop mark is based is the fact that the growth and color of a crop are greatly determined by the amount of moisture the plant can derive from the soil and subsoil. If the soil depth has increased by digging features such as pits and ditches and then filling them

69

in, or by heaping up additional earth to form artificial banks or mounds, the crops growing over such abandoned structures are high and well nourished. The converse is also true in areas where soil has been removed and the infertile subsoil is near the surface, or where there are impenetrable surfaces such as paved streets below ground level and crops are stunted. Thus a dark crop mark can be taken for a ditch or pit, while a lighter line will define a more substantial structure. Soil marks result from ploughing soil from such features as banks, which show up as a lighter color, in contrast to the darker deeper soil around them. Crop marks are very useful in chalk country, where the subsoil is a brilliant white. Infrared photography is now being used to locate field systems for the first time.[21]

Much of the world has been covered by military photographers, normally from an altitude of around 24,000 feet. These mosaics are most often used by expeditions to remote areas who want to survey a large tract of country at minimum expense. A classic example of air photograph usage was provided by Gordon Willey who used a standard Peruvian Air Force mosaic of the cultivated valley bottoms and margins of the Virú Valley in northern coastal Peru to survey changing settlement patterns there.[22] Willey employed these photographs as the basis for a master site map for the Valley, and was able to plot many different archaeological features. Three hundred and fifteen sites in the Virú Valley were located, many of them stone buildings, walls, or terraces which showed up quite well on the mosaics. Some much less conspicuous sites were also spotted, among them midden heaps without stone walls, refuse mounds which appeared as low hillocks on the photographs, and small pyramidal mounds of insignificant proportions. Adobe houses did not show up as clearly as stone structures. An enormous amount of time was saved, time which otherwise would have been spent walking over rough countryside. The aerial photographs enabled Willey and his team to pinpoint many sites before going out in the field. The finds were later investigated on the spot. The result was the fascinating story of shifting settlement patterns in Virú over many thousands of years, which has become a classic study of its kind.

ACCIDENTAL DISCOVERIES

The ingenious gentlemen who calculate such things estimate that something like a quarter of all archaeological sites have been discovered because of nature's or humans' activity. Whole chapters of man's past have emerged through accidental discoveries of sites, spectacular artifacts, or skeletons. A famous and flamboyant archaeological discovery was made by a girl named Kirsten Svendsdatter at Gallehus, Denmark, in August, 1639.[23] She stumbled over a root and found a curved golden horn, over two and a half feet long and elaborately embossed with decoration in high relief. The horn found its way into the royal treasury and was almost forgotten until, ninety-five years later, a smallholder named Erik Lassen found a second, incomplete but slightly heavier horn of the same metal. It joined its companion in the royal library in Copenhagen, where the horns remained on exhibition for sixty-eight years. In 1802, tragically, they were stolen and melted down before the thief was apprehended; this left notes and drawings as our only record of them, from which silver gilt copies were made in 1861. The Gallehus horns bear runic inscriptions and decoration which date them to the period A.D. 400–450, an unsettled time in Western European history. One horn bears the runic inscription: "I Laegaest son of Holte made the horn," and they are thought to be of ceremonial origin.

The Gallehus horns are one of many discoveries of cached weapons, coins, smiths' tools, and sacrificial objects found in the fields of the Western world. Ploughing, peat cutting, road-making, and other day-to-day activities have been a fruitful source of archaeological discoveries. Industrial activity, highway construction, airport expansion, and other destructive pastimes of twentieth-century man have unearthed countless archaeological sites, many of which have to be investigated hurriedly before the bulldozers remove all traces of the site. Deep ploughing, freeway construction, and urban renewal are bitter enemies of the past. Yet dramatic discoveries have resulted from man's despoiling of his environment. Some states require highway contractors to allocate a proportion of their contract budgets for the investigation of any archaeological sites found in the path of their freeways—this at least permits some investigation of accidentally discovered settlements. But many construction programs pay little heed to the pleas of the archaeologist and bulldoze away the past with minimal concern.

An example of a startling accidental discovery was that made on a ridge named Ingombe Ilede in the Middle Zambezi Valley, Central Africa, in 1960.[24] A water storage tank and pump house was to be built there to supply water to the many villages in the vicinity. In digging the foundations of the water tank bones were discovered. Fortunately, a local government officer happened to pass by and collected the finds, including some copper ingots and gold beads. Due to his urgent telephoning, archaeologists launched a rescue excavation on the site and recovered a series of eleven richly decorated burials from the summit of Ingombe Ilede. The skeletons, probably buried in the fifteenth century A.D., bore ornaments of copper, gold, and iron, as well as glass beads, remains of clothing, and necklaces of seashells imported from the East African coast over 400 miles away. Without the government officer's action, a major chapter in African history would never have been written, and we would know almost nothing of early commerce in south-central Africa before the Portuguese arrived at the mouth of the Zambezi River in the late fifteenth century.

Hydroelectric schemes in developing countries are a major source of site destruction, and yet have stimulated much intensive survey. The Aswan Dam scheme in Nubia provided a rare opportunity for intensive investigation of Pleistocene geology and Stone Age sites in the areas now flooded by the Nile waters.[25] Kariba dam and lake in Central Africa inundated a vast tract of the Zambezi Valley which could only be surveyed in haste months before the Valley was flooded. In both these areas, as well as with Ghana's Upper Volta scheme, much archaeological information has been lost forever.

Nature itself sometimes uncovers sites for us, which are located by a sharp-eyed archaeologist looking for natural exposures of likely geological strata. Erosion, flooding, tidal waves, low lake levels, earthquakes, and wind action can all lead to the exposure of archaeological sites. A most famous site is Olduvai Gorge in Tanzania,[26] a great gash in the Serengeti Plains, where nature, through earth movement, has sliced through hundreds of meters of Pleistocene lake bed to expose numerous living floors of early man. Fossil animal bones were found in the Gorge's exposed strata by Professor Kattwinkel as early as 1911, which led to a fossil-hunting expedition under Professor Hans Reck, and ultimately to Dr. and Mrs. Leakey's long and patient investigations in the Gorge. The results of their excavations are spectacular—a series of living floors stratified one above another upon which hominid fossils, broken animal bones, stone implements, and even traces of possible structures have been found and dated to ages ranging from 400,000 for *Homo erectus* to 1,750,000 years before the present for living floors in the earliest bed of the Gorge.

Most finds exposed by nature are not so spectacular. For example, in 1641 a great storm ravaged the coasts of the Low Countries, and laid bare the long buried shrine of a Roman goddess, Nehalennia, on the island of Walcheren, now once again covered by the North Sea.[27] Inland, the forces of nature have exposed a multitude of archaeological sites. The great river valleys of Europe, Africa, and Asia are filled with extensive deposits of water-laid alluvium and gravel, exposed when the vegetation is low in the dry season or uncovered by erosion and commercial work. Boucher de Perthes found his hand axes in the Somme River quarries; for many years the relative chronology of African prehistory and the European Lower Paleolithic rested on cultural sequences derived from the terraces of the Somme, Thames, Nile, Zambezi, and other rivers. Erosion gullies and sand dunes are also likely geological contexts for the field archaeologist to examine; these are particularly common in subtropical areas where erosion is often uncontrolled and results in the rapid destruction of valuable agricultural land. In 1951, a schoolmaster named MacLennan was driving from Nairobi to Johannesburg along the Great North Road which winds over thousands of miles from Capetown to East Africa. He noticed a series of large erosion gullies to the east of the road at Isimila near the small town of Iringa, central Tanzania, and stopped to explore the sandy deposits left standing by centuries of water erosion. MacLennan returned to his car with twenty-six beautiful Acheulian hand axes which he had picked up on the gully slopes. Fortunately he reported his finds to a South African archaeologist who published them. Six years later a team of University of Chicago archaeologists under F. Clark Howell excavated at Isimila, exposing a series of well-preserved Acheulian living floors in the walls of the eroded ravines. Such occupation areas have been found only at a handful of sites in Africa, Europe, and the Near East, most of which will be referred to in this book. At Isimila, surface erosion made a major contribution to prehistoric research.[28]

In late 1957, another remarkable discovery was made, this time in the semiarid country in southeastern Colorado.[29] Wind erosion exposed what appeared to be five separate piles of bison bones in an arroyo near Kit Carson. Some projectile points were also found with the bones. The bone bed at what became known as the Olsen-Chubbuck site lay in a filled buffalo trail, of a type which crisscrossed the plains in early frontier days. The bones were carefully excavated, and shown to come from *Bison occidentalis*, an extinct species. Separate piles, made up of different bone types such as limb bones, pelvic girdles, etc., gave a clue to the hunters' butchery techniques. They had cut up the carcasses systematically, piling the detached members in the arroyo in separate heaps, dismembering several bison at a time. The remains of nearly 200 bison came from the arroyo, but only a proportion was fully dismembered. Clearly the arroyo was a trap into which the beasts had been stampeded. (They have a keen sense of smell, but poor vision; a lumbering herd of these gregarious beasts can be readily stampeded into an abrupt declivity, and the leaders have no option but to plunge into the gully and be immobilized or disabled by the weight of those behind them.) So vivid a reconstruction of the Paleo-Indians' hunt could be made that the excavators were even able to guess at the direction of the wind on the day of the stampede. The vivid traces of this hunt of 6500 B.C. were buried in the arroyo by nature, and exposed again eight thousand years later, to be discovered by the vigilant eye of an amateur archaeologist.

ARCHAEOLOGICAL SURVEY

Most sites are found by skillful survey and thorough examination of the countryside for both conspicuous and inconspicuous traces of the past. The first stage in an archaeological survey involves work in the laboratory. Geology, soils, water supplies, and vegetation have all played their part in determining prehistoric settlement patterns and the location of ancient settlements. Maps and air photographs are assembled; the scientific literature on the region is perused. After some days, one goes into the field armed with an intimate knowledge of the survey area, its topography, geology, soils, vegetation, hydrology, and population. The result is a minimum of wasted time, for many areas—as discovered in the laboratory—may be quite unsuitable for prehistoric settlement.

An example of a find through such survey lies in southern Zambia, where the Southern Province of the country extends from the Kafue River in the north to the Zambezi in the south, a distance of some three hundred miles (Figure 3.2).[30] Most of the province is undulating plateau covered with savannah woodland, with an average altitude of 4,000 feet (1,220 meters). The savannah woodland of the highlands is dotted with prehistoric farming sites, many of which were occupied for several hundred years. Soils are moderately fertile, grazing grass is abundant, and the environment abounds in wild vegetable foods and game for the hunter. But both sides of the plateau are bounded by belts of country inhospitable to the farmer. The eastern borders of the highlands abut a steep escarpment of dry, stony hills, which plunges over 2,000 feet (610 meters) to the floor of the Zambezi Valley, 1,200 feet (365 meters) above sea level. Water supplies among the hills are minimal except in one or two deep valleys, and human settlement is a horrendous undertaking for subsistence farmers. Our survey area was thus delimited to the east by natural topographic features, while the western boundary was marked by a band of infertile agricultural country where a *mopane* (evergreen woodland) flourished on a deep, hard, clayey soil which is infertile to prehistoric farmers with only limited bush-clearing equipment and a simple agricultural technology. Thus our search for archaeological sites in southern Zambia was largely limited to the highland areas of the plateau and to the Kafue and Zambezi valleys. We were able to eliminate much of southern Zambia from intensive survey attention by dint of careful

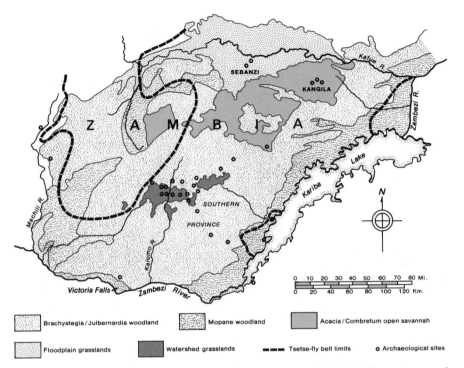

Fig. 3.2   Southern Zambia, showing vegetational zones, some archaeological sites, and areas of settlement.

laboratory research beforehand. The highland areas themselves have yielded over thirty large farming villages built on low ridges on the woodland and occupied intermittently over many generations by farmers equipped with simple iron tools. They kept cattle, small stock, and dogs and cultivated cereal crops; they lived in small mud-and-stick huts with thatched roofs, which were built on traditional village sites near good grazing areas in the savannah woodland. The thirty sites already known are but a fraction of the settlements that await discovery.

Field surveys are always conducted systematically, with careful reference to the preparatory work in the laboratory. The chosen country is traversed by automobile, on horseback or camel, by bicycle, or, most effectively, on foot. Most famous field archaeologists of this century have been avid walkers. In fact, one well known archaeologist used to boast that he had walked off the feet of certain colleagues in pursuit of the past. Footwork is important, for it enables the archaeologist to develop an eye for topography and the relationships of human settlement to the landscape. He watches for the soil colors underfoot in modern farming villages—is the grey organic soil underfoot likely to have formed in prehistoric settlements? Are abandoned recent village sites characterized by a certain vegetational cover which may also be found on the surface of much older sites? Ploughed fields may display telltale traces of ash, artifacts, or hut foundations. Vegetation may grow more lushly on areas where the subsoil has been disturbed or the nitrogen content of the soil is greater.[31] Soil discolorations in ploughed land or exposures of eroded soil may yield broken bones, stone implements, potsherds, or other evidences of prehistoric occupation. The local inhabitants, too, may provide information about places where "ancient bones" or traces of old settlements have been found. Every area has its folklore of "warriors' bones" or spectacular artifacts found during ploughing or digging house foundations. Some are founded on fact. Observation is the key to finding archaeological sites. Heinrich Schliemann's discoveries at Troy and those of Arthur Evans at Knossos in Crete resulted from judicious use of historical sources and careful observation. The prehistorian has less conspicuous signs to guide him. Grey soil from a rabbit hole, a handful of humanly fractured flints in river gravel, a blurred mark in a ploughed field— these are the signs of antiquity which he seeks. In doing this, he is following in a tradition of archaeological field survey with roots in the travels of Camden and the curiosity of medieval scholars.

Chapter 4

Excavation

A romantic atmosphere with images of elderly men in sun helmets, sweating natives, great pyramids, and buried treasure surrounds the popular view of archaeological excavation. Yet, though the image may remain, the techniques of modern excavation are rigorous and demanding, requiring long training in practical field techniques. We cannot compare archaeological digging with clearing a drainage ditch or digging up an acre of potatoes, although regrettably some excavations of my acquaintance bear such a resemblance. Archaeological excavation has certainly come a long way since the eighteenth century when it first became a serious tool of students of the past. Most early excavators were little more than treasure hunters ardently searching for antiquities for their cabinets—archetypes for the helmeted archaeologist of cartoon and popular legend. Many nineteenth-century excavations were almost carnivals, where several burial mounds would be opened in the course of a day while the supervisors of the excavations would "continue to pass our time, at intervals between digging and pic-nicing, in games of various descriptions—not exactly such as those which the builders of the mound celebrated when they laid the deceased on his funeral pile" (Figure 4.1). The antiquarian Thomas Wright, who wrote these words, and his colleagues of the 1840s led strenuous lives, as his description of an 1844 burial excavation reveals:

> Between 9 and 10 o'clock, the members assembled on the Breach Downs to be present at the opening of some barrows under the superintendence of the noble President. The workmen employed had previously

77

Fig. 4.1   Nineteenth-century barrow excavation.

excavated the barrows to within a foot of the place of a presumed deposit. Eight barrows were examined ... most of them contained skeletons, more or less entire, with the remains of weapons in iron, bosses of shields, urns, beads, fibulae, armlets, bones of more animals, and occasionally more vessels.... After the examination of these barrows, the whole party visited the mansion of the noble President, at Bourne, and having inspected his lordship's interesting collection of antiquities, and partaken of a substantial repast, attended the excavation of two barrows in his lordship's paddock, forming part of the group of which some had been recently opened. . . .[1]*

At the same time, the great civilizations of the Near East and Egypt were being unearthed from millennia of oblivion, with Henry Layard, Auguste Mariette, Heinrich Schliemann, and others hastily uncovering and removing literally tons of antiquities from their proper archaeological context. "Nothing was done with any uniform plan," complained Sir Flinders Petrie, doyen of early Egyptologists, of Mariette's work in the Nile Valley in 1883, "It is sickening to see the rate at which everything is being destroyed, and the little regard paid to preservation."[2]

But a century before, Thomas Jefferson, third President of the United States and author of the Declaration of Independence, had spent some time investigating burial mounds in Virginia. He excavated one such mound, and wrote a careful description of the layers and burials in it, drawing conclusions from his finds and noting their relationship to local theories about the mounds. Jefferson's perceptive observations and the lighthearted adventures of Victorian antiquarians together represent a polarity of curiosity about the past which forms one of the roots of archaeological scholarship.

The foundations of modern excavation lie in many beginnings. They have roots in the enthusiasm of Heinrich Schliemann, discoverer and excavator of prehistoric Troy, in the dedication of Sir Flinders Petrie, who brought order to Egyptian archaeology, and especially in the work of European archaeologists. In 1873, the Austrians under Alexander Conze began excavating at the Sanctuary of the Great Gods on the island of Samothrace. The dig lasted two years; the team of scientists included a photographer and two architects—and a man-of-war. The report was beautifully illustrated and full of accurate plans, one of the first modern archaeological monographs. The German Ernst Curtius began digging at Olympia in 1875, and worked there for six seasons. His excavations were conducted with Teutonic thoroughness, with careful planning of the architecture and detailed studies of the stratigraphy. New methods of digging and recording were developed, soon to be disseminated by Curtius's colleagues, among them Wilhelm Dorpfeld who turned Schliemann's excavations at Troy from "digging to dissection" of a complicated sequence of stratified layers.[2]

The sense of purpose and discipline the Germans and Austrians

* See pages 325–326 for notes to Chapter 4.

inculcated into the digging process was also practiced by a military gentleman in Britain. General Lane Fox retired from active duty in 1880 and succeeded to the Rivers estate in southern England, changing his name to Pitt Rivers. The General was a man of many parts, who had already studied the evolution of firearms and other artifacts and gained wide anthropological interests. He devoted the last twenty years of his life to a detailed exploration of the archaeological sites on or near his estate with a scientific thoroughness that had firm roots in his military training. Pitt Rivers' methods were elaborate and pains-taking; he recorded every object found in his trenches in such a manner that its exact find spot could be identified in the future, with reference to sections and plans of the dig. Three-dimensional recording was a cornerstone of his excavations, as were accurate stratigraphic profiles with the finds recorded on them, a large and competent staff, and prompt and meticulous publication of his results. The General is a colossus in the history of archaeology—the labor involved in producing the elegant blue and gold monographs describing his excavations must have been enormous.[4]

The lessons learned from the Pitt Rivers campaigns fell on many deaf ears, but were heeded by other pioneers. Pitt Rivers, the Germans, and Egyptologist Sir Flinders Petrie led a revolution in Old World archaeology that gradually steered the discipline away from treasure hunting to the study of people, their artifacts, and environment. But the early years of the twentieth century saw little progress, with wholesale digging of precious sites on both sides of the Atlantic and scant regard for stratigraphy or accurate record. New World archae-ology had entered a "descriptive-historic" period with the beginnings of potsherd stratigraphy and the excavations by Kidder at Pecos.[5] But excavation techniques were still primitive, and often hair-raising by modern standards. In the 1930s, however, scientific excavation again became a serious concern. Sir Cyril Fox and Sir Mortimer Wheeler excavated a series of important sites in Britain, basing their methods on those of Pitt Rivers and the Germans. Gerard Bersu in Germany, Howard Carter in the Valley of the Kings, and Sir Leonard Woolley in Iraq, all played their part in the development of modern excavation in the Old World, while W. S. Webb in the southeastern United States and Glenn A. Black in the Midwest helped advance scientific digging in the New World. The excavators of the 1930s changed the face of archaeological digging. The sweating graduate student digging for cultural sequences in the Peruvian rain forest inevitably applies many basic recording techniques developed by Pitt Rivers and his successors. In like manner, the excavator of Colonial Williamsburg or a Paleolithic cave in the Near East records his stratigraphic profiles and small finds according to principles enumerated by the remarkable General and refined thirty years ago.

A great exponent of the art of excavation has been Sir Mortimer Wheeler, whose short monograph *Archaeology from the Earth,* is an elegant and lively part of any archaeologist's library. Wheeler's digs were organized on basically military lines. The techniques of Pitt Rivers and his successors were refined and applied with consistent energy; the central emphasis in excavation shifted from finding objects to developing a strategy for an excavation campaign oriented toward the solution of archaeological problems, rather than discovery for discovery's sake. Wheeler's forthright denunciation of shoddy methods in archaeological fieldwork rubbed off on a generation of students who dug with him on the chalk downs of England or in India, and then applied his methods in remote parts of the British Empire, as well as at home. The past decade has seen great refinement of Wheeler's methods both in Great Britain and on the Continent, where particular attention has been paid to urban archaeology. Martin Biddle in medieval Winchester and Barrie Cunliffe at Fishborne, England, are among the excavators who have improved Sir Mortimer Wheeler's recording and digging methods. In the United States, Ivor Noël Hume has used meticulous excavation methods in his study of Colonial Williamsburg. The following section on excavation owes much to Wheeler and those who have followed him.

EXCAVATION METHODS

The last century has seen a transformation from treasure hunting to scientific investigation with a battery of well-disciplined methods, from curiosity to problem-oriented excavation. Archaeologists are digging up the past at a ferocious rate in all corners of the world. Dr. and Mrs. Leakey are exploring Olduvai Gorge in Tanzania with its rich storehouse of early living floors and hominid fossils. Professor Jelinek of the University of Arizona is reexcavating a Paleolithic cave at Mount Carmel in Israel. Martin Biddle is working with a large team of volunteers on the archaeology of medieval Winchester in England. Summer archaeology field schools are being conducted all over the United States, and American expeditions are working in Guatemala, Kenya, and Peru. All this activity will result in publications, reports, analyses, and descriptions of a multitude of different archaeological sites, prehistoric peoples, and research problems. But most professional archaeologists now understand the responsibilities and basic principles of excavation—guidelines developed in over two hundred years of archaeological exploration.[7]

The first lesson that any budding excavator learns is that his work is potentially destructive. Excavation is destruction—the archaeological deposits so carefully dissected during any dig are destroyed forever, and their contents removed. Here, again, there is a radical difference from history and other subjects. A scientist can readily recreate the conditions for a basic experiment; the historian can return to his archives for a reevaluation of the complex events in a politician's life. All that remains after an excavation is the finds from the trenches, the untouched portions of the site, and the photographs, notes, and drawings that record the excavator's observations for posterity. Thus, accurate recording and observation play an overwhelmingly vital role in the day-to-day work of an archaeologist, not only for the sake of the accuracy of his own research, but because he is creating an archive of archaeological information which may be consulted by others. Most of the basic handbooks on excavation refer to this need for discipline and meticulous recording during the unavoidable destruction of a chosen site.[8] Good excavators generally do not dig an entire site, but deliberately leave part of it for workers who come along later with new ideas and methods. Numberless different sites have been excavated during the past fifty years in every extreme of environment and with a bewildering array of research problems or preservation conditions that confronted the investigators. Yet all sites have fundamentally similar recording problems, whatever the reason they were excavated. The finds from any site are useless unless considered with reference to their context. *Context* means stratigraphy, chronology, and association—the three basic attributes of any find. Apart from the basic motions of uncovering a site, the crux of serious excavation is in the observation and ongoing interpretation of the significance of the layers being dissected by shovel, pick, and trowel.

Belzoni, Mariette, and those nineteenth-century barrow diggers were looking for archaeological treasure. But Thomas Jefferson spent some summer days in 1784 excavating for information about the inhabitants of Virginian burial mounds. Today, we follow in Jefferson's footsteps and search for the past in the widest sense, excavation being but one method at our disposal, even if it is a vital one. Archaeological research, like any scientific inquiry, is concerned with problems, models, and hypotheses that are constantly tested against new and existing evidence. Thus, any excavation is planned around a set of problems, and the objectives and strategy of the dig depend to a great extent on the dictates of the wider research project.

The research plan can be a simple one, and can involve simple propositions to be tested against excavated evidence. How old is that burial mound? Who occupied that shell midden, when, and what did they live on? What is the cultural sequence at Olduvai Gorge? Or, most fundamental of all—what is that site? What can we find out about its inhabitants? Such questions are normally asked during the first stages of a field campaign when a site has been located but no trenches sunk into it. As investigations proceed, stratigraphy is established, and dates obtained, then the research objectives may change and become highly specific and extremely complex.

The end products of even a month's excavation on a moderately productive site are a daunting prospect. Box upon box of potsherds, stone tools, bones, and other finds are stacked in the laboratory, the contents to be cleaned, sorted, marked, and studied. Hundreds of slides and photographs await processing and cataloging. Rolls of drawings, compiled with care in the field, contain important stratigraphic data without which the finds are meaningless. Cartons of soil and pollen samples, burials, radiocarbon samples, and other sources of information are piled up for eventual dispatch to specialists who will evaluate them. One expert excavator once told me that he estimated that a month's fieldwork meant a minimum of six months' laboratory work. My own experience suggests he cannot be far wrong. Excavation costs are such that problem-oriented digging is now the rule rather than the exception, with the laboratory work forming part of the ongoing evaluation of the research problem. The large piles of finds and records accumulated at the end of even a small field season contain a bewildering array of interdigitating facts which the researcher has to evaluate and reevaluate as his inquiry proceeds. He is constantly arranging his propositions and hypotheses, correlating his observations, and reevaluating his interpretations of the archaeological evidence. His boxes and plans are the basis of his research strategy and affect his fieldwork plans for the future. The days when a site was excavated because it "looked good," or because sheer lack of imagination precluded the development of a research strategy, have been replaced by a process of constant reevaluation of research objectives.

An early example of archaeological strategy was the discovery of the Minoan civilization. Sir Arthur Evans, son of the John Evans who was a central figure in the establishment of man's antiquity, was one of the greatest archaeologists of all time, combining organizing genius with scholarly integrity and brilliant insights, the latter perhaps the most important quality for any archaeologist.[9] In 1894 he visited Crete, determined to dig at Knossos, legendary site of ancient Cretan civilization. For many years, he had been interested in Mycenaean gems and had become interested in the origins of writing, convinced that a picture script was a precursor of literacy. His researches on gems led him to Crete, where he found that others had been stopped from digging at Knossos, although finds from it were in antique dealers' stores. After protracted negotiations, lengthened by uprisings and civil turmoil, he began digging on March 23, 1899. By April 13 he had discovered Linear B tablets, the mysterious Minoan script that was not deciphered until more than fifty years later, and was on his way to the unearthing of Minoan civilization, almost forgotten since Bronze Age times. Throughout the five years of excavation which followed, he issued annual summary reports, realizing in 1905 that a major study of the finds was necessary. Unlike many other spectacular excavations, the Palace at Knossos was fully published, with a minute attention to detail remarkable for the time. The *Palace of Minos* began to appear in 1921, the last volume in 1935, when Arthur Evans was seventy-nine years old. It is a magisterial work, the culmination of forty years of Cretan research which was pursued with relentless rigor and meticulous care. The result—a new civilization described for science through rudimentary research strategy, even if Knossos sits at the center of numerous other localities whose significance has not been coordinated with the finds from the great Palace itself. Although the descriptive genius of the Minoan discoverer excites the layman, the sound research tactics shine through the great work.[10]

One's research strategy depends considerably on the facilities available, the time at one's disposal, and the nature of the research problem. The only general rule is: no excavation is carried out without a strategy behind it and without attention to day-to-day tactics. To quote Sir Mortimer Wheeler again: "The excavator without an intelligent policy may be described as an archaeological food-gatherer, master of a skill, perhaps, but not creative in the wider terms of constructive science."[11]

TYPES OF EXCAVATION

Thus, strategy and problem-solving are two factors that determine the dig's layout. While the size and character of the site also play their part, and sampling techniques, if used, will affect digging plans, I have always mentally made two fundamental distinctions as far as trench layout is concerned, for excavations can be either selective or total. Since the settlements of prehistoric man are frequently sizable, complete excavation is a rarity, even if a considerable area of the site is investigated. Selective investigation is commonplace. Trenches are limited, the dig's objectives are often limited to stratigraphic and chronological considerations, or the solution of specific research problems to amplify larger digs elsewhere. A cross section of pottery, stone tools, and animal bones from a site are obtained from a selective

dig, perhaps as a lead-in for future investigations, or as a trial stratigraphic sequence to test against other sites where similar types of
excavation are planned. Surface features can be tested by selective
trenching in advance of a major dig.

The layout of small digs is determined by the surface topography,
density of finds, sampling factors, electronic survey,[12] or visible features
on the site. Selective excavation has the advantage that it is much
cheaper than larger-scale digging. If the excavation is planned carefully
many complex problems can be solved with a minimum expenditure
of time and money. In a world where fieldwork costs are escalating
rapidly, this is an important consideration; the days of larger excavations are probably behind us except under exceptional circumstances.
The high cost of excavation means careful planning and coordinated
strategy so that no trench is wasted and the maximum information
obtained. But, with a possibility that large-scale excavation will take
place later, trenches must be carefully sited to avoid hindering any
such future excavation.

Some of the world's most important sites have been excavated
selectively, using the concept of *vertical excavation* where limited areas
are excavated for specific information (Figure 4.2). Selective excavation
has also become a powerful technique often widely used when "rescue" digs are carried out in advance of construction work when there
is no time to carry out large-scale operations.

Area excavation is on a much larger scale and is naturally far more
expensive. An area dig implies *horizontality*—covering large areas to
recover building plans or the layouts of entire settlements (Figure
4.3). While stratigraphy and chronology are still vital, the primary
concern of area excavation is either settlement pattern, houses and
other structures, or horizontal relationships. The only sites that are
almost invariably totally excavated are very small hunting camps,
isolated huts, and burial mounds. The problems with horizontal digs
are exactly the same as those with any excavation, those of stratigraphic
control and accurate measurement. Figures 4.4 and 4.5 show three-
dimensional recording and ways in which archaeologists measure their
sites and record their field data. In a horizontal excavation, hundreds
of meters of ground are removed to expose large complexes of structures like, for example, the rooms of a pueblo. The former palace
at Nonsuch in southeastern England is a famous example, where the
ground plan of the entire palace, which had been lost, was recovered
by horizontal excavation, adding a new portrait to the already glittering
history of Henry VIII's reign.[13]

Area excavations imply the exposure of large open areas of ground
to a depth of several meters. A complex network of walls or post

Fig. 4.2   A vertical excavation at Maiden Castle, Dorset, England.

holes may lie within the area to be investigated. Each feature relates to other structures, a relationship which must be carefully recorded to interpret the site correctly, especially if several periods of occupation are involved. If the entire area is uncovered, it is obviously difficult to measure the position of the structures in the middle of the trench, far from the walls at the excavation's edge. To achieve better control of measurement and record, it is better to use a system that gives a network of vertical stratigraphic sections across the area to be excavated. This is normally done by laying out a grid of square or rectangular trenches with walls several centimeters thick between each square (Figure 4.6). Such areas may average 3.7 meters (12 feet) square in size, or larger. As Figure 4.6 shows, this system allows

Fig. 4.3   A horizontal, grid-type excavation at Maiden Castle.

Fig. 4.4   A site grid. Every spot within the grid, which is usually extended over the entire site, can be
measured in two directions. The trenches are laid out with reference to the grid, and the
finds in them can be assigned exact, three-dimensional measurements—two giving an
object's spot within the site and the third giving its depth.

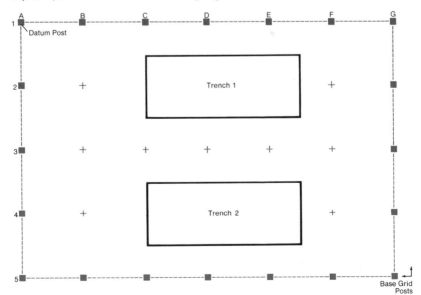

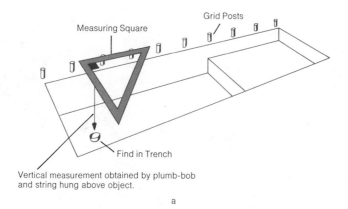

Measuring Square

Grid Posts

Find in Trench

Vertical measurement obtained by plumb-bob
and string hung above object.

a

Grid Posts

90°
angle

Vertical measurement
taken from this arm
with plumb bob held
over object

Measuring
square (held
horizontally)

Trench

Horizontal measurement
taken from this arm
(distance from grid
post line)

b

Fig. 4.5   *Three-dimensional recording. (a) The use of a measuring square. (b) A close view of the
square from above. The horizontal measurement is taken along the edge, perpendicular to
the grid post line, and the vertical measurement from that arm with a plumb bob.*

stratigraphic control of considerable areas, and ground does not have
to be removed except in areas where the finds are especially important.
Large-scale excavation with grids is extremely expensive and time-
consuming and is difficult to use in areas with irregular ground, but
it has been employed with great success at many excavations, being
used to uncover structures, town plans, and fortifications.

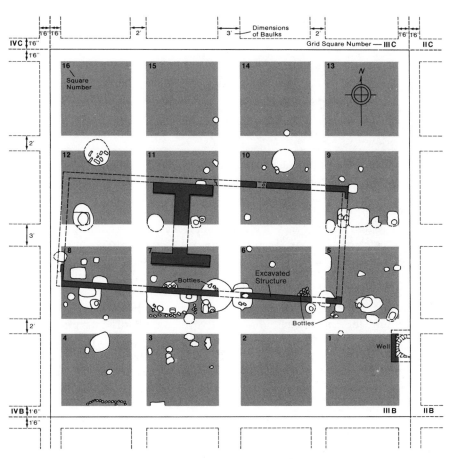

Fig. 4.6   A horizontal grid excavation, showing the layout of squares relative to an excavated structure at Colonial Williamsburg.

SAMPLING

Some archaeologists are beginning to use sampling techniques, too. They argue that, since we are relying more and more on statistical approaches to archaeological data in the reconstruction of prehistoric lifeways, the effects of uncontrolled bias in excavation are more noticeable. For example, if we are interested in past adaptations to environmental conditions, we must sample different types of sites in each environmental zone, and not merely those that "look important" or could yield spectacular finds. Unfortunately, resources are limited, and we obviously cannot dig all the sites in an area where hundreds may occur. Thus, these archaeologists argue, we must use sampling techniques to ensure a statistically reliable basis of excavated data from which we can make generalizations about our research problem.

Sampling has been defined as the "science of controlling and measuring the reliability of information through the theory of probability."[14] American archaeologist Lewis Binford has explored this subject, and in several articles argues against conscious or unconscious bias in selecting which site, or part of a site, should be excavated. Bias might consist of logistical convenience, destruction of the site, close proximity of a base camp, or a multitude of unconscious but pervasive factors. Yet we cannot assume that the sites which our bias leads us to select are the same as those which we did not select. Thus, Binford suggests, if the "universe" we seek to study—perhaps a region, a site, or a "culture"—represents similar kinds of archaeological unit and is "homogeneous," then we can use sampling techniques to choose our units of study free of selective bias.

This is achieved by assigning numbers to all units being studied, deciding how many can be dug with the resources available, and then selecting that many units from a published list of *random* numbers. Such a technique can be used only if all units are homogeneous, and in cases in which each possible sampling unit has an equal probability of being selected for excavation by random methods. If the "universe" is not homogeneous, perhaps consisting of ceremonial sites, villages, and burial grounds, or of sites of widely differing size, or of settlements in different ecological zones, then "stratified sampling" is employed. Each category of site or unit is treated as a separate homogeneous universe, which is selected randomly, with care taken that the numerically less common universes are proportionately adequately represented among the excavated units.

Sound sampling procedures, it is argued, permit generalizations about archaeological units to be made with confidence. Valid generalizations are not possible if all sites excavated, for example, came from areas chosen because they were near paved roads—that case is only generalizing on the basis of chosen bias. With random sampling, sites near the road are no different from those away from tarmac, and some activities are not represented in a site, not by accident but because they did not take place. And with sound sampling procedures, statistical tests can evaluate the confidence to be placed in generalizations made.

Sampling technique is new to archaeology, and as this methodology is developed and applied more widely, excavation methods will change, especially on sites which lend themselves to quantitative investigation, such as shell middens, living floors, caves, or town sites.

HOW DO YOU DIG?

What tools does the archaeologist use?[15] The traditional archaeological symbol is the spade, which has a flat back and straight edge, and is used for cleaning walls. Shovels, with their scoop-like shape, are used for piling up earth in a trench preparatory to its being sorted, and have innumerable applications in cleaning straight edges and tidying trenches; shovels are the principal working tool of the archaeologist under conditions where much ground has to be uncovered.

The principal tools for loosening soil are the pick, the mattock, and the fork. The pick and the mattock may be considered together because they are variants on the same type of tool; when used with care, they are a delicate gauge of soil texture, an indication much used in larger sites. But the most common archaeological tool is the diamond-shaped trowel, its straight edges and tip having innumerable uses: soil can be eased from a delicate specimen; the edges can scrape a feature in sandy soil into higher relief; and as weapons of stratigraphic recording, they can trace a scarcely visible stratum line or barely discernible feature. In addition, they are used for clearing postholes and other minor work, so much so that they are rarely out of a digger's hand on smaller sites.

Another important small tool is the brush, which of course has its greatest application on dry sites. The most commonly used brush is the household type with fairly coarse bristles; it can be held by the handle or the bristles and, wielded with short strokes, effectively cleans objects found in dry and preferably hard soil. The excavator uses various paintbrushes for more delicate jobs. The one-inch or one-half-inch domestic paintbrush has wide application in the cleaning of animal bones and more coarse specimens. Fine, camel's hair artist's brushes are best for most delicate bones, beads, and fragile ironwork. Many other small implements, some improvised on the site, aid in brush work. Six-inch nails may be filed to a point and used for delicate clearing jobs on bones and other fragile artifacts. The needle is another tool to clear soil from such delicate parts of skeletons as the eye sockets and cheekbones. One of the most useful digging tools is the dental pick, available in a bewildering variety of shapes. Often, dental picks can be obtained without charge through dentists, who discard them as soon as they show signs of wear. Continental European archaeologists have used a small, hooked digging tool, called a *crochet*, for many years; this is widely used for those excavations where a trowel is too big but where smaller tools are too slow and inefficient. The screen is another important tool because many finds, such as coins, glass beads, shells, small tacks, nails, and other small artifacts are miniscule. Most deposit from sites where small artifacts are likely to occur is laboriously sifted through fine screens, of one-half to one-eighth-inch size.

The archaeologist's surveying instruments normally include linen or metal tapes, plumb bobs, string, spirit levels, drawing boards, drawing instruments, a plane table, and a surveyor's level and compass—all essential for accurate recording of site plans and sections, and for setting up the archaeological archive.

RECORDING

As noted earlier, excavation is destruction, and an artifact's context is as important as its typological features.[16] Detailed records and accurate measurement are the foundation of sound, scientific excavation, and some understanding of site records is as important as a grasp of the principle of superposition—indeed the director of an excavation spends more time writing and drawing than he does digging. He maintains a number of different notebooks throughout the excavation, including the site diary or day book. This large notebook records all events at the site—the amount of work done, the daily schedule, the number of people on the digging team, and any labor problems that may arise. Dimensions of all sites and trenches are recorded. Any interpretations or ideas on the interpretations, even those considered and then discarded, are meticulously recorded in this book. Important finds and significant stratigraphic details are also noted carefully, as is much apparently insignificant information, which may, however, prove to be vital in the laboratory. The site diary purports to be a complete record of the procedures and proceedings of the excavation. The site diary is more than an aid to the fallible memory of the excavator; it is a permanent record of the dig for future generations of scientists who may return to the same site to amplify the original findings. Site diaries can be a most important tool in the hands of later researchers—for instance, the Knossos site diaries kept by Sir Arthur Evans as he uncovered Minoan Civilization for the first time, which have been used again and again by later investigators in Crete.[17]

A "small-finds" register is important in the records on any dig. But in many cases, while some artifacts such as pottery or stone implements may be very common, others, such as iron tools or beads, will be extremely rare and have special significance. So a "small-finds register" is maintained. Each "small find" is given a special number and labelled with its level, trench number, and depth below surface; additional information relating to the layer in which the object was found is also noted. This procedure provides a permanent record of significant artifacts that must be described individually in the final report and whose preservation is important. The researcher also lists the bags of finds made during the excavation in the same book. Each bag, especially of common artifacts like pottery, animal bones, and stone implements, receives a serial number and is recorded in a list in the back of the small-finds register.

The recording methods mentioned so far are basic ones used by archaeologists during excavation. But the recording both of the site plan and of its structures, as well as of stratigraphic sections, is just as important. The site plan may vary from a simple contour plan for a burial mound or occupation midden (Figure 4.7), to a complex plan of an entire prehistoric town or of a complicated series of structures.[18] Accurate plans are important, for they provide a record of the measurement and recording grid, set up before excavation to provide a metrical framework for the trenching (Figure 4.6).

Drawing stratigraphic profiles is a complex process and requires not only skill in recording but considerable interpretative ability. The difficulty of recording a section varies with the site's complexity and with its stratigraphic conditions. In many cases, the different occupation levels or geological events are clearly delineated in the section and it is easy to record the limits of particular levels with light lines drawn with a trowel. On other sites, however, the sedimentary record may be much more complex and less visible, particularly in drier climates where the soil's aridity has tended to leach out colors (Figure 4.8).[19] The recording method varies according to the profile's complexity. With smaller and more simple sections, it normally is possible to set up a horizontal datum string on the wall, the depth of which is measured carefully below the datum point for the entire site. All features on the profiles and the depths on the cutting are carefully recorded with reference to vertical measurements taken from the datum line. The whole of the section is therefore automatically measured relative to datum. On larger sites, where the stratigraphy is complex and on a large scale, a surveyor's level may be used for greater accuracy. Photography is extensively used in stratigraphic interpretation (Figures 4.9 and 4.10). Stratigraphic profiles present a most critical operation in archaeology, rivalled only by the necessity for accurate and dispassionate observation of the excavated evidence.

Three-dimensional recording of major features or important artifacts is another vital part of the excavation process. Many huts, pits, or burial groups are important merely because of their association with other features or artifacts. Such information can only be recovered by three-dimensional measurement, where the feature's horizontal and vertical coordinates are recorded with reference to the site grid.

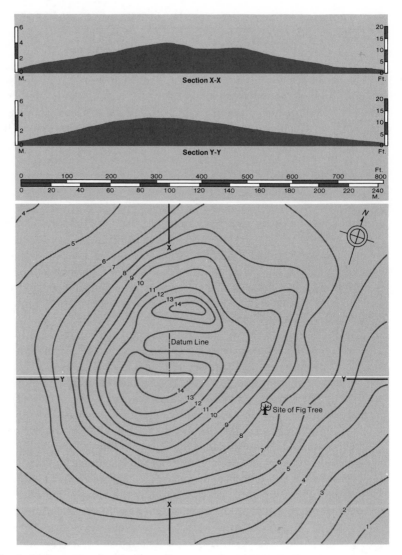

Fig. 4.7   A simple contour plan of a large village mound at Kalomo, Zambia.

ORGANIZATION OF AN EXCAVATION

The director of an archaeological field expedition needs skills in addition to those of a competent archaeologist. He has to be an accountant, politician, doctor, mechanic, personnel manager, and even a cook. On a large dig, though manual labor may not be his respon-

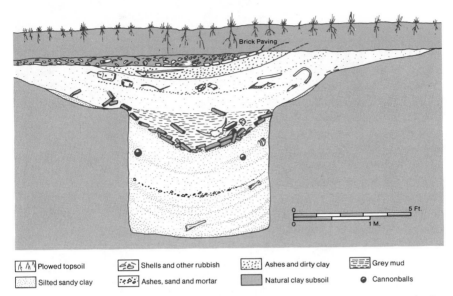

Plowed topsoil | Shells and other rubbish | Ashes and dirty clay | Grey mud

Silted sandy clay | Ashes, sand and mortar | Natural clay subsoil | Cannonballs

Fig. 4.8   A section through a seventeenth-century ice-house pit at Colonial Williamsburg, showing
the way in which the strata settled. The figure illustrates the complexity of archaeological
stratigraphy.

sibility, his logistic problems are compounded and he will head a
staff of site supervisors, artists, photographers, and numerous minor
functionaries who form the excavation team on a city dig or a field
school.[20]

In these days of rising costs and financial stringencies, most excavations are on a comparatively small scale, a team of students or laborers
under the overall supervision of the director and perhaps one or two
assistants; the assistants may be graduate students with some technical
training in archaeological fieldwork and can take some of the routine
tasks from the director's shoulders, allowing him to concentrate on
general supervision and interpretative problems. But in many cases
the director will not only be in charge of the research and the arrangements for the excavation, he will also personally supervise all trenches
excavated on the site. On him, therefore, devolve the tasks of recording, photography, drawing, measurement, and labor supervision. He
may also take his turn at the recovery of fragile burials and other
delicate objects that he cannot entrust to his students or workmen;
he is also responsible for maintaining the excavation diaries and find
notebooks, the storage and marking of artifacts, and the logistics of
packing finds and shipping them to the laboratory. So varied are

Fig. 4.9   A stratigraphic profile from Kalundu mound, Zambia. The scale is in feet, and the labels
denote excavated layers.

the skills of the excavator that much of a professional archaeologist's training in the field is obtained as a graduate student working at routine tasks and gaining experience in the methods of excavation and site-survey under experienced supervision. For the director, such students provide not only useful supervisory labor but also an admirable hone upon which they can try out their favorite theories and discuss in ruthless detail the interpretation of the site. Many an

Fig. 4.10 A stratigraphic profile through a ditch at Maiden Castle.

elaborate and much cherished theoretical model has been demolished over a disputed profile or an evening camp fire! Opportunities to gain excavation experience are always open, and notices of digs can be found on many college and university bulletin boards. The comradery and happiness of a well-run, student-oriented excavation is one of the more worthwhile experiences of archaeology.

Chapter 5
Excavation Problems

OPEN HUNTING CAMPS

The remains of temporary hunting camps should, theoretically, be the most common archaeological sites, but undisturbed examples are rare and consequently assume great importance. Land surfaces occupied by hunting bands are the most useful source of information on the life of early man. Living-floor archaeology has become a most important type of excavation in recent years, revolutionizing our ideas on early human cultural evolution. Until recently most evidence for the early stages of cultural evolution existed in isolated artifacts found in river gravel beds and alluvia associated with a jumble of fractured animal bones and other artifacts. The picture has changed in recent years, with greater emphasis being placed on the excavation of living-floor sites found in lake-bed deposits, undisturbed since their occupation in the Lower or Middle Pleistocene.[1]* Hunting camps come from later contexts, as well. The Star Carr encampment has been mentioned in earlier chapters,[2] while extensive Upper Paleolithic mammoth-hunting sites have been discovered in Czechoslovakia and eastern Russia.[3] Numerous examples of kill sites come from the New World.[4] All are open-air sites, which are particularly difficult to locate because their occupants left few traces of their presence during their short stay and had few material possessions. The thickness of the occupation deposit may not be more than a few centimeters, and

* See pages 326–328 for notes to Chapter 5.

Fig. 5.1   Olduvai Gorge, Tanzania.

several settlements may be placed one above another, representing different visits to the same locality over a period of years. Most sites were occupied for a short period and the localities were chosen for pragmatic reasons—the butchering of a large mammal, availability of water or vegetation, or an abundance of tool-making stone.[5] A few important open-air hunting sites were occupied again and again, and were often situated in areas of particular richness in game or vegetable foods.[6]

Olduvai Gorge in Tanzania contains many early hunting sites which have been excavated over many years by the Leakey family (Figure 5.1).[7] The living floors are buried under tons of overburden which has to be removed before the last few centimeters of deposit above the occupation level are carefully removed with trowel and brush. A grid network is laid out over the floor, so that each artifact, bone fragment, or natural stone can be plotted in position on a master plan before removal. Thus, the associations of each object on the floor are carefully recorded for posterity.

The results of the Olduvai excavations have been spectacular. The remains of both a robust and a gracile form of Australopithecine have been found on living surfaces in Bed I at Olduvai,[8] in direct association with stone chopping tools and broken bones of small animals. A cranium of *Homo erectus* has been found in overlying Bed II, in levels potassium argon dated to *ca.* 400,000 years ago, where stone hand axes and large mammal bones have been found.[9] Early hunting camps have also been found at Olorgesaillie in Kenya,[10] Kalambo Falls in Zambia,[11] in northern Malawi,[12] at Isimila in Tanzania[13] as well as in Syria[14] and Torralba, Spain.[15] In all these sites the tools of early man were uncovered in direct association with the remains of the game he hunted. Stratigraphic information, dating samples, and a settlement pattern were obtained by careful area excavation, the tools being plotted in position and photographed carefully before being lifted for further study in the laboratory. Figure 5.2 shows the complexity of such sites.

In the New World, horizontal excavation has also yielded significant results, especially where the kills of early man, mammoth-hunters in particular, are concerned.[16] A primary objective here has been to study the association between early man's tools and the extinct animals he hunted. Area excavation has been particularly used for this purpose; an example is the bison-kill site in Colorado excavated by Joe Ben Wheat, who found that a narrow arroyo was used as a death trap for a herd of bison (see Chapter 3).[17]

Living-floor excavations are normally on a large scale (Figure 5.3), and frequently involve the services of a Pleistocene geologist. Hunting-camp excavations aim at uncovering settlement patterns and structures as well as the dating or stratigraphy of sites. Concentrations of dismembered animal carcasses,[18] sleeping places, hearths, the remains of windbreaks,[19] or piles of flaked stone debris[20] are all elements of a settlement pattern on a living floor that should be considered in relation to one another. The potential for complete reconstruction of the environment and subsistence patterns of hunting-camp inhabitants is excellent, especially if preservation conditions are good, as they were, for instance, in the case of Star Carr (Figure 5.4) or the second millennium B.C. Stone Age hunting camps at Gwisho hot springs in Zambia. The latter were sited in the middle of a hot springs complex, overlooking the floodplain of the Kafue River. Wooden digging sticks and arrowheads, as well as thousands of animal bones and seeds, were found in association with traces of a windbreak and other structures, and some detailed analogies with modern Bushman subsistence

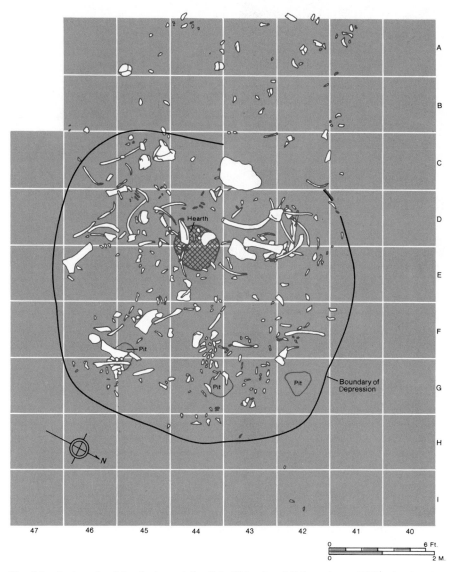

Fig. 5.2 *A plan of a living horizon at the Paleolithic site of Tel'manskaya, USSR, showing the scattering of debris and a structure. The letters and figures at the edges of the drawing refer to the grid squares laid over the site. For example, the hearth is found in square 44DE.*

patterns were made,[21] for the ancestry of the modern hunting population of southern Africa is known to lie with the Bushmen.[22] Recent intensive investigations of the !Kung Bushmen of the Kalahari Desert

Fig. 5.3 Visiting scientists inspecting the excavations in Olduvai Gorge, Bed I, with Dr. Leakey (right).

have focused on their ecology, subsistence, and settlement patterns to such an extent that an archaeologist accompanied the anthropologists in the field to study modern abandoned Bushman hunting camps from the archaeological standpoint.[23] Research like this has obvious application to the archaeology of open hunting camps.

CAVES AND ROCKSHELTERS

The mouth of a cave or a rockshelter overhang was a favorite home of prehistoric man. Both give shelter from the elements and shade on hot days. Caves and rockshelters are common where geological conditions—especially granite or limestone outcrops—permit. The river valleys of the Dordogne in southwestern France are lined by great rockshelters and deep caves in the high forested cliffs overlooking

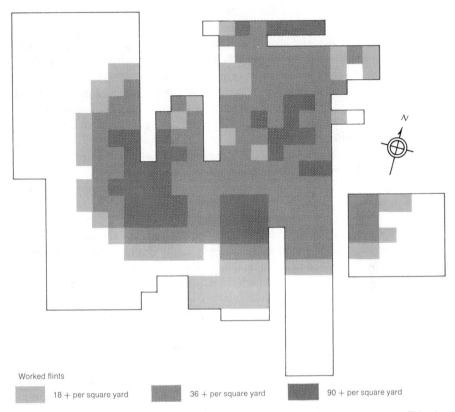

Worked flints

18 + per square yard   36 + per square yard   90 + per square yard

Fig. 5.4   *Densities of artifacts on living floors are frequently plotted square by square. This plan shows the distribution of worked flint on the Star Carr site in England.*

lush floodplains.[24] Prehistoric hunters lived in the Dordogne rockshelters for over 40,000 years, leaving behind dense layers of occupation. The dolomitic limestone of Mount Carmel in Israel formed caves that were Middle and Upper Paleolithic man's home for thousands of years, and his burials in the caves have been uncovered to add a new chapter to the story of human evolution.[25] Rockshelters and caves in the New World have also yielded key cultural sequences. Danger Cave on the western edge of Great Salt Lake Desert in western Utah was occupied by prehistoric man from about 9000 B.C. until recent times.[26] The cave mouth was choked with 3.9 meters (13 feet) of occupation debris, representing five periods of use over thousands of years. Lovelock Cave is another important site, where caches of tools for fishing and duck-hunting were found, dating to about 2500 B.C.[27] Weasel, skunk, mink, antelope, and other mammal bones were discovered, and in addition, the dry conditions at Lovelock preserved many grasses and vegetable foods.

Cave and rockshelter excavations are some of the most common digs, and certainly some of the hardest to carry through successfully. The ground below the cliff overhang at the cave mouth usually consists of ash and other debris piled up through successive human occupation, intercalated with sterile layers where geological phenomena have added to the deposits (Figure 5.5). A few millennia of hard frosts and hot summers, or cold rain, will cause cliff fragments to split off in angular chunks and fall to the ground, perhaps forming a sterile layer of debris. Layers of windblown sand sometimes seal off human occupation levels, both assisting and complicating stratigraphic observations.

Excavation of caves or rockshelters is slow and meticulous work. The size of trenches is normally constricted by the dimensions of the site, and digs tend to be selective rather than area-oriented, except at the largest rockshelters where there is room to move and the occupation has been concentrated under different parts of the overhang. The stratigraphy is often compressed or made up of a series of fine hearth lines, abandoned camp fires of visiting hunting bands. Figure 5.6 shows a stratigraphic profile from Haua Fteah Cave in Libya, a large site where the stratigraphy is level but still extremely complicated.[28]

Cave and rockshelter excavations are normally oriented toward chronological and stratigraphic problems. Accurate digging and meticulous recording of data are essential, and are based on small-scale grids. In caves where stone implements are rare and it is important to obtain stratigraphic evidence for them, the position of each artifact may be measured exactly. The Upper Paleolithic hunters of Britain were few and are imperfectly known from rockshelter excavations, most of which were conducted in the late nineteenth century. Compared with the rich French rockshelters of the Dordogne, most British caves yielded a scatter of tools and some fossil animal bones, enough to give a shadowy picture of a hunting culture known as the Creswellian, named after a cave in Derbyshire. Some years ago, C. B. M. McBurney excavated several caves in South Wales that contained Upper Paleolithic implements in very small numbers, but associated with important geological evidence, and fractured animal bones.[29] So little was known of the stratigraphic associations of the Creswellian that McBurney and his team recorded the exact position of every flint chip or stone implement found in the deposits of the Cat Hole and other rockshelters he excavated. The result—a better definition of the Creswellian and its geological and chronological associations.

Fig. 5.5   Haua Fteah Cave, Libya.

An interesting example of a large-scale rockshelter excavation is the work of Professor H. L. Movius of Harvard University at the Abri Pataud in Les Eyzies, France, the Mecca of Stone Age archaeologists.[30] Abri Pataud is being excavated on a coordinated, master-plan basis, involving not only archaeologists, but also geologists, botanists, chemists, paleontologists, and numerous other specialists. Over 6 meters (20 feet) of deposit have already been meticulously removed, occupation layer by occupation layer, using a lateral excavation method developed by the Chinese archaeologist Kwang-Chih Chang. Every hearth, major find, and artifact has precise recorded coordinates and is carefully described on a card index. Excavation is slow work. Trowels, crochets, dental picks, and brushes are used to ease the dirt away; a constant record is being kept of soil color, texture, and the slopes of natural layers in the deposit. The Abri Pataud has already yielded six layers of Upper Paleolithic occupation (9,000–40,000 years ago), including both Perigordian (Gravettian) and Aurignacian horizons,

105

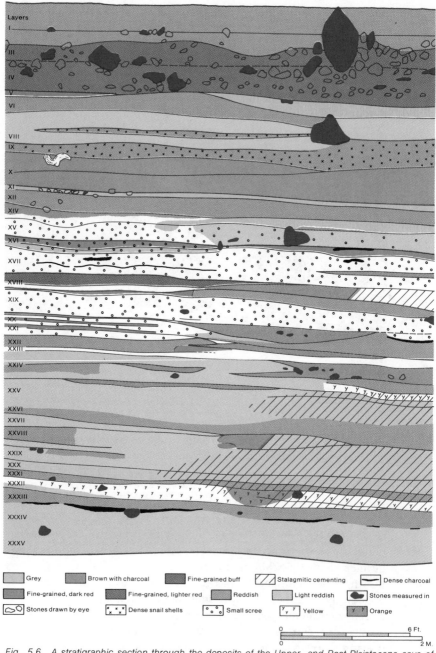

Grey   Brown with charcoal   Fine-grained buff   Stalagmitic cementing   Dense charcoal

Fine-grained, dark red   Fine-grained, lighter red   Reddish   Light reddish   Stones measured in

Stones drawn by eye   Dense snail shells   Small scree   Yellow   Orange

0   6 Ft.

0   2 M.

*Fig. 5.6   A stratigraphic section through the deposits of the Upper- and Post-Pleistocene cave of
Haua Fteah. The drawing shows a complex sequence of layers and lenses, most of them
associated with cultural material; the key gives the colors of the earth.*

Fig. 5.7   Abri Pataud rockshelter, Les Eyzies, France.

through which the archaeologists have traced minute changes in tool types, excavating to a far higher standard and resulting in more basic information than ever before obtained (Figure 5.7).

STRUCTURES AND DWELLINGS

For much of his history, man lived in simple windbreaks, skin tents, or portable structures that leave little trace in the archaeological record. But, with the advent of food production and more permanent settlement, his housing became more permanent and is more frequently discovered in excavations. Dwellings may vary from a simple round hut with pole walls and a thatched roof (Figure 5.8)[31] or a mud house with a flat roof and an entrance through the roof[32] (Figure 5.9), to an elaborate stone farmhouse or a palace[33] (Figure 5.10). In the larger house, the normal household activities—living, sleeping, cooking, storage—took place in separate rooms, but in a smaller one, these activities, reflected both in artifacts like cooking utensils and in features like hearths or sleeping platforms, occurred within a single area. Discovering the relationship between different rooms and separate

107

Fig. 5.8   A pole and mud hut, typical of the Zambezi Valley, Zambia.

Fig. 5.9   A schematic reconstruction of houses and shrines from Level VI at Çatal Hüyük, Turkey, showing flat-roof architecture and roof entrances. (After James Mellaart, Çatal Hüyük, Fig. 12. Copyright © 1967, Thames and Hudson Ltd. Used with permission of McGraw-Hill Book Company; London: Thames and Hudson Ltd.)

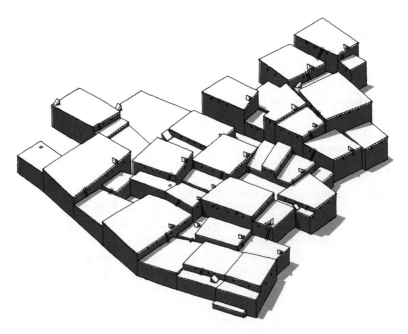

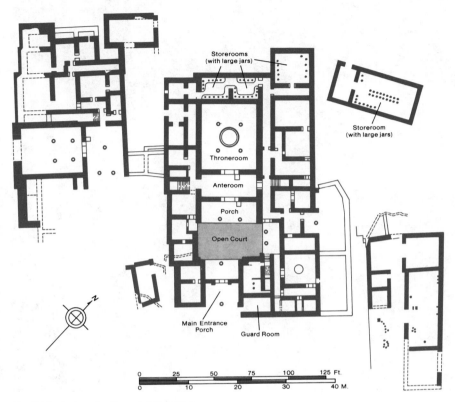

Fig. 5.10 A plan of a Bronze Age palace.

activities is as important in the excavation of a house as establishing its dating and the method of construction.

Grid excavations are normally used to uncover structures of any size (Figure 5.11).[34] These allow stratigraphic control over the building site, and especially the study of successive occupation stages. In many cases, the structures may have been built of perishable materials like wood or matting. Wooden houses are normally recognized through the post holes of the wall timbers and sometimes foundation trenches (Figure 5.12). Clay walls collapse into a pile when a hut is burnt or falls down (Figures 5.13–5.15); the wall clay may bear impressions of matting, sticks, or thatch. Stone structures are often better preserved, especially if mortar was used, although sometimes the stone has been removed by later builders and only foundation trenches remain (Figure 5.16). Stratigraphic cross sections across walls given an insight into the structure's history. The dating of most stone structures is compli-

Fig. 5.11 *Horizontal excavations at the site of the Old Minster, Winchester Cathedral, England.*

cated, especially when successive rebuilding or occupation of the building is involved.[35] Obviously, excavating a stone structure by following the walls around its perimeter is a mistake (Figure 5.16) because this destroys the complicated history of the building and the vicissitudes through which it has passed. For example, this would ruin the means of telling who the original builders were, when the structure was destroyed, and when it was rebuilt. Careful stratigraphic control through horizontal excavation is essential to gain these insights.

The dating or cultural setting of any building is based ideally on three categories of objects.[36] The first are those that come from the levels accumulated before the building was constructed; the second are contemporary with the structure; and the third are the finds made in the levels that overlie the structure and perhaps bury it. All these finds have a chronological relationship to the building: the first are

110

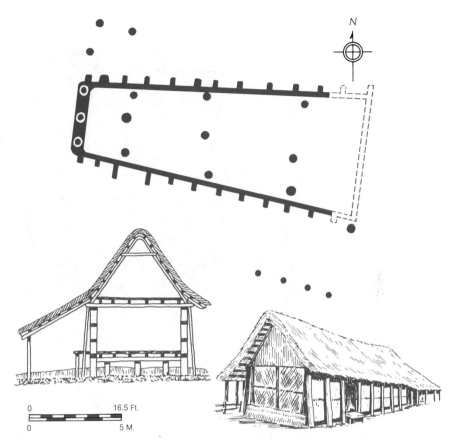

Fig. 5.12   The plan and reconstruction of a trapeze-shaped Neolithic house in Deiringsen-Ruploh, Germany. (After Buttler.)

earlier, the last are later, and those in the middle are contemporary with the building. The object of excavating stone structures is not merely to trace a building's outline, and then to reconstruct its plans, but also to reconstruct its history, understand its architecture, and establish how it was built.

Some of the most spectacular structures include those that have left few traces on the surface. European archaeologists have scored many notable triumphs in recovering timber structures from sandy soils where only traces of post holes and house foundations remain. At Koln-Lindenthal in Germany, an early farming village of at least twenty-one households was discovered which had been successively rebuilt some seven times.[37] The early farming communities that oc-

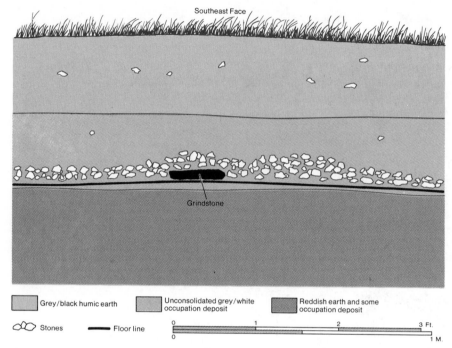

Fig. 5.13 The collapsed remains of a pole and mud hut, overlaid with occupation deposit, in Kangila site, Zambia.

cupied Koln-Lindenthal and other similar sites in the fifth millennium B.C. lived in huge long houses with massive timber framing; they measured up to 30.5 meters (100 feet) long and 7.6 meters (25 feet) wide, and had clay daubed walls. These remarkably standardized dwellings are known to us almost entirely from the post holes and bedding-trenches found in the sandy soils which the inhabitants favored for settlement and agriculture. The plan of an early farming settlement at Sittard in the Netherlands shows the complexity of such a constantly reoccupied longhouse settlement (Figure 5.17). Many farming villages of timber houses are known from prehistoric Europe. The timber-built settlement at the Wasserburg in southern Germany[38] dates to the twelfth to ninth centuries B.C.; an island settlement with timber palisades, its first phase contained thirty-eight small rectangular houses, replaced later on by nine big houses with a hall, wings, and associated byres. One such structure had six rooms and a main hall.

Wagon burials are found in Czechoslovakia and the Upper Danube, dating from 700 B.C.[39] The dead were deposited in wooden mortuary

Fig. 5.14 Pole and mud houses and grain bins—from the Middle Zambezi Valley, Zambia. (Compare with Figure 5.15.)

Fig. 5.15 A clay floor overlaid by wall rubble in a village mound at Isamu Pati, Zambia, showing the archaeological evidence for houses of the general type in Figure 5.14.

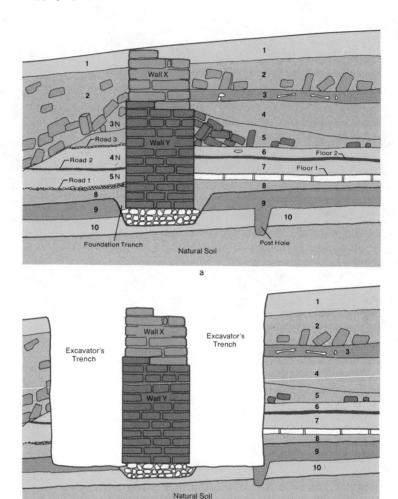

Fig. 5.16 *The stratigraphy of walling showing the foundation trench and the relationship of the archaeological strata to the wall. (a) A stratigraphic cross section from use of correct excavating methods. (b) The same section, showing how much information is destroyed through excavation by following the wall.*

houses, often sunk in the ground and buried under earth mounds (Figure 5.18). A spoked four-wheeled vehicle, sometimes used as a hearse, commonly accompanied the body. The horses were not buried with the wagon, but their harnesses and yokes were laid in the grave—often two sets, one for the cart horses and one for the warrior's own steed. Skillful excavation, allied with excellent preservation con-

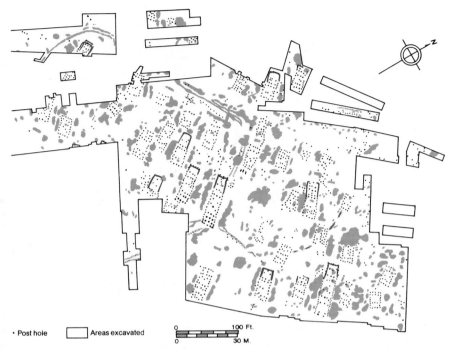

• Post hole   ☐ Areas excavated   0   100 Ft.
                                    0   30 M.

Fig. 5.17 Ground plans of longhouses at Sittard, Netherlands, built by Danubian people.

ditions, has permitted the reconstruction not only of the funerary wagons but also of the horse harnesses, as well as the armament and ornamentation of the wagon's owner. Impeccable plans of the various artifacts' positions and of the wagon components were necessary before the burials were lifted. The great tombs of the Shang civilization of northern China are another example of complex tombs where able excavation recorded many features that would otherwise have been lost. The shaft, axle, and lower parts of the chariot wheels are visible as discolored areas in the ground, which were excavated to recover the dimensions and character of the chariots in which the charioteers were buried to accompany their masters; these chariots were found at the entrance ramps of the great Shang tombs.

Storage pits are commonly found on prehistoric farming sites, and many reach several meters in depth (Figure 5.19).[40] Their contents furnish important information on dietary habits gleaned from food residues or caches of seeds. Trash pits are even more informative (Figure 5.20). Garbage pits and privies at Colonial Williamsburg have yielded a host of esoteric finds, including wax seals from documents

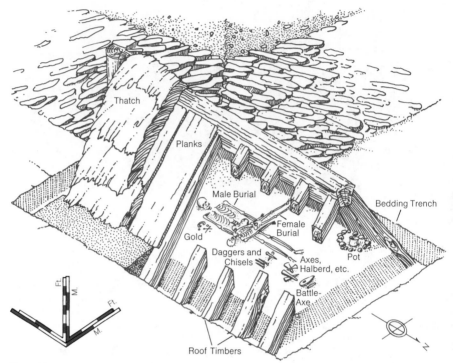

Fig. 5.18   A wooden mortuary house from a barrow at Leubingen, East Germany.

used as toilet tissue.[41] Some historic pits can be dated from military buttons and other finds.

VILLAGES AND TOWNS

Prehistoric communities may vary in size from a cluster of buildings (Figure 5.21) to a complete medieval or Colonial town. Horizontal grid excavation combined with trial excavation is the only approach to settlement problems of this type, for problems of relationship over large areas of ground are involved and accurate stratigraphic control is again essential. Obviously, total excavation is out of the question on the largest sites; instead, archaeologists try to excavate examples of all existing varieties of structure or groups of buildings (Figure 5.22). One town or village can include not only dwelling units, but also markets, reception halls, palaces, shops, government offices, workshops, law courts, and drainage systems.[42] The main excavation

Fig. 5.19 A double pit at Maiden Castle, Dorset, England, which is cut into chalk subsoil.

problem revolves around disentangling different periods of each successive occupation in situations where the stratigraphy has been complicated by extensive disturbance of underlying strata by later and
modern activity (Figure 5.23).[43] Urban archaeology has become increasingly important in recent years as many long-established cities
like England's Colchester, Winchester, and London have been rebuilt
after World War II, or as early Colonial buildings destroyed by
industrial activity in the eastern United States are traced. A remarkable
example of this type of archaeology came from Winchester, where
the history of a row of cottages, eleven houses, and two churches

117

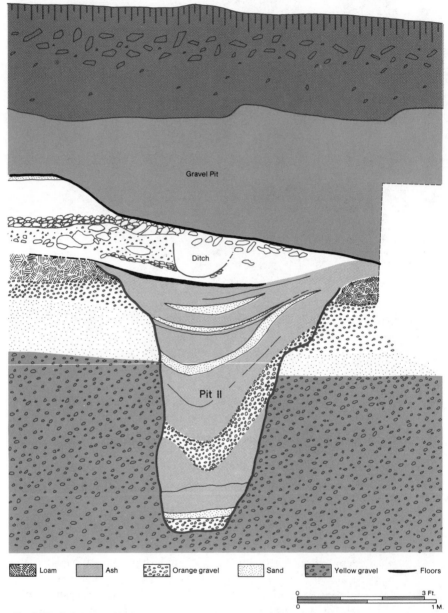

Fig. 5.20 *A Roman rubbish pit overlaid by house floors found at Storey's Paddock, Cambridge, England.*

was recreated from documents and archaeological research.[44] The Brooks area of Winchester was formerly a cloth-working area where dyeing and fulling took place. The Brooks houses had workrooms

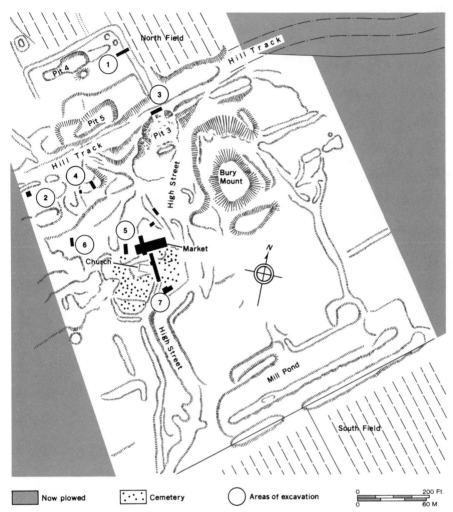

Fig. 5.21 A plan of the deserted medieval village at Clopton, England, showing that limited excavations
(black areas) have established many main features.

and shops facing the street with the water channels for the dyeing
process penetrating the front walls; working and living quarters were
behind or on top of the shop. A title deed to one house shows that
by 1366 it was owned by Richard Bosynton, a leading fuller of his
day, who became City Cofferer (treasurer) in 1380/81. Bosynton
appears as a strong character, who was fined sixpence in 1390 for
polluting the stream that ran by the Brooks houses with dyer's waste.
He sold part of his house in 1407 when he retired, and the surviving
deed describes the house in detail at the time. Another house was

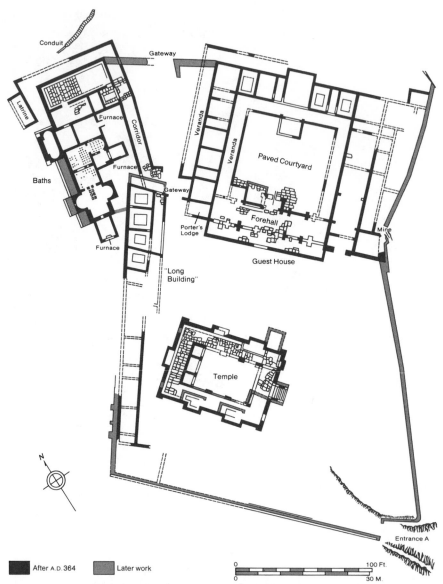

Fig. 5.22 *A Roman temple and its precincts at Lydney, England. Consider how you would excavate this site to obtain information about the different structures involved.*

owned by William Bolt, a vigorous business man, who evicted a feckless tenant named John Shovelar from it in 1402 as a result of a complex law case. Shovelar had been in trouble with the courts for, among other offenses, erecting a public urinal on his property—urine was a vital ingredient in the fulling process, acting as a

Fig. 5.23 Views of Brooks site, Winchester, England: above, the outlines of the thirteenth-century cottage walls and of small rooms are clear, as is the small lane in front of the houses; below, a vertical view of three-dimensional recording of features of the thirteenth-century cottages. The circle of stones is a nineteenth-century well. Note the baulks and the use of the recording grid.

type of soap. In this and other instances at Winchester, documents and excavations were linked to provide a remarkably graphic picture of life in a medieval town.

MOUND SITES

Mounds of varying size or shape are among the most common archaeological sites. Burial mounds, sometimes called barrows or tumuli (especially in Europe), are the first type that comes to mind when such sites are mentioned. But many mounds are habitation sites, or tells; others, especially in America, comprise the foundations of temples; still others have accumulated due to refuse-dumping or shell-fish-collecting. Excavation methods for dissecting these mounds radically differ according to the size and character of the site.

Many human settlements have occupied the same site for centuries or even millennia, with successive generations living on top of earlier occupation levels. In other cases, the same site may be used by different peoples who may have no knowledge of each other, or instead who have succeeded each other because of battle or political action; the later change is reflected in differing material culture, architecture, or economic practices.

Settlement sites occupied over long periods of time often form mounds of occupation debris and subsoil, often deliberately accumulated by the inhabitants to raise the level of their settlement. Traditional village sites are occupied again and again for many reasons. The low ridges formed by earlier occupation may serve to elevate the new settlement above floodwaters, or provide a better drained or cooler dwelling place. The low hill formed by an earlier settlement may have strategic advantages in flat country. The site may lie near one of the few permanent water supplies for many miles, so that the inhabitants move from the settlement only when their grazing grounds or gardens are exhausted. Whatever the reason, mound sites are commonly discovered and investigated largely because they frequently yield stratigraphic information, valuable especially for establishing local cultural sequences in little-known areas. Although Indian mounds in the Ohio Valley received attention from early nineteenth-century archaeologists, the most famous settlement mounds are probably the tells of the Near East, a favorite target of nineteenth-century antiquarians who plundered them unmercifully. Sir Henry Layard made spectacular finds at Nineveh in the mid-nineteenth century, uncovering the marvels of a long-abandoned city.[45] In more recent times, the Indus civilizations have been uncovered from the mounds at Harappa and Mohenjodaro in Pakistan, while the origins of food production and urban life in the Near East have been wrested from the deposits of such tells as Jericho, Jarmo, and Ubaid.[46]

The logistics of excavating mound sites can be enormous, especially where the settlement extends over many acres as it often does in the Near East. The depth of the mound can vary greatly as well. Mound sites from central Zambia range between 1.1 meters (3.5 feet) and 5.5 meters (18 feet) in depth, the latter presenting considerable excavation problems.[47] The truncated pyramidal mounds of the Mississippian peoples of North America were part of huge religious complexes; they center around the rich floodplains of the St. Louis, Missouri, and Natchez, Mississippi, areas.[48] Clusters of mounds were arranged around a plaza, some consisting of eight to ten construction phases with mud and thatch temples built on top. The mounds were enlarged by destroying the temple on top, and encasing the mound in another layer of earth. The largest known is that at Cahokia, Illinois, near St. Louis; 30.5 meters (100 feet) high, it covers an area of sixteen acres. A height of 15.2 meters (50 feet) is common at lesser sites, creating formidable problems even for the determined excavator. Some clay, stone, and stucco pyramids and mounds of Mexico also reach impressive size.

Clearly, with sites of these great dimensions, only a sampling of the deposits and stratigraphy can be made without prohibitive expense. Some idea of the general layout of the settlement can be obtained from a careful plot of the exposed surface features and air photographs of the site, but excavations are inevitably expensive and extremely difficult. Although both vertical and horizontal excavations have been applied to mound sites with success, the most important objective is a clear understanding of a mound's stratigraphy.

Many archaeologists glibly describe mound excavation as the process of stripping successive layers from a cake. This simplistic analogy is partly true, but many factors are at work in the formation of a tell. The inhabitants may first pile up a small hill of subsoil before living on their new site. Alternatively, they may live there and build it up systematically at the same time; this will result in artificial expansion of the culture layers, which are thickened by sterile subsoil. Such an instance occurred with two large mounds in central Zambia, occupied by subsistence farmers and ironworkers over a millennium ago, where it was estimated that the mound's height had been increased by a third during the occupation by deliberate accumulation of subsoil. The result—a lower density of finds and a chronological time span in 5.5 meters (18 feet) similar to that found in 10 feet of mound deposit in neighboring areas.

Mound stratigraphy is rarely simple, for both man and animals complicate it. Burrowing mammals stroll through the soft soil of the occupation levels, disturbing burials, huts, and the complex layering of consuming interest to the excavator. Rubbish, burial, and storage pits are dug into lower levels; drains, new street levels, and house foundations disturb natural accumulations. As Braidwood and Howe, the excavators of the early farming village at Jarmo in the Near East remarked: "The . . . strata of the archaeological sites may pitch and toss in ways their surface contours seldom suggest. . . ."[49]

Mounds are accumulated by many natural and artificial processes still imperfectly understood. The tells of the Near East reach great heights mostly because of the decay of mud-brick houses. In the warm climates of the Mediterranean and Near East, prehistoric and indeed modern peoples extensively use sun-dried mud and poles to build their houses, as have many Africans within the past two thousand years. The houses are abandoned, often the poles are removed to be used again in other structures, the gaunt walls eventually collapse and form piles of mud, upon which, perhaps, a later generation builds. Whole cities were constructed in this way and over many generations, with the need for defensive walls and increased shortage of agricultural land, people continued to live in the same place as their ancestors. Thus, the mound villages that litter the plains of the Near East today were formed. Mounds in other parts of the world probably developed by similar processes, even though deliberate accumulation and other factors may have contributed more to their height.[50]

A mound excavation is normally carried out in three ways. A vertical trench or series of cuttings may be made to establish the stratigraphy and sequence of a site's cultural layers. This technique requires meticulous observation of the layering, especially if there are disturbances of the soil. The stratigraphy has to be studied three-dimensionally to establish the orientation and slope of the strata. Furthermore, as Figure 5.24 shows, there is no guarantee that a trench has penetrated the mound's core and sampled the earliest occupation. The logistics of digging small cuttings at great depth are also formidable, so much so that most excavations on large mounds, short of tunnelling, must be on a fairly large scale.

A trench may be sunk against a vertical face, starting the excavation of a level at the edge of the mound, and then removing it horizontally across the site before starting the underlying stratum. The end result of a vertical face dig is normally a large stepped trench with a gradually diminishing area size for the lower strata. Ideally, the technique should be combined with vertical test-trenching so the strata can be studied on a small scale and structures or major changes in the stratigraphy can be anticipated.

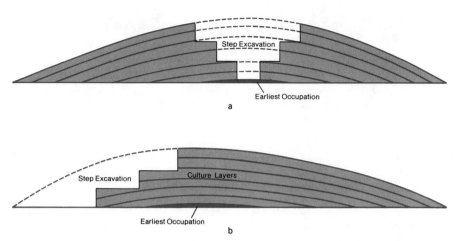

Fig. 5.24   Some approaches to mound trenching (not to scale). (a) A stepped trench from the summit exposes a small amount of the original occupation, if this is at the mound's center. All earth must be lifted out. (b) A stepped cutting at the mound's edge may miss the core occupation, but soil is easily disposed of. In both (a) and (b), stepping of the walls prevents collapse.

Another way of excavating mounds is to carry out a conventional grid or horizontal excavation, stripping large areas of the mound down to bedrock. This is enormously expensive, but useful when major settlement patterns or large areas of houses are to be studied. Wheeler has used this technique with success in Pakistan, where he was able to recover a vivid picture of the Indus civilization.[51] Much of Wheeler's success was due to his penchant for carefully selecting significant areas of the city for excavation by surface observation. At Harappa and Mohenjodaro, great citadels and ceremonial centers dominate extensive cities laid out on a grid pattern; some houses still stand to the first-floor level (Figures 5.25 and 5.26).

BARROWS, OR SMALL BURIAL MOUNDS

Burial mounds, or barrows, are found throughout the world in an infinite variety of forms.[52] The so-called round barrow of Europe may be up to 36 meters (120 feet) across and about 4–5 meters (15 feet) deep. A long type, up to 90 meters (300 feet) in length, has a basically rectangular ground plan.[53] Some mounds contain one interment; others, several deposited at different times; and some, numerous burials such as occur in the frequently used Megalithic tombs of Western Europe.[54]

In the nineteenth century and, alas, upon many occasions in the twentieth, the dead were removed from barrows by means of a hastily dug pit or trench (Figure 4.1). But now excavators realize that the

Fig. 5.25 A portion of the mud-brick defenses at Harappa, Pakistan.

burial itself is only part of a burial place's history, for the graves form an integral part of the structure and have a definite relationship to the barrow's stratigraphy. The objectives of burial-mound excavation include obtaining details on sepulchral customs, dating the burials, and recovering as much information as possible on climatic conditions, vegetational cover, and the soil chemistry of the mound.

A common way of digging a round barrow is by the "quadrant"

Fig. 5.26 *A brick revetment of the defenses at Kaushambi, India.*

system.[55] The mound is dissected like a large cake (Figure 5.27); vertical profiles are left along both axes of the barrow to establish the mound's stratigraphy, and the associations of the burials. The original ground surface under the barrow is carefully uncovered, and pollen samples taken from the base as well as from the body of the mound. Palynology determines the flora present on the site when the mound was built, locates the old land surface under the barrow, and if possible sheds light on the materials from which the mound was constructed. By no means are all mounds conducive to the survival of pollen spore—in many cases the grains are leached out by acid soils. There is the

127

Fig. 5.27 A quadrant excavation on a round barrow from Wiltshire, England, photographed from above.

danger of differential destruction of pollen grains, too, so the results must be interpreted with care.

A 2.4 meter-high burial mound (8 feet) near Portesham in southern England was excavated in 1955, and found to have a core of turfs, about 13.7 meters (45 feet) in diameter.[56] Although no traces of a main interment were found, the excavator recovered four cremation urns of Late Bronze Age form, all secondary burials. Pollen samples were taken through the mound, both from the surface under the barrow and the turf core, as well as from the upper levels. Geoffrey Dimbleby, who analyzed the samples, found that an early period of oak, lime, and birch forest had given way to more open country where bracken, grass, and cultivation weeds were frequent—the change obviously the result of agriculture. Ivy was also common; he found that this species was common in the turf levels, as if the turfs had been cut near the mound.

As noted above, burial mounds vary widely in shape, size, and mode of construction. Not every barrow is totally excavated, but enough has been learned to demonstrate how important stratigraphic profiles and processes of mound-building are in studying these conspicuous sepulchral monuments.

CEMETERIES AND SKELETONS

Burial grounds are a specialized form of site, dug for specific purposes—to obtain information on burial customs and population statistics[57] from large numbers of skeletons, or to recover pots, weapons, and other tools from sealed graves for typological purposes.[58] The best way to excavate a cemetery is on a grid pattern, with stratigraphic control over the whole site, to establish whether the cemetery was used at different times, the relative ages of the skeletons found there, and the relative positions of the burials. If a skeleton projects into a baulk between two trenches, it can still be recovered by removing the wall when the recording process has been completed. Accurate three-dimensional recording is essential if the grave goods and bodies are to be recorded for posterity. Some idea of the problem's complexity can be gained by looking at Figure 5.28 which shows a series of richly decorated burials from a Zambian trading village.

The unearthing and recording of human burials is considered by the layman to be one of the most romantic aspects of the archaeologist's job. No doubt this is true when the skeletons are adorned with an array of rich grave goods. But, in fact, the excavation of burials is a difficult and routine task which must be performed with care because of the delicacy and often bad state of the bones. The record of the bones' position, and the placement of the grave goods and the body ornaments is as important as the association of the burial, for the objective is reconstructing burial customs as much as establishing chronology.[59] Skeletons are normally buried in grave pits, coffins, or sometimes more elaborate structures. Most commonly, however, in prehistoric times, human burials were deposited in shallow pits dug into underlying strata. The position of the bones and grave goods is recorded as well as the burial's stratigraphic position relative to the strata around it. In multilevel occupation sites, later burials may be dug into underlying horizons, confusing the stratigraphic picture. All too often, this particular aspect of a burial has been ignored in

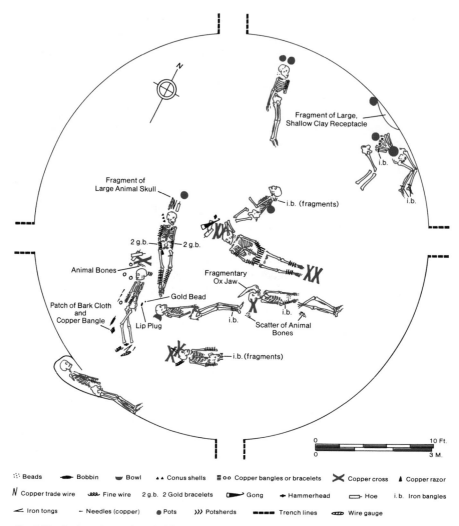

Fig. 5.28 A plan of a series of richly decorated burials at Ingombe Ilede, Zambia, showing the association of grave goods and bodies.

excavation reports, making it difficult to date a skeleton with any degree of accuracy.[60]

A burial is normally located from a surface feature such as a gravestone or pile of stones, or from an accidental discovery during excavation. Once the grave outline has been found, the skeleton is carefully exposed from above. The first part of the skeleton to be identified will probably be the skull or one of the limb bones, and the main outline of the burial is traced before the backbone, ribs, feet, and finger bones are uncovered (Figures 5.29 and 5.30). The greatest care is taken not to displace the bones, or any ornaments or grave goods that surround them. In many cases the burial is in a delicate state and the bones may be soft, so the bones are exposed gradually, giving them time to dry before they are coated with a suitable chemical such as polyvinyl acetate or bedacryl. The hardened bones can then be removed to the safety of the laboratory.[61] Normally, the undersurfaces of the bones are left in the soil so that the skeleton may be recorded photographically before removal. The photography of skeletons requires careful use of the camera to avoid parallax errors and a scale so that the scale of the photograph may be apparent to the viewer. The burial is either removed bone by bone, or is surrounded with a cocoon of plaster of paris and metal strip, the inside of which is packed with earth; the whole structure is then transported to the laboratory where it is cleaned at leisure. This technique is expensive in time and labor and is normally only used when a skeleton is of outstanding scientific importance or to be displayed in a museum. Normally, however, the bones are carefully removed, one by one, hardened with chemicals and then packed in cardboard cartons or wooden boxes with cotton, wool, and straw for transport to the laboratory.

FORTIFIED SETTLEMENTS AND EARTHWORKS

Fortified settlements and earthworks still conspicuous in the landscape today form an important category of archaeological site. Their excavation is invariably a large-scale operation, requiring sophisticated planning and a careful blend of horizontal and vertical trenching. Few have been excavated adequately. Earthworks are a common feature of the Early and Middle Woodland Adena and Hopewell cultures of the eastern United States.[62] The Hopewell Adena heartland is in the central Ohio Valley where many sites are characterized by vast high narrow ridges of earth that enclose large "fields." The enclosures can be circular, square, or pentagonal; their earthworks often border cliffs or promontories along rivers and creeks. Burial mounds are found inside these enclosures, and Adena funerary customs are well known. The Adena people are estimated to have been living from about 1000 B.C. to A.D. 200. They were less sophisticated culturally than their Hopewell contemporaries, and their economy was based on collecting and on maize agriculture. Unfortunately, the significance of their earthworks is still unknown, for no one has yet carried out large-scale excavations on them—a potentially expensive project but one worthy of long-term research.

Fig. 5.29 An Iron Age war casualty from Maiden Castle, holding the remains of a leg of lamb in his hand.

Fig. 5.30 An infant burial at Ingombe, Ilede, Zambia, dating from the seventh century A.D., or later. (The scale is in inches.)

Fig. 5.31   An Iron Age earthwork at Maiden Castle.

The serried ditches and banks of Maiden Castle in southern England[63] (Figure 5.31) or of the Heuneburg in Germany,[64] required a combination of vertical and area excavation to establish the stratigraphy and chronology of the earthworks and also the layout of the houses and wooden palisades at the entrance to the settlements. Sir Mortimer Wheeler's description of the battle that led to the sack of Maiden Castle is a classic of archaeology; the story of a desperate defense of the town is preserved in the strata of the site's entrance, which disclosed a series of hastily buried war casualties and burnt houses.[65] "Causewayed camps" in southern England, the huge ditch-enclosed settlements of early farmers in southern Italy, or the standardized square ramparts of Roman legionary forts (Figure 5.32) dot the European landscape and provide a fruitful source of inquiry for the student of earthworks.[66] The dating of earthworks, their use and mode of construction, and the history of the site itself are primary concerns in such excavations. Careful cross-sectioning of banks and ditches is an effective way of dating many earthworks.[67] When a deep

133

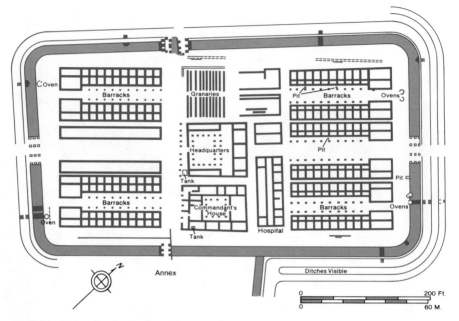

Fig. 5.32   A plan of a Roman fort at Fendoch, Scotland.

ditch is dug, its bottom is clean and regular, but very soon some natural silting of the walls takes place, as a result of rainstorms, wind, and other climatic or human factors. Such silt can normally be identified at the bottom of the stratigraphic section of a ditch and is known as "primary silting" (see Figure 4.10). Obviously, any artifact, like a potsherd, found in this layer provides a date *after which* the ditch cannot have been built. This primary silting is overlain by the secondary filling which, of course, is later than the date of construction and primary silting. Unless the ditch has been filled deliberately, this silting is entirely natural and gives a clue as to the later history of the settlement. A cross section of ramparts may also yield dating evidence, for accurately dateable artifacts, like imported pottery, coins, or charcoal which can be radiocarbon dated, can occur in the silt layers (Figures 5.33 and 5.34).

Earthworks and forts often have buildings with them that require area excavation.[68] Barrack blocks, houses, roadways, and guard huts, as well as refuse pits, are only a few of the structures that may await investigation. Some idea of the problem can be gained from an examination of Figure 5.32. Here, obviously, the location of the roadways is important, with selective excavation of each type of structure located

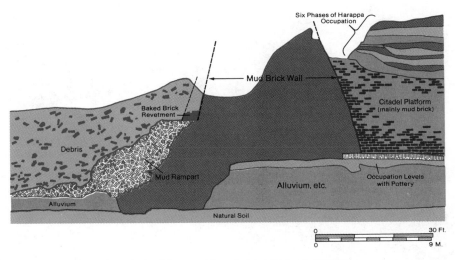

Fig. 5.33 A section through the defenses of the citadel at Harappa, Pakistan.

Fig. 5.34 Dating the construction and the destruction of a building by its associated artifacts—at Colonial Williamsburg.

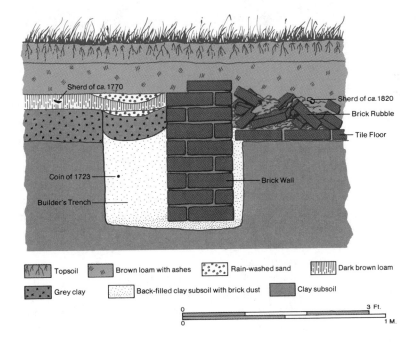

Fig. 5.35 Excavations on the Galatea Bay midden. North Island, New Zealand.

inside the fort. Aerial photographs or electronic survey may be useful in establishing the interior layout, too.

SHELL MIDDENS

Shell middens are common in coastal areas, especially in the southeastern United States, California, New Zealand, and South Africa.[69] The kitchen middens of Denmark were already being investigated on a large scale in the nineteenth century, and were vividly described by Sir John Lubbock in his *Prehistoric Times*, surely one of the best books on prehistory written in the nineteenth century. Remarkable results have been obtained from shell-midden excavations, especially in the reconstruction of diet, which is referred to in future chapters. The excavation problem is not so much one of identifying features as

one of obtaining statistically reliable samples of the food and occupation residues in the body of the midden. E. W. Gifford calculated
the relative proportions of various elements in some California shell
middens many years ago and obtained the following figures:[70]

Fish remains	0.031%	Charcoal	0.220%
Shell	52.070%	Stone	7.500%
Ash	12.270%	Bones of vertebrates	0.055%
Soil	27.840%		

The figures indicate the types of finds in such sites, for adequate
samples of the various constituents of the mound are needed for
detailed analysis in the laboratory. Apart from the sampling question,
concentrations of artifacts or food residues may provide evidence of
specialized economic activity or insight into the settlement pattern
of the users of the midden. Although some shell midden digs are
designed purely to sample the deposits, many shell midden investigations in recent times have been horizontal digs, either laid out on
a grid pattern, as for example at Galatea Bay in New Zealand (Figure
5.35),[71] or by systematically removing the midden, square by square,
as has been practiced at Robberg Cave in South Africa.[72] Another
classic shell midden excavation was carried out by Clement Meighan
on Catalina Island off Los Angeles.[73] Sites like these, found on many
shores, can give a good picture of riverine and seaside strandlooping
economies like those also recorded in historical descriptions of prehistoric peoples in South Africa, California, and elsewhere.[74]

Stratigraphy and settlement patterns, chronologies and cultural sequences, strategy and careful survey—again and again we come back
to the principles of excavation so carefully enumerated by Pitt Rivers,
Wheeler, and other leading excavators over the past eighty years.
Though individual methods may vary from site to site and from area
to area, and their effective application depends on the archaeologist's
ability, no one denies that the fundamental purpose of excavation
is recovery of information and the solution of specific research problems.

Part Two
Analysis of the Past

Like earnest mastodons petrified in the forests of their own apparatus the archaeologists come and go, each with his pocket Odyssey and his lack of modern Greek.
Diligently working upon the refuse-heaps of some township for a number of years
they erect on the basis of a few sherds or a piece of dramatic drainage, a sickly
and enfeebled portrait of a way of life. How true it is we cannot say; but if an Eskimo
were asked to describe our way of life, deducing all his evidence from a search
in a contemporary refuse dump, his picture might lack certain formidable essentials.

Lawrence Durrell, *Prospero's Cell*

Chapter 6

Environment and Subsistence

Ever since the early hominids camped by African lakes, human societies have been vehicles whereby man has adapted himself to his
ecosystem. Modern societies function within an environment to which
they have adapted their culture and which they exploit to the limits
of their day-to-day requirements and technological competence.

The anthropologist studies the societies within their environment,
evaluates the adaptations they have made, and identifies the factors
that act on them. Animal societies fit into their respective ecosystems
in a simple manner.[1]* They maintain an equilibrium with other animals
and plants in the system, an equilibrium which is, however, subject
to constant readjustment as all elements in the system change. Human
societies also live in ecosystems, as animals do, but the instinctive
reactions of the latter are, in the case of man, modified by the inherited
behavior of preceding generations. We eat with a knife and fork,
use iron tools, or undergo complicated initiation rites at puberty—all
these culture traits are inherited from earlier generations.

Cultural inheritance has become an increasingly powerful factor
in human history. The earliest Australopithecines lived in small bands
and enjoyed the simplest of cultures;[2] their inherited cultural heritage
was small. As speech, art, and writing were developed, however,
human society was increasingly shaped by inheritance, and culture
became more effectively disseminated and transmitted to a growing
world population.

* See pages 328–331 for notes to Chapter 6.

Our relationship to our ecosystem is determined by our culture. Through the millennia of human history, our control over the environment has increased to the extent that today we completely dominate it and are destroying it. Our culture now shapes our ecosystem, for all aspects of it react to the diverse changes that we impose. Thus, studying man's history is, to a considerable degree, the examination of ecosystems within which human culture has flourished and of the increasing control exercised by man over his environment. We learn not only about cultural process in the past, but also about the conditions under which prehistoric peoples developed their culture and utilized their environment.

Understanding paleoecology is vital not only to the understanding of cultural process but also in the finding of archaeological sites in the field, where preservation conditions also play an important part. Before finding our sites, we must establish something about their ancient environmental setting, even if the finer details of the picture must await excavation.

RECONSTRUCTING ANCIENT ENVIRONMENTS

The glacials and interglacials provide us with a broad canvas of climatic phases and broad environmental generalizations for the Pleistocene. We know, for instance, that Western Europe had an Arctic climate in 33,000 b.c. and that a warmer regimen existed in Central Europe 100,000 years ago. Such broad categories of climate are adequate for geologists but too imprecise for archaeologists concerned with the minutiae of human adaptations within a limited area around a prehistoric hunting camp over a very short period of time. Some broad indications on environment can be obtained from animal bones. Many southwestern French caves were occupied 15,000 years before Christ by reindeer hunters, who also pursued mammoths, woolly rhinoceros, and wild horses. They were obviously living in an Arctic, tundra type of environment, whereas the hunters of Swanscombe in the Thames Valley during the Mindel-Riss Interglacial were living off animals that favored warm climates, such as the rhinoceros and various deer. Such major climatic subdivisions are readily identified, especially in glaciated areas, where the geological record shows much contrast and traces of glacial activity. Animal bones are far harder to use in Mediterranean or tropical areas where the major climatic changes of the Pleistocene were reflected in rainfall and temperature changes rather than the advance of ice sheets. Many animals taken by Paleolithic hunters were comparatively tolerant of temperature change, and even of increasing aridity, making environmental reconstruction more difficult.

The Haua Fteah Cave east of Benghazi on the coast of Libya is an excellent example of how animal bones are used to study paleoecology.[3] Charles McBurney, who excavated the Haua, found a huge sequence of Stone Age cultures, beginning with Middle Paleolithic levels at the base estimated to date to about 90,000 b.c., and passing through the Upper Paleolithic to agricultural peoples and the remains of historical occupation. Enormous numbers of broken animal bones were found in the levels of Haua Fteah, and a simplified graph of the finds shows major fluctuations (Figure 6.1). There are three main food animals in the Haua collections. The gazelle, a small antelope, requires little water and would be more common when desert conditions encroached near the cave. Barbary sheep, another important quarry, tolerates widely ranging conditions, and could endure a wide range of climates. In contrast, large bovines such as wild cattle cannot flourish without perennial water supplies, and are highly sensitive to climatic change. Haua Fteah has an annual rainfall of 500–550 millimeters (20–22 inches), and lies within a narrow coastal belt of bush country with pine trees. This gives way south of the site to cypress and more high country, abruptly changing from bush to desert steppe some 40 kilometers inland, and to stony desert in another 40 kilometers. Today, cattle are kept within the coastal bush country, sheep and camels live in the desert steppe, and gazelle are common eating on the desert fringes. Because cattle, sheep, and gazelle bones are all found in Haua Fteah, and major fluctuations in the Saharan climate are known to have occurred during the Pleistocene, it is believed that proportions of game animal bones in the cave fluctuated with climatic change, as the vegetational zones shifted with changes in rainfall. Hunting preferences cannot be regarded as a reason for the fluctuations because changes in animal counts do not coincide with cultural changes. Furthermore, it is unlikely that the Haua Fteah hunters would have neglected such readily available quarry as the wild ox if it lived in the area.

The graph of the game animals shows that wild bovines were abundant in the Middle and in the early part of the Upper Paleolithic. About 30,000 b.c., however, the hunters took more and more wild sheep and increased numbers of gazelle and horses, a trend that lasted into historic times; the increased cattle values in the late Upper Paleolithic reflect some minor increase in rainfall. Gazelle were very important in the early part of the sequence but decreased in significance sometime before 80,000 b.c. Haua Fteah is so close to the sea that fluctuations in the Mediterranean's temperature, measured accurately by use of deep sea cores, can be extrapolated against the radiocarbon-dated cultural sequence in the cave. The periods of warmer seawater temperature coincide with times when the large bovines were common,

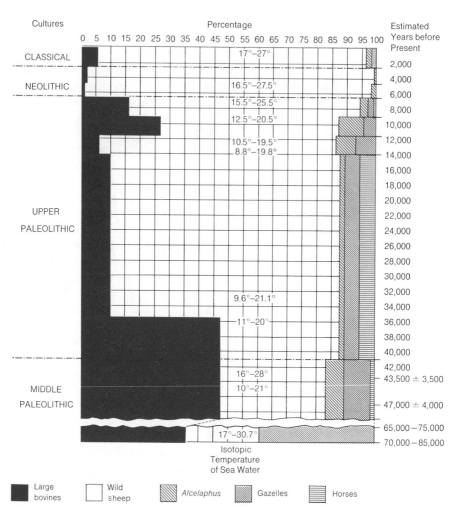

Cultures   Percentage   Estimated

Fig. 6.1   The main mammals at Haua Fteah, Libya, plotted against a radiocarbon time-scale, and
isotopic temperature readings from deep-sea cores in the Mediterranean. The earliest dates
are little better than estimates.

whereas the colder ocean temperatures pertained when the hunters
were not taking wild cattle. Thus, bovines were common at Haua
Fteah in periods of warmer, drier conditions, probably moving south-
ward, away from the coastal belt, into the present desert steppe areas
when the climate became colder and wetter, times when standing
water may have been available in the Sahara for much of the year.

Such generalized reconstructions of ancient environment are based on diverse evidence in addition to the animal bones. The climate and vegetation pattern at the present day is projected into the past, with calculations as to the probable effects of a major increase or decrease in rainfall. The ecological niches of the animals, even small rodents, whose remains are found in the sites, are carefully studied; their needs, such as dependence on regular water supplies, are taken into account. If possible, geological or related data, as with the sea cores at the Haua, is related to the human occupation.

But the character of the vegetation is left to intelligent guesswork for projections of present floral conditions. This is through no fault of the excavators, who rely on the evidence from the deposits available to them. In some caves or other sites, remains of nuts, berries, or even wood are found, and can be used to identify a few tree species in the area at the time of occupation.[4] The evidence is frequently sparse and reflects only those species collected by the inhabitants, rather than giving a complete picture of the microenvironment around the cave. Fortunately, however, the technique of palynology has led to tracing the vegetational history for much of Europe and North America from pollen grains found in bogs, clays, and other similar deposits.

PALYNOLOGY

The basic principles of pollen analysis are described in Chapter 2. Palynology has obvious applications to paleoecology, and can supply a vivid picture of the environs of a prehistoric settlement, especially if combined with other evidence. While man had little effect on the natural vegetation until he began forest clearance and food production, pollen analysis can measure such effects and date the appearance of agriculture and forest clearance.[5]

The Stone Age hunting camp at Star Carr, England, is a classic example of pollen analysis being applied to date and reconstruct the ecology.[6] This small prehistoric settlement consisted of little more than a platform of birch brush sited in some reeds at the edge of a small lake, and was occupied in the eighth millennium B.C. The deposits were peaty, and pollens as well as wood were preserved in the deposits. Star Carr's pollen diagram is illustrated in Figure 2.9, with the occupation level indicated (see page 47). At the time the camp was occupied, birch trees were common around the site, with some pine and willow. Elm, oak, and hazel were almost nonexistent. The stratigraphic profile from Star Carr clearly shows the sloping edge of the lake, with the occupation deposits spreading out into deeper water. Traces of reeds in the deposit were common, evidence that the platform was thrown down in the reed swamp at the lake's edge (Figure 6.2) and probably lay within the reeds and at the edge of the forest, resting on a muddy gravel. Water plants, as well as fungi, were found in the occupation levels, together with abundant remains of forest game animals like the red deer. We shall return to Star Carr later in this volume.

Pollen analysis is also used for environmental reconstruction in less temperate areas of the world. A famous instance is the Kalambo Falls prehistoric site on the border of Zambia and Tanzania in East Africa.[7] J. Desmond Clark found a long sequence of Stone Age occupation sites flooded by silts and gravels from a Pleistocene lake which formerly flourished in a shallow valley behind the 665 meter-high Kalambo Falls (726 feet). Hand-axe makers, whose living floors are more than 55,000 years old, were the first known occupants of the lake shore, to be followed during subsequent millennia by later hunters and gatherers as well as farmers. The Acheulian people who lived at Kalambo settled in temporary hunting camps on the lake's edge. The horizons in which their living floors are found were partly waterlogged, which preserved a large quantity of organic materials including tree trunks, leaves, twigs, and lumps of organic deposit from which numerous pollen samples were taken. The spore counts showed that the area, now under savannah woodland, had had a denser rain forest cover when Early Stone Age hunters lived there. Unfortunately, examples like Kalambo Falls and Star Carr are rare, and our picture of prehistoric ecology is almost always incomplete and inadequate. But more and more attention is being paid to palynology in prehistoric research.

SUBSISTENCE

The ways in which man has obtained his food since the Lower Pleistocene have affected not only his survival, but nearly every aspect of the society and culture in which he lives. Man's long history covers a period of over four million years of food-getting, beginning in the earliest times with simple gathering and hunting economies that evolved to more specialized subsistence patterns of the same type, and later, more rapidly developed to food production by highly advanced methods of agriculture and stock-raising. The prehistory of man is the story of his diverse adaptations to world environments and of his increasing control over the same, to the extent that today we have caused a serious ecological crisis.

But in Stone Age times, when man was a hunter and gatherer, his subsistence patterns were intimately tied to his environment. The

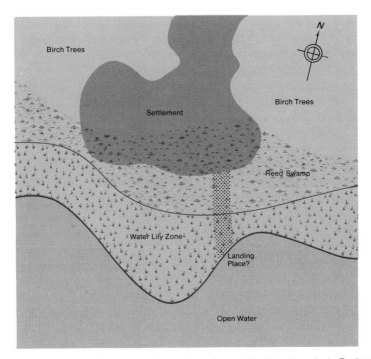

Fig. 6.2 A reconstruction of the vegetational surroundings of the Star Carr site in England.

migrations of game, the seasons of vegetable foods, and the availability of permanent water supplies during dry periods of the year—even salmon runs—vitally affected how hunters obtained their food, influenced their weapon design, and were reflected in their settlement patterns, architecture, and material culture. Nevertheless, while the availability of food supplies and water, as well as climate and soils, did set broad limits on how prehistoric peoples could make their living, a wide range of choices was still available to those living in a particular environment. These choices in turn were limited by the societal constraints of the community. Furthermore, the development of prehistoric economies and of new techniques of making one's living depended not only on changes in the natural environment and in the people's habitats, but also on the creation of more effective means of obtaining food, especially in producing it rather than merely gathering it. Both social evolution and density of population bear a direct relationship to the effectiveness of hunting or subsistence agriculture.

We considered paleoecology briefly in Chapter 3, and will now look at the methods developed for studying subsistence activities.

Although nineteenth-century archaeologists examined the bones from French caves or Indian mounds and eager scientists described the mollusca in Danish shell middens, only in recent years has the archaeology of subsistence become a major field of research. A natural preoccupation with chronology and classification was characteristic of archaeology until the 1940s, when pioneers such as Grahame Clark began to emphasize the ecological approach to prehistoric archaeology.[8] No one disputed that man has either been a hunter-gatherer, a pastoralist, or a farmer during his early history. Many scholars felt that such broad categories of subsistence activity were quite adequate, and that there were higher priorities in research than the minutiae of animal bones or vegetal remains.[9]

A greater understanding of ecology and its implications to archaeology led people to view man and his culture as merely one element in a complex ecosystem.[10] Immediately, detailed information on subsistence activities within an individual site or culture assumes great importance, for we have to view the inhabitants' relationship with their ecosystem, and study not only their subsistence activities, but their environment as well. Many fundamental questions require answers. The following are merely a selection: What was the role of domestic animals in a mixed farming economy? How important was fishing to a shellfish-oriented population living by the sea? Was the site occupied seasonally when the inhabitants engaged in a specialized economic activity? Did old habits of hunting and gathering persist as a new economy based on food production was introduced? What systems of agriculture were used and how was the land cultivated? What species of domestic animals were present and what plants were grown? Were domestic stock kept for breeding, meat, or draught purposes? What effect did the subsistence pattern have on permanency of settlement? This chapter reviews some ways in which the answers to questions such as these are sought.

The tangible evidence for prehistoric subsistence consists not only of artifacts, but also of food residues left by prehistoric populations, as well as contemporary drawings or paintings of economic life.[11] How much survives is dependent on the soil and climatic conditions. All too often the evidence is incomplete, one-sided, or trivial rather than important. The picture of human subsistence yielded by artifacts is necessarily limited. Flint axes, pressure-flaked arrowheads, iron hoes, or digging-stick weights may indicate the outlines of the picture, but hardly clothe it with substance and intricate detail (Figure 6.3). So many critical artifacts used in the chase or garden were made from perishable materials such as basketry, wood, or fiber that few details of economic life can be obtained from man's more durable achieve-

Fig. 6.3   A reconstructed Neolithic chert axe with a wooden handle of ash wood (approximate length, 30 inches). The handle is a copy of an example found in a Danish bog; only the stone is original, which illustrates how little of an artifact survives under normal conditions.

ments in stone or metal (Figure 6.4). Food residues from prehistoric sites also survive unevenly and differ widely, their abundance being a direct reflection of the preservation conditions. Mammal bones, the

Fig. 6.4   Some iron arrowheads from a thousand-year-old farming village in Central Africa (one-half actual size).

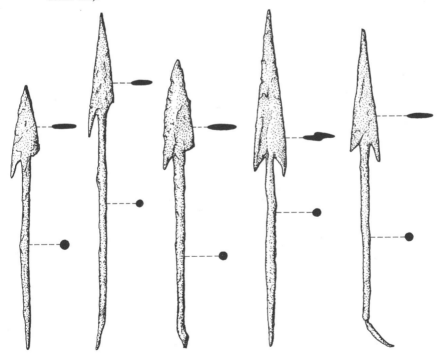

remains of animals butchered for food or ritual purposes, are the most common economic data, while bird and fish bones and the remains of invertebrates like beetles or frogs are not uncommon. Carbonized seeds occur in many hearths or cooking pots and provide a momentary insight into collecting or agricultural habits, while dry or wet sites may yield large collections of vegetal remains in a fresh state. Human feces and palynology are other sources of economic evidence, as are fresh or seawater mollusca and the stomach contents of bog corpses. Rock paintings can give a pictorial representation of subsistence activity, another source of evidence about prehistoric economy.

ANIMAL BONES

Sorting and Identification

Broken food bones are probably the most tangible remains of human subsistence patterns to survive from the past. Bone is one of the more durable raw materials and survives in various environments either in a fossilized or fresh form. Most people think skeletal remains occur in a more or less complete state, but rarely does an animal obligingly lie down and die in an archaeological site. Indeed, about the only mammals to do so are small rodents[12] who have died in their burrows or domestic animals like dogs that were not normally eaten.

All other faunal remains are usually fragmentary, coming from dismembered carcasses butchered either at the archaeological site or at the hunting grounds. To some degree, how much of the carcass is carried back to camp depends on the animal's size. Small deer may be taken back whole, slung from a pole carried by two hunters. A hunting band may sometimes camp at the site of the kill of a large animal, both eating their fill and drying parts of the carcass for later use. Almost invariably, however, the bones found in occupation sites have literally been sliced to ribbons. Every piece of usable meat is stripped from the bones: sinews are made into thongs, and the skin becomes clothing, or containers, or sometimes housing. Even the entrails are eaten. Limb bones are split for their delicious marrow: some bones are transformed into tools like harpoon heads, arrow tips, or leather working tools (Figure 6.5). The fragmentary bones found in an archaeological deposit represent the byproducts of many subsistence and cultural activities that can only be inferred from a detailed study of the bones. The archaeologist's job is attempting to conjure up a picture of the animal that was hunted or kept by the site's inhabitants from the fragmentary bone they dropped into

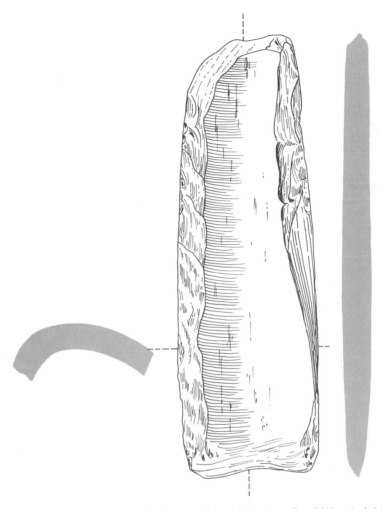

Fig. 6.5   A leather-working tool from Star Carr, made of wild ox bone (two-thirds actual size).

their occupation layer. But he also has to envisage the role that mammal played in the economy and culture of those who killed it—a difficult problem for the difference between the "actual animal" slaughtered by prehistoric man and the "archaeological animal" found, identified, and studied by the archaeologist is considerable.[13]

Animal bones are rarely found in articulation in an occupation level, unless one is excavating a kill site or finds some extremities of a fore or hind limb detached from the long bones in one piece. The fragments occur throughout the deposit, at some places in signifi-

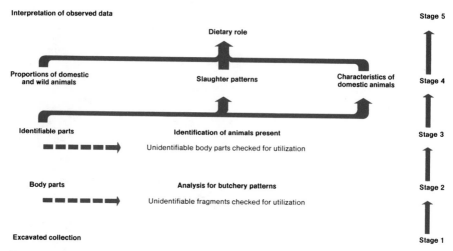

Fig. 6.6   Animal bone analysis.

cant concentrations, at others merely scattered over a living area. Bone distributions are carefully plotted on living floor sites to show any significant associations of body parts with artifacts, windbreaks, or other structures. But unless a living floor is definitely identified, the fragments are normally handled in bulk and bagged carefully for laboratory study.

The study of animal bones is traditionally regarded by archaeologists as the preserve of the zoologist and osteologist. But, in fact, this particular aspect of archaeology is by no means difficult; methods of day-to-day identification and analysis can readily be learned by anyone with a bent for examining osteological remains. Zoologists, indeed, are often so busy that more and more archaeologists are identifying their own faunal collections, using both comparative collections and numerous excellent osteological manuals that have appeared in recent years.[14] But mammalogists are always glad to assist with difficult identification problems and to discuss the implications of findings from the taxonomic or ecological viewpoint.

The first step in analysis is the cleaning and basic sorting of the collection (Figure 6.6). All fragments are examined; those that can be assigned to a body part are put on one side for further examination and counting. The unidentifiable fragments are counted, checked for signs of use as tools, and then discarded or put on one side.[15] This leaves a much smaller collection to handle, and the body part counts can be entered on a suitable form for more detailed analysis of butchery practices at a later stage. Some skeleton parts can positively

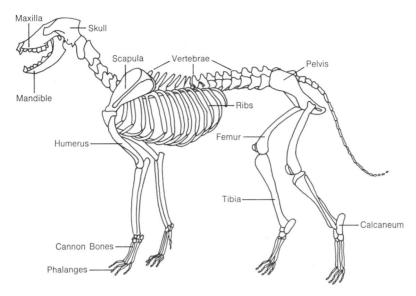

Fig. 6.7 A dog skeleton showing the most important body parts from the osteological viewpoint.

identify the animal to which they belonged, but only a small proportion of the body parts in a collection are sufficiently characteristic for this purpose. As an example, only 2,128 fragments of a collection of 195,415 from a Stone Age hunting camp in Zambia could be identified;[16] a further 9,207 could be assigned to a particular body part. The remainder of the collection had been smashed into small pieces by hunters in search of marrow, sinew, or meat. The skeleton of a dog in Figure 6.7 illustrates a typical mammal skeleton. Small skull fragments, vertebrae, ribs, scapulae, and pelvic bones are normally of little use to identify a domestic as opposed to a wild animal, or to differentiate one species of antelope from another. Upper and lower jaws and their dentition, individual teeth, the bony cores of horns, and sometimes the articular surfaces of long bones are susceptible to identification.[17] Teeth are identified by comparing the cusp patterns on their surfaces with those on comparative collections carefully collected from the site area (Figure 6.8). This task is made harder by the fragmentary nature of the material, for often individual teeth are relied on to identify an entire animal. In some parts of the world, the articular ends of long bones can be used as well, especially in regions like the Near East or parts of North America where the indigenous mammalian fauna is somewhat restricted.[18] It is even possible to distinguish the fragmentary long bones of domestic stock from

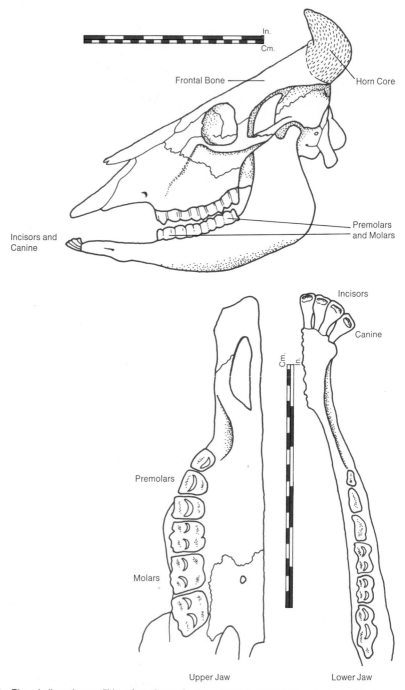

Fig. 6.8   *The skull and mandible of a domestic ox, showing important osteological features (one-fourth actual size).*

those of wild animals of the same size in the Near East, provided that the collections are large enough and the comparative material sufficiently complete and representative of all ages of individual and of variations in size from male to female individuals. But in other areas, such as sub-Saharan Africa, for example, the indigenous fauna is so rich and varied, with such small variations in skeletal geography, that only horn cores or teeth can distinguish between different species of antelope and separate domestic stock from game animals. Even the dentition is confusing, for the cusp patterns of buffalo and domestic cattle are remarkably similar, often only distinguishable by the smaller size of the latter.[19]

Most bone identification is by direct comparison, and is a fairly simple process, easily learned by anyone with sharp eyes. Statistical techniques are being used more frequently for comparing long bones as well as teeth, especially where fine distinctions between individual species are involved, or male/female size differences are a problem.[20] The identification stage of a bone analysis is the most important of all, for several fundamental questions need answering: Are domestic and wild species present? If so, what are the proportions of each group? What types of domestic stock were kept by the inhabitants? Did they have any hunting preferences that are reflected in the proportions of game animals found in the occupation levels? Are any wild species characteristic of vegetational associations no longer found in the area today?

The first stage in attacking these problems is a complete listing of the animals in the collection and a count of identifiable fragments of each represented. Although these can be counted and expressed as a percentage of all identified bones, such figures are meaningless. We have to equate the "archaeological animal" as represented by the bones with the game animal or domestic beast killed by the man who dropped the remains of his meal. No one has yet succeeded in developing a technique for overcoming this problem.[21]

Game Animals

Though the listing of game animals and their habits gives an insight into hunting practices, in many cases the content of the faunal list gains particular significance when we seek to explain why the hunters concentrated on certain species and apparently ignored others.

The dominance of a particular game species can result from economic necessity, convenience, or a matter of cultural preference. Many societies restrict the hunting of particular animals or the consumption of certain game meat to one or the other sex. The !Kung Bushmen of the Dobe area of Botswana have a complicated series of personal, age specific, and sex specific taboos in eating mammals.[22] No one can eat all twenty-nine game animals regularly taken by the Bushmen; indeed no two individuals will have the same set of taboos. Some mammals are eaten by everyone, but with restrictions on what part they may eat. Ritual curers will set personal dietary restrictions on other animals, although no one eats primates and some carnivores. Such complicated taboos are repeated with innumerable variations in other hunting and agricultural societies, and have undoubtedly affected the proportions of game animals found in archaeological sites.

Examples of specialized hunting are common, even if the reasons for the attention given to one or more species are rarely explained. Upper Paleolithic hunters of Solutré in southwest France concentrated on wild horses, apparently driving them over cliffs in large herds.[23] At the eighth millennium B.C. hunting camp of Star Carr in northeast England, Grahame Clark found the remains of a minimum of eighty red deer in the occupation levels, while roe deer, thirty-three individuals, was the next most common game.[24] The Archaic Riverton culture peoples of the central Wabash Valley, Illinois,[25] hunted the white-tailed deer as the basic meat staple in their diet, to the extent that the remains of this mammal were more numerous than those of any other species in the sites, including in most cases birds, fish, and turtles as well. The specialized big game hunting economies of the Plains Indians are well known, reflected in the archaeological record by spectacular bison-kill sites in Colorado, at Plainview, Texas, and at Folsom, New Mexico.[26]

Another factor is overhunting, or the gradual extinction of a favorite species. One well known example is the history of the North American bison, a major food source for all Plains tribes until its near extinction in the late nineteenth century.[27] *Bos primigenius*, the European aurochs or wild ox, was a major quarry of Upper Paleolithic hunters in Western Europe, and was still hunted in Post Glacial times and after the advent of food production (Figure 6.9).[28] The last aurochs died in a Polish park in 1627, and we know from illustrations and contemporary descriptions what these massive animals looked like. The bulls were large, up to six and a half feet at the shoulder, and often wore very long horns. The male coat was black with a white stripe along the back and white curly hair between the horns. Professor Lutz Heck of Berlin has tried to reconstitute the aurochs, by crossing breeds of cattle that exhibit certain characteristics of the wild ancestor. Heck's experiments were most successful, forty "reconstituted aurochsen" living by 1951. The mental characteristics of the aurochs reappeared together with the physical appearance. "Reconstituted aurochsen" are fierce, temperamental, and extremely agile if allowed to run wild. The German experiments have provided a far more convincing reconstruction of a most formidable Pleistocene mammal than any number of skeletal

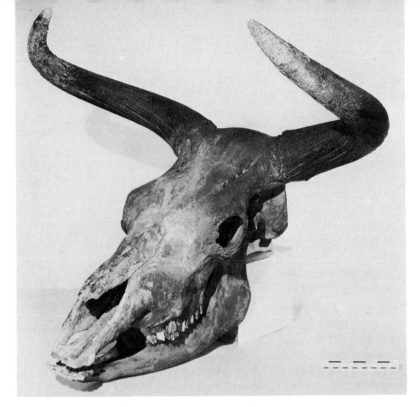

Fig. 6.9   *A* Bos primigenius *skull from Cambridgeshire, England.*

reconstructions or artists' impressions (Figure 6.10). Hunting habits changed radically at the end of the Pleistocene with the onset of warmer climatic conditions and greater forest cover, causing the retreat of the Arctic fauna, and their replacement by temperate species like the red and roe deer and the elk. Again, hunting activities have changed as drastically in the past century. Richard Lee records how the older Bushmen state that in earlier times there were more game animals and a higher hunting population in the central interior of Botswana.[29] Their forefathers used to hunt in large groups, killing buffalo, giraffe, and elephants. Today their descendents have a predominantly gathering economy, supplemented by the meat of twenty-nine different mammals, mostly those whose carcasses have a relatively high meat yield. Hunting is a common pursuit, the warthog being the most important source of meat, together with small game. This change in hunting habits directly results from the importation of Victorian rifles and early hunting safaris, which decimated the wonderful African fauna within three generations.

Domestic Animals

Apart from identification difficulties, the bones of domestic animals present more problems than those of wild species. If the population is obviously fully domesticated, the characteristics of the species

157

Fig. 6.10 A wild aurochs, as depicted by S. von Heberstain in 1549.

present must be studied to establish distinctions in breeds.[30] With early farming sites, however, where the transition from the wild to domestic state was still in progress, the osteological problems are formidable, for domestication transformed man's relationship with the animals he tamed, his food supplies stabilized, and he made more intensive use of the species involved.[31]

Nearly all domestic animals originated from a social wild species, in other words, a species with an inclination to be sociable, facilitating an association with man. Domestic animals did not all originate in the same part of the world, but were always domesticated in their natural area of distribution in the wild. Scholars have assumed that the domestication of wild animals takes place when a certain level of cultural achievement is reached. Domestication everywhere seems to begin when a growing population changes over to a more settled and culturally higher form of life. A regular food supply is needed for larger groups of people; domestication is dependent on such conditions and, at the same time, is a prerequisite for further cultural progress.

Wild animals lack many characteristics valuable in their domestic counterparts. Thus, wild sheep have hairy coats, but their wool is not the type produced by domestic sheep, which is suitable for spinning; aurochs, ancestors of the domestic ox, and wild goats produce sufficient milk for their young, but not in the quantities so important to man. Considerable changes have taken place during the course

[handwritten marginal note: These processes go hand-in-hand.]

of domestication, man developing characteristics in his animals that often render them unfit for survival in the wild.

The history of the domestic species is based on fragmentary animal bones found in the deposits of innumerable caves, rock shelters, and open sites.[32] Osteological studies of wild and domesticated animals are inhibited both by the fragmentary bones in most sites and by the much greater range of sexual and growth variation in domestic, as opposed to wild, populations. Nevertheless, a number of sites have produced evidence of gradual osteological change toward domesticated animals.[33] If the bones of the wild species of prehistoric domesticated animals are compared with those of the domestic animals through time, the range of size variations first increases and eventually a selection in favor of smaller animals and less variation in size appears.[34] This transition is, however, fluid and it is difficult to identify wild or domestic individuals from single bones or small collections. The bones of domestic animals demonstrate that a high degree of adaptability is inherent in wild animals. Man has found it necessary to change the size and qualities of animals according to his need, with corresponding effects on their skeletal remains. Different breeds of cattle, sheep, and other domestic animals have developed since the origins of domestication (Figures 6.11 and 6.12). The humped zebu ox of Asia can be identified in faunal collections from the characteristic bifid spinal process that forms on the neck vertebrae.[35] Humped cattle are pictured in Egyptian tombs (Figure 6.13),[36] and everyone is familiar with the Jersey and Guernsey breeds of modern times.

Slaughter Patterns

The next step after identification of the bones is analyzing the age at which the animals were slaughtered and the butchery techniques used. Age is determined by examining the eruption and wear patterns of teeth, as well as the epiphyses of long bones. The latter may be unfused or partially joined in the case of immature animals, and although these make a useful criterion, it is not so significant in areas like Africa or Asia where the osteology of long bones and other extremities is less well known. Some Near Eastern sites have yielded such large collections that higher proportions of immature epiphyses were used to show the threshold of domestication—the period when the inhabitants of such sites as the Belt Cave in Iran systematically began to kill goats at a younger age than they did when they were hunting the wild species.[37] Most aging is determined by studying the dentition, using complete jaws so that the eruption formulae can be compared. Sometimes single teeth are used, the wear on the cusps being measured by a standard scale, but this method is less reliable.

Fig. 6.11 A Minoan bull and dancers, as painted on the walls of the Palace of Knossos. The ox has a piebald coat and was a domesticated form. (After Arthur Evans.)

The assembled data are then tabulated in graph or table form, ready for interpretation. Some cases of slaughter pattern graphs appear in Figure 6.14—obviously, large samples are essential.

The interpretation of slaughter patterns is fairly straightforward when hunting economies are involved. Most hunting societies were skilled in the chase, taking animals of all ages with a preference for individuals in their prime which yield tender meat (Figure 6.14a). Less able hunters might concentrate on immature or old animals that were easier to trap or run down. Mass game drives of large herbivores like the bison or buffalo yield a more even curve with all ages of beast represented. Hunters tend to select animals with a high meat yield rather than older or younger beasts.[38]

Fig. 6.12 A herd of buffalo grouped around a structure of marsh reeds, from a clay impression of a Sumerian seal.

Fig. 6.13 A stele of Bebwawi, Amarna, Egypt, from the Eighteenth Dynasty, including a zebu bull.
(After N. de G. Davies.)

Domestic animals, being a controllable meat supply, are subject
to quite different selection criteria. In more advanced agricultural
societies, cattle or horses might be kept until old age for draught
purposes, surplus males being castrated and females being retained
until they stopped lactating or were of no further use for breeding
or ploughing. Even if riding or work animals were not kept, the
problem of surplus males persists. The ratio of male to female in
any cattle population is 1:1, with the result, of course, that there are
far too many males for breeding purposes. This male surplus represents an abundant source of prime meat, and was often slaughtered
at early adulthood. Cattle stood for wealth in many traditional societies,
as they do in some today, but were slaughtered on special occasions
like funerals or weddings; the herd surplus was consumed in this
manner, and the owner's obligations were satisfied. Thus, a population
of cattle jaws found in a site may reveal a characteristic curve (Figure
6.14b) showing that surplus males and females were slaughtered at

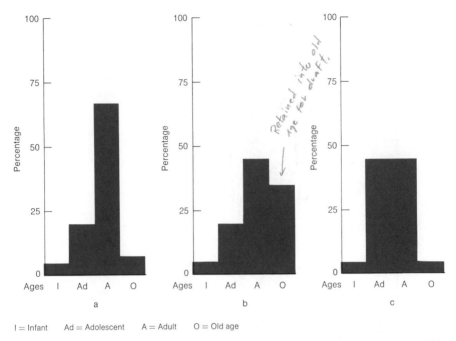

I = Infant   Ad = Adolescent   A = Adult   O = Old age

Fig. 6.14 Aging graphs for hypothetical—and ideal—cases. (a) Hunting population slaughtered by skilled hunters. (b) Typical domestic cattle population. (c) Typical domestic goat population.

different ages. Or perhaps the remains of a herd of goats yield a simple graph (Figure 6.14c), reflecting circumstances in which small stock were slaughtered in their prime for meat purposes. These situations are by no means universal, but offer examples of factors that can affect slaughter pattern data.

Butchery

The fragmentary bones in an occupation level are the end-product of the killing, cutting up, and consumption of domestic or wild animals. To understand the butchery process, the articulation of animal bones must be examined in the levels where they are found, or a close study must be made of the fragmentary body parts. For instance, kill sites occur at Olduvai Gorge and Torralba, Spain, and in the American West, to name only a few. Such areas were occupied by hunters who camped beside their kill, removing the skin and meat from the carcass of a large mammal, and perhaps drying some surplus meat for later consumption. The butchering tools used by the skinners are found in direct association with the bones, so that the excavations preserve the moment of butchery for posterity. Such an incident is illustrated in Figure 6.15 in which the sequence of dismembering a

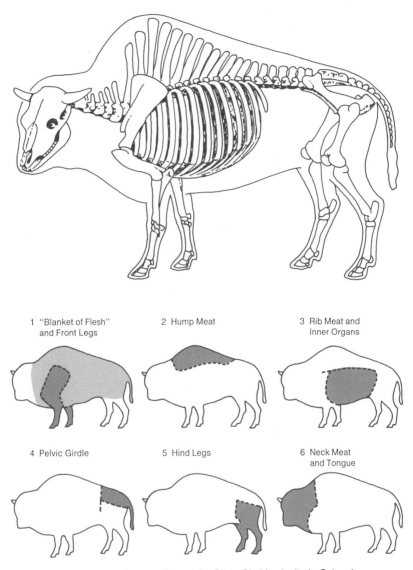

Fig. 6.15 Butchering practices of Paleo-Indians at the Olsen-Chubbuck site in Colorado, as recon-
structed from the archaeological evidence and historical butchery data. (From "A Paleo-
Indian Bison Kill," Joe Ben Wheat. Copyright © January 1967 by Scientific American,
Inc. All rights reserved.)

bison carcass has been reconstructed from an accumulation of bones
at a kill site in Colorado.[39]

Deciphering butchery techniques becomes more complicated at a
base camp or more permanent village where meat was brought onto

the site or slaughtered nearby. In one method, body part distributions are reduced to proportions of the most common bone present.[40] The technique was developed by Theodore White who applied it with success to bison kill sites in the Great Plains, where preservation conditions appear comparatively even. Many sites are larger, however, and soil conditions are such that some more delicate body parts may disintegrate more swiftly than others, to result in a distorted picture of the skeletal remains left on the site by its inhabitants. The bones of the forelimb and extremities are most frequently found, whereas those of the skull, vertebrae, and innominate parts are less common. This pattern is remarkably consistent over many sites and must, to some degree, reflect the selection practices of the butchers. The animal's size may effect how many bones are found at a base site. Goats, chickens, or small deer may be carried to the village as complete carcasses, but usually only small portions of larger beasts are brought in—this is especially true of those with a high meat yield because these are often consumed where killed and every scrap of flesh and entrails utilized.

VEGETAL REMAINS

Gathering and agriculture are two major components of prehistoric subsistence almost invariably underrepresented in the archaeological record. Seeds, fruits, grasses, and leaves are among the most fragile of organic materials and do not survive long unless they are carbonized or preserved under very wet or arid conditions. As early as the mid-nineteenth century, scientists were identifying fruit and cereal crops from the deposits of the Swiss lake dwellings exposed by the especially low waters of the lakes.[41] Some carbonized grains were recorded by Pitt Rivers in his excavations, and plant remains were discovered at an early date in the dry caves of the western United States. Vegetal remains, dried by the arid climate of the Nile Valley, were found in the Desert Fayum by Gertrude Caton-Thompson in the 1920s.[42] Exceptional finds like these helped to found our knowledge of prehistoric food crops. But in recent years, more and more attention has been paid to flotation techniques (see page 166) for recovering large samples of seeds from superficially unproductive sites.[43] Others have used the grain impressions on pots[44] to base a provisional botanical history of Europe; palynology has provided insights into forest clearance dates and agriculture's introduction to many parts of modern Europe.[45]

Carbonized seeds are normally found in cooking pots or among the ashes of hearths where they have been dropped by accident. Though the preservation conditions are not ideal, it is possible to identify both domestic and wild plant species from such discoveries.[46] Much early evidence for cereal cultivation in the Near East comes from carbonized seeds. Many more unburnt vegetal remains occur in waterlogged sites and in dry caves. The Star Carr site in northeastern England yielded a range of fungi and wild seeds, some of which were eaten until recently by European peasants.[47] A Stone Age hunting camp at Gwisho hot springs in central Zambia situated on the edge of a tract of savannah woodland rich in vegetal foods contained quantities of seeds and fruit preserved by the high water table in the springs.[48] Ten thousand identifiable vegetal fragments came from the occupation levels at Gwisho, many of them from six edible species still eaten by southern African hunters; this represents a remarkable continuity of subsistence pattern over more than 4,000 years.

The dry caves of the western United States and Mexico have provided a great quantity of dried vegetal remains. Tularosa Cave in New Mexico is important for its documentation of the transition from the Archaic to Formative stages.[49] Cochise occupants of Tularosa were harvesting primitive corn by 2000 b.c., and their Mogollon successors employed horticulture fully. The dry deposits in the cave contained much organic material, including moccasins, sandals, and hunting implements. The lower levels, occupied by Archaic hunters, yielded the remains of no less than thirty-nine species of wild flora used for food, tools, and raw materials; edible plants included yucca seeds, cacti, walnuts, and various grasses. Tularosa gave a remarkable picture of the introduction of cultigens into the Southwest. Maize, beans, squash, and gourds were found in the Cochise Archaic levels, adding a new dimension to our knowledge of the area's gathering economy. A primitive corn was being grown by the Cochise by 2000 b.c., and a millennium later, squash and beans were being cultivated. Although the origins of agriculture in this area plainly lie to the south in Mexico, the Tularosa finds indicate cultivated crops were introduced into more northerly areas before domestic plants had completed evolving from the wild to the domestic state. The process of economic transition was completed by 300 b.c. when pottery was introduced to Tularosa. Corn has been found even earlier at Bat Cave, northeast of Tularosa, where it has been dated to *ca.* 3500 b.c.[50]

Danger Cave, on the western edge of the Great Salt Lake in western Utah is another large dry cave occupied from about 9000 b.c. until recent times.[51] Over thirteen feet of rich deposit, mostly consisting of dust and chaff, contained one of the most complete cultural inventories ever recovered from the western United States. Sixty-five plant species, all found in the area today, were recovered from the site. Other desert caves in Nevada, such as Lovelock and Gypsum,[52] contain desiccated occupation layers or numerous caches of artifacts. Some hoards include pine nuts, edible seeds, and the raw materials for toolmaking.

The Tehuacán Valley in the state of Puebla, Mexico, has provided a record of continuous human occupation from the earliest times to the Spanish Conquest.[53] Early inhabitants of the valley lived mainly by hunting rabbits, birds, and turtles, but later, about 6700–5000 B.C., their successors subsisted mostly on wild plants like beans and amaranth. These people, who lived in caves during the dry season, began to cultivate squashes and avocados; maize pollen occurs in their cave deposits, and a few small wild maize cobs occur at the end of their occupation. Grinding stones, pestles, and mortars were in use for the first time, indicating that seeds were being ground for food. Richard MacNeish has excavated over a dozen sites in Tehuacán, five of which contained the remains of ancient corn; 80,000 wild plant remains and 25,000 specimens of corn came from the sites, providing a detailed picture of agriculture's origins in highland Mexico. The small wild maize cobs came from the lowest occupation level in San Marcos Cave, and were no more than twenty millimeters (0.78 inches) long. Coxcatlan Cave contained important botanical evidence, too, for by 5000 B.C., although the inhabitants of this and other sites were still gathering most of their vegetal food, 10 per cent of the deposits came from domestic cultivation—gourds, squashes, beans, chili peppers, and corn. A third of Tehuacán subsistence was based on agriculture by 3400 B.C., a period when the domestic dog first appeared; permanent settlement first began soon after this. Pottery was being manufactured by 2300 B.C., and more hybrid types of corn came into use. So many vegetal remains were found in the settlements of Tehuacán that the history of domestic corn in this area can be written in quite astonishing detail (Figure 6.16): abundant at first, wild corn became virtually extinct two thousand years ago, as did the early cultivated varieties, which were superseded by more modern forms. Botanical evidence of this complexity and completeness is unique in the archaeological record.

Flotation techniques have been employed systematically to recover seeds in central Illinois, and also at Ali Kosh in Iran. The method uses water or chemicals to free the seeds, often of microscopic size, from the fine earth or occupation residue that masks them: the vegetal remains float while the residue sinks. Although this technique enables us to recover seeds from many sites where it was impossible before, by no means can it be applied universally, as its effectiveness depends on soil conditions. Through flotation, Stuart Struever and his colleagues recovered over 36,000 fragments of carbonized hickory nut shell from ovens, hearths, and storage-refuse pits in the Apple Creek

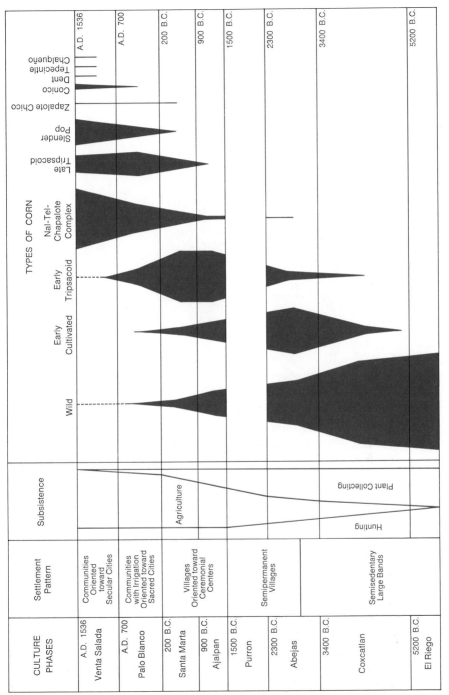

Fig. 6.16 The evolution of maize in the Valley of Mexico.

Fig. 6.17 (a) The wild ancestor of einkorn (Triticum boeoticum). *(b) Cultivated einkorn* (T. monococ-cum). *(Both two-thirds actual size.)*

site in the Lower Illinois Valley.[54] This Late Woodland settlement also yielded 4,200 fragments of acorn shell, as well as over 2,000 other seeds from at least three species. Few cultivated seeds were found, which indicated that the inhabitants relied on hickory nuts and acorns for much of their vegetable diet.

Frank Hole's experiments with flotation at the Ali Kosh site in Iran were also successful, indeed the results were dramatic.[55] After the first season of excavations, Hole and his colleagues stated confidently that "plant remains were scarce at Ali Kosh." Two years later they used a modified version of Struever's flotation technique and recovered over 40,000 seeds stratified throughout the cultural sequence at the Ali Kosh mound. The data gave a startlingly complete botanical history for the site, showing the increasing importance of emmer wheat and two-row hulled barley and the effects of irrigation (Figure 6.17).

Apart from the seeds themselves, which reveal what the food plants were, grain impressions in the walls of clay vessels or adobe brick help uncover the history of agriculture or gathering. The microscopic

Fig. 6.18 A grain impression from a Neolithic pot at Hurst Fen, Cambridgeshire, England.

casts of grains that adhered to the wet clay of a pot while it was being made are preserved in the firing process and can be identified with a microscope. Numerous grain impressions have been found on European handmade pottery from the end of the Stone Age (Figure 6.18). Indeed, a remarkably complete crop history of prehistoric Europe has been pieced together from grain impressions. The most abundantly cultivated cereal in prehistoric Europe was emmer wheat (*Triticum dicoccum*); wheat was the most important grain during early farming times, but barley rose into prominence during the Bronze Age. Some typical grain impression figures follow:[56]

	Stone Age		*Bronze Age*		*Pre-Roman Iron Age*	
	Wheat	Barley	Wheat	Barley	Wheat	Barley
Britain	17	9	23	223	19	15
Denmark	35	54	22	214	1	30

Grain impressions have been studied in the Near East, and western Sahara,[57] whereas some related work on adobe bricks has been carried out in the western United States.[58]

Palynology has been an invaluable tool to study European forest clearance. Many years ago, Danish botanist Johannes Iversen was studying the pollen diagrams from Scandinavian peat sequences when he noticed that there was a remarkably sudden change in the composition of the forests in the beginning of the sub-Boreal period (Blytt and Sernander, zones VII–VIII).[59] The elements of high forest—oak, ash, beech, and elm—simultaneously declined, while, at the same moment, the pollens of grasses increased sharply. At one locality, he found a charcoal layer immediately underlying the zone where forest trees declined. The increase in grass pollens was also associated with the appearance of several cultivation weeds, including *Plantago*, which is characteristically associated with cereal agriculture in Europe and went with European farmers throughout the world, even to North America. Iversen concluded that the tree cover vanished as a direct result of farming activity—man's first major imprint on his environment (Figure 6.19). Similar pollen curves have been plotted from data gathered elsewhere in Europe. The first human clearance of forests has also been dated in Uganda where deep pollen cores from Lake Victoria show a sudden drop in forest cover about 3,000 years ago.[60]

However effective the recovery techniques used for vegetal remains, the picture of either food gathering or agriculture is bound to be incomplete. A look at modern hunters reveals the problem.[61] The !Kung Bushmen of the Kalahari Desert in southern Africa are classic examples of hunter-gatherers who appear in every book on ethnography, and yet until comparatively recently, little was known of their ecology or subsistence patterns. Many early writers on hunters assumed the !Kung relied on game alone and lived in a perennial state of starvation that was relieved periodically by meat-eating orgies. Nothing, in fact, could be farther from the truth. Much subsistence activity of Bushmen and other hunters is conducted by the women who gather the wild vegetable foods that comprise a substantial part of their diet. Many early observers were naturally preoccupied with hunting techniques and more spectacular subsistence activities, for, in former times, many hunting peoples pursued larger game, often cooperating with other bands in the chase.

Today, vegetable foods play a leading part in Bushman diet and have presumably increased in importance as the large game herds have diminished. The Bushmen know of at least eighty-five species of edible fruit, seeds, and plants; of this enormous subsistence base, they eat regularly only some nine species, noticeably the *Bauhinia*.

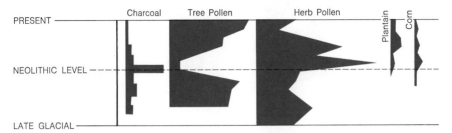

Fig. 6.19 Fluctuation in the frequencies of charcoal and fossil pollen brought by Neolithic coloniza-
tion: Ordrup Mose, Denmark. The amount of grass pollen rises sharply as the forest
decreases. (After Iversen.)

In a famine year or when prime vegetable food sources are exhausted, they turn to other species, having an excellent cushion of edible food to fall back on when their conventional diet staple is scarce. Theoretically, therefore, the Bushmen can never starve, even if food is scarce at times. Their territory, of course, is delineated in part by available sources of vegetable foods as well as by water supplies; its frontiers in many cases represent a day's walking distance out to the gathering grounds and back to the base camp.

AGRICULTURE AND DOMESTIC AND WILD ANIMALS

Very few subsistence-farming peoples have ever relied on agricultural products or their herds alone to provide them with food the year round. Hunting, fishing, and gathering have always supplemented the diet, and in famine years or times of epidemic the people have fallen back on the natural resources of their environment for survival (Figure 6.20). Since, however, food production has led to increased population densities, famine often ensues because the resource base for farmers remains the same as that which may have supported a smaller hunter-gatherer population in comfort.[62] Even in times of plenty, most food producers rely on game for some of their meat, evidenced by the bones of wild animals in faunal collections where cattle and small stock are also present. The proportions of domestic and wild species in such a collection are considerably important in assessing the roles of hunting and pastoralism in the economy. If such figures are based on how many individuals are represented in the collection, or on some sound formulae, the results can be revealing, especially when a series of collections are available from a cultural sequence extending over several hundred years.

Prehistoric stockbreeding in Europe has been studied intensively,

Fig. 6.20 A woman of the Leya tribe, Zambia, pounding wild nuts for food.

using large bone collections and statistical techniques. Charles Higham[63] used Swiss collections and modern comparative material to document the history of stockbreeding. He combined the faunal analyses with pollen studies and found that the aims of stock-raising were closely integrated with the agricultural methods and technological attainments of prehistoric societies in Switzerland. Higham points out, for example, that bovines and sheep find only limited feeding in mixed oak forest and that a damp, forested environment is difficult for sheep, who are susceptible to blow-fly attacks and other diseases in warm humid weather and who also have a natural antipathy to woodland. Consequently, any diminution in forest acres through agricultural bush clearance encouraged the keeping of domestic herbivores. Higham convincingly argues that any prehistoric tribe, which encouraged stock-raising and agriculture by removing the factors in the environment limiting such activities and by conditioning the "mix" of its herds to the man-modified environment, promoted its chances for

survival by increasing its productivity. The earliest Swiss farmers |
settled near lakes, positioning their villages where the environment
best suited their activities. Most sites bordered shores where rich
lacustrine soils and a more favorable climate encouraged agriculture.
Lake plants gave vital early spring fodder, whereas the undergrowth
of the nearby mixed oak forest provided supplemental feed for domestic stock and acorns for pigs.

Early farming was confined to open areas favorable to this activity,
but this kind of land rapidly became scarce. Metal tools added a
new factor to the situation, and aided in forest clearance. The destruction of forests gave greater areas of pastureland, and removed a major
barrier to prehistoric farming. Herbivores became more important
because the hay raised in these lands allowed stock to overwinter.
In this, as in so many other instances, the economic strategy of the
prehistoric farmer integrated with the limiting factors of his environment and his technological abilities to produce a distinct pattern of
economic evolution. Behind the proportions of fragmentary bones lie
the unconscious and deliberate subsistence strategies of man, the
discovery of which is the ultimate goal of the scholar of prehistoric
economies.

While one may argue, as Higham does, that the most significant
change in prehistoric Europe was the decline in importance of the
pig and rise of sheep and horses due to progressive forest clearance,
in other areas different factors may affect the content of domestic
herds. The inhabitants of the Deh Luran Plain in Iran first began
to cultivate cereal crops and keep goats sometime before 7000 B.C.
The first food production involved plants and animals introduced from
the mountains to the rolling steppe of Deh Luran. As the excavators
point out, "What man did, before 7000 B.C., was to domesticate the
annuals he could eat, and then domesticate the animals who lived
on the perennials."[64] The cultivation system was expanded so that
domestic grains increased from 5 per cent of the vegetal remains to
about 40 per cent between 7000 and 6000 B.C. But this early domestic
plant and animal complex, based as it was on upland-mountain environmental adaptations, inhibited rapid population growth. Even so,
the vegetational pattern of the steppe was altered as field weeds were
established and land clearance and grazing removed the natural grass
covering.

Between 5500 and 5000 B.C., some simple irrigation techniques were
introduced that took advantage of the local drainage pattern. Barley
cultivation became of prime importance, and the cultivation areas
expanded. Sheep increased in importance and cattle were introduced,
the latter only assuming a vital role in the economy when ploughs

began to be used around 2000 B.C. Each gradual or rapid change in the subsistence pattern or environment of Deh Luran instituted by man led to a complicated chain reaction affecting every sector of the inhabitants' culture.

The farmers of the Batoka Plateau in southern Zambia were also cattle owners; abundant grazing grass and good supplies of perennial water make the region a prime cattle area today. By excavating a series of settlement sites, the evolution of cattle herding was traced over a period of 1,300 years.[65] In the seventh century A.D. and in earlier centuries, the farmers of the plateau had few cattle, relying on game for much of their protein. By A.D. 1000, cattle represented about 60 per cent of the food bones at several sites, whereas two hundred years later they were overwhelmingly dominant in some sites, and in a single nineteenth-century settlement represented over 90 per cent of the animal bones.[66] The increase in cattle is thought to be connected with natural increases in herd surpluses rather than with any major changes in economy or culture, for there has been a basically similar, mixed farming economy on the Batoka Plateau since the advent of metallurgy eighteen hundred years ago, and population densities have been too low for major modification of the vegetational cover.

The rates of herd growth and the importance of pastoralism are affected by many factors, among them endemic stock disease, the nutrient qualities of grazing grass, the availability of water supplies, and, in some areas, the distribution of the dreaded tsetse fly, carrier of trypanosomiasis which is fatal to cattle and harmful to man.[67] Similar factors also affect the growth rate of domestic stock, because the size of cattle or smaller stock can vary widely from one environment to another.

BIRDS, FISH, AND MOLLUSCA

Bird Bones

Bird bones have been sadly neglected in archaeology, although some early investigators realized their significance. Japetus Steenstrup and other early investigators of Danish shell middens took care to identify birds, including those of migrants.[68] Many Maglemose camps in Denmark have been recognized as summer settlements, where cranes and mute swans were taken and where winter species are absent. In contrast, coastal shell middens of the Ertebølle type were occupied all year, with most fowling taking place in the winter.[69] In 1902 the famous Peruvianist Max Uhle dug a large Indian mound on the eastern shores of San Francisco Bay. The site was excavated again in 1926, and Dr. Hildegarde Howard studied a large collection of bird remains from the dig;[70] her report illustrates the potential importance of bird faunas in archaeology. She found that water birds were the predominant species, especially ducks, geese, and cormorants; land birds distinctive of hill country were absent. All the geese were winter visitors, mostly found in the Bay Area between January and April each year. The cormorant bones were nearly all immature, suggesting that the Indians had been robbing cormorant rookeries; most of the cormorant bones equalled an adult bird's in size, but ossification was less complete, equivalent to that in modern birds about five to six weeks old. Dr. Howard examined rookery records and estimated that a date of *ca.* June 28 each year would be the actual time when rookeries could be raided. Thus, from the evidence, she concluded that the Emeryville mound was occupied both during the winter and the early summer, and probably all year.

Bird hunting has often been a sideline in the struggle for subsistence. In many societies, young boys have hunted winged prey with bows and arrows, while training for larger game. A specialized bird-hunting kit is found in several cultures, among them the Post Glacial hunter-gatherer cultures of Northern Europe. Though bows and spears were used in the chase, snaring was obviously practiced regularly. The birds found in some African hunting and farming sites are almost invariably species like guinea fowl who fly comparatively rarely and are easily snared.[71] No traces of the snares have been found in excavations, for they are normally made of perishable materials. Surprisingly little has been written on prehistoric fowling, perhaps because bird bones are fragile and present tricky identification problems.

Fish

Fishing, like fowling, became increasingly important as man began to specialize in different and distinctive economies and as his environmental adaptations became more sophisticated and his technological abilities improved. Evidence for this activity comes from both artifacts and fish bones.

Freshwater and ocean fish can be caught in various ways. Nets, basket traps, and dams were methods in wide use from Post Glacial times on, but their remains rarely survive in the archaeological record except in dry sites or waterlogged deposits. Basket fish traps have been found in Danish peat bogs, dating to the Atlantic vegetational period.[72] The ancient Egyptians employed somewhat similar traps which are depicted in Old Kingdom tomb paintings (2660–2180 B.C.). Nets remain the most popular fishing device and were used in Northern Europe in Post Glacial times, too. Seine nets, which captured surface-swimming fish by surrounding them, have been found in two localities in Finland and Estonia; the damp conditions preserved not only the pine-bark floats, but also parts of the fiber net and stone weights.[73] A large fishweir, constructed of vertical sticks 1.2 to 4.9 meters long (4 to 16 feet), sharpened on one end with a stone axe, enclosed an area of two acres at Boylston Street, Boston.[74] The weir was built about 2500 B.C., and was probably the work of coastal Archaic people. Such traps were evidently widely used along the Atlantic Coast, built in estuary areas where tidal currents were strong. In the Boston weir, brush and flexible withies were placed between the stakes; fish were diverted into the enclosure by "leaders," also made of brush, leading to the trap mouth. Considerable community effort must have been necessary to build this weir, which provided an almost inexhaustible food supply for its designers.

Fishhooks, harpoons, and barbed spearheads are frequent finds in lake- or riverside encampments. The earliest fishhooks had no barbs, but did have a U-shaped profile (Figure 6.21). Post Glacial hunting peoples like the Maglemose folk of Denmark used such artifacts in the seventh millennium B.C., in all probability to hunt the pike, a prized freshwater fish in prehistoric times.[75] Bone and antler harpoon heads, common in Magdalenian deposits from southwest French caves, may sometimes have been used for bottom fishing.[76] The Maglemose peoples of the Baltic Sea area certainly spear fished. Numerous barbed bone points have been recovered from the bottom of an old lake at Kunda in Estonia, two of them associated with pike skeletons. Many pike bones were found at the Mesolithic site of Svaerdborg, Denmark, together with numerous barbed spear-points. North European methods of fishing are vividly described by J. Scheffer in his portrayal of the Lapps: "Their way of fishing alters with the season, in the Summer usually with drag nets, between two boats, or else with spears like tridents, but that they have more teeth. With these they strike pikes, especially when they lie sunning themselves near the top of the water: they do the same by night burning dry wood at the prow, by which light the fish are enticed thither."[77]

Scheffer's words are apt, for artifacts alone tell us little about the role of fish in prehistoric economy or the fishing techniques of prehistoric peoples. Did they fish all year or only when salmon were running? Did they concentrate on bottom fish or rely on stranded whales for fish protein? Such questions can only be answered by examining the surviving fish bones themselves. Unfortunately, piscine remains are among the most fragile in archaeology, and are susceptible to destruction by many corrosive factors. Once recovered, however, fish bones

Fig. 6.21 Bone fishhooks of the Maglemosian culture from Northern Europe (two-thirds actual size). (After Clark.)

are readily identified and are often informative. The Stone Age hunters of Gwisho in central Zambia lived near the floodplain of the Kafue River in the third millennium B.C., a vast, seasonally inundated area where fish abound.[78] Each dry season the waters of the Kafue recede, leaving isolated pools that survive long after the river has gone. Many catfish are stranded in the depressions, lurking in the soft mud. The local inhabitants trap the fish or spear them as the pools dry up, eating some of their catch fresh and drying the rest for later consumption. The hunting camps contain catfish bones in overwhelming numbers, whereas other species, normally caught by rod and line or more sophisticated methods, are almost nonexistent. The conclusion reached was that Gwisho hunters were taking bottom fish to the virtual exclusion of other species because they were the easiest to catch, especially as the Kafue's waters were several miles away and other food sources more convenient.

The Chumash Indians of Southern California were remarkably skillful fishermen, venturing far offshore in frameless plank canoes and fishing with hook and line, basket, net, and harpoon. Their piscatory skill is reflected in the archaeological sites of Century Ranch, Los Angeles,[79] where the bones of such deep-sea fish as the albacore and oceanic skipjack were found, together with the remains of large deep-water rockfish that live near the sea bottom in water too deep to be fished from the shore. Five other species normally occurring offshore, including the barracuda, were found in the same midden. The bones of shallow-water fish among them the leopard shark and

California halibut were discovered in the same sites, indicating that both surf fishing and canoe fishing in estuaries with hook and line, basket, or net were also practiced.

The degree to which a community depends on fishing can be impressive. Lake- or seaside fishing encampments tend to be occupied on a more permanent basis than hunting camps, for the food supply, especially when combined with the collection of shellfish, is both reliable and nourishing. The "Later Stone Age" fishing camp at Lothagam in northern Kenya, dating to the fourth millennium b.c., yielded the remains of over 10,000 fish bones, nearly all Nile perch, a species that grows to an enormous size. Only some 250 mammal bones were found in the site, which was certainly occupied over a long period of time.[80]

Mollusca

Shellfish from seashore, lake, or river have formed an important part of prehistoric diet for many thousands of years. Augustin de Beaulieu, who visited the Cape of Good Hope in 1620 with a fleet of ships from Honfleur, France, was a curious and perceptive observer whose wanderings over the Cape Peninsula enabled him to describe the Khoi-Khoi, the indigenous cattle herders and gatherers: "Also they go along the seashore where they find certain shell fish, or some dead whale or other fish, however putrefied it may be, and this they put on the fire for a little and make a good meal of it."[81] The identification of the mollusca in shell middens is a matter for expert conchologists, who possess a mine of information on the edibility and seasons of shellfish. With such data, it was determined that the Khoi-Khoi seem to have depended on shellfish at dry times of the year when inland pastures were parched and vegetable foods in short supply. Other peoples subsisted on mollusca for most of the year, accumulating gigantic piles of shells at strategic places on the shores of lakes or oceans near favored rocky outcrops or tidal pools.

A century ago, the Danes were discussing the distribution of Baltic oysters found in seaside middens near Copenhagen,[82] and the study of prehistoric mollusca has continued since then. Modern midden analysis involves the systematic sampling of the deposits, and the counting and weighing of the various constituents of the soil. The proportions of different shells are readily calculated, and their size, which sometimes changes through time, easily measured. California shell middens have long been the subject of intensive research, with the changes in frequency of mollusca projected against ecological changes in the site areas.

The La Jolla Culture middens of La Batiquitos Lagoon in San Diego are a notable example of such analysis. Claude N. Warren[83] took column samples from one shell mound and found that the remains of five species of shellfish were the dominant elements in the molluscan diet of the inhabitants. The changes in the major species of shellfish were then calculated for each excavated level. They found that *Mytilus*, the bay mussel, was commonest in the lower levels, gradually being replaced by *Chione*, the Venus shell, and *Pecten*, the scallop, both of which assumed greater importance in the later phases of the site occupation, which has been radiocarbon dated from the fifth to second millennia B.C. Warren found that *Ostrea*, the oyster, a species characteristic of a rocky coast, was also most common in the lower levels, indicating that the San Diego shore was rocky beach at that time, with extensive colonies of shellfish. By about 6,300 years ago La Batiquitos Lagoon was silted to the extent that it was ecologically more suitable for *Pecten* than the rock-loving *Mytilus*. Soon afterward, however, the lagoons became so silted that even *Pecten* and *Chione* could no longer support a large population dependent on shellfish, which then had to move elsewhere. Similar investigations elsewhere in California have also shown the enormous potential of mollusca in studying prehistoric ecology.

Both fresh and seawater shells had ornamental roles, too. Favored species were traded over enormous distance in North America, Europe, and Africa. *Spondylus gaederopus*, a mussel native to the Black Sea, the Sea of Marmora, and the Aegean, was widely distributed through human agency as far north and west as Poland and the Rhineland by early Danubian farmers in the fifth millennium B.C.[84] The shells were used as pendants, beads, or bracelets and are ubiquitous in Danubian country. As the Danubians expanded northward and westward into their new territories, they began to trade the shells to perpetuate the ornamental tradition of their homeland. On the other side of the world, baler shells from the coast of Cape York in northern Australia were chipped and ground to form oval ornaments that were passed from hand to hand across the continent to South Australia by hunting bands—a remarkable example of the high value of seashell ornaments to some communities.[85] The *conus* shell, common on the East African coast, was widely traded, finding its way into the African interior and becoming a traditional prerequisite of chieftainly prestige. The nineteenth-century missionary and explorer David Livingstone records his visit to Chief Shinte in western Zambia in 1855: the going price for two *conus* shells at that time was a slave, or five for a tusk of elephant ivory. Archaeological digs have indicated that *conus* shells were handled in the Zambezi Valley seven hundred years earlier, reflecting a long history of trade in such prestigious ornaments (Figure 6.22).[86] Indeed, as late as 1910, enterprising merchants were trading china replicas of *conus* shells to the tribesmen of Central Africa.

Fig. 6.22 Ingombe Ilede burial with conus shells, *ca. fifteenth century* A.D. *(The shells are the circular objects around the neck, numbered 1–4.)*

ROCK ART

Rock art is a major source of information on economic activities. Some years ago, African archaeologist J. Desmond Clark published an account of "Late Stone Age" hunting practices in southern Africa in which he drew heavily on the rock art of Rhodesia and South Africa (Figure 6.23). The paintings depict the chase, weapons, collecting, camp life, and sometimes domestic animals. Clark remarked, "In the rock art there is preserved an invaluable record of the people's hunting methods, the different kinds of weapons and domestic equipment they used, their customs and ceremonies."[87]

The rock paintings of Natal, South Africa, provide fascinating information on fishing practices and the boats associated with them. Patricia Vinnecombe recorded a fishing scene in the Tsoelike River rockshelter in Lesotho, southern Africa (Figure 6.24).[88] The fishermen, armed with long spears, are massed in boats, apparently cornering a shoal of fish which are swimming around in confusion. Some boats have lines under their hulls which may represent anchors; the fish cannot be identified with certainty, but may be freshwater catfish or yellowfish. Vinnecombe's paper generated considerable discussion—some authorities argued that the boats in the paintings were probably made of bark.[89] Another famous scene from the Cape Province of South Africa depicts a group of ostriches feeding peacefully,

Fig. 6.23 A running hunter from Ho Khotso, Lesotho, southern Africa, shown in a Late Stone Age drawing painted in purple-red. The figure is 21 centimeters (about 8 inches) high.

and among them lurks a hunter wearing an ostrich skin, his legs and bow protruding beneath the belly of an apparently harmless bird. Such vignettes of prehistoric hunting life add enormous insight to

Fig. 6.24 A rock drawing depicting a fishing scene from Lesotho, southern Africa.

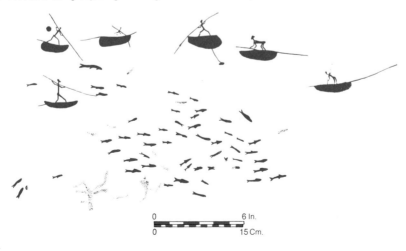

Fig. 6.25   *Deer being driven toward bowmen, an Upper Paleolithic wall-painting (dark red) in the Cueva de los Caballos, near Albocácer, Castellón. (After Obermaier.)*

data obtained from the food residues recovered from caves and rock-shelters (Figure 6.25).

PREHISTORIC DIET

So far, information on prehistoric subsistence has been that gleaned from various archaeological finds. The ultimate objective of economic archaeology is not only to establish how man obtained his food, but also to reconstruct his actual diet. Dietary reconstruction is difficult, largely because of incomplete economic information. Yet the problems involved are fundamental. What proportion of the diet was meat? How diverse were dietary sources? Did the principal sources of diet change from season to season? To what extent did the people rely on food from neighboring areas? Was food stored? What limitations or restrictions did technology or society place on diet? All these questions lie behind any inquiry into prehistoric subsistence.

The most complete reconstructions of diet come from the remains of meals in the stomachs of prehistoric corpses and from human feces found in dry caves and occupation sites, especially in the western United States. The last meal of a bog corpse from eastern England found in 1911 consisted of blackberry seeds, rose haws, and other wild vegetal remains.[90] The stomach of Tollund man, who was executed around the time of Christ, contained the vegetable remains of a finely ground meal made from barley, linseed, and several wild grasses; no meat was found in the contents.[91]

Many American scholars have studied coprolites from dry caves in the United States and Mexico. Seeds, nuts, deer hair, feathers, and chips of bone have been identified in feces from Danger Cave in Utah, and pollen analysis is now being applied to human excrement.[92] Most analyses have consisted of dry sorting and microscopic analysis, but more advanced techniques are being developed. Robert Heizer and his colleagues have analyzed numerous stratified coprolites from the Lovelock Cave in central Nevada.[93] Most of the 101 coprolites analyzed contained bulrush and cattail seeds; they also showed that Lahontan chub from the waters of nearby Humboldt Lake were regularly eaten. Undoubtedly caught with fiber dip nets found in the cave, they were eaten raw or toasted. One coprolite contained the remains of at least fifty-one chub, calculated by a fish expert to represent a total fish weight of 3.65 pounds. Adult and baby birds, the water tiger beetle, and possibly freshwater gastropods were also eaten. Collecting vegetable foods seems to have been done on a casual basis, and the remains of large mammals were not found in the feces. Unfortunately, however, identifying large mammals is particularly difficult except from hairs or splinters of heavy mammal bones.

Coprolites have been analyzed from stratified cave sequences in the Tehuacán Valley. A diet of grass seeds and a starchy root known as *Ceiba* came into vogue at the beginning of the incipient agriculture stage;[94] this diet continued in use almost up to the Spanish Conquest. Maize is conspicuously absent from the Tehuacán Valley cave coprolites, as though the crop was grown for tribute purposes and not eaten by the inhabitants—or, alternatively, ground so finely that the meal was digested without trace. Coprolites, like other economic evidence, must always be considered in conjunction with other information sources.

Food residues from living floors or occupation levels are less satisfactory. Animal bones, fish bones, or shells, are almost invariably the most common food remains to be found, and tend to be overemphasized in reconstructing an economy, even if accompanied by quite a collection of vegetal remains. Early literature bulges with examples of this emphasis, propounded by investigators who were bemused and delighted by large bone middens; when reinvestigation later revealed that, in fact, collecting or agriculture had formed a major part of the economy. Surprisingly little attention has been paid to prehistoric diet, largely because obtaining the data is difficult. The nutritional factors involved in diet have been seldom studied, and the full potential of this approach to archaeology has not been realized. Californian archaeologists have attempted to study the relative weights of different food sources in shell middens,[95] but the methodological difficulties are considerable. But basically, information on prehistoric diets comes from the analyses and the identification procedures described in this chapter. Since the ultimate objective is explaining how man lived in the past, new theoretical frameworks, systematic use of ethnographic analogy, and quantitative methods will, it is hoped, intensify research on the dietary requirements of prehistoric man.

TRADE

Human subsistence is based on natural resources and on the exploitation of the environment, whether or not man produces food. Many hunting cultures were self-sufficient in their dietary requirements and only used the raw materials within their regular hunting territory. Their knowledge of their environment was detailed and resource-oriented; indeed, trade may have been generated when man moved to a new territory where a formerly abundant raw material did not exist, but was still needed. Contacts between neighboring bands were fleeting and sporadic, and though sometimes based on the exchange of food and raw materials, these contacts could also have a ritual nature. The systematic barter of raw materials may have begun with the exchange of stone for implement-making and stone axes. Several sources of tough stone for axe and adze blades were exploited by Australian stoneworkers, although the extent to which these were traded is a matter for further research.[96] Certainly, stone axes were a primary trade item in early food-producing societies in Western Europe. The yellow nodules, *livres de beurre*, of Grand Pressigny flint are found in early farming sites through France. Petrological analyses of stone axe blades in England have revealed a complex network of quarries and trade routes for the diffusion of tough cutting edges through much of the country.[97]

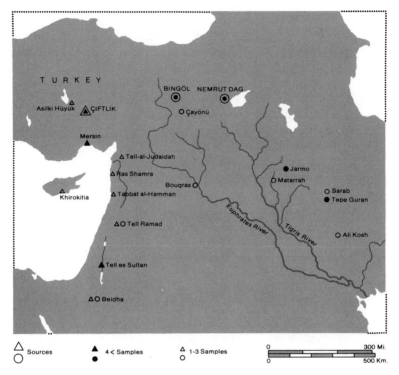

Fig. 6.26 Obsidian trade in the Near East in the sixth and seventh millennia B.C.

With the advent of food production and metallurgy, the demands for raw materials increased and transcended the limited territory of the hunter-gatherer. Skins, hut poles, grain, ornamental materials, and metal ores were soon being handled over enormous distances. British archaeologist Colin Renfrew and a number of colleagues have harnessed scientific technology to study obsidian trade in the Near East.[98] Obsidian is a fine black volcanic glass, eminently suitable for the manufacture of stone tools and mirrors. Only a limited number of obsidian outcrops occur in the Near East and Mediterranean basin (Figure 6.26), and it is possible to identify the source of an obsidian artifact by studying the trace elements both in the source ores and in the finished tools found in sites many miles from the outcrops. Renfrew and his colleagues have reconstructed the history and extent of obsidian trade over the critical period of time when food-producing societies were establishing themselves in the eastern Mediterranean. Obsidian trade helped to widen human perspectives and to develop the complex trade routes so much a part of the growth of urban society and literate civilization.

Trade is normally recognized in the archaeological record by the discovery of objects exotic to the material culture or economy of the host society. Glass, for example, was not manufactured in sub-Saharan Africa before the advent of European rule, yet imported glass beads are widespread finds in archaeological sites of late first millennium A.D.[99] The natural copper outcrops of the Lake Superior region were exploited to make hammered ornaments found in Archaic sites as far away as the southeastern United States.[100] Amber from the shores of the Baltic reached the Mediterranean by regular trade routes as early as the sixteenth century B.C.—the attractive substance was used to adorn wealthy Mycenaeans.[101] The amber trade is thought to have been handled by middlemen who were trading German metal to the vigorous metallurgists of Denmark, southern Sweden, and northern Germany, areas where copper and tin had to be imported for the smiths' use.[102]

Complicated barter networks extended over much of Europe and the Near East in later prehistoric times; the peoples of the African interior knew of and prized seashells from the Indian Ocean. The Hopewell Indians of Ohio traded obsidian, mica, and other exotic raw materials which are found from the Rockies to the Atlantic Coast.[103] Although much prehistoric trade was indirect, was based on prosaic objects, and was bartered between villages, the contacts of early man widened rapidly once regular trade began. The perspectives of farmer and hunter widened as trading became more and more important in supplying raw materials and supporting specialized craftsmen. The transactions between man and his environment and his increased exploitation of the latter were refined and encouraged, as they are today, by intensified local and long-distance trade.

Chapter 7

Technology and Artifacts

"Whatever the ultimate inspiration or the intermediate cause, it was by their hands that the early Europeans dragged themselves out of the primeval mist of savagery, struggled up the long slopes of barbarism and ultimately attained to some kind of civilised existence."[1]* Grahame Clark's words from his classic study of prehistoric Europe provide us with ample justification for studying the technology of the ancients. The tools that man has manufactured throughout his long history were the means by which he augmented his limbs and extended the use of his environment. Other animals beside man use extraneous objects to achieve subsistence objectives and display considerable evidence of behavioral adaptability. But man differs from other animals not only in possessing culture but in the degree to which he has come to depend on it.

Man's physical evolution helped make dependence on his culture possible, but was itself affected by cultural development.[2] Man's success and continued survival has been due to his remaining an unspecialized organism, adaptable—in the main—to changing environmental conditions through his culture and capable of far more rapid change and adjustment to an enormous range of environmental conditions. Biological evolution has proceeded alongside cultural evolution, the two processes interacting with each other. Man adopted an upright posture, freeing his hands for toolmaking and becoming adapted to life in open country where vegetable foods and tree-climbing were

* See pages 332–334 for notes to Chapter 7.

less important. His brain became larger, a trend encouraged perhaps by the use and manufacture of tools. Human awareness and man's culture were shaped by the human brain, working with man's hands to enrich his life experience to an extent unknown in other primates. His technological achievements over the three million years that he has been a toolmaking mammal are both impressive and terrifying. Twentieth-century technology is developing at an almost uncontrollable speed. We can land a man on the moon, transplant human hearts, and build sophisticated computers. Yet our ability to adapt to the quickened technological pace of the 1970s and our society's capability to handle these staggering advances have lagged far behind, nor have we yet developed mechanisms whereby our society can live with twentieth-century technology to the best advantage. Our contemporary armory of computers, atomic bombs, household appliances, and every conceivable artifact designed for a multitude of specialized needs has evolved in a direct, albeit diversely branching, line from the first simple tools made by early man. Archaeologists study the material remains of human activity in their attempts to write culture history and reconstruct cultural process, and artifacts are a primary item they study. Any form of artifact is the end product of well defined and instinctive human behavior. It constitutes its maker's definite idea of the proper way of making the tool concerned, whose form is dictated by definite conventions. In other words, an implement represents not only the level of technological achievement of the society in which its maker lived, but also a vast amount of inherited information and experience passed on to its user from earlier generations. Thus, man's technological achievements are as important to us as his quest for subsistence, and the increasing sophistication of his craftsmanship and increasing diversity and ingenuity of his industrial skills have played a major part in human cultural and physical evolution (Figure 7.1).

STONE TECHNOLOGY

Certain categories of rock have, with bone and wood, been the primary raw materials for man's technology for most of his existence on earth. The advent of metallurgy is but a recent development, and stone tools have provided the foundation for the classification of many prehistoric cultures since scientific archaeology began. The raw material itself has set severe limits on the extent of man's technological achievements for much of his history, and the evolution of stoneworking over the millions of years during which it has been practiced has been infinitely slow—man eventually exploited almost every possibility afforded by suitable rocks for making implements by various techniques.

Fig. 7.1 Australopithecus africanus. *(After extensive research, artist Jay H. Matternes drew this portrait of an* Australopithecus *group.)*

The simplest way of producing a stone that will cut or chop, surely the basic tool produced by prehistoric man, is simply to break it in half and use the resulting sharp edge. But to produce a tool that has a more specialized use or can be employed for several purposes requires slightly more sophisticated flaking technique. First, an angular fragment or smooth pebble of suitable rock can be brought to the

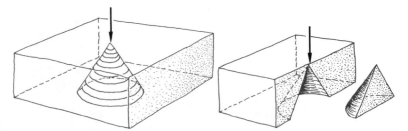

Fig. 7.2   How stone fractures: (left) when a blow is struck on flinty types of rock, a cone of percussion is formed by shock waves rippling through the stone; (right) a flake is chipped when the block (or core) is hit at the edge and the stone fractures along the edge of the ripple.

desired shape by systematically flaking it with another stone. The flakes removed from this core or lump are then primarily waste products, whereas the core becomes the implement that is the intentional end product of the stonemaker. Furthermore, the flakes struck from the core can be used themselves as sharp edged knives, or further modified to make more formal artifacts. From this simple beginning, many and complex stone industries have evolved, the earliest tools being simple—many of them virtually indistinguishable from naturally fractured rock.

Identifying man-made implements as distinct from naturally broken rocks is something that can only be learned by experience in handling many artifacts, but here is a generalized description of the principles of stone-implement manufacture.[3] Generally, Stone Age man and other makers of stone tools chose flint, obsidian, and other hard homogeneous rocks to fashion their artifacts. All these rocks break in a systematic way, like industrial glass. A sharp blow directed vertically at a point on the surface of a slab of suitable stone knocks out a solid cone, with its apex at the point where the hammer blow hit the slab. This effects a "conchoidal fracture" (Figure 7.2). When, however, a blow is directed at a stone slab obliquely from the edge and the break occurs conchoidally, a flake is detached. The fractured face of the flake has a characteristic shape, with a bulge extending from the surface of the piece outward down the side. This is known as the "bulb of percussion"—there is a corresponding hollow or flake scar on the core from which the flake has been struck. The bulb of percussion is readily recognized, as the accompanying text figure (Figure 7.3) shows, not only because of the bulge itself but also from the concentric rings that radiate from the center of the impact point, widening gradually away from it. Such deliberate fractures by man are quite different from those produced by natural means like frost,

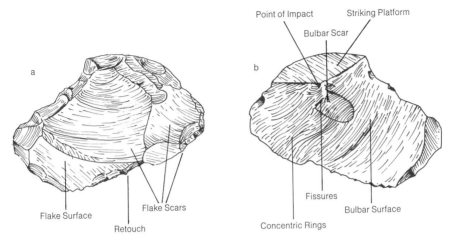

Fig. 7.3   The component parts of a flake tool. (a) Flake surface. (b) Bulbar surface.

extreme heat or cold, water action, or stones falling from a cliff and fracturing on large boulders below.[4] In these cases the rock may sometimes break in a similar manner, but most of the flake scars are irregular, and instead of concentric rings and a bulb of percussion, there is often a rough depressed area on the surface with concentric rings formed around it.

Careful examination is needed to distinguish human and naturally fractured stones one from another, a particularly acute problem with tools of the earliest men.[5] In many cases, their artifacts were made by the simplest of hammerstone techniques, resulting in the removal of two or three flakes from the pebble (Figure 7.4). This produced a jagged edge that was effective, so experiment shows, in dismembering carcasses of game.[6] There have been several famous controversies over alleged "artifacts" found in Lower Pleistocene deposits in Europe and Africa that are contemporary with periods when hominids were already flourishing elsewhere. A celebrated furor arose over a series of alleged tools, named "eoliths," found early in this century in Lower Pleistocene horizons in eastern England.[7] These were championed as early evidence of human occupation for many years until reexamination of the geological contexts and accurate measurements of the flaking angles on the "eoliths" demonstrated that they were probably of natural origin.[8] Under such circumstances, the only sure identification of humanly fractured stone implements is to find them in association with fossil human remains and broken animal bones, preferably on a living floor.

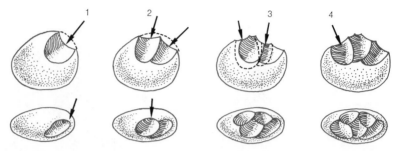

Fig. 7.4 *Chopping tools were made by a simple process. Side view (top row): first, two flakes were struck off (1 and 2); second, the stone was turned over and two more flakes were removed (3); and third, a fifth flake completed the tool, giving it a sharp edge. The bottom row shows the process from above.*

Several different methods of flaking stone were used during prehistoric times. The most common and the earliest used was direct fracturing of the stone with a hammerstone. The core was held in the hand and repeatedly struck with a hammerstone at selected points to produce a steep or sharp edge (Figure 7.5). The angle at which the blow was delivered determined whether the flakes removed were shallow and long or steep and short. In a variant on this technique, the core was swung against an anvil, removing a series of large flakes, a method known as the "block on block." These techniques produced the chopping tools and flakes found at Olduvai Gorge and other Australopithecine living sites (3 million–*ca.* 70,000 B.C.).[9] *Homo erectus* began to make tools flaked on both surfaces (Figure 7.6), such as the Acheulian hand axes of the Middle Pleistocene (400,000–70,000 B.C.), from sites like

Fig. 7.5 *Stoneworking techniques. (a) Using a hammerstone. (b) The anvil technique.*

a   b

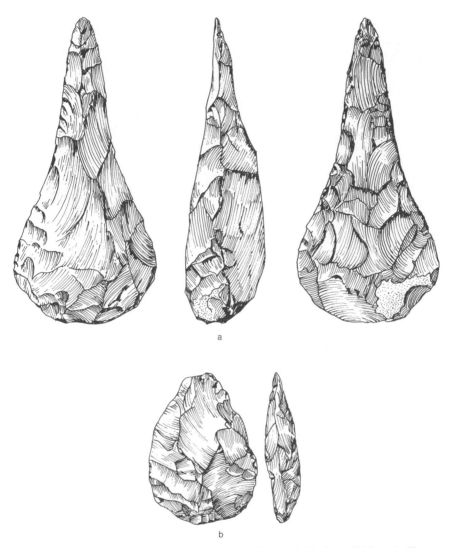

a

b

Fig. 7.6   Two Acheulian hand axes (three views of a, and front and side views of b) from the Thames Valley, England (one-third actual size).

Kalambo Falls, Isimila, Torralba, and Swanscombe.[10] Many later hand axes were finely trimmed by using a piece of hardwood or bone to remove fine skim flakes from the edges of roughly shaped tools. The "cylinder hammer" technique produced sharp tough edges, a refinement from the crude multi-purpose tools of the Lower and early Middle Pleistocene (Figure 7.7).

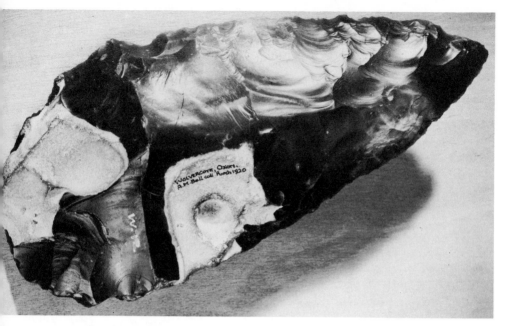

Fig. 7.7 An Acheulian hand axe from Wolvercote, Oxford, England.

During the Upper Pleistocene (later than 70,000 B.C.), man became a more skillful hunter and developed a need for more specialized stone tools. He began to think about shaping cores to produce specific types of flake intended for special purposes such as spearheads. Some people shaped cores to a tortoise shell form so that one flake could be removed from the convex face in a shape ready for immediate use. "Levallois" tortoise cores are widely found in Europe and the Near East where flint was abundant, and were used to produce points and scrapers; the technique was named after a Paris suburb where it was first recognized (Figure 7.8). Other, widely used prepared cores include disc types, where more than one flake was removed from the trimmed core; these have appeared with frequency in Africa, as well as the Near East and Europe, made by Middle Stone Age and Mousterian stoneworkers (ca. 70,000–35,000 B.C.).[11]

Some thirty to forty thousand years ago, man began to make blades with a punch as opposed to the percussion techniques. Many blades were long parallel-sided artifacts produced with great regularity and skill by a punch placed between the hammerstone and the core. Experimental studies indicate that a chest punch could have been used, the core being held between one's feet while resting it on the ground (Figure 7.9). A wooden staff with a hard tip exercised pressure at a specific point on the core's edge, thereby producing a long

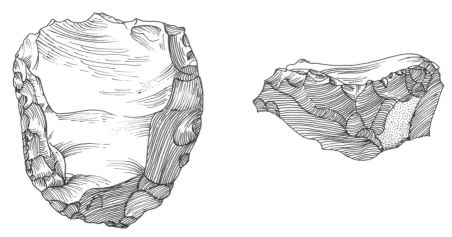

Fig. 7.8   Two views of a Levallois tortoise core from the Thames Valley (one-half actual size).

Fig. 7.9   Two uses of the blade technique, employing a punch.

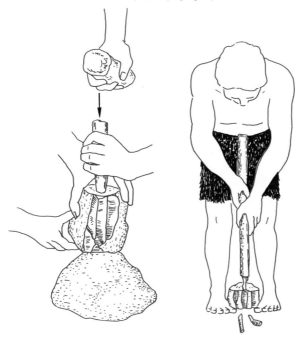

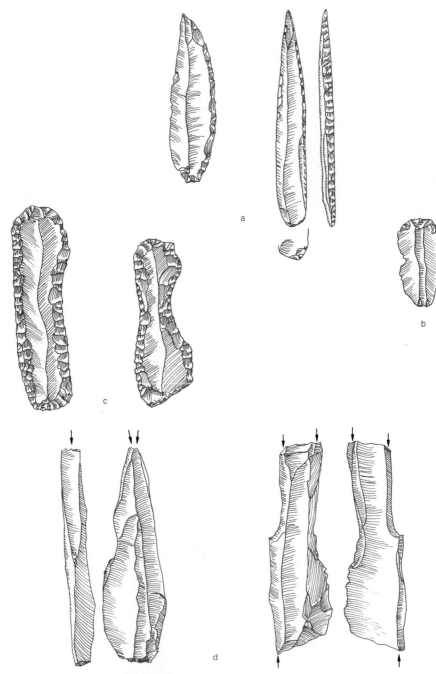

Fig. 7.10   Some major Upper Paleolithic tools (actual size). (a) Backed blades. (b) End-scraper. (c) Sharpened and notched blades. (d) Burins.

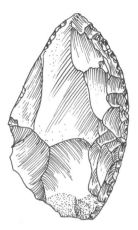

Fig. 7.11 Mousterian side-scraper with step retouch (one-half actual size).

parallel-sided blade. By thrusting his chest down on the punch, the stoneworker could produce a beautiful knife blade of flint or obsidian up to several centimeters long.[12] The knife blades were roughed out and later trimmed to form scrapers, knives, projectile points, and engraving tools—the latter used in Western Europe for carving on antlers and rocks (Figure 7.10). Thus, a much greater variety of specialized tools was made. Developed in the northern parts of Africa, Europe, and southwest Asia, blade tools spread as far as 55° North in European Russia and as far east as Japan and northeastern Siberia; the tools' production was the first stone technology, as far as can be established, to be introduced into the New World and spread there across the Bering Straits.[13]

The secondary trimming of flakes and blades was achieved in numerous ways. In some cases, the blade's side was battered with a stone or a piece of wood to produce fine flake scars to sharpen or blunt the edge. More often, the stoneworker would take a piece of bone or wood, or another stone fragment, and press it against the blade's surface removing short steep step flakes that both sharpened and toughened the working edge (Figure 7.11). Another method was to notch the edge by pressing it against a piece of stone or wood, thereby forming a notched blade or flake that could be used as a hollow scraper for woodworking (Figure 7.12).[14] One way of retouching stone tools was by nibbling the edges with the teeth, a method used by Australian aborigines. But the most famous and most common technique in the later periods of prehistory, especially in the New World, was pressure-flaking. The stoneworker used a small billet of wood or antler and pressed it against the working edge in such a

Fig. 7.12 The stoneworking technique of pressure-flaking.

way that he exerted pressure in a limited direction to remove a fine shallow parallel-sided flake. This formed one of a series of flake scars that eventually covered most of the implement's surfaces (Figure 7.13). The advantage of pressure-flaking is that it facilitates the production of many standardized artifacts with extremely effective working edges in a comparatively short time. In southwest Asia, Europe, and many parts of Africa and south and eastern Asia, small blades were fashioned into minute arrowheads, barbs, and adzes, known as microliths; these

Fig. 7.13 Paleo-Indian pressure-flaked points. (a) Clovis point. (b) Folsom point. (c) Scottsbluff point. (d) Eden point. (Used with permission of McGraw-Hill Book Company and Thames and Hudson Ltd.)

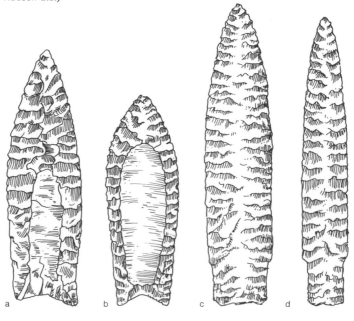

a   b   c   d

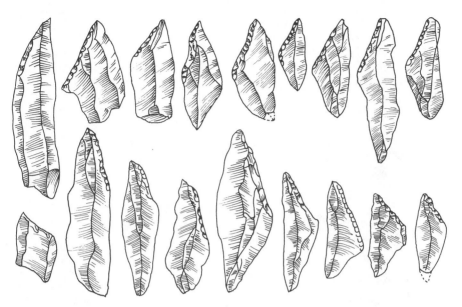

Fig. 7.14   Microliths from Star Carr (actual size.)

were often made by a characteristic notching technique (Figure 7.14),[15] and also spread into Arctic America and Australia.

Early farmers began to polish and grind stone to produce implements for use where a sharp working edge was required that would not wear as quickly as one produced by merely flaking the stone (Figure 6.3). The edges were shaped by rough flaking, and then laboriously polished and ground against a coarser rock such as sandstone to produce a sharp tough working edge. Modern experiments have demonstrated the greater effectiveness of polished stone axes in felling forest trees, the toughened working edge taking longer to blunt than that of a flaked axe.[16] Polished stone axes became important in many early peasant societies, especially in Europe, Asia, Mesoamerica (Figure 7.15), and parts of temperate North America. They were not only used in New Guinea, Melanesia, and Polynesia for agriculture, but also in the manufacture of canoes which were essential for fishing and trade.[17]

Early students of Stone Age archaeology were preoccupied with stone tools and their classification. Complicated hierarchies of functional types such as scrapers, arrowheads, points, hand axes, and choppers were carefully erected, and used to study the evolution of prehistoric culture. The French prehistorian Gabriel de Mortillet formulated

Fig. 7.15 *Ceremonial Olmec axe head, depicting a god who combines the features of a man and a jaguar. His face is stylized, with flame-like eyes and a drooping mouth.*

a sequence of Old Stone Age cultures in 1881,[18] based on evolutionary principles and series of stratified "type fossils." This provincial classificatory scheme had wide acceptance until the 1920s, albeit in modified form, until archaeological research in many other parts of the world showed how parochial de Mortillet's scheme was. The latter was based on finished tools, each cultural stage having certain typological characteristics and type implements associated with it. The various "epochs" of the Stone Age evolved slowly from one into another, the implements changing in each stage. For example, the hand axe or core tool was characteristic of the Acheulian culture in the Lower Paleolithic. In the Middle Paleolithic, there were spearpoints of Mousterian type, which in turn were succeeded by the blade and antler tools of the various stages of the Upper Paleolithic, such as the Aurignacian, Solutrean, and Magdalenian (Table 7.1). The use of "type fossils" continued in the 1920s, and only began to disappear with the development of more sophisticated methods of typological

Table 7.1   Western European Paleolithic Cultures[a]

Paleolithic stages	Cultures	Stages recorded	Approximate dates
UPPER PALEOLITHIC[b] (*ca.* 35,000– 12,000 years before the present)	Magdalenian	I–VI	15,000 B.C.
	Solutrean	3 to 4 stages recognized	17,000 B.C.
	Later Perigordian	up to 5 variants recognized	25,000 B.C.
	Aurignacian	up to 4 stratified stages known	30,000 B.C.
	Early Perigordian	1 or 2 stages	*ca.* 35,000– 32,000 B.C.
MIDDLE PALEOLITHIC (*ca.* 70,000– 35,000)	Mousterian		± 70,000– *ca.* 35,000 B.C.
LOWER PALEOLITHIC (±2.5–5 million– *ca.* 70,000)	Acheulian and Clactonian Oldowan (not common in Europe)		*ca.* 400,000 B.C. ± 2–5 million B.C.

[a] Greatly simplified.
[b] Many archaeologists use another terminology for the Upper Paleolithic of France:

Alternate Terminology	French Terminology
Gravettian	Later Perigordian
Aurignacian	Aurignacian and Perigordian
Chatelperronian	Early Perigordian

The British tend to think of three distinct cultures (alternate terminology) during Aurignacian times, while others think of two contemporary traditions, the Aurignacian dying out as the Perigordian continued.

analysis, as some scholars began to realize that full understanding of stone technology involved the study not only of the finished implements but also of the cores and waste by-products formed by the industrial activity itself.

Their ideas were stimulated by ethnographers who described stone-working techniques among the extinct Tasmanians, the Australian aborigines, American Indians, and South African Bushmen.[19] Gunflint makers were sought out and interviewed; the Brandon flint makers in Suffolk, England, even obligingly made some hand axes.[20] Archaeologists began to experiment with stone themselves; some like the celebrated Monsieur Coutier became expert flint knappers. Dr. Louis Leakey has used hand axes and cleavers to skin antelope, and the French prehistorian François Bordes and his American colleague Don Crabtree have made films documenting the techniques of stone tool manufacture.[21] Because of these and other experiments, stone tool manufacture is understood far better, and the emphasis in analysis has moved toward developing quantitative techniques. Early workers began by calculating the percentages of artifact types in different sites and then comparing the figures. More refined analyses are now fashionable, using cumulative curves[22] and attribute analyses in which different features of stone implements are correlated in clusters with the use of computers.

Other archaeologists have begun to study the edge wear on stone tools as an adjunct to basic typological classification. Soviet archaeologist S. A. Semenov pioneered this field;[23] edge wear is also being studied in Africa as well as the New World.[24] There are several factors that control edge damage. These include the tool's material, the cross section of the edge, and the mode of use together with the material upon which the artifact was used. The unknown variable is normally the material worked by the tool, so it is difficult to say precisely what any artifact's mode of use was. But the study of edge wear does have considerable potential.

With more sophisticated analytical techniques, many classical definitions of Stone Age cultures have been found to be inadequate. Forty years ago, people assumed that many Stone Age cultures, like geological eras, occurred in a standardized form over large parts of the world—the hand-axe culture of Africa, Europe, and Asia, for example, forming one vast monolithic continuum. More detailed studies and analyses, particularly of living floors, have revealed numerous regional variants within this vast distribution of hand-axe sites.[25] These differences are due to variable raw materials, a wide range of differing ecological adaptations, and the infinite variability of human achievement. The study of stone implements is an inquiry into only a part of human behavior, and to draw, as earlier prehistorians did, far-reaching conclusions about the rate of cultural change on the basis of stone tools alone is unwise, for the most durable tools sometimes had lesser significance than other, more perishable aspects of human culture.

WOOD

Nonhuman primates sometimes use sticks to obtain grubs or for other food-getting purposes, so it is logical to assume that since the earliest times man must have used sticks also, and begun to shape them casually into convenient tools. Wooden artifacts form an important part of the material culture of many hunting peoples; occasional, tantalizing glimpses of prehistoric wooden artifacts have come down to us when preservation conditions have been favorable. As mentioned earlier, wooden implements were found on an Acheulian living floor at the Kalambo Falls site in northern Zambia some years ago, in a context that has been radiocarbon dated to about 53,000 years ago.[26] The tools consisted of several pieces of wood, some water worn, including possible digging sticks and a club. In England, a fire-toughened spearpoint was found at the Clacton Channel site which dates to the Mindel-Riss interglacial (*ca.* ?150,000 B.C.) (Figure 7.16). A Middle Paleolithic spear was found at Lehringen, Germany, in association with an elephant skeleton;[27] the creature had been killed by a wooden spear driven into his belly, probably from underneath—a technique sometimes used by the pygmies of the Congo forest. Still another wood artifact was a fragment of a throwing stick which came from the Middle Stone Age site at Florisbad in South Africa.[28] Wooden digging sticks and arrowheads were found at the Gwisho hunting camp in Zambia that dated to *ca.* 2800 B.C.[29] (see Figure 7.17).

Numerous wooden artifacts have been found in dry sites in North America, especially in the Southwest, where Basketmaker settlements have yielded wooden canes, arrow foreshafts with flaked projectiles mounted in them, musical instruments, and other tools.[30] Burials both in the Southwest and in coastal Peru have also yielded wooden artifacts.[31] In addition, the wooden objects found in the Bronze Age graves of Jericho, Ur of the Chaldees, and Tutankhamen's tomb in Egypt are well known.[32]

Normally, however, the use of wood can only be deduced from more durable artifacts. Stone axe blades or arrow barbs are often found, but their wooden hafts have perished; reasonable speculation about the method of mounting the blade or tip is permissible. Thousands of metal axe and adze blades have been found in European

Fig. 7.16 *Wooden spearhead from Clacton, England, of the Lower Paleolithic period—76 centimeters (about 30 inches) long.*

Bronze Age sites but only a small proportion of them, mostly from northern bogs or the Swiss lake sites, still retain their wooden handles (Figure 6.3).[33] These finds show that the hafting of the bronze heads evolved from a simple binding to the socketed axe in the later Bronze Age.

BONE

Bone as a material for toolmaking probably dates to the very beginnings of human history, but the earliest artifacts apparently consisted of little more than fragments of fractured animal bone used for purposes that could not be fulfilled by wood or stone implements. South African anatomist Raymond Dart has alleged that *Australopithecus* had a fully fledged bone culture and he systematically fractured such bones as jaws and limb bones to form clubs, scrapers, and other artifacts. Dart's[34] "osteodontokeratic"—bone, teeth, horn—culture has been the

Fig. 7.17 *A technician demonstrating the use of a Late Stone Age digging stick from Gwisho hot springs, Zambia.*

subject of much controversy, and most scholars reject his hypothesis on the grounds that other, natural factors could have caused such systematic bone fractures (Figure 7.18).[35] Formal bone tools are rare on the Olduvai living floors but several bone fragments show systematic utilization as though they were used for scraping skins and similar purposes.[36]

The earliest standardized bone tools date from later prehistoric times. Splinters of bone were sharpened and used as points in many societies, but bone and antler artifacts were especially favored by the Upper Paleolithic Magdalenian peoples of southwestern France some 12,000–14,000 years ago and by Post Glacial hunter-gatherers in Scandinavia.[37] Bone tools dating to as early as 8800 B.C. were found at the Lindenmeis location in Colorado.[38] Many bone tools were either

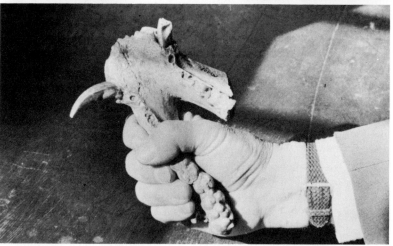

Fig. 7.18   Osteodontokeratic "artifacts" from Makapansgat, South Africa. Raymond Dart believes that the teeth, limb bones, and tusks of pigs, antelopes, and gazelles were used as tools.

ornamental artifacts or formed projectile heads. Splinters from long bones were ground and scraped, as well as being hardened in the fire and polished with beeswax, to produce arrowheads, spearpoints, and other artifacts. Bone was also carved and engraved, especially during Upper Paleolithic times in Western Europe, as was reindeer antler.[39]

Deer antler was an even more important material than bone for some later hunter-gatherers. Fully grown deer antler is particularly suitable for making barbed or simple harpoons and spearpoints. One well known technique involved a beam of reindeer or red deer antler: a series of parallel grooves were made with a suitable stone graver, the resulting splinters being levered from the beam and fashioned into barbed arrowheads or spearheads used for fishing, hunting, and other purposes.[40] Bone and antler were much used in prehistoric times for harpoons for fishing and for conventional hunting. Numerous harpoons are found in Magdalenian sites in Western Europe (Figure 7.19) and also in Eskimo settlements in the Arctic, where they form an invaluable index of cultural development, analogous to that of pottery in the American Southwest.

Fig. 7.19 Magdalenian harpoons from France.

Bone tools do not throw much light on the material culture of peoples to whom the by-products of game animals were not particularly important. In woodland areas where timber is abundant, the tendency is to use wood at the expense of bone and antler. But in the Arctic, bone and ivory are of critical importance, elaborate typological studies have been made of the stylistic and functional changes in such diverse items as the harpoons and the winged ivory counterweights fastened to the butts of harpoons (Figure 7.20). Artifacts include picks made of walrus tusk, and snow shovels and wedges made of ivory and bone—as were drills and domestic utensils. Studying such a range of bone artifacts is complicated by elaborate and variable engraved designs on some artifacts, but H. B. Collins and others have been able to trace the development of the harpoon of the Northern Maritime Eskimo from the elaborate types of the Okvik and Old Bering Sea phases to the simpler forms characteristic of the Punuk phase and modern Eskimo weapons.[41]

With bone tools, functional classification is easier, especially in areas like the Arctic and southern Africa where contemporary ethnographic accounts are available for fruitful analogies. But, as with stone and wooden implements, the study of the by-products is as important as a close scrutiny of the implements, so that one may understand the role of bone technology in the material culture as a whole.

CLAY

Receptacles for carrying food or water must have been in use since the earliest times. Animal skins, bark trays, ostrich eggshells, and wild gourds have also been used in recent times for carrying loads outside the immediate surroundings of a hunting settlement, and must have a long history. Such informal vessels have the advantage of portability and are easy to replace or to improvise with.

The clay pot is one of the most common and imperishable archaeological finds, but has a comparatively recent history. Pottery is almost invariably an attribute of food production, coming into use under conditions where more permanent settlement patterns permit a more elaborate material culture, a more varied diet, and possibly the brewing and storage of fermented gruels or liquids. At one stage it was thought that the advent of pottery coincided with the origins of food production; we now know that agriculture and pastoralism were practiced in the Near East from the eighth millennium B.C., if not earlier, and pottery does not appear until slightly earlier than 6000 B.C. at such early agricultural settlements as Jarmo and Jericho.[42] The inhabitants

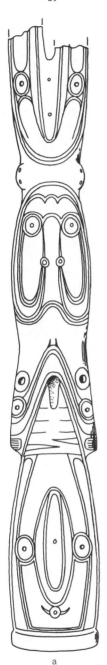

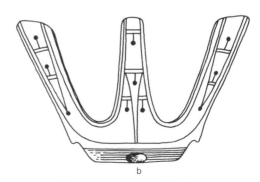

a   b

Fig. 7.20 (a) A socket-piece for a harpoon, Old Bering Sea style, 11.5 centimeters (4.5 inches) long. (b) Eskimo winged ivory object of the Punuk phase, diameter about 12 centimeters (4.7 inches). (Both after Collins, 1937.)

of the Tehuacán Valley in highland Mexico began cultivating crops several thousand years before the first pottery appeared there about 2300 B.C. Pottery was made in Japan by 8000 B.C., occurring in a context which seems to be that of hunters and gatherers.[43]

Serious potsherd archaeology in the New World began with N. C. Nelson in 1914 and A. V. Kidder a few years later, the latter producing refined potsherd stratigraphies from excavations in the rubbish mound at the Pecos Pueblo.[44] Since then, clay vessels have been the basis for innumerable regional surveys of prehistoric culture sequences in the Americas and on the other side of the Atlantic where, however, until recently potsherd archaeology was less well developed. Pottery is normally abundant in those sites where it is found, and is therefore susceptible to statistical treatment, provided that adequate sampling procedures are used in the field. Indeed, detailed analyses of potsherds fill the pages of innumerable archaeological journals; in the past fifty years,[45] an enormous literature has grown up around the subject. The classification of pottery depends on the recognition of numerous attributes found on the potsherds recovered from the ground. Common attributes are shape, dimension, decoration, decorative motif, lip form, and texture (Figure 7.21). The object of such elaborate classifications is to produce a basis for establishing the basic features of a pottery collection, which can then be compared as a whole to collections from other sites close to the original one in space and time.

Functional classification of most prehistoric pottery is an impossible task, unless the anthropological record is sufficiently complete to allow an accurate comparison to be made, or unless the prehistoric vessels are characteristic enough to allow them to be identified as pots of specialized use—perhaps employed for salt-making or some other economic activity. As indicated earlier, many variables act upon the potter and his family. Many African potters, for example, relate the shape of a vessel directly to its function. Bowls are used for cooking vegetables or eating. Pots, with their deeper bodies, are used for storage, water carrying, cooking, or even ritual purposes. Changes in shape may sometimes reflect, indirectly, a change in economic activities, but the economic evidence must be extremely complete before such conclusions can be drawn. At the Isamu Pati Iron Age mound village in Zambia, occupied intermittently for a long period from the seventh to the thirteenth centuries A.D., the uppermost levels contained a much higher proportion of cattle bones than the lower horizons.[46] At the same time, the pottery changed dramatically from a preponderance of simple bag-shaped vessels (Figure 7.22) to an overwhelming dominance of spherical pots with out-turned lips. These

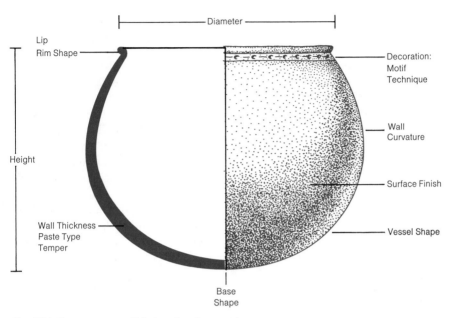

Fig. 7.21 *Some common attributes of a clay vessel.*

could only have contained liquid, and were tentatively taken to reflect a change in dietary habits, perhaps an increase in milk consumption.

The details of pottery analysis need not concern us here, as they have been well described by Anna Shepard, Frederick Madsen, and others.[47] An amazing amount of information can be conjured from

Fig. 7.22 *A Zambian Iron Age pot from the Kalomo culture (one-third actual size).*

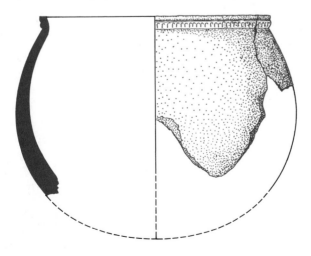

a single potsherd (Figure 7.23). Vessel shapes can be reconstructed from fragmentary potsherds that bear a sufficient portion of the lip profile. Both the techniques and motifs of vessel decoration are important. Decoration often varies according to the pot's shape, and is placed in a regular position on the walls of the vessel depending on its shape. The techniques of adornment are legion: painting, scratching, grooving, incision, stamping, and imprints made with such varied media as the fingernail, cords, or bird bones are all found. Normally, the technique used bears some relationship to the motif, which is restricted to some degree by how it is applied. Variations in technique and motif are reflections of changes both in vessel shape and in fashion, but usually occur gradually.

Another important aspect of ceramic typology is studying the clay's texture and finish, using microscopes and other high-powered instruments as well as elaborate chemical tests. Manufacturing techniques and evidence for trade can sometimes be obtained from detailed

Fig. 7.23 Pots are reconstructed from fragments by a technician through pottery analysis in the laboratory.

studies of clay. In many cases, such deductions can readily be made by linking trace elements in the clay with a particular locality, as in the case of stone axes.[48] Unfortunately, however, these studies only apply where pot-making was a highly developed industry and not merely an activity carried out in a village by people using available resources. There are, however, numerous examples of pottery trading that are reflected in the archaeological record by exotic trade sherds, whose decoration and form lie outside the norm for the industry. Sometimes they can be related to a primary center of pottery distribution in a nearby region.[49] The analysis of potsherds becomes increasingly complex as pottery industries become more elaborate. Particular attention has been paid in the New World and in the Near East to the styles of painted pottery and the techniques for decorating it (Figures 7.24 and 7.25). In some cases, also, a pot that is well made in one locality may be used as a horizon marker for cross-dating in another. The situation becomes much more complex in Classical times when potters, whose names are actually known and whose dates are well established, mass produced vessels that were widely traded in the civilized world and also into neighboring barbarian areas. Such vessels, like Chinese porcelain and glass, can be used to give more accurate dates to sites where no other form of chronology is available.

To assess the significance of ceramic data for cultural studies, not only archaeological evidence but also anthropological sources must be employed, as well as traditions preserved by early explorers of the peoples in the particular area being studied. From the careful use of such accounts it is frequently possible to add valuable information to the basic raw material obtained from the archaeological investigations. Unless ceramic studies lead to a better understanding of the cultural context in which they were found, potsherds form a sterile record of very limited historical value. Morphology and decorative detail are the accepted overriding criteria for establishing the relationship between different ceramic traditions. The actual materials and techniques employed by prehistoric man have only been seriously considered in cases where a particular group of pottery so differs from others in the same archaeological context that it requires detailed analysis.

Potsherds, whether made locally or traded into an area, were originally parts of pots made by inhabitants of a site and used in their daily life. Describing them is an essential part of cataloging prehistoric material culture. The makers were influenced by numerous different factors that are not reflected directly in the archaeological record, such as customs, beliefs, taboos on particular usages, and also the environment and level of economy and technology under which they were made. The closest way to analyzing those factors not reflected

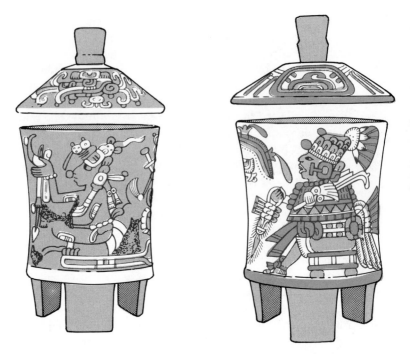

Fig. 7.24 Cylindrical tripod jars from the Early Classic Period at Kaminaljuyú, Guatemala. The decoration is in painted stucco. Left, a Mayoid motif in light green and dark red; right, a Teotihuacánoid motif in buff, light green, and dark red. (After Kidder, Jennings, and Shook, 1946.).

in the record is by analyzing the pottery in its constitutent parts and establishing the norms for each element of these parts, i.e., to produce modes that are the averages of behavior for the potting industry.

Surprisingly little attention has been paid to the social, cultural, and economic settings of pot-making in modern populations. As a result, it is difficult to draw meaningful conclusions, even in areas where the anthropological investigation is comparatively complete. Most descriptions of pottery, both in archaeology and anthropology, deal with techniques and processes of manufacture and with the design elements. They may tell us something about the division of labor in the making of pots, but they reveal little about the potters' status in their own society, their attitudes artistically and in terms of fashion, the economic role of pottery, nor the way in which potters are trained. From the archaeological viewpoint, important factors are the variability found within a potting community and the processes that bring about change in a pottery tradition, as well as stability in it.

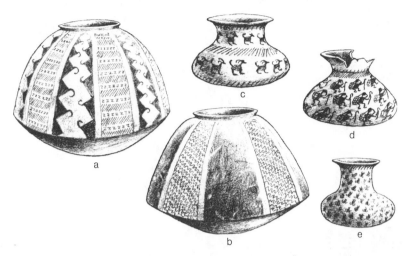

Fig. 7.25 Hohokam painted pottery from the southwestern United States. Pots a–c, about 46 centimeters (18 inches) high; remainder, about 14 centimeters (5.5 inches) high. (From Prehistory of North America by Jesse D. Jennings, Fig. 7.9. Copyright © 1968 by McGraw Hill, Inc. Used with permission of McGraw-Hill Book Company.)

METALLURGY: IRON AND COPPER

The study of metallurgy and metal objects found in archaeological sites is limited on one hand by the state of the material's preservation and on the other by our knowledge of primitive metallurgy as a whole.[50] Preservation of metal tools in archaeological horizons is dependent entirely on the soil's acidity. In some circumstances iron tools are preserved perfectly and can be studied in great detail. In other cases, soil acids have completely reduced the iron to a rusty mass that is almost entirely useless. Copper and gold normally survive somewhat better (Figures 7.26 and 7.27). The former was one of the earliest metals smelted by man, for the ore requires a lower melting point than iron does, and is readily shaped into artifacts.

Although native copper was hammered into simple ornaments in the Near East before 5000 B.C., copper smelting and casting only became commonplace in the third millennium, in Pre-Dynastic Egypt and also Sumer.[51] Elaborate castings of stags and cattle were found in the Royal Tombs at Alaca Hüyük, Turkey, dating to the late third millennium B.C. Copperworking was well established in Europe before 2000 B.C., but intensive activity was concentrated in areas where the ore is abundant, namely Spain and Transylvania.[52] In contrast to fine quality stone and iron, copper ores are rare and normally concentrated in well-defined regions. The metal was normally, but not invariably,

Fig. 7.26 Gold beads from Central Africa were a common trade commodity in later prehistoric times; gold was handled either in the form of dust or finished ornaments.

alloyed with tin, which is even rarer; bronze produces a harder metal tool and makes casting much easier, so this alloy was more extensively used than the pure metal.

Rich sources of copper ore were rare enough to stimulate constant demand both for the metal and for finished objects. It is thought that the techniques of copperworking spread to temperate Europe through early trading contacts forged with the more sophisticated societies of the Near East.[53] Copper mining and trade formed one foundation of the Luba Kingdom of the Congo in Central Africa whose influence spread far beyond the boundaries of its homeland in the closing centuries of African prehistory.[54] The Indians of Lake Superior in the New World exploited the native copper ore deposits on the southern shores of the lake, and the metal was widely traded and cold-hammered into artifacts in Archaic times (Figure 7.28).[55] During the European Bronze Age, many day-to-day objects, especially spearheads, swords, axes, and brooches were produced and traded (Figure 7.29), but these tools were comparatively valuable, and many people still used stone tools. After the production of iron, bronze was relegated to a more ornamental role but bronze ornaments were still traded.

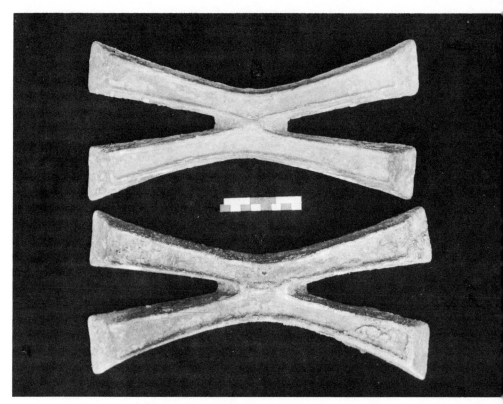

Fig. 7.27 Two copper ingots from a burial in Central Africa. Each weighs about eight pounds (3.6 kilograms), and is of standard form for trading. Presumably they were carried in lots on pairs of sticks wedged into the forks of the ingots. The scale is in centimeters and inches.

Indeed, many prehistoric peoples received copper and iron together, the former being an ornamental or ceremonial metal, the latter more functional.

Much research has been devoted toward the typological classification of copper and bronze artifacts, especially in Europe and the Near East where elaborate classifications of Bronze Age swords, axes, and safety pins dominate the literature. Little is known, however, about the technology of bronzeworking or about how prehistoric man organized the extraction of metal and the production of tools. Analyses of trace elements in the metals, studies of technological variation and of artifact types made by the blacksmiths are as important as the strict archaeological classification of the material. Copper mines were developed in many parts of the Old World and provide a fruitful field for the student of metallurgy to investigate. The most elaborate European workings are in the Tyrol and Salzburg areas,[56] and many

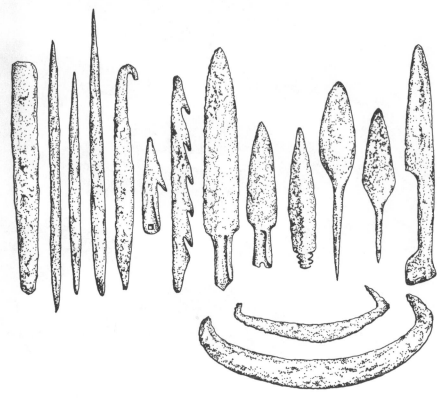

Fig. 7.28   Copper artifacts from the Archaic period in North America. (After Jesse D. Jennings, Prehistory of North America, Fig. 4.8. Copyright © 1968 by McGraw-Hill, Inc. Used with permission of McGraw-Hill Book Company.)

were oval workings entered by a shaft from above. Fire-setting was used to exploit the lodes of copper ore, and at Mitterburg, Austria, the miners drove shafts into the hillside with bronze picks, extracting the copper by elaborate fire-setting techniques. Many early copper-workings have been found in southern Africa, where the miners followed surface lodes under the ground. Fortunately, the traditional Central African processes of copper smelting have been recorded:[57] the ore was placed in a small furnace with alternating layers of charcoal, and smelted for several hours at high heat maintained with goatskin bellows; the furnace was destroyed after each firing, and the molten copper dripped onto the top of a sand-filled pot buried under the fire.

Iron is a more prosaic metal, lacking the lustrous color of fresh

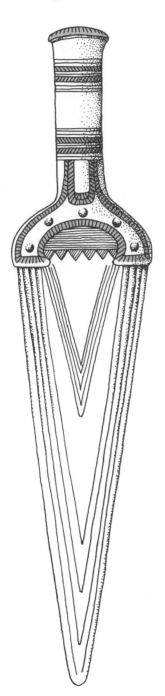

Fig. 7.29   A bronze metal-hilted dagger from Lustenitz, East Germany, second millennium B.C.

copper or bronze, but it yields more effective cutting edges and thus had a far more revolutionary effect on human cultural development than its ornamental relative. Iron tools were first made on a large scale south of the Black Sea in the second millennium B.C., but objects made of the new metal were uncommon for several centuries. The military advantages of the new metal may have been appreciated by the Hittite kings. Even so, iron spread slowly to other areas. Egyptians were working iron by the seventh century B.C., whereas iron artifacts are found in Greece and Crete in eleventh-century B.C. contexts. Iron-working was first established on a large scale in continental Europe in the Seventh century B.C. by Hallstatt peoples. In earlier times iron had played a comparatively limited economic role, most artifacts being slavish copies of bronze tools before the metal's full potentials were realized. Weapons like swords and spears were the first artifacts to be modified to the new material, and specialized ironworking tools, such as tongs, and a range of woodworking artifacts began to be used as soon as iron's qualities were recognized.[58]

Iron ore is much more abundant than copper in a natural state, being readily obtained from surface outcrops and bog iron deposits. Once its potentialities had been realized, the metal's use became so widespread that stone and bronze ceased being employed for essential artifacts and were relegated to a subsidiary, often ornamental role. Iron ore was usually obtained from local deposits, and industrial activity tended to be regional until, with the growth of more concentrated settlements, blacksmiths began to congregate in areas of richer outcrops and specialize in iron tool production. The products of Hallstatt peoples of the European Iron Age (sixth century B.C. and later) are particularly famous and brought a rapid acceptance of iron technology by most of prehistoric Europe.

The impact of iron was immense, for it made available abundant supplies of tough cutting tools for agriculture. Charcoal was needed for smelting, and population pressures in temperate Europe meant that man was beginning to clear heavier and more forested soils. With iron tools, essential forest clearance became easier and man achieved even greater mastery over his environment. Ironworking profoundly influenced the development of literate civilizations, which developed more fully the basic technology of early European and Classical smiths. In sub-Saharan Africa, ironworking played an important role in the expansion of Bantu-speaking peoples over much of the subcontinent, but the craft did not reach southern Africa until less than two thousand years ago (Figure 7.30).[59] Some peoples, like the Australian aborigines and the New World Indians, did not discover iron's potential until they came into contact with European explorers.

The functional classification of iron tools is generally a simple matter, for many basic tool types made in prehistoric times are still being used today, either in primitive technology or in our own society. Elaborate typologies of iron artifacts have been formulated, especially in Europe where Hallstatt ironwork has been studied in depth. Iron technology requires many more techniques than the copper or bronze smelting, for high temperatures have to be maintained for many hours to reduce the ore. Prehistoric man normally used an elaborate furnace filled with alternate layers of charcoal and iron ore, which was fired with the use of bellows.[60] The amount of metal produced in a single smelting was comparatively small and the techniques very wasteful in terms of this resulting quantity of iron. Many tools were made by such cumbersome methods, and they were shaped by forging or

Fig. 7.30 An African ironworker using a goatskin bellows.

hammering into simple forms. But tough working edges could only be produced by quenching or tempering the metal or by adding carbon to produce steel.

Surprisingly little is known about the techniques of prehistoric iron technology. Present evidence is inadequate, but Stuart Piggott has postulated that European iron technology remained almost static between 600–700 B.C. and medieval times; tempering and quenching were unknown.[61] Thus, the typological study of iron objects goes much further than merely classifying the artifacts. What was the level of technological achievement? Were the blacksmiths using techniques such as tempering or quenching? Did they strengthen the blades of weapons, and how? Chemical analysis and a careful review of manufacturing techniques can answer most of these questions. Once again, the primary question is not tool types, but the role of the iron artifact in the culture of its makers.

CLASSIFICATION OF ARTIFACTS

Our attitude toward life and our surroundings is one that involves constant classification and sorting of enormous quantities of data. We classify different types of eating utensils: knives, forks, and spoons—each type has a different use and is kept in a separate compartment in the drawer. We group roads according to their surface, finish, and size. A station wagon is classified separately from a truck. In addition to classifying artifacts, life styles, and cultures, we also make choices among them. If we are eating soup, we choose to use a spoon. Some people eat rice with a fork, some use chopsticks, and others have decided that a spoon is more suitable. In this case, there is a variety of available choices, the final decision often dictated by cultural usage rather than functional pragmatism.

Other criteria for choice and classification also exist. Buying an automobile is almost an American national occupation. A visit to a car dealer has all the aura of ritual and gamesmanship associated with religious ceremonies in other societies. Yet the final choice of model and color is dictated by many factors, some of them logical, others less so. The car's size may be affected by the number of people in a family, but one body style may be chosen over another, as may a color, according to the vibrations between the style and color and the family, rather than for any pragmatic reason. The horsepower of the engine and the options added to the car may be partly pragmatic—airconditioning for coolness in a hot climate or a small engine for economy—while others, such as superior upholstery, racing stripes, or revolution tachometers, are added for prestige reasons or simply because custom or tradition has dictated that a car have these accessories. We live in a world of choice and classification, and our sense of choice and classification is constantly being titillated by advertisement, political exhortation, and even education.

CLASSIFICATION IN ARCHAEOLOGY

The archaeologist is an experienced classifier in everyday life and is merely applying to archaeological evidence behavior that, to a considerable extent, is instinctive even though some choices he makes are difficult and are made over a long period of time. In our daily life we habitually use classification as a tool and part of our life style, and like a computer, we should employ it as a servant rather than a master. Sometimes our classifications of good and bad—for example, those based on color of skin or on our definitions of what is moral or immoral, pornographic or acceptable—are made and then adhered to as binding principles of life without ever being questioned or modified, however circumstances may change. Dogmatism and rigidity result from these attitudes and are as dangerous in archaeology as they are in life. In archaeology, classification is a research tool, a means for ordering data, and the objectives of classifications may change according to the problems being investigated.

The archaeologist deals with the fossilized results of human behavior in the form of man's artifacts and in the variations in his tools, so he classifies them as an essential part of archaeological analysis. The classification of archaeological finds proceeds from the simple to the complicated. In the field, the different broad categories of cultural material are classified separately for laboratory analysis. Obviously, animal bones are analyzed in a different manner than stone tools are; glass requires special treatment, as do radiocarbon or pollen samples. This kind of elementary classification is one of convenience for the excavator and laboratory technician, quite divorced from the ultimate goal of discovering the history of the site inhabitants.

An archaeologist's classifications are intended to simplify comparison between tools from different layers or sites. They are designed to help him understand chronological or cultural relationships. Archaeologists erect series of "types" that may cover a bewildering range of artifacts: huts, arrowheads, axes, baskets, fish-spears, shields, bone harpoons, and pots are but a few categories of human remains to have been so classified. F. Hole and R. F. Heizer, in their comprehensive review of archaeology, put the point succinctly: "A *type* is the most frequently used unit of comparison with artifacts. By the word 'type' we mean a particular type of artifact ... in which several attributes combine or cluster with sufficient frequency or in such distinctive ways that the archaeologist can define and label the artifact and can recognize it when he sees another example."[62]

The term "typology" simply refers to the classification of archaeological artifacts. An archaeologist classifies his collection into similar groups, such as projectile points, scrapers, and potsherds, in much the same way as a zoologist would classify a group of bovids as elk, deer, and antelope—and calls each group of artifacts a "type."[63] A list of the types found at a site thus is a description of what has been found there. The value of typology is that it allows the archaeologist to compare what has been found at two different sites or in different levels or areas within a settlement in order to reach some conclusions about the site's nature and its age. The whole process enables comparisons of archaeological types from one site with those from others. Typology, as James Deetz puts it, has as its main aim "classification which permits comparison ... Such comparison allows the archaeologist to align his assemblage with others in time and space."[64] Equivalent assemblages of artifacts from other sites can be equated with those from one's own settlement by typological comparison, using the arbitrary classification used on either site. Sequences of types can be constructed by ordering the assemblages of artifacts through time, and placing collections in relative chronological order.

Using classification as an archaeological tool involves as much research strategy as is needed in the field because of the complex set of variables. A collection of stone tools or potsherds on the laboratory table represents the fossilized remains of human behavior, the products of a prehistoric society and culture which placed a series of complex limitations and technological boundaries around the artifacts. The owners of the tools classified them into different groups for themselves, each one having a definite role in the society. This "functional" classification is the same as ours, i.e., we assign different roles in the eating process to a knife, fork, and spoon. Knives cut meat; the prehistoric arrowhead is employed in the chase. Fish knives are used in eating seafood; one type of missile head is used to hunt deer, another type to shoot birds. Such functional classifications are an intimate part of the culture of the people who made them. The uses of an artifact may be determined not only by convenience and practical considerations, but also by custom or regulation. The light barbed spearheads used by some Australian hunting bands to catch fish are too fragile for dispatching kangaroo; the special barbs enable the impaled fish to be lifted out of the water. Pots are made by women in most African or American Indian societies, which have division of labor by sex; each has formed complicated customs, regulations, or taboos, that, functional considerations apart, categorize clay pots into different types with varying uses and roles in the culture.

Furthermore, each society has its own conception of what a particular artifact should look like. Americans prefer larger cars, Europeans small ones. These preferences reflect not only pragmatic considerations of road width and longer distances in the New World, but also differing attitudes toward travelling and, on the part of many Americans, a preoccupation with prestige and driveway display, manifested in chromium plate and style changes. We think that a car should have a color-coordinated interior and a long hood to look "right." The steering wheel is on the left, hood ornaments are preferred, and a speedometer is required by law. In other words, we know what we want and expect an automobile to look like and possess, even though minor design details change through time—as do the lengths of women's skirts and the widths of ties. So each society, in making its own classifications, has its own "mental template," as Deetz named it,[65] not only of an object's design, but also of its function. Even the Australopithecines must have had a crude conception of what it was to handle a tool and shape it for a definite objective in their quest for food.

The archaeologist seeks to reconstruct cultural history and process and uses artifacts to help do so. Ideally, his classification of the finds should reflect the precise roles and functional classifications made by the members of the society from which they came. Needless to say, such an objective can never be achieved, both because of incomplete preservation and the lack of written records. We have no means of visualizing the complex roles that some artifacts achieved in prehistoric society, nor of establishing the verbal restrictions placed upon their use by the particular society. Although in some cases obvious functional roles like that of an arrowhead for hunting or warfare or of a pot for carrying water can be correctly established in the laboratory, functional classifications are necessarily restricted and limited. For example, we shall consider the case of a Scandinavian flint dagger (Figure 7.31)—a beautifully made, pressure-flaked tool, a copy of the bronze daggers fashionable at that time in Central Europe. This has been classified by generations of archaeologists as a dagger, by implication a weapon of war and defense, worn by Scandinavian farmers who still had no metals and made in a slavish imitation of a more advanced tool. While this instinctive designation may be correct and near the mental template of its owner's expectations and those of his society, we really do not know if our functional classification was correct. Was the dagger actually used in warfare and for personal defense? Was it a weapon or purely an object of prestige for the

Fig. 7.31 A pressure-flaked Scandinavian flint dagger (one-half actual size). (After Oakley.)

owner, perhaps with some religious function? Did it signify the rank of its wearer? What other uses did it have? Did men and boys wear them, but not women? We cannot answer these questions except by using common sense, ethnographic analogy, or various types of multi-variate analyses—sometimes based on the quantification of large samples of major and minor artifact attributes and associations.[66]

The only instances where a classification related to that of the owners themselves can be developed is where the material culture of a modern people shows continuity with the cultural traditions in the archaeological sites excavated. This situation exists in many parts of the world—among the Indians in the southwestern United States and other areas of North America, the hunter-gatherers of the Kalahari Desert in southern Africa, many agricultural peoples of Bantu Africa, and the Australian aborigines. Even in these cases, functional clas-sification is difficult, for human society is infinitely changeable, and many complex factors can affect the ways in which people look at their culture. Each artifact has many attributes or features that identify it to its owners: these may be the profile or lip of a pot, the decoration on the shoulder, or a certain shape of handle. While many attributes may be obvious to us as well, and we may use them to describe the object, many characteristic features of the artifact in the maker's eyes may elude us—important to them because of social traditions or pragmatic functional dictates that never occur to twentieth-century archaeologists.

How is a category of artifact developed by its owner? What consti-tutes the variations within one artifact type, and the borders between one type of clay vessel and another? How does man decide upon and maintain an artifact "type"? These are questions best considered by taking an example, succinctly described by James Deetz—the case of a basket made by the Chumash Indians of Southern California (Figure 7.32).[67] The mental template of this basket has been reproduced in tangible form by weaving with plant fibers; the template itself has been formed in the maker's mind by several factors, the most important of which is the tremendous reservoir of inherited cultural experience that the Chumash have acquired, generation by generation, through the several thousand years they lived in Southern California. The mental templates of their baskets are almost unconscious, and relate both to the feeling that such and such a form and a color are "correct" and traditionally acceptable. But there are more pragmatic

Fig. 7.32 A typical Chumash parching tray.

and complex reasons too. This Chumash basket bears a band of decoration around the inside of the rim and rectilinear stepped patterns and diamond patterns on the body of the basket. The basket is flat and circular, with a simple rim. Each feature mentioned above can be described as an attribute of the basket, distinctive ones which combined to give the Chumash receptacle its characteristic form. All these attributes formed part of the mental template of the basket as well. Each has a good reason for its presence, whether traditional, innovative, functional, or imposed by the technology used to make the basket. As Deetz points out, the band of decoration around the rim of the basket is a feature of the decorative tradition of the Chumash and occurs on most of their baskets. Its rich red-brown color, not mentioned before, is caused by the species of reed used in its manufacture—the best material available. The flat round shape is determined by its use, for such trays were used for roasting seeds by tossing them with red embers. While the step-like decoration on the body was dictated by the sewing and weaving techniques of all basketry, the diamond motifs between the steps are unique to this particular basket. The woman who made the diamonds was an innovator; her personal stamp on the basket might be a single occurrence unless it was adopted by others—then over several generations, it might become an integral part of the mental template of the basketry tray made by every woman in the group.

The mental template of this type of Chumash basket and the attributes that comprise the template and the object resulting from it are subject to constant change and are influenced by many factors, some pragmatic, some traditional. The Chumash parching tray is the product of a set of distinctive attributes, and is very similar to others produced by the same mental template of a basket made by other members of the same culture. The baskets of neighboring groups may be basically similar, but the varying attributes of the basket types of the Chumash culture's neighbors reflect different sets of factors and a slightly different mental template. The Chumash example serves as a warning that the variations in human artifacts are both complex and sometimes subtle. Our task as archaeologists is to measure these variations and to establish the causes for and directions of change.[68]

Chapter 8

Ordering and Interpretation

Artifacts and other material remains of the past function within a historical context made up of several variables, the principal of which are time, space, and "culture." Although chronology has been discussed at length in Chapter 2, time and the other variables that affect the finds studied in earlier chapters are explored here.

ARTIFACTS AND TIME

Archaeological contexts have a long history, beginning with Christian Thomsen and the Three-Age System and assuming an increasing importance as early scholars wrestled with problems of stratigraphy, association, and classification. They had a particular concern with ordering of artifacts through time. As early as 1849, Sir John Evans described the *stater* of Philip II of Macedon (Figure 8.1) and its progressive alteration in the hands of British coiners who had little interest in the Greek prototype. Evans noted the degeneration in the design and used it to devise a chronological sequence for the coins.[1]*

Toward the end of the nineteenth century, many scholars, among them the celebrated General Pitt Rivers, began to study the evolution of artifacts. If animals evolved, why not artifacts, they argued. But they soon found that many variables affect changes in tool design, among them improved efficiency, stylistic degeneration, or simply popularity. Pitt Rivers was the first to use the term "typology" to

* See pages 334–336 for notes to Chapter 8.

Fig. 8.1   The derivation of the British stater from the stater of Philip II of Macedon, as studied by Sir John Evans. The original faces of the Macedonian coin are at the left.

refer to the employment of methods used in natural science to work out relationships in the form and structure of organisms within an evolutionary sequence, but applied to humanly made objects. Pitt Rivers's typologies were based on another important principle, the fact that certain technological trends are irreversible. To take an obvious example, an aeronautical enthusiast, given the photographs of a series of aircraft types dating from the beginnings of aviation up to the present could place them in approximate order, even if he had no idea of the photographs' dates. But it would be impossible to envisage a typological sequence in which the first aircraft was a supersonic airliner and the latest a Bleriot monoplane of 1912. The modifications needed would be both illogical and incredible.

The humble stone-chopper of the Australopithecines, however, stands in a direct-line relationship to the latest and most sophisticated computers—a platitude, perhaps, although the measurement of technological change over the millennia is a logical step from the study of "types." Early archaeologists like Evans and Pitt Rivers were concerned with a series of objects whose evolutionary direction through time was known; methods of artifact ordering through time were a logical step from their work.

Another scholar, the Egyptologist Sir Flinders Petrie, also contributed much to the early study of artifact chronology. In 1902 he wanted to arrange a large number of Pre-Dynastic tombs from the Nile Valley in chronological order. He eventually placed them in sequence by studying groups of pots found with the skeletons, arranging the vessels in such a way that their stylistic differences reflected gradual change.[2] The handles on the jars were particularly informative, for they changed from functional appendages into more decorative handles, and finally degenerated into a series of painted lines. Flinders Petrie built up a series of pottery stages at Diospolis Parva to which he assigned "sequence dates," the fifty stages running from ST 30 to ST 80. ST 30 was the oldest, for Petrie assumed correctly that the earliest of his wares was not, in fact, the most ancient Egyptian pottery. His sequence dates were subsequently applied over wide areas of the Nile Valley, providing an admirable relative chronology for early Egyptian pottery that remained in use for many years.

Determining the direction of development within a typological series—deciding whether a process of progressive evolution or degeneration is taking place—is not always easy. The flat and flanged axes of the European Bronze Age are obvious examples of tools whose evolution was in the direction of improved efficiency (Figure 8.2). In other cases, the picture can be complicated by deliberate invention, the impact of higher cultures or new economies from outside, and many social restrictions acting on the material culture of its members.

The Law of Association is the key to the study of typological series. Danish archaeologist J. J. A. Worsaae first stated the principle in 1843: the objects accompanying a burial are in most cases things that were in use at the same time.[3] When certain artifact types are found together in grave association after grave association, and when more evolved forms of the same tools are found in association with other burials, the reliability of any typological sequence based on theoretical lines of evolutionary development is enhanced. The basic typology of the European Bronze Age is based almost entirely on the study of grave associations and abandoned hoards of bronze objects buried in times of stress by itinerant merchants or smiths. Many types of hoard are known from European soil—those of traders, religious offerings, votive hoards, and small collections of tools abandoned or lost in a bog or thicket. Merchants' hoards, whose rapid turnover of stock meant a more or less contemporary content, are more useful than religious collections which may contain heirlooms. Grave associations have also been used with success in Peru where a stylistic sequence of spouted pottery bottles found in Moche graves on the north coast confirmed a hypothetical sequence for the Moche pottery style proposed some years earlier.[4] John Rowe and his associates then extended the sequence to other shapes of pottery vessel by means of a complicated series of analyses. Had other types of artifacts been present, such as carvings, textiles, and other tools, they could have proceeded to make typological and chronological studies of a wider range of artifacts until they had a basis for discussing cultural change.

An exemplary case of problem-oriented research into grave-lot chronology using the latest methods of problem-oriented archaeology

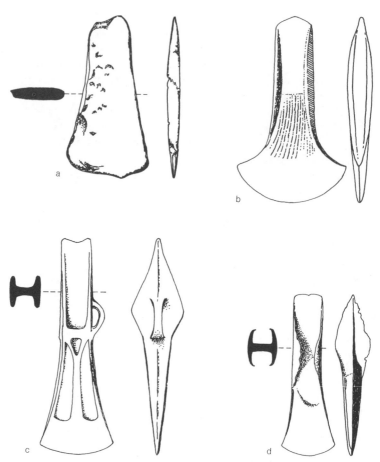

Fig. 8.2   Bronze axes from Europe (one-third actual size). (a) Flat axe. (b) Axe with step ridges and raised side flanges. (c) Palstave with loop for hafting attachment. (d) Wing-flanged axe.

has recently been published by British archaeologist Roy Hodson.[5] The Iron Age La Tène cemetery at Munsingen-Rain, Switzerland, lies on a narrow ridge on the Swiss plateau. With lateral space for the cemetery limited, the burials were packed closely in a form of horizontal stratigraphy along the ridge. The earliest, fifth-century B.C. graves are at the north end of the cemetery; the latest, deposited in the second century B.C., in the south. Hodson's study was devoted entirely to distinguishing the successive chronological horizons of the La Tène burials. He did this by laying down some well defined, basic assumptions at the beginning of the project, then carrying out a highly rationalized, formal analysis. Clusters of thoroughly studied artifact attributes were grouped into types, their reliability as chronological horizon indicators assessed carefully, and a refined chronology built up from the groupings. Hodson's study is an example of applying the latest quantitative methods to the study of grave chronology. His refined analyses permitted chronological phases of less than a century to be detectable, admittedly on material that lies at the very end of unwritten history in Europe.

The last fifty years have seen a rapid development in techniques of seriation, or chronological ordering, of artifacts based on Petrie's principles. Recent studies of seriation are based on the assumption that popularity of any artifact or culture trait is a transient thing. The mini skirt becomes the midi or maxi, dancing styles change from month to month, records hit the top forty but are forgotten within a short time, and each year's automobile model, hailed as "brand new," is soon relegated to the secondhand lot. Other traits may have a far longer life. The chopper tools of *Australopithecus* were a major element in early man's tool kit for hundreds of thousands of years. Candles were used for centuries before kerosene and gas lamps came into fashion. But each had its period of maximum relative frequency, or popularity. Figure 8.3 shows how such popularity distributions are made up, using bar graphs plotted against strata or other archaeological associations. Each distribution of artifacts or culture traits plotted has a profile that has been described as resembling a large battleship's hull viewed from the air.

The technique of seriation is based on the assumption that the popularity of pottery types, stone artifact forms, or other culture traits peaks in a "battleship curve," the widest part of the graph representing the period of maximum popularity. Thus, it is argued that sites within a restricted and uniform geographic area showing similar plots of pottery or other artifact types are of broadly the same relative date. A series of sites or surface collections can be linked in a relative chronology, even though, without absolute dates, one cannot tell when they were occupied, provided that the samples of artifacts used are statistically reliable. Edwin Dethlefsen and James Deetz tested the "battleship curve" assumption against some historical data, using a series of Colonial gravestones from a New England cemetery (Figure 8.4).[6] The gravestones, dated by the inscriptions on them, show three decorative styles—death's head, cherub, and urn and willow—that yield an almost perfect series of battleship curves following one upon the other. Seriation is also applied to stylistic change within a single series of artifacts that may in themselves form a "battleship curve";

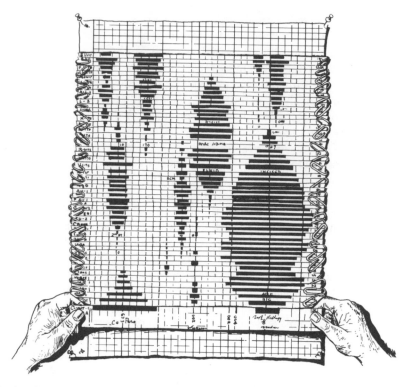

Fig. 8.3 A seriation graph in the making. Each strip of paper represents a stratigraphic unit, with a bar graph of the pottery counts for each type plotted on it. These are being placed in order to produce the most viable seriated sequence. The strips are placed in position with paper clips on a piece of graph paper pinned to a back board. This diagram is almost complete.

the same principle, used by Petrie with his Pre-Dynastic jars, applies and a battleship curve results. Deetz and his colleague tested this assumption against dated death's head gravestones (Figure 8.5) and found it valid.

Seriation has become a powerful research tool especially in sites where pottery or other sensitive culture traits are common. A seriated sequence of types or styles from a series of stratified and perhaps dated sites can serve as a yardstick for fitting many surface sites in the same area into a relative sequence. Today's seriators use sophisticated statistical techniques to assess the viability of their conclusions.[7] Sound sampling procedures are obviously essential if seriation is to be used extensively, so it is necessary to establish that the samples collected were selected randomly.[8]

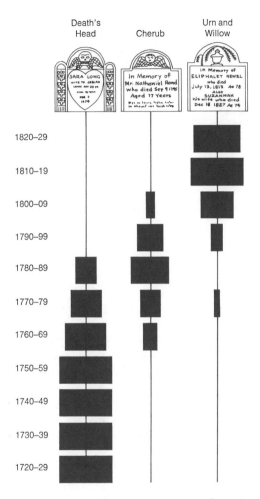

Fig. 8.4 *Typical seriated stylistic sequences of New England gravestones from Stoneham, Mass.*

ARTIFACTS IN SPACE

Time is a vital dimension of archaeology—so is space. Both represent contexts within which the archaeologist groups his artifacts and other culture traits for purposes of classification and comparison. Space implies distribution and the use of distribution maps.[9] In Chapter 7 we made the basic assumption that most artifacts were used for rational purposes and that characteristic groups of them were used for particular activities like ironworking, butchery, and hunting. Arising from this, similar patterned groups of artifact types may be found on other living sites of the same people, which, although the artifacts

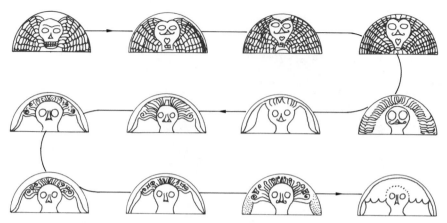

Fig. 8.5   The seriation of stylistic change within a single New England tombstone motif.

may differ in detail, obviously resulted from basically similar activities. Provided that the tools from the other sites are in a contemporary context and within a restricted geographic area, archaeologists accept them as being representative of similar "cultures," a term that has come to imply "tribe," although this is a gross generalization. During the earlier millennia of the Stone Age, cultural similarities were wide-spread—similar hand axes occur in Europe, Africa, and India. But archaeological cultures have proliferated as the man's diversity was accentuated, and considering space in terms of defining cultural boundaries is vital in examining more recent archaeological periods.

ARCHAEOLOGICAL UNITS

Typology is a method of describing the form of one artifact, or a collection of them. The spatial and temporal relationships of the same collections are established by distribution maps on the one hand and by use of absolute and relative chronology on the other. The relationships just mentioned have to be integrated with one another in meaningful terms, a process that is carried out by formulating several archaeological units. The units must be "characteristic, recurrent, and internally consistent, and relate to one another in such a way that one can assume that they are concrete expressions of common social traditions."[10]

Archaeological units[11] are formulated by combining typological data, distributions of sites, and the timespan of the proposed unit. The hardest problem is fixing the dimensions of time and space. The contents of a possible unit formulation have to be defined in terms of earlier and later occupation levels at a site, for the artifacts in this unit may merge into material found in lower or upper levels, whereas earlier or later artifacts may persist or originate in this middle unit. Such problems sometimes must be solved by studying the external relationships of the artifacts to establish their true context. To some extent, of course, the definition of any archaeological unit is arbitrary, and this is acceptable, provided that the archaeologist retains awareness of this and softens the rigidity of his formulations as necessary. The problem, indeed, is the same as that encountered with types.[12]

Many different archaeological units have been utilized by field-workers in different parts of the world, for no one has yet succeeded in applying a single terminological scheme to both Old and New World prehistory. Archaeological taxonomy had its origins in the work of Gabriel de Mortillet, J. J. A. Worsaae, and Oscar Montelius in Europe and of Kidder and others in the New World. More attention has been paid to taxonomic problems in North America, where classification became a major preoccupation after the First World War. The present, most commonly used North American terminology had its ancestry in the so-called Midwestern Taxonomic System, and in the work of Willey and Phillips after the Second World War, both attempts to synthesize cultural sequences over large areas of the Americas.[13]

All terminologies of proposed archaeological units are merely suggested labels that try to define groupings of artifacts and other traits in space and time, and represent attempts to reconstruct the prehistoric past by using cultural data. How closely these terminologies relate to actual prehistoric societies is difficult to assess with our present, somewhat crude techniques of reconstructing the past. Much depends on the complexity of the society being reconstructed. Small hunting camps obviously provide an excellent chance to study intact societies, for a single camp was normally occupied by a band of several families enjoying close social relations and a well-knit society. But larger, agricultural settlements offer social situations that are far beyond the capabilities of the archaeologist's spade and interpretative skills because many different factors interact to form a more complex society and there is greater contact between societies which may be trading essential commodities. The archaeologist's *phase, culture, horizon,* and *component* represent, like types, an attempt to organize cultural data as part of the reconstruction of the way prehistoric peoples lived. Archaeological units are also designed to present data in a form suitable for studying prehistoric culture change.

ARCHAEOLOGICAL CULTURES

Definitions of *culture* in anthropology are legion, although everyone agrees that they use it to refer to a distinct human phenomenon. Culture may be qualified to refer to an individual culture such as "Western European," "Middle Class American," or "Nuer." The qualification conjures up certain characteristic attributes or behavior patterns typical of those associated with the cultural label. Each human culture is distinctive, having different features of behavior and artifacts; all cultures are made up of a myriad of tangible and intangible traits, some inherited from earlier generations, others unique to the culture itself—the content of any culture resulting from a complex adaptation to a wider range of ecological, societal, and cultural factors. Human culture is unique because much of its content is transmitted from generation to generation by sophisticated communication systems that permit complex and on-going adaptations to aid man's survival as well as to help rapid cultural change take place—for example, when less advanced societies come into contact with higher civilizations.[14] We would be helpless without our cultural equipment (houses, axes, ploughs, and hunting weapons), and we survive because of our culture. Over twenty-five years ago Clyde Kluckhohn and William Kelly defined culture as "historically created designs for living, explicit and implicit, rational, irrational, and non-rational, which exist at any given time as potential guides for the behavior of man."[15]

Cultures are made up of human behavior and its results, and obviously consist of a complex and constantly interacting set of variables. Human culture is never static, always adjusting to both internal and external change, whether environmental, technological, or societal, and has been referred to as an organized system. Archaeologists study early cultures by working with the tangible remains of human activity, with the artifacts, food residues, and other culture traits discussed in these pages. Archaeological "cultures" are part of terminological usage. They consist of material remains of human culture preserved at a given point in space and time at several sites, in other words "an assemblage of artifacts that recurs repeatedly associated together in dwellings of the same kind and burials of the same rite. The arbitrary peculiarities of all cultural traits are assumed to be concrete expressions of the common social traditions that bind together a culture." Gordon Childe continues, "Artifacts hang together in assemblages, not because they were used in the same age, but also because they were used by the same people, made and executed in accordance with techniques, rites, or styles, prescribed by a social tradition, handed on by precept and example, and modifiable in the same way."[16]

Thus archaeological culture represents a social system, defined in a context of time and space that has come down to us in the form of artifacts and other durable culture traits. Unless we have historical records of the owners, we must give it an arbitrary name—many have proliferated as archaeologists dig up the past. The Acheulian Culture was named after a village in northern France, the Desert Culture after a well-defined geographic area in western North America; others have been called after characteristic tool types. The geographic boundaries of archaeological cultures are arbitrary; so are the artifact classifications of which they consist—it follows that precise definition, not only of the space and time dimensions, but also of content is a prerequisite to comparisons of neighboring cultures or of cultural change in the past. Earlier in this book some methods of analysis and comparison employed to establish the convergence and divergence of different archaeological cultures were reviewed.

CULTURE CHANGE: INVENTION, MIGRATION, AND DIFFUSION

Although the classification of artifacts and prehistoric cultures in time and space have been discussed, the troublesome subject of cultural change has not. The principal agents of cultural change—invention, migration, and diffusion—are surrounded by a voluminous and often controversial literature,[17] in which people have sought to establish criteria for identifying the three processes in the archaeological record. Some history of archaeological theory is traced in Part 3 of this book, so only a brief consideration of invention, migration, and diffusion as they are recognized in practice is included here.

Invention involves the creation of a new idea, and the transformation of it, in archaeological contexts, into an artifact or other tangible innovation that has survived. Many inventions such as new social institutions, religions, or ideas leave little tangible trace in the archaeological record. An invention implies either the modification of an old idea, or series of ideas, or a completely new concept; it may be made by accident or by intentional research. The atom was split as a result of long and patient investigation with the ultimate objective of fragmentation in view; fire probably accrued to man's armory as a result of accident.[18] Inventions spread, and if they are sufficiently important, spread widely and rapidly. The transistor is in almost universal use because it is an effective advance in electronic technology; ploughs had an equally dramatic effect on agriculture in prehistoric Europe. How inventions spread has been studied extensively by archaeologists and anthropologists. Inventions spread and gain acceptance because of diffusion, a label that refers to the processes by which new ideas or cultural traits spread from one person to another or from one group to another. Diffusion depends greatly on the acceptance of the trait, for new traits must be evaluated in terms of their recipients' needs and social context, with the result that some societies may reject an invention while others accept it avidly. Archaeological finds normally reflect technological development; the acceptance of a diffused cultural trait often depends entirely on its effectiveness as a method of controlling one's environment or raising the standard of living. The advent of ironworking led to more intensive agriculture and the clearance of large woodland areas in Iron Age Europe. Warfare became more effective with iron weapons and a greater factor in political maneuver. Once in use, iron was rapidly recognized as a radical improvement on any other known toolmaking substance, and soon came into common use—a classic example of the rapid diffusion of a significant new invention.[19]

Diffusion is really the spread of ideas that are adopted by other people. It is quite distinct from the spread of commodities or new artifacts from commercial activity, which normally involves the receivers of the new tool using it and not learning to make it themselves. Segmented faience beads were widely traded through Europe from the eastern Mediterranean during the Bronze Age. These objects were made from fine quartz grains cemented together, glazed, and colored blue in XVIIIth Dynasty Egyptian workshops before being brought to Mycene and then onward into barbarian Europe. But the European farmers who received them did not manufacture such beads themselves, obtaining the ornaments by commercial means rather than by diffusion.[20]

One idea may be diffused, or many traits together—perhaps ones that are not even vaguely related. The manufacture of bronze weapons, for example, presupposes that the makers have a knowledge of metallurgy and a conception of the design and use of bronze artifacts. All these traits form a logical pattern of diffused ideas, each dependent on one another. Other traits apparently unconnected may travel together simply because they have been adopted through contact of one group with another; sometimes, indeed, a whole culture may be diffused and adopted by another group, a process described by Alfred Kroeber as "assimilation."[21]

Diffusion often involves the spread of ideas over long distances; these ideas are socially transmitted from individual to individual and ultimately from group to group, but do not involve the actual movement of many people. The process of migration does. A whole society can move, expanding its sphere of influence into new areas. English settlers moved to the North American continent, taking their own culture and society with them; the Spanish occupied Mexico. The results of such population movements were not only a diffusion of ideas, but a mass shift of people, involving social and cultural changes over a wide front. One can argue that these processes are really modified diffusion, but most archaeologists make a distinction between the two.

Distinguishing between independent invention, diffusion, and migration from archaeological evidence is, to put it mildly, a tricky business. Independent invention is usually identified by the isolation of exotic objects in an archaeological component, which cannot have been introduced by trade, and involve a radically new technological concept or idea outside the normal cultural behavior at the time or perhaps related to some earlier experimentation. Many such minor inventions are unusual objects that are made once and then fall into oblivion. A toolmaker may momentarily visualize the possibilities of a new artifact type or raw material, but his product is unacceptable, or he loses interest. Many inventions are believed to have earlier prototypes; clay-lined baskets are thought to have been the forerunners of clay pots in Yugoslavia, Egypt, and other areas, but it is impossible to control the data sufficiently to prove this, and the theories at best are speculative. Examples of revolutionary inventions are legion: bows and arrows, bronze and iron smelting, agriculture, and the domestication of animals are all obvious cases. The evidence for most of these traits is so diffuse that the task of identifying the exact point of invention in time and space is impossible.

Migration and diffusion are equally hard to deduce from archaeological evidence. Both are recognized through evidence of major cultural change within a short period of time at a stratified site. Do these changes result from local invention, diffusion of a cluster of cultural traits that were rapidly adopted, or wholesale population replacement? Distribution maps are a fundamental tool for studying diffusion and migration, but must be used with great care. The plotting of find spots on a map must be carefully controlled, both the exact traits plotted and the chronological range involved. Obviously, a map of a characteristic type of bronze safety pin is useless unless all the pins belong to a narrow segment of prehistoric time, so the artifacts are delineated in space and time.

On the assumption that a trait—let us say swordmaking—was invented in a single village and that the utility of the new design was quickly recognized, we would expect to find the distribution of these swords to expand in a circular pattern on the ground from the village. But time is advancing inexorably, and those settlements at the outer limits of the distribution received the sword at a later date than those in the middle. So the effect is like that of a cone, as the accompanying illustration shows (Figure 8.6). In fact, the cone shape is distorted by many factors like geographical barriers and the degree of acceptance of the new weapon by different peoples. As Deetz urges, the archaeologist in fact looks at distributions in two dimensions, space and time, and the effect is triangular.[22] Under favorable circumstances, with accurate spatial and chronological control, it may be possible to obtain a chronological gradient away from the point of origin. In general terms, for example, food production is accepted as having spread westward into the Mediterranean basin and Europe over a period of several thousand years. The chronological gradient is there, but not nearly as accurate as we would wish.

One of the most famous historical reconstructions based on the diffusion of traits is Leslie Spier's study of the Sun Dance among the Plains Indians of North America.[23] The Sun Dance was a long, important ritual carried out by many North American tribes of the Great Plains and Plateau. Dancers fasted for several days prior to the ceremony. A large center pole was erected in the place designated for the dance and sometimes decorated with buffalo hide. The dancers themselves pierced their backs and chests, making slits through which leather thongs were passed. The thong ends were tied to the center pole or to heavy buffalo skulls that were then dragged after the dancer. Spier divided the Sun Dance into discrete elements such as the decoration of the center pole, use of a specially designated area for the dance, and the amount of fasting beforehand, and he compared individual ceremonies throughout the area where it was in use. He found the most elaborate Sun Dance complex to have been practiced among the Cheyenne Indians and therefore designated the Cheyenne as the originators of the ceremony. Later, archaeologists and ethnographers studied the history of the Cheyenne, and found that they had not moved to the Great Plains until after 1750, a date long after the Sun Dance had been adopted by other Plains groups. Elaboration, then, is not necessarily a good indication of where a culture trait originated.

In cases where such traits as food production have discontinuous distributions, with a development of agriculture in several different areas, the situation is even more controversial. Some say that man is basically an unambitious animal who rarely made drastic discoveries; thus, if he did, the major inventions of mankind were made but once—a school of thought that flourished at the beginning of this century. Scholars like Elliot Smith believed that all civilization derived from the Nile Valley; later discoveries have thrown the basic assumptions of this school of thought into disrepute.

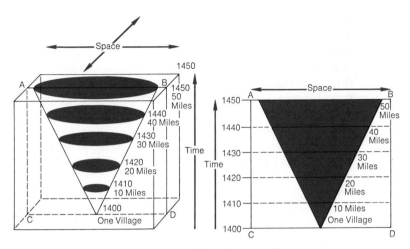

Fig. 8.6 *The spread of a culture trait in space and time—the cone effect.*

Kroeber, whose knowledge of primitive society was encyclopedic, observed that where two cultures, even those widely separated in time were facing the same problems and were in many degrees similar, they tended to invent new ideas along parallel lines. The similarities may result from environmental patterns or from an ultimate, and often very remote, common origin. Thus, he argued that independent invention of a wide range of significant culture traits is quite possible, and indeed likely. The situation is a flexible one, and requires detailed historical or archaeological information to resolve it, as well as a profound knowledge of the phenomena of culture change. Clearly, speculations based on inadequate archaeological evidence or knowledge of historical connections are doomed to failure.

In archaeological terms, several criteria must be satisfied before we can decide whether a series of artifacts in archaeological sites distant from one another are related to each other in meaningful historical terms. First, the traits or objects must be sufficiently similar in design and typological attributes to indicate that they probably have a common origin. Second, the traits must be shown not to have resulted from convergent evolution. The earlier development of the trait, perhaps as generalized as a form of architecture or a domestic animal, must be carefully traced in both cultures. Third, the distributions of the surviving traits must be carefully studied, as well as those of their antecedents. The only acceptable evidence for the diffusion of a trait, or its transmission by migration, is a series of sites that show, when plotted on a map, a continuous distribution for the trait or perhaps a route along which it spread. Accurate chronological control is essential, with either a time-gradient from either end of the distribution, or one toward the middle. In many cases, the archaeological criteria may be difficult to establish, but the importance of reliable evidence is obvious. These criteria are rarely satisfied, and the interpretation of the prehistoric past suffers as a result. Theoretical speculations are all very well, but may result in completely false conclusions, sometimes supported by uncritical use of scanty archaeological evidence.

How do we distinguish between diffusion and migration in the archaeological record? There are so many different ways in which culture can change. A population may totally replace another by driving out the former inhabitants. This phenomenon is rare, but may occur where two populations live next to each other. Theoretically this may be reflected by a complete change in the material culture, but in practice this is rare. Again, rigid criteria have to be satisfied. Many sites must reflect the same change to demonstrate a population shift over a larger area than one site. Continuous occupation is important, for a vital stage in an evolutionary process may be missing if only a few sites are examined. Every aspect of economic and technological evidence must be examined to avoid a one-sided interpretation of the archaeological record. The more sudden and dramatic the change, the better. Perhaps the most conclusive argument for migration is the abrupt replacement of the existing population by a new racial type; proof of this involves the careful use of data from physical anthropology. A useful indicator of migratory change is evidence of widespread destruction of the earlier occupation by invaders with a completely different material culture. Here again, the evidence must be well-documented and widespread in space. On a wider scope, we must prove that the new culture originated in another area and document the distribution of the new population outside the area of replacement. What migration route did they follow? Were geographical and climatic conditions favorable to the movement of population? In other words, the new and possibly intrusive culture must be viewed within the widest environmental and historical framework to minimize the dangers of unwarranted speculation.

Another common form of migration causing culture change is the movement of a small population group into a new area over which they gain political control, subjecting the indigenous population either by force, economic power, or ritual ability. The native culture may continue to flourish, but the old and new cultures will tend to blend into one, even though rigid social distinctions between the two populations persist. The degree of blending depends on many intangible factors, for each group plays an important role in the total culture and society. Six hundred years ago, the Karanga Kingdom between the Zambezi and the Limpopo rivers in south-central Africa was ruled by a series of hereditary chiefs, who controlled trade and religion, while the indigenous population of farmers mined gold, copper, and other raw materials for long-distance and domestic trade networks. The archaeological record reflects a blending of pottery styles and other culture traits that increased as the kingdom developed after the fifteenth century A.D.[24]

The criteria for studying partial replacement of population are even more rigid than those for total change. Both elements in the blended culture must be isolated by excavation of pure components of each, dating to the time before which the blended culture flourished. In other words, the two populations and their culture must be accurately defined so that the contribution of each to the blended culture can be measured. The intrusive culture must be particularly carefully described, and established as being of nonlocal origin. As with total replacement, the migration route and place of origin must be established. Unless the intrusive culture is well defined, it is only too easy to assign all cultural changes found in a prehistoric sequence to intrusive peoples when in fact they evolved locally without foreign impetus. Another difficulty is demonstrating that the area was settled by foreigners with permanent settlements, and especially to illustrate the gradual process of cultural blending from the archaeological record. To set up these criteria is hard, for the process of blending is often swift and all too few traits are preserved. Accurate dating of individual traits and detailed stratigraphic analyses are essential parts of the criteria, for sometimes one can show that a particular trait, thought to be associated with an intrusive people, in fact appeared at a different time from the others.

Several other migratory situations can occur. Invaders may move into a new area and adopt the material culture of those already there. Families or individuals may move in as settlers, refugees, or perhaps specialist craftsmen; communities of slaves may settle in a new area without having a major impact on the area's native culture.[25] All these processes are subtle ones that are rarely reflected in archaeological sites. The presence of foreign craftsmen might be recognized through a concentration of exotic houses or workshops containing artifacts of foreign design.

Invention, diffusion, and migration are some principal agents of cultural change, and the archaeologist studies them using his observations and analyses as basic raw material. But even if he employs all ecological, archaeological, linguistic, biological, and historical evidence, his data are often inadequate to understand fully the motives of the humans who used the artifacts, structures, and settlements that he has studied. Artifacts result from human behavior, and each one had a definite role in its own culture. Discovering these roles and the part played by innovative traits can at least take us some distance along the route toward understanding the prehistoric past.

SOCIAL ORGANIZATION

The more intangible aspects of human society, including both social organization and religious systems, are difficult to deduce from archaeological data. Many minor differences between prehistoric peoples, those of speech, religion, and social organization, for example, are seldom obvious in the archaeological record—and traditional definitions of culture in archaeology are such that we can only recognize differences when they are detectable in the data obtained through excavation, analysis, and induction. Archaeological cultures are quite different from those of anthropologists and do not necessarily coincide with the boundaries that the owners of a culture may recognize themselves, frontiers imposed by such subtle criteria as hostility, linguistic difference, or diverse religious beliefs.

The starting point for any investigation of social structure must be basically socioeconomic,[26] and consider the minimal economic group—usually the nuclear family—found in the archaeological record. We can hypothesize that the nuclear family occupies a dwelling unit, preserved in the form of floor plans (Figure 8.7) of structures in which

Fig. 8.7   The plan of an Upper Paleolithic hunters' longhouse at Kostenki IV, USSR.

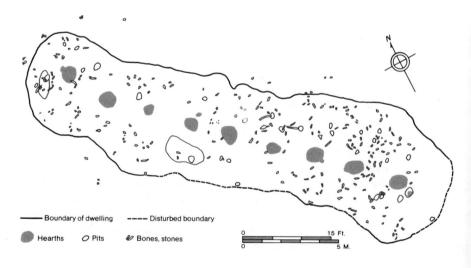

———— Boundary of dwelling   - - - - Disturbed boundary

⬤ Hearths   ○ Pits   ✎ Bones, stones

0 ———— 15 Ft.
0 ———— 5 M.

the minimal unit lived. Unfortunately, so many variables beyond that of the nuclear family, such as kinship, temporary residence, marriage customs, and descent laws, can affect the make-up of a household that the generalization is hardly a reliable one except when a site has a known historical association, or good ethnographic information is available. Lewis Binford was able to make this assumption at the Late Woodland site at Hatchery West, Illinois,[27] and using experimental techniques, he obtained complete data for features at the site and identified the remains of four district communities. The earlier, La Motte, periods of summer and winter occupation were associated with "corporate work areas for the preparation of food."[28] The later, Mississippian settlement was a single-family house, part of a more dispersed settlement pattern than that of the La Motte occupations. The Hatchery West Mississippian occupation was only a segment of a very different community type produced by adaptive changes that resulted in the emergence of the Middle Mississippian in the Midwest.

Binford used artifact patterning as a basis for inferences about prehistoric social systems.[29] Artifact patterning, i.e., combinations of artifacts isolated in excavations, can reflect the activities of individuals or minimal groups of interacting individuals—such as families, lineages, or ironworking teams.[30] The artifact patterning of a whole community is discernible in any single occupation settlement site where structures are present, and the behavioral patterning of an entire society is also best investigated in terms of settlement patterns (Chapter 9).

James Deetz has published a series of papers that deal with artifact patterning in terms of inference of residence and descent in prehistoric societies.[31] His study of the change in patterning of ceramic attributes among the Arikara Indians of the Missouri Valley was based on both archaeological and historical evidence. The excavations revealed three levels of occupation, with the earliest inhabitants of the site having lived in large houses and made fine pots of uniform standard. Such large houses gave shelter to several families who farmed together, the women traditionally doing most of the food production as well as making the pots. But Deetz found that house sizes were smaller in the later levels, and his carefully seriated types from the lower horizon fell into disarray, for styles were much more variable as though the "mental templates" were less rigorously adhered to. The written history of the Arikara provided a possible interpretation, for from the sixteenth century the people had moved more and more frequently as they moved up the Missouri Valley into more open country. As time passed, the men began to act as middlemen in the trade in horses and guns between Plains Indians and white traders, and the role of women changed as farming became less vital. The matrilocal houses of earlier times gave way to mixed settlement, reflected in more variable pottery traditions and other changes in artifact patterning.

Evidence for specialized roles in society and for social stratification is more readily obtained, especially from sites like Harappa or Mohenjodaro where laborers had their own quarters, or from richly furnished graves like those of the Royal Cemetery at Ur or of the Shang chieftains in China.[32] Tattooing, religious objects, or richly ornamented artifacts are all signs of rank, although, unless the associated materials are particularly informative, the amount of additional data obtained is limited.[33]

Much research into social organization in prehistoric societies has derived from studies of relationship and association of artifacts in the field; people are beginning to look at prehistoric social systems within the context of anthropological theory.

RELIGION AND RITUAL

The anonymous cynic who wrote that "religion is the last resort of troubled excavators" hit the nail on the head. Inferences about religion or ritual are bound to be highly speculative, even though artifacts or sites of obvious religious association are found or investigated.[34] Places of worship include Greek and Roman temples, sacred hills, and Mexican religious complexes. The "Venus" figurines of the European Upper Paleolithic have widely been interpreted as fertility symbols,[35] and later human figures have also received similar interpretation[36]—but the ritual associations of such objects are in doubt. The cave art of Altamira and Lascaux has been called a manifestation of "sympathetic hunting magic" by many observers, and new investigative methods are dealing with this interpretation.[37] Burial mutilations, oral tradition, and even astronomy[38] have been used to infer religious activities from archaeological data. Mother Goddess cults, Baal-Astarte rituals, and earth worship are a few of the fascinating manifestations of ritual found in archaeological literature—a delight to the eccentric and entertainment to the serious student of prehistory. Perhaps the best opportunities for the study of prehistoric religion lie in the area of analogy, for example, the case of the red deer antler frontlets from Star Carr.[30]

ANALOGY IN ARCHAEOLOGY

The term "analogy" infers that a relationship exists between two or more phenomena because the same relationship may be observed in similar situations. Our abilities to reason by analogy are often tested in aptitude examinations by such questions as: "A fish is to water as a bird is to: (a) a tree (b) a house (c) air (d) grass seed." Obviously, if we grasp the relationship between fish and water, we will not have any trouble completing the question. Analogy in archaeology involves inferring that the relationship between various traces of human activity in the archaeological record is the same as, or similar to, those of similar phenomena found among modern primitive peoples. Thus, on a very simple level, archaeologists infer that small pointed pieces of stone are projectile points because there are ethnographic records of peoples making small pointed pieces of stone for the tips of lances or arrows. Reasoning by analogy has enjoyed a long history in archaeological interpretation.

In Part 3, the discussion about early unilineal evolutionists shows they considered living tribes to be good examples of successive stages of development in culture history. Each stage of cultural development was correlated with a stage of technology, a form of the family, a kind of religious belief, and a type of political control that could be observed in some living group of people. Because the stages of technology were readily observed in the archaeological record, archaeologists had only to identify the stage of technological development in their sites and then infer by an analogy to some living group the kind of social organization and religion appropriate to the stage, as provided by the unilineal scheme. Thus the Bushmen, Australian aborigines, and Eskimos, who retained a hunting and gathering way of life, manufactured stone tools, and had no knowledge of metallurgy, were considered to be living representatives of Paleolithic peoples. The geologist, W. J. Sollas, made direct analogies between Upper Paleolithic hunters and modern hunting groups.[40] Many early investigators thought that the most primitive Stone Age peoples were matriarchal, had no government, and believed in numerous spirits. The archaeologist who dug a Paleolithic site would interpret his findings by analogy to the unilineal scheme; if he wanted to interpret details not in the scheme, such as the meaning of a particular form of burial, he would turn to the literature of the Bushmen, Australian aborigines, and Eskimos for the "correct" interpretation.

Since the early unilineal schemes have largely been abandoned by Western archaeologists, this kind of simplistic analogy is not often encountered today. In the Soviet Union, however, unilineal schemes of evolution form an important part of Marxist-Leninist doctrine. Even recent Soviet monographs still employ analogy to the "correct stage of development" in order to interpret the social structure of archaeologically known peoples. For example, S. I. Rudenko, writing about the origin of the Eskimo, chides Western scholars for not attempting to describe the development of Eskimo socioeconomic structure. This failure, he writes, "is to be explained by the very simplistic approach of foreign investigators to Eskimo culture, caused by their disregard of the authentic scientific outlook of Marxism-Leninism."[41] Rudenko then postulates that the first stage in Eskimo development was characterized by primitive communism and a matriarchal form of the family. Although he admits that all known Eskimo groups are patrilocal, he sees this as a recent development due to the introduction of trade by American sailors. He then cites the fact that three very important Eskimo spirits are female and leaps to "the conclusion that the Eskimo were matriarchal in the remote past."[42]

Outside of the Soviet Union, the selection and evaluation of appropriate analogies is a far more complicated problem, and one to which several possible solutions have been offered. The thinking of the cultural relativists, especially of the American historical school, is evident in three different approaches to the analogy problem (see Chapters 10 and 11). Cultural relativism proposes that each culture is uniquely composed of ideas and traits and that no two cultures can be compared on any scale due to their uniqueness, a quality that can only be understood subjectively. One relativist approach maintains that all interpretations by means of analogy are assertions that cannot be proved or disproved and for this reason, archaeologists, in order to be scientific, should abandon analogy completely and just report what they find.[43] Thus, finding a small pointed piece of stone is one thing, and calling it a projectile point is quite another. Perhaps, in this particular, archaeologically known culture, such pieces of stone were used as amulets and not as projectile points. Perhaps by calling them projectile points we may be deluded into assuming that they played the same role in the thinking of the people who made them as they do in that of people known from ethnographic literature. Culture relativists would consider this an erroneous conclusion because, since every culture is unique, the role played by an artifact or culture trait in any individual culture must also be unique. It would be a mistake then to infer that a small sharp piece of stone had only utilitarian value to its maker; it may also have been an art object or have had ritual significance. Thus, we cannot use analogy to interpret the ways in which such artifacts are thought of or used in any known culture. The logical conclusion to the relativist view is, of course, that archaeologists cannot interpret anything they find or compare their discoveries to anything else. This train of thought would, if followed to its conclusion, end archaeology completely.

At every step of his investigation, however, the archaeologist must make inferences about human behavior, and these are largely based on analogies with living groups. The very act of distinguishing man-made artifacts from natural objects is guided by analogic reasoning. We know from observations of human behavior that man-made objects are patterned in certain predictable ways. If we did not let this assumption guide our thinking, we could never tell a hand axe from the gravel surrounding it. Abandoning analogy does not seem to be a workable solution to the problem.

The stamp of cultural relativism is also seen in a second approach: archaeological interpretation through analogy should be restricted to the technology of the cultures the archaeologist is studying.[44] Enough small pointed pieces of stone have been found imbedded in the bones of animals and men for us to safely acknowledge that such tools were most likely projectile points. Still, we have no way of knowing if the points were a part of ritual activity as well as the hunt. Similarly, the archaeologist will have information about how houses were constructed and what they looked like, what plants were grown and how these were prepared for food, and perhaps some information on grave furniture. But he will not know what the people who lived at his site *thought* a proper house should look like or which relatives would be invited to help build a house, or what spirits were responsible for making crops grow, or who in the house customarily prepared the food, or whether or not the people believed in life after death. According to the relativist view, the ideas, beliefs, and customs of any people are uniquely their own and not related to either the natural environment or to their hereditary makeup. Although the archaeologist does have direct access to the part of culture that is technological in nature, he has no way of knowing anything about a people's beliefs and ideas; thus, any analogy drawn from the ideas and beliefs of real people is probably incorrect.

This view of archaeological interpretation is implicit or explicit in many archaeological writings. R. H. Thompson, in a widely read article on analogy in archaeology, presents an explicit statement of this viewpoint.[45] He argues that an archaeologist's first inferences *must* be based on technological generalization, and warns that anything beyond this is almost completely subjective and depends on the archaeologist's abilities and competence. But how are we to judge the ability and competence of the archaeologist whose interpretation we are reading? Thompson does not offer a solution to this problem. Under his criteria, archaeologists must then be restricted to talking about technology unless we feel that a particular archaeologist is competent to make other generalizations.

The cultural relativists' third solution is related to that of the historical schools in ethnography as well. European archaeologists typify this as the folk-culture approach;[46] New World scholars call it the direct historical one (see Chapters 10 and 11). On both sides of the Atlantic, this approach uses the simple principle of working from the known to the unknown. In archaeological problems, the known are the living people with written records of their way of life, and the unknown are their ancestors for whom no written records exist. Thus, the archaeologist first excavates historically known sites and determines the inventory of cultural debris in them. Because these are historic sites, the archaeologist freely resorts to written records when he interprets his finds. For example, archaeologists working at the historic site of Fort Raleigh in North Carolina[47] found small lead alloy tokens stamped with the names Hans Schultes and Nuremberg. Normally, without written records, one would not know whether these tokens were pendants, coins, or IOUs for trade with Herr Schultes. The historical records tell us, however, that such lead alloy tokens were used for counting by Elizabethan merchants; the tokens were moved across a board marked off into rows like an abacus. Historians also tell us that Hans Schultes of Nuremberg made lead counters that were very popular on the Continent and in England. The archaeologists who discovered the tokens at Fort Raleigh confidently interpreted their finds as counters, and inferred that the colonists expected to engage in commerce not only with the Indians but with their neighbors and Europe. This kind of archaeological interpretation is often described as "text-aided" research. The only analogy involved is the comparison of the archaeological material to the historical texts of the appropriate period.

Once the historic period is well-known, the archaeologist starts investigating older sites—defined as those most similar to the historic sites in their material content. He continues to draw on the historic material for analogies, but as sites become more and more remote in time from the historical record, his interpretations become less and less reliable. Some archaeologists distinguish between "parahistoric" and "telehistoric" sites to clarify the degree of remoteness of the settlements from historic documents.[48] Parahistoric sites belong to peoples who had no knowledge of writing themselves but who are contemporary with literate societies; their customs or affiliations may be mentioned in the written accounts of their literate neighbors. The Iron Age inhabitants of Maiden Castle in Dorset, although illiterate themselves, were subdued by the legions of a thoroughly literate Roman Empire; the conquerors left numerous traces of their campaigns both in documentary records and in the archaeological record. Sir Mortimer Wheeler's fine description of the investment of Maiden Castle in the first century A.D. owes much to the Roman records of the conquest.[49]

Telehistoric sites are those far removed from written records. Star Carr, the Olsen-Chubbuck bison-kill site in Colorado, and Olduvai Gorge are all "telehistoric," and remote from documentary evidence of the human past. According to proponents of the folk-culture or direct historical approach, confidence in the interpretation of past lifeways diminishes as we move from historic to parahistoric to telehistoric sites; analogies to living peoples become less and less secure the more remote we become from written records. Although this would seem to be a completely sensible attitude, the archaeologist generally infers a great deal about behavior from nondocumentary sources. Is the prehistoric bison kill described by Joe Ben Wheat any less vivid than the siege of Maiden Castle described by Sir Mortimer Wheeler even though the kill site is telehistoric whereas Maiden Castle is parahistoric? Although it would seem that text-aided archaeology is certainly useful, confidence in particular interpretations of past lifeways seems to depend on more than the presence or absence of written documents.

The emphasis on functionalism in ethnology has also influenced archaeological thinking about the use of analogy and behavioral interpretation (see Chapters 10 and 11). Functionalist ethnographies integrate various aspects of culture with each other and with the adaptation of the culture as a whole to its environment. Functionalism stresses the notion that cultures are not made up of a random selection of traits, but that cultural traits are integrated in various ways and influence each other in fairly predictable ways. Functionalist thinking is evident in the way that many archaeologists select analogies from the ethnographic data to help them interpret their archaeological finds. Given that several ethnologically known cultures might provide reasonable analogies, functionally oriented scholars suggest selecting those that most closely resemble the archaeological culture in subsistence, technology, and environment—and those that are the least removed from the archaeological culture in time and in space. As an example, let us say we wish to find ethnographic analogies for the Desert Culture sites—the term "Desert Culture" refers to the very old (10,000 B.C. to *ca.* 500 B.C.) occupations of the arid western United States.[50] The archaeological remains in these sites—grinding stones, basketry, sandals, cores, choppers, and some stemmed projectile points—indicate a reliance on gathering food and small game hunting; signs of pottery and agriculture are lacking. The desertic environment was harsh but not infertile as food resources. The functionalists would argue that appropriate analogies might be drawn from the literature on the Bushmen of the Kalahari Desert in southern Africa or on the desert Australians, both of whom rely on gathering and small game hunting in desiccated regions. But the Bushmen and the Australian aborigines are far removed from the Desert Culture in both time and space when compared with the modern Pueblo Indians of the southwestern United States who inhabit some of the same territory once occupied by Desert Culture peoples. The Pueblo are, in fact, probable descendents of Desert Culture peoples and might for this reason provide appropriate analogies. But they have adopted pottery, agriculture, and a settled, village way of life, and their entire adaptation to desert conditions differs from that of their desertic, hunter-gatherer ancestors.

We might go so far as to assume that we might use the Bushmen and Australians for analogies regarding subsistence and technology, but for a Desert Culture trait not obviously dependent upon subsistence or technology, the Pueblo Indians might provide the more appropriate analogy. The problem is that we often do not know which aspects of culture are most closely integrated in a functional manner. For example, perhaps we want to know about the role of sandal-making among the Desert Culture people—whether sandals were produced by men, women, individuals on their own initiative, or formal groups working together. If we consider sandal-making an aspect of technology, we might turn to the literature on Bushmen or Australian material culture in which sandals are sometimes featured. Among both the Bushmen and Australian aborigines, domestic tasks are generally done by women working alone or with one or two helpers. The analogy might lead us to argue that sandal-making was regarded as a domestic task by Desert Culture people and carried out by women who usually worked alone. On the other hand, weaving is men's work among the Pueblo Indians and is carried out in special ceremonial rooms; since much ritual performed there today reflects very ancient Pueblo Indian practices, we might be led to infer by analogy that in Desert Culture times, the weaving of sandals was not regarded as a domestic task and was carried out by men. No matter which alternative we chose, we would probably not have much confidence in our choice.

The most recent literature in archaeology reflects a different attitude toward the use of analogy in archaeological interpretation. The selection of possibly appropriate analogies from the ethnological literature is increasingly being seen as only the first step toward interpretation. Once several different analogies are chosen, the implications of each one are explicitly stated and should be tested against the archaeological data.[51] In our example of sandal-making among Desert Culture peoples, the ethnographic literature provided conflicting analogies. If we want to gain confidence in selecting one or the other analogy, we must state explicitly the implications each would have for the archaeological data and then examine the latter again in the light of each implication. If sandal-making were a domestic task done by women working alone, we might expect to find the raw materials for sandal manufacture associated with tools that more surely represent women's work, such as grinding stones for food preparation. We might also expect to find tools for sandal-making (such as awls and scrapers for preparing fiber) among the debris of most domestic sites. We could anticipate that women working alone might introduce more variation into the finished product than might be the case in products made by group effort or by individuals working in the company of other specialists. A contrasting list of implications for the possibility that men produced sandals could also be made, and both sets be tested against the archaeological data.

Devising test implications is not an easy task. For example, to find a measure for the amount of variation in a finished product one would expect under certain production conditions requires sophisticated measurements, various statistical tests, and often experimentation among groups of living people. Archaeologists willing to make the effort entailed in this approach, however, have found that they are able to discover more about ancient societies than was previously thought possible. Reasoning by analogy is, of course, an important part of this process, but it is only one step in the archaeologist's task. Analogies provide the material from which test implications are drawn; they are no longer ends in themselves.

The use of analogy as only one phase of the interpretative process in archaeology is demonstrated by James N. Hill's analysis of room variability at the Broken K Pueblo site in Arizona.[52] Broken K is a ninety-five-room, one-story pueblo that was occupied from A.D. 1150 to 1280. Hill's excavations revealed that three types of rooms were present at Broken K: large rooms containing ventilators, firepits, and mealing bins; small rooms with none of the preceding features; a third type similar to the large room in all respects and with special features like wall niches, benches, and slab-lined floors. Hill turned to the ethnography of living Pueblo peoples and found there were three kinds of rooms in modern pueblos, used for three purposes. Large rooms without special features serve as living areas where most domestic activities are conducted; small rooms are primarily for storage; some large chambers serve as special ceremonial rooms. Hill then hypothesized that the differences among the room types at Broken K reflected the differences in room functions as observed in the modern pueblos. To test this, Hill turned to the ethnographic data for test implications of the functional differences in rooms, and listed sixteen different implications that could be tested against the archaeological data. For example, if the small rooms were used as storage areas, they would be expected to contain large quantities of food remains, such as corncobs, seeds, and pollen; on the other hand, small rooms should not contain evidence of food preparation or eating, such as small grinding stones, animal bones, and charred food remains. If the large rooms were living space, they should contain a greater variety of cultural debris than the small rooms. If the large rooms with special features were ceremonial in function, they should have no evidence of food preparation, although they might contain serving bowls and certainly some traces of ritual paraphernalia. Hill tested each implication of functional difference against the archaeological data and found that most implications were confirmed. Drawing an analogy between Broken K and modern pueblos provided only the clues that then had to be tested by scientific method.

Chapter 9

Settlement Archaeology

The houses of the Latookas are generally bell-shaped, while others are precisely like huge candle-extinguishers, about twenty-five feet high. The roofs are neatly thatched, at an angle of about 75°, resting on a circular wall about four feet high. . . . The town of Tarrangollé is arranged with several entrances, in the shape of low archways through the palisades; these are closed at night by large branches of hooked thorn. . . . The main street is broad, but all others are studiously arranged to admit of only one cow, in single file, between high stockades; thus, in the event of an attack, these narrow passages could be easily defended.[1]*

Sir Samuel Baker was a practical, down-to-earth Victorian explorer who discovered Lake Albert and investigated the sources of the Nile River in the 1860s. He also happened to write good books, and his accounts of the African interior still sparkle with life more than a century after they were penned. Baker wrote of African life, of architecture and village layout, of strange customs, and of diverse ecological adaptations, even though he did not construe them as such. Much of the archaeologist's work is with the reconstruction of prehistoric settlement patterns, environmental adaptations, and house styles—his objective is the piecing together of a far more complete account of the peoples he studies than that of Sir Samuel Baker, which, while vivid, is at best superficial.

Earlier chapters covered observation and organization of archaeological data, including the classification of artifacts, the erection of

* See pages 336–337 for notes to Chapter 9.

typologies, and the study of subsistence patterns. Houses, architectural styles, storage pits, temple layouts, and city street plans are recovered from excavations too, and described as individual units in the analysis. But they have a context and a relationship to one another, to the artifacts associated with them, and to the people who built and used them. Settlement archaeology is about these relationships.

Settlement patterns are determined by many factors, by the environment, economic practices, and technological skills.[2] Inherited cultural patterns and established networks of human behavior have an impelling influence on settlement patterns in some societies. The distribution of Bushmen camps in the Kalahari Desert is dependent on the availability of water supplies and vegetable foods; ancient Maya settlements in Mexico were laid out in segments dictated by political and religious organizations. Village layout may be determined by a necessity for protection of stock against animal predators or war parties; other settlements may be strung out at intervals along an important trade artery like a river. Population growth and herd density increases can overload the capacities of hunting grounds or grazing areas, leading to new adaptations and alterations in the settlement pattern. Even the positioning of houses is dictated by a complex variety of social, economic, or even personal factors that may defy explanation, especially when the trowel is the only weapon at the anthropologist's disposal.

Settlement archaeology is part of the analysis of adaptive interactions between man and his environment. Thus, like many problems affecting the study of man, the ones involved are multi-disciplinary and complex. The houses and villages of a prehistoric society, as much as the artifacts found in their settlements and the food residues by their hearths, are part of the settlement pattern. This pattern, by its very nature, involves relationships among people who decided on the basis of practical political, economic, and social considerations to place their houses, settlements, and religious structures where they did. Thus, settlement archaeology offers the archaeologist a chance to examine social organization.

Although archaeologists had long stressed the important role played by environment and technology in determining human settlement patterns, systematic research in this field is a comparatively recent development. Several persuasive scholars had approached settlement archaeology from the archaeological standpoint, making a simplistic assumption that settlement patterns directly resulted from interaction between environment and technology. This form of "ecological determinism" was favored by some scholars but has recently fallen into disfavor as the complex factors involved in settlement archaeology become better understood. Gordon Willey, one of the first to study settlement patterns in the New World, investigated sites in the small Virú Valley in northern coastal Peru soon after World War II.[3] Willey's use of aerial photography to locate the numerous sites in the Valley has already been mentioned. His survey traced the changes in distribution and layout of settlement during several millennia of prehistory during which the Valley's economy changed drastically from early farming times up to the Spanish occupation and beyond. The Virú study related the settlement patterns obtained from aerial photography and ground survey to historical events, economic evidence, and social factors. Willey studied the settlement pattern as a reflection of the environment and the technological level of each Virú population, as well as of its social organization and intercourse, all of which affected the sites built. He realized that the Virú settlement patterns resulted from a far wider spectrum of factors than merely environment and technology, and that the study of broad settlement patterns was not a new approach to archaeology but merely a logical extension of the existing methodology. Settlement archaeology has become a fashionable research objective because of Willey's work and the development of sophisticated computer technology which allows far larger bodies of data to be handled than ever before.

The study of settlement patterns involves examining the degree to which human settlement reflects a society and its technology's adaptation to a specific environment. The social, religious, or political aspects of settlement patterns are also important, and many scholars have not only studied the distribution of sites and the sizes of human settlements, as well as minor details of interior layout within houses or settlements, but also tried to reconstruct the more intangible social factors from archaeological data. This approach involves statistically ordered patterning of artifacts and other culture traits within single settlements, an experimental approach that shows great promise and is dependent to some degree on sophisticated use of computers and other mathematical tools through which the data is not only quantified but also analyzed as to its probable reliability. Bruce Trigger carefully defines three levels of settlement pattern, each of them "shaped by factors that differ in quality or degree from the factors that shape other levels."[4] These are, first, the single building or structure, second, the arrangement of such structures within individual communities, and third, the distribution of communities against the landscape. The object of the exercise is not only to study settlement patterns as a basis for interpreting cultures, but also as an aspect of a total view of prehistoric society. Understanding factors that interact to determine a settlement pattern at any of these three levels of abstraction is vital, and is best obtained from anthropological analogy with modern societies. At this level of interpretation, opportunities exist for the careful correlation of archaeological and anthropological data to amplify the raw facts of prehistory.

STRUCTURES

Studying settlement patterns begins with the individual structure. Houses, huts, windbreaks, and other dwelling places have infinite variety, from the crude shelters of grass and sticks used by Stone Age hunters and Australian bands to the elaborate villas of Imperial Rome and Henry VIII's palaces. Temples, fortifications, and even cattle pens are all forms of structures. Domestic architecture may be standardized or differ according to strict modes of variation, some dictated by society, others by the environment. Both societal and environmental factors as well as economic pattern are the most vigorous dictates of single structure design. Rain and snowfall, temperature variation, wind direction and strength—all play their part in determining house design. The mammoth hunters of the western Russian plains 20,000 years ago lived in semisubterranean dwellings with roofs made of skins and mammoth bones, with hearths inside the houses.[5] Theirs was a treeless and Arctic environment and they made full use of the by-products of a resource abundantly available to them, the mammoth. On the other hand, the Tonga subsistence farmers of the Middle Zambezi Valley in Africa live where the midday temperature is often over 100°F, and the nights are hot most of the year.[6] They spend more of their lives in the shade of their pole-and-mud huts than they do in them, the thatched roofs project beyond the walls to form wide verandas; some houses are built on poles to allow passage of the wind under them.

Those with nomadic ways of life tend to make less permanent and elaborate structures. The !Kung Bushmen, hunters of the Kalahari Desert, Botswana, erect small windbreaks of grass and sticks to protect themselves from the prevailing winds and provide shade in the hot months;[7] they abandon the structures when they move camp. The Plains Indians, on the other hand, have their tepees, which are erected wherever a new camp is pitched and are sturdy enough to be used for many years.[8]

Available raw materials are of paramount importance. Mud brick was used to build the earliest cities in the Mesopotamian delta, for stone was not available. Ugandan farmers live in huts with thatched roofs and stake walls, the latter plastered with anthill clay—structures that survive for many years in the subtropical environment. The clay renders the walls waterproof and more resistant to the ravages of white ants. Central Eskimos make igloos out of snow blocks simply because it is the most readily available material; their houses are easy to erect and to heat. The Indians of the American Southwest build homes with heavy walls of stone and clay that absorb the sun's heat and insulate the inhabitants against the extreme cold of nighttime. The architectural style of buildings also depends on the builder's skill, the available raw materials, and the general technological level of his society. Some schools, such as the European and suburban American, build houses that, for the most part, have their weight concentrated in the walls, whereas other styles, such as the Far Eastern, support the roof on a framework of beams and use lighter walls that almost hang from the roof.[9]

In many societies, the limited economic opportunities and an even distribution of wealth result in standardized house plans. The building's size or the rooms in it may reflect such groupings as nuclear families. But as societies and cultures become more sophisticated, so do the wealthier citizens, or those of higher rank, who often live in more elaborate structures, and religious activities or specialized trades such as ironworking, trading, or construction work are concentrated in special buildings. In more sophisticated archaeological sites, the recognition of places of worship or special quarters of a town is a fairly easy matter. Many societies had special structures associated with ritual, readily identified in the archaeological record. The temples of the Classic Maya, exemplified by the pyramids at Tikal (Figure 9.1), rise over 60 meters (about 200 feet) above the plaza floors. Small buildings of one to three rooms were placed at the top of the pyramids, which had rectangular plazas enclosed on three or four sides by large mounds. Numerous carved stelae and altar stones were erected in the plazas; the temples surmounting the mounds were elaborately decorated.[10] The ritual purpose of these structures is obvious, but this fact does not reveal the religion, which is a subject in itself. Historical documents and oral traditions may give insights into the character of the religious ceremonies held at a ritual center, but the interpretation of religion from archaeological evidence is a cautious and speculative business.

Some religions, or peoples, do not have conspicuous ritual centers. Many African societies, for example, have monotheistic cults, associated with a supreme being whose priests often have intercessionary powers with him through ancestor cults. Six hundred years ago, the Karanga peoples of what is now Rhodesia worshipped a god named *Mwari*, with whom they communicated through their ancestors. The priests of *Mwari* were the religious and political leaders whose dwell-

Fig. 9.1   Tikal was the greatest of the Mayan ceremonial centers and was inhabited as early as 600 B.C. This temple dates to the Late Classic, ca. A.D. 700.

ing places were hilltops upon which they lived in splendid isolation from the common people. Two such hills are the famous archaeological sites of Zimbabwe and Mapungubwe in the Limpopo Valley, where rich finds have been made although much of the *Mwari* cult is lost to the archaeologist.[11] Simple rainmaking ceremonies are often carried out in normal dwellings or in temporary shelters; many African groups build spirit houses—small temporary shelters—that vanish completely from the archaeological record. The extent to which religion can be reconstructed from excavated sites depends greatly on the type of structures with which the religion is associated.

Artisans' houses and trading activities can be identified by concentrations of specialized artifacts found in caches in otherwise undistinguished structures. Such hoards should include at least a proportion of unfinished objects to show that toolmakers lived there. In more elaborate sites, trading and workshop areas and even streets have been uncovered. At the early town of Hacilar in Turkey, James Mellaart found potters' workshops in a settlement dating to *ca.* 5435–5250 B.C.[12] At Thebes and El-Lahun in Egypt, minor craftsmen lived in houses of two or three rooms within a walled enclosure, depended on others for their food, and often organized into shifts; information about their activities has come down to us in records from Deir El-Medina, Thebes, where generations of workers who built the Pharaohs' tombs lived for over 400 years.[13] Here again, the historical record allows amplification of elaborate archaeological finds.

How much can be deduced about social and political institutions from house architecture? The size and layout of a building may reflect the family organization of the occupants. Societies may be monogamous or polygamous; in the latter case each wife would have her own kitchen or even her own hut. Some houses may be occupied by nuclear families. In South America, long houses are often associated with lineage organization, and sometimes, with controlled use of anthropological data, particular house types can be related to particular forms of family organization. The problem is complex, for even a standardized house type may have important auxiliary roles, such as the men's clubs found in parts of Melanesia which are long houses. The answer to the above question is to consider all the structures in a site in relation to one another rather than individually, for relationships between structures are sometimes more significant than the houses themselves. Within a single house, a family unit can only be distinguished by interpreting the use of the artifacts found in it, in order to identify different rooms, especially the individual cooking areas.

COMMUNITIES

The layout of communities, using the latter word in Murdock's sense of a "maximal group of persons who normally reside in face-to-face associations" is a greater problem.[14] Both environment and economy limit the size and permanence of a settlement because the ability to gather food and store it is as important as the technology necessary to transport food and process it into edible units. These two major factors are vital, for they determine whether a community lives in one place permanently or must shift camp at regular periods during the year to subsist. How long Bushmen camps are occupied is limited by the availability of water, game, and vegetable foods near the site—so the camp moves at regular intervals. Preliterate Uruk and Ubaid city dwellers in Mesopotamia (*ca.* 4000–3000 B.C.) who used irrigation in their agriculture had no need to move regularly to achieve a stable subsistence cycle.[15]

While the permanence of human settlement is affected by subsistence ecology, the layout of a community is greatly determined by social and political factors, particularly by family and kinship considerations. On a large scale, whole sectors of towns may be reserved for religious or ethnic groups living under the protection of the city rulers. Foreign traders may live in their own quarter, reflected in the archaeological record by exotic objects, unusual houses, or many store rooms. Islamic settlements on the East African coast dating to the late first millennium A.D. contain a proportion of indigenous African pottery, reflecting a cosmopolitan population living under the rule of the merchants at Kilwa and elsewhere.[16] Bruce Trigger cites the presence of Huron captives in historic Seneca Indian villages, attested by many Huron-style potsherds among the Seneca materials,[17] but, without the backup of historical records, these might have been described as trade potsherds and their real social significance misinterpreted. The great cities of Harappa and Mohenjodaro flourished in northwestern India during the third and second millennia B.C., with rigid law, standardized architecture, and utilitarian material culture. The agricultural output at Harappa was under municipal control, flour being produced by organized coolie labor housed in rows of identically planned, squalid two-roomed tenements in a special sector of town. The Indus civilization must have been depressingly efficient and slightly terrifying in its standardized heyday.[18] The relationship of one house to another or of a group of structures to other similar groupings forms the basis for interpreting community settlement patterns. Marriage customs may multiply the number of houses associated with one family unit; a father may live in a cattle camp with his sons, and their families occupy houses within his enclosure. Landownership systems may be reflected in community layout, or perhaps the need for mutual protection against animal predators or humans may be uppermost in the minds of the community. The archaeologist looks for systematic and statistically probable associations of settlement attributes—in the same way he looks for artifact attributes—that may indicate a grouping of social units.

A general systems theory context for these types of study only recently developed in archaeology, but it is serving to structure several important settlement pattern studies involving community layouts and the human rationale behind them, as well as the ecological and other factors affecting them. Work along these lines is flourishing in the

New World. George Cowgill and René Millon have begun a detailed mapping and survey project of the urban area of Teotihuacán,[19] the principal ceremonial center and political capital of the Classical Period in the Valley of Mexico. The size and complexity of the site have meant that an enormous amount of information is available from the innumerable features found at Teotihuacán. Records are being built up on all features detected on the surface; the collections of artifacts from 5,000 separate structures are also being correlated with the aid of computer programs. The major aim of the work is a better understanding of Teotihuacán as a going concern throughout its history, and answers to several questions are sought. What were the number and characteristics of the social classes in the city? Were they rigidly delineated? What specialized crafts were practiced and where? What were the social functions and uses of the different artifacts and structures? Discovering the organization, administration, and population grouping of the city is vital, as is the degree of decentralization of ritual, political, and economic power. Also important are the changes taking place through the period *ca* A.D. 100–700 when Teotihuacán flourished.

William Longacre studied the Carter Ranch Pueblo in east-central Arizona[20] in an attempt to determine changes in human adaptation over the period of occupation from A.D. 1050–1200. The Pueblo consists of a U-shaped block of rooms facing a courtyard, containing such facilities as storage areas, cooking places, and religious structures. A mound of trash lies just east of the site and yielded many burials. The Pueblo as a whole is orientated to the east, and the interior features of the site are generally lined up from west to east. There were at least five periods of construction, and the Pueblo expanded for the most part to the east and south. Thousands of potsherds, complete vessels, stone and bone tools, and other cultural remains were found scattered throughout the site. A conventional analysis of the artifacts suggested that Carter Ranch site belongs within the "late Mogollon" culture, but the problem was to "isolate and explain certain organizational features of the sociocultural system as an initial step toward gaining a better understanding of adaptive changes made by the society to environmental stress."[21] Longacre took Lewis Binford's view of culture as a point of basic theoretical assumption, viewing culture as a "systematic whole composed of interrelated subsystems, such as the social system, the technological system, the religious system, etc."[22] Thus, he had to consider the nature and interrelations of the component parts of the sites or cultures under study and relate them to the region's ecology. He was trying to isolate cultural processes and the means by which cultures change or remain stable.

Before analysis of the Pueblo began, the investigators postulated a research design and set up a series of testable hypotheses. Their central argument was that if "there was a residence rule which led to related families living in the same locale through several generations, then ceramic manufacture and decoration would be learned and passed down within the context of this residence unit (assuming female potters). Non-random preference for certain designs might reflect this social pattern."[23] They also assumed that the "patterning of material remains in an archaeological site is the result of the patterned behavior of the members of an extinct society, and that this patterning is potentially informative as to the way the society was organized."[24]

The Carter Ranch study was undertaken to determine more precisely the environmental and cultural changes of the east-central Arizona region between A.D. 1050 and 1200. Palynology has shown small but significant shifts in the vegetational cover to have taken place from A.D. 700 or earlier. The upland regions of east-central Arizona are dotted with prehistoric sites, dating from about A.D. 700–ca. 1000, whose inhabitants cultivated corn. The uplands can now support only marginal agriculture, and cultivation is confined to irrigation in deep stream valleys. Between A.D. 600–1100, the population was scattered in small communities living in hamlets of three to twenty rooms, linked to the arable lands in the many small floodplains in the area. Overpopulation of a particular village led to the creation of a new one on unexploited land. About A.D. 1100 or slightly earlier, a minor shift in rainfall and slight decrease in mean annual temperature is indicated by pollen diagrams, probably resulting in a shorter growing season and making many upland agricultural plots marginal. People began to converge on the deeper valleys where temperatures were higher, and villages coalesced to form larger communities with more than one residence unit. Great kivas, or ceremonial centers, began to appear at a few sites around A.D. 1000–1100, representing an attempt to integrate the separate villages in the single settlement into a more coherent whole by religious or ceremonial means. This process culminated in the development of a few very large pueblos, each composed of many small villages integrated into a single unit. Carter Ranch straddles the period when this was first taking place.

Longacre and his colleagues used relatively sophisticated computer-calculated statistical operations to analyze 175 design elements, and groups of elements were defined, using more than 6,000 potsherds. Then the counts of elements from occupation floors in the rooms examined at Carter Ranch were correlated with each other using a "multiple regression analysis" and an IBM computer. Two distinct clusters of rooms were identified, one at the south end of the pueblo and the second associated with a kiva at the north end. The thirty-four burials found in the midden east of the pueblo were subjected to design element analysis and it was found that the northern burials were related to the northern room cluster, whereas the more southerly skeletons belonged to the southern group. Burials in the center of the midden were mixed as to design distribution, ceremonial grave offerings were common, and the graves contained design elements from both clusters. The investigators considered this area to be a burial ground for high status individuals.

The two clusterings of architectural units were associated with kivas: burial areas and middens. If the hypothesis that women were the potmakers was correct, the distribution of clusters suggested there was postmarital residence near the wife's female relatives, where ceramic decoration was learned and inherited through the residence unit. Stratigraphic analyses of the potsherds in the trash heaps supported the notion of design continuity. The system of postmarital residence suggested by the patterned distributions implied also that rooms, burial rights, and other nonportable objects were inherited within the residence units, probably in the female line. The archaeological evidence, in the form of kivas, associated burial practices, and jointly used storage areas, favored a corporate residential area maintained by a social unit larger than a family. The inference of descent from archaeological data is extremely difficult, but the corporate residence units and pattern of matrilineal inheritance led Longacre to argue that the residence units may represent localized matrilineal descent groups.

The residence unit is a comparatively large social group. But households, the basic economic and landholding unit, are harder to determine from the archaeological record at Carter Ranch Pueblo; they probably consisted of groups of adjoining rooms forming residence areas. Longacre analyzed the rooms' contents thoroughly in an attempt to discover whether the different chambers had specialized functions or were multi-purpose dwelling areas. He studied the correlation of pottery classes with room types and found, for example, that the pottery types found in kivas or other ceremonial structures were less common on household floors. Brown textured jars showed evidence of having been burned over fires—therefore in use as cooking pots—and were very common in rooms with circular floor pits, as were storage pots; perhaps such chambers were used primarily for cooking and storage. The same rooms also contained evidence of general household activities, as though they had one prime purpose, but other uses as well. Painted pottery, on the other hand, showed no signs of smoke, but the bowls, pitchers, and jars made with painted motifs may have served in the preparation and serving of food; they seemed to be associated with rooms having square firepits and mealing bins. Thus, the Carter Ranch rooms appear to have had a multi-functional use, even though different structures had varying primary roles, a pattern found in modern Western Pueblo architecture today. As a result, the household unit is hard to delimit at this site, in contrast to settlements where the rooms' activities tend to be more specialized.

We have dwelt on the Carter Ranch site at some length, for it demonstrates the effectiveness of the new approach to settlement patterns and social organization in archaeology. Carter Ranch dates to a transition period for the farmers of this Southwest region. Statistical analyses have revealed two distinct residence units that have occupied a single site; the farming population has begun to cluster, drawing in from the scattered village units of the previous 500 years. Palynology has given a tentative explanation of the cause—environmental stress—for establishing a settlement pattern of fewer and larger sites. At Carter Ranch, detailed archaeological analysis has documented the first set of adaptive changes that led ultimately toward the cultural system of the modern Western Pueblos.

Analyses of the type used with Carter Ranch and Teotihuacán are in early stages of development, but have tremendous potential in answering some of the obvious and more sophisticated questions posed by settlement patterns. Why were ceremonial Maya pyramids placed where they were in relation to the rest of the settlement around them? Why was the citadel of Harappa in the Indus Valley placed to one side of the city? What effect did political organization have on the growth of specialized communities? Why were fortifications built, and to protect what? What was the importance of trade in the siting of a village or town? Was it built on a particular site to take advantage of raw materials? Was trading the responsibility of some families, or a universal activity? What were the effects of warfare on a high population of animal predators? The archaeologist is only just developing effective methods and techniques to deal with these problems, for, ironically, much basic evidence of use in settlement pattern analysis already appears in scientific monographs or is buried in dusty museum store rooms.

POPULATION DISTRIBUTIONS

The density and distribution of settlements and population are determined to a considerable extent, as is obvious from the Carter Ranch example, by the natural resources of the region under examination and by the economy and technological level of the population. The requirements of hunters differ from those of agriculturalists, and pastoralists have still different preferences—abundant water supplies and grazing grass. In Africa, for example, the distribution of cattle is determined by the zones of tsetse-fly-infested country, for the insect's bite is fatal to stock and dangerous to men; thus, pastoral populations tend to concentrate in fly-free grassland areas where surface water is readily available.[25] The density of agricultural populations is determined by equally critical factors. The shifting cultivator, for example, the Bemba farmer of northern Zambia, has an understanding of his environment that is astonishingly profound; he can rate a plot's fertility and its suitability for one of his crops by examining the vegetational cover and the soil's physical characteristics.[26] Critical factors are the land's staying power, the number of seasons during which it can be cropped with satisfactory results, and the fallow period required before it can be reused. The "climax" vegetation (mature forest cover) indicates fertility, whereas the successive stages of regeneration of vegetation in an abandoned garden show its readiness for recultivation. Farmers and hunters have equally detailed knowledge of their environments, including medicinal and nutritive uses of many plants, and the stock-raiser possesses a remarkable knowledge of the food values of grazing grasses.

The interaction of many complex factors including those mentioned and other, more subtle ones, such as the carrying capacity of agricultural land, provides a backdrop that the student of prehistoric settlement patterns cannot afford to ignore. Archaeologists and geographers have made numerous successful studies of the relationship between prehistoric settlement patterns and environments, such as the Carter Ranch analysis. Sir Cyril Fox made a pioneer study of prehistoric settlement patterns in England on a countrywide scale with his classic monograph *The Personality of Britain*, published in 1932, in which he studied prehistoric population distributions against a base map of the reconstructed vegetation of prehistoric times and modern topography. He distinguished zones of prehistoric population and an increasing penetration of England's highland areas through time. Other studies have skillfully used settlement pattern distributions to correlate, for example, the earliest farming settlement of Central Europe with the loess soils of the plains occupied by Danubian farmers before 3000 B.C. Work on an even larger scale has been carried out in sub-Saharan Africa from which Desmond Clark and his colleagues have produced an *Atlas of African Prehistory;* this plots the distribution of most known Stone Age sites of all periods on translucent sheets that can be laid on base maps of ancient and modern climate, vegetation, and other critical factors. Distribution studies of this magnitude reflect to some degree the distribution of archaeological research rather than of prehistoric settlement patterns, but the ultimate objective is to produce a basic source in which distributional information is available.

Large-scale studies of geographical settlement patterns depend on thorough site survey and are most effective within narrowly defined regions. Several factors may affect the changing settlement patterns of an area. Apart from natural factors like water supplies or game population, a region may change from being self-sufficient to becoming dependent on trade for such basic raw materials as iron ore or ornamental metals. Some inhospitable regions may support flourishing towns purely on the basis of raw materials, and the population relies on trade to exchange its precious materials for food. Trade increased in importance in Central Africa, for instance, as soon as there was a substantial and regular demand for raw materials above the inter-community level. Traders from India came with the monsoon winds to visit the East Coast of Africa in search of the soft ivory of the African elephant. A regular trade in tusks and metals resulted in exploitation of the far interior, with important trading and religious centers emerging as new centers of population.

Political organization may also affect population distribution, as will warfare. Sotho Chief Mosheshwe of what is now Lesotho in southern Africa saved his people from destruction in the mid-nineteenth century by occupying a fortified hilltop named Taba Bosiu.[27] In preceding decades the Sotho had lived on fertile lowlands west of the Lesotho Mountains. A study of their prehistoric settlement pattern would reflect the major shift in population from the lowlands to the bases and tops of fortified hills like Taba Bosiu because of warfare and political factors. A powerful centralized political organization like that of the Romans is reflected in various types of settlement which, under favorable circumstances, can be related to one another on the basis of architectural style, size, and distribution of population. The size and distribution of Mayan ceremonial centers is an example of archaeological evidence that shows, by the placing of minor ceremonial centers, a relationship between subordinate religious sites and the major one in the center.

SUMMARY

Ecology, warfare, and religion all influence settlement patterns, whether architecture, village or town layout, or wider population distributions. Buildings and town plans are more susceptible to the influence of minor social conventions and whims than the major zone distributions are. A settlement pattern results from a people's adjustment to factors of varying importance that interact with each other.

The three levels of studying settlement patterns—the individual house or structure, the community or settlement as a whole, and the distribution of population within a large zone—yield different data about prehistoric society because of their relationships with each other and the environment. Houses contain information on specialized activities, household units, and family organization. Residence units or communities can be analyzed for data on warfare and trade, religious practices, and even lineage organization and political authority. Larger units of human population add data on the exploitation of natural resources, commerce, and major political groupings. Archaeology is becoming increasingly preoccupied with research projects oriented toward these problems as being essential adjuncts to the analysis of artifacts and occupation residue. The systems approach and new quantitative methods offer exciting prospects for future studies in this field.

Part Three

Frameworks for the Past

The Four Stages of Public Opinion

I (Just after publication)

The Novelty is absurd and subversive of Religion & Morality. The propounder both fool & knave.

II (Twenty years later)

The Novelty is absolute Truth and will yield a full & satisfactory explanation of things in general—The propounder man of sublime genius & perfect virtue.

III (Forty years later)

The Novelty won't explain things in general after all and therefore is a wretched failure. The propounder a very ordinary person advertised by a clique.

IV (A century later)

The Novelty a mixture of truth & error. Explains as much as could reasonably be expected.

The propounder worthy of all honour in spite of his share of human frailties, as one who has added to the permanent possessions of science.

Notes by Thomas Huxley, 1873

Chapter 10

Intellectual Frameworks:
Mercati to Durkheim
(with Linda Cordell)

The archaeological record gives us a broad and tantalizing view of man's diverse adaptations and cultural evolution through the dimensions of time and space. Looking at our long ancestry, we realize that the artifacts of the first toolmaking Australopithecines are the ultimate ancestors of our complex twentieth-century machine tools and computers. We can appreciate the vast amount of time required for man to develop more specialized tool kits, articulate speech, social structure, religious beliefs, and all the other attributes of self-awareness that are distinctively human. More than ever before, in a world of jetliners and instant communication, our knowledge of the unwritten past and of the varied world community combine to reveal the sheer diversity of human experience and life-styles from one end of the world to the other.

This diversity has accelerated in recent millennia. Half a million years ago stone hand axes or chopping tools were in daily use throughout the world of *Homo erectus*. In 1000 B.C., bronze was used by many European societies, iron tools were in use in the Near East, sub-Saharan Africa had no metallurgy and little agriculture, the very early Olmec Civilization was developing in Mesoamerica, and Polynesia was as yet uninhabited by man. Human cultural diversity has mushroomed since then.

The sweeping perspectives of prehistoric time are indeed awesome, and the methods employed to reveal them are well-developed, complex, and widespread. More and more details of man's cultural history are recorded each year, and the pace of discovery threatens to overwhelm us as a "knowledge explosion" occurs in archaeology. Modern cities are constantly expanding as populations increase and man's rapacious demands for living space seek to be satisfied. Housing developments, freeways, dams, pipelines, and other urban phenomena bury the past or destroy it with the blade of a bulldozer. Our knowledge of the past will never be "complete," and if it ever did become so, this objective of archaeology would be insufficient. The facts gleaned from site surveys, excavations, and artifact analyses, and carefully deposited in the pages of learned journals or monographs are meaningless unless they are interpreted, questioned, and tested against general or specific research hypotheses; these, in themselves, form part of the problem-oriented research strategy formulated when site survey or excavation began.

Our discussion so far has been with basic information, the archives of the past that end up in museum storerooms or in excavation notebooks. Regrettably, many archaeological reports go little further than listing facts and cautiously interpreting the finds. Yet these facts should be related to research objectives and conscious hypotheses, for archaeology, as part of anthropology, asks questions about societies and cultures—how they operate, how they change, and what general rules they follow. Archaeologists have an obligation to interpret their data to explain cultural processes and the large- and small-scale changes they detect in the prehistoric past. Indeed, from the beginnings of archaeology, scholars have been trying to reconstruct human history with descriptive models of the past; in this chapter we shall examine more recent attempts to do so. Julian Steward and Frank Setzler posed the question as long ago as 1938: "Shall we hope that the future Darwin of anthropology will interpret the great historical scheme we've erected?"[1]*

RATIONALISM, SCEPTICISM, AND A
NATURALISTIC PHILOSOPHY OF EVENTS

Archaeologists have so far been primarily concerned with "structure"—with the description of forms, be these hand axes, pots, or villages, as they occur in time and space. We have built, like pre-Darwinian biologists, elaborate classifications of prehistoric artifacts based on structural similarities. What then, we may legitimately ask, is the relationship between the different classes of artifacts laboriously erected and actual human behavior? What can we learn of human motives and cultural process? To phrase the question in another way,

* See pages 337–338 for notes to Chapter 10.

we know that human culture has changed in the past three million years, a dazzling palimpsest of stone artifacts, cave art, agricultural societies, and urban complexes—but can we explain how and why this change took place? Archaeologists have addressed themselves to this problem in many different ways and have viewed their role in answering the question in an equally diverse manner.

The interpretation of archaeological data of any kind depended greatly on the notions of the world held by its discoverer. Thus, the medieval peasants who discovered Paleolithic hand axes in the great river valleys of France and England interpreted their finds in the context of their folk beliefs; the hand axes became celestial thunderbolts with magical properties, a reflection of the parochial perspectives of the average peasant and writer of the time. The French farmers knew nothing of the tremendous diversity of mankind that existed beyond the frontiers of their fields and markets, and were shackled by the biblical story of the Creation. Man had fallen; since the Fall in the Garden of Eden when the world was perfect, things had been in a state of decline. Nothing in their world had prepared them to accept the idea that the thunderbolts they cherished were made by men who did not even possess the rather unsophisticated technology of medieval Europe.

The horizons of the European world began to widen very gradually in the eleventh and twelfth centuries. The Crusaders and ambitious travellers, such as Marco Polo (1254–1324), returned with exciting tales of the wonders of the great civilizations of China and the peoples of the Near East. Trade routes, closed since the advent of the Dark Ages, were reopened, with important consequences for the intellectual climate of the later Middle Ages. European scholars were gradually exposed to Muslim scholarship, which had retained an interest in the Classical writers of Greece and Rome, and developed the disciplines of mathematics, geography, and natural sciences far beyond the limited achievements of the Classical civilizations. Trade with the East also stimulated the development of more urban centers in Europe, and an increasingly wealthy urban middle class of merchants emerged. These families found ways to increase their wealth and power outside the rigid frameworks of both the church and the agrarian feudal aristocracy. Intellectually they were far more sceptical than their predecessors, with greater secular concerns and more pragmatic explanations for the past. Thus scholars of the later Middle Ages, such as the Italian Michael Mercati (1541–1593), proposed that the "thunderbolts" found by the European peasants were artifacts produced by men before they knew how to make tools out of iron.[2] The objects themselves, thunderbolts or artifacts, had not changed; they were interpreted differently because man's ideas about his world had changed. Celestial magic was not popular with sceptical fourteenth-century naturalists, although Mercati did not have much evidence to support his interpretations. He did have the writings of Greeks and Romans who speculated about stages in the development of weapons from nails and teeth to stone and wood, to bronze, and finally to iron. A collection of stone artifacts made by American Indians and Asian natives had been brought back to Rome by some explorers and submitted to him for examination. His evaluation of the archaeological finds from European gravels was based on simple analogy rather than supernatural belief.

Today, of course, we have considerably more evidence about the past, much of it based on careful stratigraphic excavations, a battery of dating techniques, and sophisticated laboratory analyses. Yet, perhaps one reason why archaeologists have accumulated evidence in favor of Mercati's interpretation of archaeological finds rather than celestial magic is that we, as scholars, are heirs of the sceptical intellectual climate that sprang up in part from a new awareness of the tremendous diversity of human experience.

Surrounded as we are by the technological accomplishments of twentieth-century technology, it is difficult for us to realize how slowly modern scientific inquiry evolved, and how recently the basic principles of scientific research were developed. The social sciences in particular have been brain children of very recent times, and the archaeologist as a student of human behavior in the past leans heavily upon the research of scholars concerned with the ways in which people behave. Prehistoric research developed hand in hand with the newly fledged field of anthropology, both of them given great impetus by *The Origin of Species*, the acceptance of the Antiquity of Man, and Victorian imperialism, which revealed with even greater clarity the brilliant diversity of man.

Anthropology itself developed out of the radical political and social climate of eighteenth-century Europe. Enlightened writers like John Locke, Thomas Hobbes, Voltaire, and Jean Jacques Rousseau were interested in how they could improve their own society and philosophized about the rules and laws necessary to perpetuate a sophisticated civilization. The naturalistic interpretation of stone artifacts resulted in part from the influence of Newton and Locke who viewed the universe as running like a clock rather than through the hand of God. Did man need despotic government or a minimum of social control? What was the basic nature of man? Man "in a state of nature" did not have the benefits of eighteenth-century European government and civilization. Such peoples' exotic customs and strange appearance were being immortalized by Captain James Cook in the South Seas and Australia and by early travellers in South Africa and North America (see Figures 10.1 and 10.2).[3] The romantics of eighteenth-century Europe depicted contemporary savages in book and lithograph as dancing in Eden-like innocence among pastoral groves. Rousseau particularly glorified the life of "savages," insisting that men would be much better off without the institutions, rules, and repressions of civilization. Hobbes, on the other hand, depicted man in a state of nature as being in constant strife and turmoil; he felt that an absolutist state was necessary for men to live together peacefully. In any case, the eighteenth-century philosophers were aware of mankind's diversity, although their knowledge of other peoples was cloaked in fantasy. The same scholars also questioned their own institutions and held the working assumption that man, thinking rationally, could humanize his government. People like Locke and Anne Robert Turgot (1727–1781) were sceptical of mystical interpretations of the past, and conceived of human society in rational terms. Apparently they were largely motivated by a revulsion against the clerical establishment; they argued both explicitly and implicitly against the church and its interpretation of the world and its history.

By the eighteenth century, European natural science had developed to such an extent that people became aware that the results of science might be applied to the betterment of human life. The explorations of Cook and others had led to some knowledge of primitive societies flourishing at various levels of cultural development. Therefore, a theory of human progress was necessary if men were to improve their lot by formulating better social institutions, and to explain how they had achieved a diversity of life-style far removed from that of the South Sea Islanders.

DEGENERATION AND PROGRESS

Enlightenment thinkers viewed human history in terms of progress, but their ideas were challenged in the closing decades of the eighteenth and the first half of the nineteenth centuries. These were turbulent years, when the French Revolution and campaigns of Napoleon shattered eighteenth-century illusions that man's rational behavior led to improvements in the world. The potency of rational thought was rejected by war-torn and disheartened European intellectuals who doubted the notion of human progress. Scholars like Immanuel Kant (1724–1804), Johann von Herder (1744–1803), and William Godwin (1756–1836) retreated from rationalism in literature, history, and art toward philosophical idealism and romanticism. For the Romantic

IN.ALLAGO

Fig. 10.1 A family of Khoi-Khoi pastoralists from the Cape of Good Hope.

writers, the present was not of particular concern; they retreated into an imaginary past when conditions were better and man's behavior was clothed in glory. During the Napoleonic Wars and the uncertainties caused by the rise of a European industrial society, ideas of

Fig. 10.2 An Australian aborigine with his lightweight hunting kit.

progress and evolution dropped out of sight. Philosophers sought "understanding" through emotional introspection, a theme well illustrated by the emotional romantic poetry of early nineteenth-century Europe. This was the philosophical climate into which Darwinism was born, one of considerable introspection, scientific scepticism, and restless scientific inquiry.

The concept of human progress almost disappeared during the Romantic period only to resurge in popularity in the mid-nineteenth century. Orthodox religious interpretations of the past were widely accepted during the 1920s and 1930s, and the decline of man since Adam's Fall was a logical extension of Romantic philosophy. But the Industrial Revolution and the explosion of scientific knowledge in many fields, among them geology and paleontology, gave rise to a renewed scepticism about religious dogma and simplistic explanations of man's early history. This time, there was a difference—the sceptics backed their arguments with scientific fact. They proposed a rational and naturalistic interpretation of events and human affairs in which the concept of progress played an important part. The increased interest in human progress may also have resulted from a general decline in utilitarianism and religious thought.[4] People feared the threat of intellectual and moral anarchy, resulting from the decline in theological leadership.

The concept of progress, and indeed evolutionism itself, may have been a response to this intellectual and moral atmosphere. We have already traced the events that led up to the acceptance of the Antiquity of Man in Chapter 1—they were part of a long and sustained battle between defenders of the church and antievolutionists on the one hand, and the evolutionists, geologists, and archaeologists on the other. But the acceptance of the Antiquity of Man allowed a long time-scale for the diverse panorama of the prehistoric past, which, with Darwinism, led to modern anthropology incorporating both notions of progress and decline in human history. Whereas eighteenth-century cultural historians such as Jacques Turgot and Marquis de Condorcet had reconstructed human history using hypotheses that emphasized man's progress through successively higher stages of development, C. J. Thomsen, Boucher de Perthes, and other archaeologists, as well as the geologists Sir Charles Lyell and William Smith, were confirming notions of human progress in the past. Other scholars such as J. C. Prichard (1786–1848) and Gustav Klemm (1802–1867) were describing many primitive societies; the latter even proposed a three-stage scheme of human cultural development: savagery, tameness, and freedom.[5]

But the early classical works in anthropology were written after *The Origin of Species* had appeared, many dominated by the idea of evolution, even though some authors denied that they had been influenced by Charles Darwin.

EVOLUTION

Steward and Setzler's remark about a future Darwin is apt, for the natural sciences were revolutionized by his coming. The eighteenth-century Swedish taxonomist Carl Linnaeus (1707–1778) started it all by creating a system of ordered relationships for all living creatures in a great hierarchical scheme. His classificatory scheme covered the whole range of life, providing the framework necessary to science before it could advance toward the possibility of physical relationships and multiple creations. Linnaeus published his great *Systema Naturae* in 1735 (a century before Darwin returned from the *Beagle* expedition), basing his classifications on the structural similarities and differences between living organisms. Loren Eiseley has described Carl

Linnaeus as "drunk with the utter wonder of creation,"[6] an apt compliment to a classificatory genius who was, however, publicly committed to a single Creation and fixed modern species.

French paleontologist Jacques Cuvier was one of the first scholars to study mammalian paleontology and to apply Linnaean taxonomy to fossils found in geological beds. The flamboyant Cuvier described and classified thousands of fossilized bones, and yet was an ardent Catastrophist, relegating man to the period of the latest and final Creation. According to men like Cuvier, the great diversity of human and animal life had come about since 4004 B.C., classified by enthusiastic eighteenth-century scientists into a world "teeming with delighted existence."[7]

Darwin's voyage on the *Beagle,* theory of Natural Selection, and *The Origin of Species* provided a theoretical explanation for the diversity of both fossil and living forms that did not rely on supernatural intervention, hypothetical catastrophes, or other improbable and undemonstrable occurrences. Evolution, by means of Natural Selection, does not, of course, entirely explain biological phenomena. Thus, Darwin observed but could not explain variation in all forms of life. Modern genetics and biochemistry have gone a long way to fill in the gaps, even though some problems still await solution. What Darwin was able to do, however, was to describe a single process to account for biological change through time. "As many more individuals of each species are born than can possibly survive, and as consequently there is a frequently recurring struggle for existence, it follows that any being, if it vary however slightly in any manner profitable to itself . . . will have a better chance of surviving and thus be naturally selected," he wrote, propounding his theory of the "Survival of the Fittest."[8] Before Darwin's work was published, people were concerned only with the description of the structures of forms and with erecting classifications based on similarities of structure. Darwin's theory of Natural Selection was developed through his acceptance of the geological theory of uniformitarianism, confirmed by observations of fossil *Megatheria* in the Argentine and from a multitude of vivid field experiences on the *Beagle* expedition (Figure 10.3). He realized that his theories affected human history. "Light," he remarked cautiously, "will be thrown on the origin of man and his history."[9]

The long timespan of prehistory was to the Victorians a period of unknown length. Not until the twentieth century were accurate chronological methods developed. But scholars began to refine the subdivisions of prehistoric time produced by Thomsen. The Stone Age, for example, was divided into a Paleolithic and Neolithic, both of

Fig. 10.3 A Fuegan Indian of the Tekoenica tribe.

these being subdivided into various stages—the Acheulian, Mousterian, Solutrean, and Magdalenian. As these subdivisions were made, people began to ask what they meant. Did the technology, material culture, and society of prehistoric man develop and progress uniformly from the crude tools of the Somme Valley to the sophisticated iron technology of the La Tène culture of Europe? Had there been natural cultural evolution as well as biological evolution in which man had evolved through various stages from savagery to civilization?

The doctrines of social evolution were already being propounded by such prolific scholars as Herbert Spencer and others even before the publication of *The Origin of Species*. Human prehistory was seen by many as a logical extension of Darwinism, and Spencer, as long ago as 1850, had said, "Progress is not an accident, but a necessity. It is a fact of nature."[10] In 1867 there were exhibits of prehistoric archaeology at the Paris Exposition, arranged and commented upon by French archaeologist Gabriel de Mortillet, a man who declared passionately, "It's impossible any longer to doubt the great law of the progress of man."[11] He and many colleagues, intoxicated by stone tools and the richness of French archaeological sites, regarded prehistoric man in geological terms, with human culture passing through different epochs according to a universal law of progress in all parts of the world. Indeed, when prehistoric research was first extended beyond the frontiers of Europe, attempts were made to use the same rigid terminology, with, however, limited success.

De Mortillet's view of cultural process was highly evolutionary; yet at the very time it was being set up, others were questioning its validity. As archaeological research extended beyond the confines of Europe and into the New World, the diversity of early human experience began to be revealed in the archaeological record. The great civilizations of the Near East were recovered by Henry Layard[12] and others, and the great Mesoamerican religious complexes were described anew.[13] Upper Paleolithic art was accepted as authentic some years after the discovery of the Altamira paintings in northern Spain in 1875 (Figure 10.4).[14] Yet in many parts of North America and Africa there were no signs of higher civilizations. Furthermore, in the case of the New World civilizations and European cave art, man had apparently regressed. The great religious centers of Mesoamerica had been abandoned, and art equal to that from the French caves (Figure 10.5) did not reappear for many thousands of years. People became less and less certain that there was a common universal prehistory of man. The anthropologist Edward Tylor, whose aim was to sketch a theoretical course of civilization among mankind, was fully prepared to admit that human culture had regressed as well as progressed, and by the 1870s many scholars assumed that there had been regressions in prehistory similar to those in the historical period in which they were more than adequately documented. Tylor was one of many anthropologists and sociologists who were beginning to speculate about the society's development in philosophical terms, developing intellectual frameworks for the study of man.

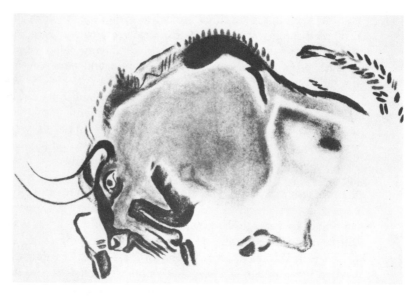

Fig. 10.4 A bison in a polychrome cave painting. The Altamira art represents the ultimate artistic achievement of the Upper Paleolithic hunters of Western Europe.

Fig. 10.5 A giant stag—from a painting in Lascaux Caves, France.

E. B. Tylor

E. B. Tylor (1832–1917) is generally credited with being one of the fathers of anthropology in the English-speaking world.[15] The son of a prosperous manufacturer, he first became interested in the development of human society on a tour of Mexico with the celebrated prehistorian Henry Christy in 1856. Tylor observed the evidence for elaborate prehistoric religion and ritual in the impressive Mayan sites and avidly chronicled the survival of folk customs in modern Mexican peoples, beginning a lifelong study of human culture.[16] At the time he began this work, the serious study of archaeology was gaining tempo, the clerics fighting a rearguard battle against the whole notion of human progress and in particular against the heretical idea that man had evolved from apes and, even worse, a primitive state of humanity comparable to that of modern savages. Tylor and Sir John Lubbock, the articulate author of *Prehistoric Times* and *The Origins of Civilization*, were in the forefront of the battle. The former was an avid supporter of human progress and, like the Enlightenment writers before him, accepted reason as a key to that progress. He took a broad overview of human development from the Paleolithic men of the Somme gravels to Victorian Englishmen, and concluded that life had improved for humanity. Anthropology was an important field of inquiry, for men could free the world from the evils of superstition and barbarism through studying the development of human institutions. Tylor was eloquent in his defense of the study of man:

> The study of man and civilization is not only a matter of scientific interest, but at once passes into the practical business of life. We have in it the means of understanding our own lives and our place in the world, vaguely and imperfectly it is true, but at any rate more clearly than any former generation. The knowledge of man's course of life, from the remote past to the present, will guide us in our duty of leaving the world better than we found it.[17]

Having concluded that man had developed upward from primitive savagery, Tylor then turned his attention to the processes by which knowledge or human skills had been transmitted and studied the causes of culture change, including both invention and diffusion, both major issues of archaeological research in succeeding decades. He sought data from various parts of the world, creating a comparative discipline out of anthropology, comparing one form of an institution with another. This is, by and large, one way in which modern anthropologists work, for they use comparative information in their search for regular associations of cultural phenomena that will help them make general statements about cultural behavior.

Edward Tylor was concerned with the origins and development of "civilized" institutions, particularly those of Victorian England. These he viewed as the highest attainments men had achieved in his day. Their origins, he reasoned, might be found in simpler institutions of ruder peoples. If the stone axes made by the natives of Australia were like the stone axes obtained from the ancient European river terraces, then perhaps the marriage customs of the native Australians were similar to those of the Paleolithic inhabitants of Europe. His data were primarily drawn from two sources: accounts of contemporary primitive peoples and the findings of archaeology. These two sets of data were then ordered to reflect a sequence of development—from the most simple to the most complex. The most complex was, of course, the way the institution existed in Victorian England, the apex of development for Tylor.

Archaeology was crucial to Tylor's search for the origins of European institutions, but little information was available in his time. Archaeologists were busy collecting facts largely obtained from hasty excavations and surface collections without regard to stratigraphic associations. Tylor's scheme of ordering data, from the most simple to the most complex, provided an intellectual framework for these facts and was meant to have universal applicability. This meant that everywhere on earth the development of institutions would be the same except that, in some places, progress had ceased and societies had remained at a lower level. The European sequence from the Paleolithic through the Neolithic to the Bronze and Iron Ages was regarded as an international model. Thus, for example, much time was spent trying to find "the American Paleolithic."[18]

Lewis Morgan

Tylor accepted the Three-Age System but distinguished three different stages of prehistoric development: savagery, barbarism, and civilization. These terms were developed even further by the American anthropologist, Lewis Morgan, who distinguished no less than seven ethnic periods of human progress, outlined in his volume *Ancient Society* in 1877. Morgan's scheme proceeded from a period of Lower Savagery which ended with the discovery of fire, through Middle Savagery culminating in the use of the bow and arrow, and Upper Savagery which achieved the discovery of pottery. Lower Barbarism ended with domestication of animals, whereas iron smelting was the ultimate achievement of Middle Barbarism. Those at a stage of Upper Barbarism invented a phonetic alphabet, and the people of his seventh stage had reached the state of civilization. Morgan has been described as a unilineal evolutionist. His scheme for the progressive cultural evolution of man was based on the assumption that his sequence had developed naturally in different regions, whereas the discoveries of Mayan cities in Yucatan in the early 1840s had precipitated anew issues of diffusion and independent development.

DIFFUSION AND RELATIVISM

Nineteenth-century and much early twentieth-century archaeology was concerned with excavation, discovery, and classification. Scholars were proposing laws of cultural process and were prepared to accept degeneration in cultural experience, and they were doing so increasingly on the basis of the archaeological record. Prehistory was becoming a record of diverse cultural achievement. It was clear that not every prehistoric hunting society had had a period of brilliant artistic achievement and that there were many different regional cultures, societies, and civilizations in prehistoric time widely distributed throughout the known world, each with different distributions, technological achievements, and settlement patterns. By the end of the nineteenth century, archaeology was becoming a record of human cultural achievement set out not as a universal cultural evolution but as a series of numerous and complex regional variations set up in time and space, documenting an immense diversity of human experience.

Cultural relativism began to reemerge as an intellectual concept, replacing the evolutionism of earlier decades. Relativism implied viewing human cultures as having a uniqueness and integrity of their own and not with reference to a single standard of evolution. There was a growth, in other words, of an interest in the specific cultures and societies and a diminishing interest in attempts to build grand schemes of evolution.

The explosion of archaeological knowledge in the late nineteenth century and in America particularly in the early twentieth, led to the gradual realization of human cultural diversity in prehistoric times, but scholars were still faced with the same questions of cultural origin. What were the origins of human culture? When and where was metallurgy introduced? Who were the first farmers? If man did not develop according to evolutionary rules, how then did culture change and cultural diversity come about?

As long ago as the beginning of the nineteenth century, Christian Jurgensen Thomsen and J. J. A. Worsaae had considered the question of cultural process and its effect on the Three-Age System. They had set out a clear role for the process of diffusion in archaeology.[19] The concept of invasions and migrating hordes became especially popular with late nineteenth-century archaeologists who were reacting against the notion of uniform cultural process and who realized that culture change had to be explained in terms of outside influence. The discovery of the new Near Eastern civilizations raised the problems of the origins of such peoples as the Mycenaeans who had been found by Heinrich Schliemann in the 1870s. Many archaeologists began to espouse diffusionist theories, especially when they compared the richness of Near Eastern civilizations with the apparent poverty of European culture. Furthermore, they argued, how could the brilliant New World civilizations of Mexico and Peru have otherwise arisen except through some long distance migration from the civilized centers of the Near East?

Diffusionism found its extreme expression in the hands of Professor Grafton Elliot Smith, who had been greatly influenced by Tylor's writings. The latter pleaded strongly in his widely read books for a study not only of existing preliterate societies, but also of the origins of man and his civilization. Tylor recognized the importance of diffusion in human history and examined in his *Researches into the Early History of Mankind* in 1865 various theories about the origins of civilization and the processes of cultural change. "Sometimes it may be ascribed to the like working of men's minds under like conditions, and, sometimes, it is a proof of blood relationship, or of intercourse, direct or indirect, between the races among whom it is found," he remarked.[20]

By the end of the nineteenth century there were two generalized explanations as to the origin of the cultural changes that appeared in prehistoric times, especially centered around the fact that similar cultural manifestations appeared in different parts of the world widely separated from each other. One theory favored independent invention and development in each area, the same idea as evolution, for evolutionary theory argued that all peoples in all parts of the world developed in a similar fashion, so that similarities are due to similar evolutionary causes. The other theorized that each culture trait had spread from its area of origin to another and so on, diffused by trade, population movement, or cultural contact. Both these theories, that of independent development and of diffusion are, of course, in themselves both entirely acceptable explanations of cultural process in the past. The controversy begins with assessing the relative importance of one or the other; much argument about cultural process in the nineteenth and twentieth centuries has been centered around the role of diffusion as opposed to evolution and the identification of the former or latter in the archaeological record.

Elliot Smith, an eminent anatomist, was the foremost proponent of the diffusionist school. He became Professor of Anatomy at the Government Medical School in Cairo in 1900 and promptly became deeply interested with Egyptology, studying long, unbroken sequences of human culture, in particular the techniques of mummification and embalming, sun worship, and monumental stone architecture. He became obsessed with the complexity of the techniques of Egyptian burial and with other achievements of Nile civilization. In his book, *The Ancient Egyptians*, first published in 1911, he argued that world civilization and much of modern Western culture was diffused from the Nile Valley. He and his disciples, notably W. J. Perry, were the chief supporters of the diffusionist view of the growth of human culture.[21] Both Elliot Smith and Perry envisaged the settlement of the world by small groups of Egyptians who carried out long maritime voyages, colonizing and civilizing the world. They thought that the Mesoamerican civilizations were derived from Egypt and abandoned all pretense at scientific method in their theorizing.

The diffusionist view of human history, like that of universal evolution, is far too simplistic but appears to have appealed widely to archaeologists simply because it was a simple explanation of what was becoming an increasingly complex picture of the human past. It was not until the 1920s that some scholars, notably Gordon Childe, investigated more closely the complexities of culture change in prehistory. The conflict between diffusionists and evolutionists was really precipitated when archaeology began to back away from its predominantly geological concept of the past. Late nineteenth-century anthropology yielded a wealth of descriptions of preliterate peoples in many different environments, and geographers were becoming aware of environment's importance to human culture. Both anthropologists and archaeologists began to realize that they were studying series of human cultures rather than series of geological epochs, the former being distributed through space and time. The early part of the twentieth century was a time of readjustment when archaeologists became preoccupied with the distribution of prehistoric cultures reconstructed through their material remains as preserved in the archaeological record. Diffusion, like relativism, stood in radical opposition to the evolutionism of the nineteenth century.

EMIL DURKHEIM AND FUNCTIONALISM

Emil Durkheim (1858–1917) was a French sociologist of great brilliance whose career began at a time when faith in reason, the order of nature, and social progress was still strong. Durkheim became an active scholar at a time when the evolutionary theories of Darwin and Spencer were the leading scientific ideas of the nineteenth century.[22] Although he espoused the evolutionary hypothesis and the use of the comparative method in both anthropology and sociology, he was critical of both and adopted an "organismic" view of society, which is, in a sense, a manifestation of the relativistic theme in early twentieth-century anthropology. Durkheim's organismic view of society stresses viewing the system as an integral whole. Hence, Durkheim's focus was generally on specific societies or institutions rather than on the total evolutionary frameworks that Tylor, Morgan, and others were attempting to construct. His methodology was aimed at making sociology an empirical study, using research methods employed in the sciences. He tried to work with social facts as "things," using data that could be observed, classified, and explained, rather than merely deduced from arbitrary postulates such as evolution. The "hard" sciences were his research model; his basic assumption was that social institutions are exterior to the individual and exercise constraint over him, and as such, they can be studied as part of the individual world. Thus social facts come to an individual from society, and must therefore be explained in terms of other social facts, not in terms of biological, psychological, or other factors.

Durkheim regarded social facts as those societal items that the individual has in common with others in his group—as society within the individual. Social facts were distinct from the biological consciousness that defines a unique individual. He defined social function: "The 'function' of a social institution is the correspondence between it and the needs of the social organism."[23] The needs of a society are related to, but on a different level from, those of the individuals in that society, and the latter are born into a social world as much as they are into a physical one. Indeed, the conditions of existence of the individual are often different from those for the existence of society, and must be studied separately.

Durkheim has been named the Father of Functionalism in the social sciences, and his functional method, based on the premise that social life is the functioning of social structure, has had a profound effect on the anthropological methodology of the twentieth century. In fact, both diffusionism and functionalism were expressions of this theme of relativity. Diffusionism led to a view of each culture as a distinct phenomenon, a product of so many historical accidents, processes of diffusion, whereas functionalism viewed each culture as a thing that needed investigation in its own terms. Both, then, rejected the single standard of evolutionism that was the hallmark of Tylor, Spencer, and the other evolutionists. Functionalism became popular in the social sciences, and many scholars were influenced by Durkheim's theories, among them Robert Lowie, Edward Sapir, Ruth Benedict, A. R. Radcliffe-Brown, and Bronislaw Malinowski.[24] The study of cultures in their "intertwined state" became a major preoccupation in anthropology and affected Childe and other archaeologists who were wrestling with large bodies of archaeological information. Malinowski (1884–1942) was the individual who made the integrated study of culture a popular method in anthropology, and practiced and preached functionalism throughout his long career. His view of functionalism in anthropology was forthright: "The functional view of culture lays down the principle that in every type of civilization, every custom, material object, idea and belief fulfills some vital function, has some task to accomplish, represents an indispensable part within a working whole."[25]

Malinowski had little concern for reconstructions of the past from archaeological evidence, advocating the functional method for studying the workings of modern culture. His own fieldwork in the Trobriand Islands, living as a Trobriander himself, had convinced him that culture can only be studied by an intimate knowledge of an individual and his cultural environment. Malinowski stands with Radcliffe-Brown,[26] a theoretician of the first order, as one of the authors of modern functionalism.

The combined approaches to the prehistoric past of limited evolutionary reconstruction, diffusionist hypotheses, and to a lesser extent, functionalism and Boasian cultural relativism led to the urgent necessity for adequate definitions of human culture both in archaeology and anthropology. This was reflected in a number of integrative schemes for prehistoric remains, a trend that started with V. Gordon Childe in the Old World and Alfred Kidder and Max Uhle in the New. Archaeologists had begun to realize that the days of great overall theoretical conceptions of the prehistoric past were over, at any rate until much more information was available.

Chapter 11

Toward Explanation: 1900 to the 1970s
(with Linda Cordell)

FRANZ BOAS AND ARCHAEOLOGY

In the first half of the twentieth century, anthropological writing began to incorporate the idea of diverse cultures, but writers on either side of the Atlantic emphasized different aspects of cultures than those that could be derived by viewing them as wholes. American scholars imbued their writing with a philosophy that was perhaps closer to the romantic and idealistic philosophy of the nineteenth century whose roots had been in European nationalism. Anthropological writings in the Old World tended to reflect not only idealist philosophies but also ideas from biology. Many prominent figures in American anthropology between the two World Wars were men who had emigrated to the United States, their families still possessing nineteenth-century nationalist philosophies.

Franz Boas

Franz Boas (1858–1942) was the dominant figure in American anthropology in the early twentieth century. He was born in Germany, of German-Jewish extraction, and received a liberal education in Europe, a training that brought much idealist, intellectual thought into his anthropological work. After writing a doctoral dissertation in physics, he developed an interest in physical and cultural geography and began his anthropological career with a trip to Baffinland in 1883. His work there was a decisive experience and he described the Eskimo as "a man as we are: that his feelings, his virtues and his shortcomings are based on human nature, like ours."[1]*

Franz Boas was a fanatical worker who trained many enthusiastic and gifted students with whom he undertook the massive task of establishing anthropology as a descriptive science. Boas maintained that anthropology had too many theories, too many broad generalizations, and too little hard data. He had a passion for collecting, classifying, and preserving vast quantities of raw data. His descriptions of such peoples as the Kwakiutl were detailed and carefully marshalled into precise categories.[2] He had a zealous concern that only the strict methods of the sciences be used in anthropological fieldwork; he grew more and more sceptical of theoretical anthropology in his later years and concentrated on intensive research within limited areas.

Boas's influence resulted in a spate of publications that would hardly appeal to the general reader. There were many ethnographies of American Indian tribes in which material cultures were described in almost pitiless detail; monographs contained detailed linguistic studies and, of course, research into culture-trait distributions. Archaeological reports of the 1920s and 1930s emphasized artifact classifications and meticulous examination of archaeological finds, with little behavioral interpretation. Although Boas for the most part was not very interested in archaeology—indeed, through the period his career covered, archaeology and ethnography tended to grow apart—he was, with his student Manuel Gamio, among the first to demonstrate a stratigraphic sequence, at an Aztec site in Mexico.[3] The Boasian influence on archaeology was a healthy one because during this time serious stratigraphic, chronological, and descriptive studies of the pre-Columbian Indian began.

Boasian anthropology tended to draw little from archaeology because archaeologists could only account for culture viewed from the outside, and Boas was interested in understanding cultures from the inside—the criteria, principles, values, and categories of the people themselves. In addition, he was interested in understanding cultures historically, i.e., how they developed. His goal in anthropology was thus twofold: subjective understanding and historical comprehension. His historical technique was that of diffusion, which allowed him to study traits objectively and not subjectively—one need not understand the subjective significance of an artifact to observe its distribution. So Boasian anthropology could expect little from archaeology to contribute to the subjective understanding of peoples, but could expect much from archaeology to understand peoples historically.

* See pages 338–340 for notes to Chapter 11.

Archaeology felt the influence of the Boasian school in a way that inhibited interpretation. The descriptive reports of the 1920s and 1930s resulted from more scientific methodology. These detailed descriptions would have significant implications for anthropology. Boas and his students were involved with publishing a permanent record of the aboriginal cultures of American Indians before they adopted Western ways. Fieldworkers spent much time taking down oral traditions and folktales, as well as enormous lists of such culture traits as types of moccasins, designs of bows and arrows, and hut styles. Much valuable information was, of course, obtained, but the interpretations of aboriginal culture were often fallacious and disproved by archaeological research. For example, American ethnographers of the time regarded the arrival of Europeans and especially of domestic horses as an event of the greatest importance, the Great Plains quickly filling with nomadic buffalo herders and raiders of the type made familiar to us by Hollywood films. The Plains were described as sparsely populated before the arrival of the horse because of a water shortage and a lack of ploughs to till the soil. Yet the work of archaeologists like W. D. Strong, who dug at Signal Butte, Nebraska, revealed that the Great Plains had in fact been inhabited by hunters and horticulturalists for many hundreds of years before the Europeans and their horses turned the plains into a macabre carnival of nomads.[4]

Archaeology, then, became a source of information against which one checked historical reconstructions produced by ethnologists, but the Boasian school considered that archaeology could only yield extremely limited kinds of information about prehistoric culture. Boas and his students, perhaps reflecting the German idealist tradition that was part of their intellectual roots, stressed an understanding of the subjective features of culture rather than its objective or phenomenal features—those that could be directly observed, such as artifacts and house types. In short, they wanted to understand culture from the inside rather than the outside. This placed severe limitations on the value of archaeological data, for the archaeologist could not come into contact with the people he studied, and, therefore, could not be expected to discover much about their subjective life. His finds were limited to the results of technological achievement, subsistence, and settlement patterns. But according to the Boasian point of view, all such cultural traits could vary randomly from culture to culture and give little insight into its spiritual and emotional basis. This approach led archaeologists to view their interpretive tasks in terms of stratified levels that become progressively more difficult to achieve. Technology was seen as easy to describe. Subsistence, at the next level, was thought to require more interpretation and to be a more difficult undertaking. The highest levels of abstraction were those of ideology and belief systems, almost impossible for the archaeologist to reconstruct from his finds.

Another implication of Boasian thinking for archaeological interpretation was reflected in the much greater concern for the construction of typologies from the 1920s onward. Archaeology began to reflect Boas's interest in the history and distribution of individual cultural traits. Descriptive typologies were developed to compare artifacts from one site with those from others; it was no longer enough to know, for example, that two sites hundreds of miles apart both contained obsidian arrowheads. If the distribution of such artifacts was being discussed, far more information was required than merely the evidence of presence at two widely separated locations. Modern typological archaeology owes much of its philosophy and importance to Franz Boas.

One problem central to Edward Tylor's interpretation of the development of institutions and also to the theories of diffusionists was a failure to emphasize that the various institutions in any human culture are normally interrelated. Early anthropologists had little notion of the many diverse cultures in remote parts of the world. In the early twentieth century, anthropological writing began to incorporate the idea of diverse cultures. Boas and his students saw human behavior as a vast spectrum of alternatives from which each group of people might select their own unique complex of behavior. For example, men might make their living by an infinite variety of means. They could, like the Fuegans, be hunters and gatherers, or alternatively, could concentrate on fishing or shellfish collecting. Others might cultivate wheat, oats, and barley, or depend on domestic stock for their livelihood. They might live in a variety of house types ranging from brush shelters to skyscrapers. Their beliefs might encompass one god or ten. The Boasians thought that each human culture selected a different configuration of institutions from the vast array of alternatives, the particular grouping they chose making that culture unique. No one set of alternatives was any better than another. The anthropologist strove to understand the society he was studying by steeping himself in its ideas and subjectively appreciating it. Because each culture was unique, it could not be compared with any others on an objective scale or be considered any better.

This notion of the incomparability of cultures is called "cultural relativism." Each culture selected traits and institutions from numerous alternatives. A given culture could be seen to accept some ideas from one of its neighbors and others from another, many traits being acquired by diffusion. The Boasians were particularly interested in the history of institutions and how these were modified by different groups of peoples; they made many field studies, of which Spier's study of the Sun Dance on the plains is a typical example (see Chapter 10). This type of historical reconstruction is one that can easily lead to erroneous conclusions. Undoubtedly, Boas's greatest contribution to archaeology was in the area of data collection, but his theory of cultural relativism, tinged with a diffusionist flavor, had a considerable effect upon archaeological thinking in the early twentieth century.[5]

V. GORDON CHILDE

Vere Gordon Childe (1892–1957) was an Australian who came to Oxford as a postgraduate student and to archaeology from comparative philology. He began studying European archaeology hoping to find the cradle of the Indo-European peoples and to identify their prehistoric culture.[6] Childe was excited by Sir Arthur Evans's discoveries of Minoan Civilization and by the prehistoric sites of Thessaly, which had been uncovered for the first time in the early decades of this century. After a brief excursion into Australian politics in 1921, Childe turned to his life's work, the study of prehistoric European civilization, a mammoth task that involved him in the identification, classification, and chronological ordering of a multitude of sites and archaeological cultures. He published his first synthesis of European prehistory in 1925, *The Dawn of European Civilization*, the sixth edition appearing in 1957, a few weeks before his death. *The Dawn* was planned to demonstrate by archaeological evidence that Europe "was indebted to the Orient for the rudiments of the arts and crafts that initiated man's emancipation from bondage to his environment and for the foundation of those spiritual ties that coordinate human endeavours."[7] This remarkable book was followed by a series of important publications including *The Most Ancient East* (1928), *The Danube in Prehistory* (1929), *Man Makes Himself* (1936), *What Happened in History* (1942), *Social Evolution* (1951), and *The Prehistory of European Society* (1957). Childe's basic conception of European prehistory was based on diffusionist principles, although he rightly eschewed the grand-scale approach of Elliot Smith and Perry, and the continuing influence of Oriental civilization on European barbarians. He was a brilliant linguist who absorbed from German scholars the concept of an archaeological culture "defined but not constituted by pottery and representing a people,"[8] and based his chronological frameworks on stratigraphic sequences of potsherds in the Danube area and by cross-connections with dated wares in the Aegean. His basic aim was to distill from archaeological remains "a preliterate substitute for the conventional politico-military history with cultures, instead of statesmen, as actors and migrations instead of battles."⁹ Childe's approach to prehistory was founded on Marxist sympathies and a firm conviction that we have meaningful lessons to learn from man's rational, intelligible progress from the earliest stages of his history.

Childe is best remembered by European archaeologists for his innovations in archaeological method, the basis of his encyclopedic syntheses of human progress. He defined cultures based on surviving, characteristic culture traits like pots, implements, house forms, or ornaments, that were constantly associated together. Such cultures were the material expression of "peoples," and might have widespread or limited distribution in time and space, although they were not a chronological concept. These firmly enumerated principles formed the basis of all Childe's work and that of his many students who were soon classifying archaeological cultures not only within Europe and the Near East, but also in widely flung corners of the British Empire where prehistoric research had begun to flourish. Childe had little interest in New World archaeology, so that the impact of his ideas was less profound in North American circles.

The modified diffusionism of Gordon Childe became standard archaeological theory in the 1930s and 1940s—but it was based on the best methodological principles then available. Cultural successions were built up within limited geographic areas and compared to those from neighboring regions, carefully checking those culture traits that have spread from one area to another. Childe's methodology has formed the basis for most modern research in the Old World, except that his diffusionism has been modified by a greater understanding of cultural evolution and independent invention as factors in Old World prehistory. He saw the emergence of food production and, later, urban, literate society in the Near East, perhaps in two great stages, those of the "Neolithic and Urban Revolutions." The modified diffusionism and concepts of Neolithic and Urban Revolutions passed imperceptibly into the textbooks and popular books of a generation of students and interested laymen. Gordon Childe himself was a superb popularizer whose accounts of European prehistory, the origins of civilization, and social evolution were widely read not only by archaeologists but by scientists and many laymen interested in a plausible account of human origins.¹⁰ Yet Childe virtually ignored the New World civilizations, and wrote a prehistory of parts of the Old World rather than a prehistory of man, a task only recently attempted by Grahame Clark and others.¹¹

Gordon Childe distinguished a general evolutionary progression in human economic and social life from the homotaxial stages repre-

sented by sequences of archaeological cultures. He visited the Soviet
Union in 1934 and discovered the potential of Marxism for explaining
the development of prehistoric cultures. He took over some Marxist
terms, actually borrowed from Lewis Morgan, and applied them to
the archaeological stages separated by his two revolutions: Paleolithic
and Mesolithic coincided with savagery; Neolithic was barbarian; the
Bronze Age in the Near East was equivalent to civilization.[12] Childe's
"Marxism" was mild and basically confined to the idea of the economy
being the integrating force in society, the structure of the latter being
determined by the mode—the means of production or technology
available for achieving society's recognized goals. Later editions of
The Dawn were as much influenced by Malinowski's functionalism.[13]
He lacked the detailed appreciation of the importance of environmental
change and ecology in prehistory that characterizes the work of such
scholars as Grahame Clark and Stuart Piggott, who followed in
Childe's footsteps, although realizing that control of the environment
through time was a vital factor in later prehistory.

To a considerable extent, Childe's work ended at the frontiers of
the present ecological approach to prehistory. He delivered a series
of lectures in Birmingham which later appeared as a book entitled
Social Evolution (1951). In this provocative volume he sought to discover,
by systematic comparisons of prehistoric cultures occupying roughly
equivalent levels of development, the regularities of cultural evolution.
His comparisons were consciously objective; he made it clear that
the technological criteria he derived from Lewis Morgan were taxonomic in nature and not processual. "Revolution," he wrote, "does
not purport to describe the mechanism of cultural change. It is not
an account of why cultures change . . . but of how they change."[14]
Thus, he recognized "correlations" between sociopolitical institutions
and techno-economic stages, but he did not attempt to choose from
these correlations the functionally interrelated institutional structures
common to each stage. Childe eschewed simple parallelism in evolutionary development, and emphasized the phenomena of cultural
convergence and divergence, thus coming close to the ecological approaches to archaeology characteristic of this decade.

Archaeology is largely a descriptive discipline, and Childe realized
that cataloging was useless unless conducted within some frame of
reference. Childe's models were really twofold, a technological-
evolutionary one, based on the familiar Three-Age System, and an
economic model in which the way of getting one's living is a criterion
for comparison. He attempted to infer social and political institutions
from archaeological data in the full realization that archaeological finds
are a limited tool for this purpose. How successful he was must await

the judgment of future scholars who work less immediately under his mighty shadow. While his interpretations of the past will provoke discussion, no one can deny his enduring contribution in the areas of classification and chronological ordering and in his insistence upon the relationship between the civilized and barbarian peoples of the Old World. Gordon Childe laid his imprint on the procedures and terminologies of Old World prehistory so firmly that his influence is likely to be felt through our lifetimes.

Those generalizing about cultural process have been concerned for the most part with a form of diluted evolutionism, modified by a modest diffusionism and an admission that independent invention and parallel evolution are sometimes possible. The schemes of V. Gordon Childe or the anthropologist Leslie White[15] are mainly so general that they are hardly significant when faced with the enormous bodies of information now at archaeologists' disposal. Childe tended to consider cultural evolution in terms of autonomous cultural principles and hence tended to ignore the more detailed interrelationships between culture and the environment.

NEW WORLD ARCHAEOLOGY: 1920-1950

In the Old World, Thomsen, Worsaae, and Montelius laid the groundwork for the predominantly stratigraphic and chronological approach to prehistory characteristic of European archaeology, which was further developed by Gordon Childe and other modern scholars. New World archaeologists, whose background was more anthropological and oriented toward data collection and the direct historical approach, had increasing difficulty communicating with one another as more and more regional cultural sequences were developed in the 1920s and 1930s. The term "culture" was used in so many diverse ways that some common yardsticks of comparison had to be devised and formal descriptive terminologies developed. The most widely used was the so-called "Midwestern Taxonomic Method" developed by W. C. McKern and others before the Second World War.[16] The Midwestern taxonomy was based on formal similarities between different assemblages and had no chronological implications. Such terms as "assemblage," "components," "foci," "aspects," and "phases" were a series of hierarchical names used only to classify sites and broader groupings of settlements. Prewar American thinking did not emphasize cultural change, for the great evolutionary sequences of Old World prehistory appeared telescoped in the Americas, where few societies had moved beyond hunting and gathering or simple agriculture. The major preoccupation was with ethnographic description, with classification, and with working backward from known historical sites into prehistory.

This "direct historical approach" probably owes its origin to the Boas school and to W. D. Strong's work in the plains of Nebraska. It involves working from the known, historic period sites to the unknown, prehistoric settlements, preferably those of known peoples. The historical sites provide a fixed datum point to which earlier sequences can be tied, and a series of specific problems that serve to link archaeology and ethnography in the search for solutions to common cultural problems. This approach was applied with success to the Inca Civilization of Peru, where the continuity of prehistoric culture was emphasized rather than its discontinuity, with rewarding results (Figure 11.1).[17]

The regional specializations of the 1930s were less fashionable by 1940 when James Ford, James Griffin, and Gordon Willey began a massive synthesis of unpublished archaeological data from hundreds of sites excavated during the Depression.[18] Their studies of the eastern parts of the United States revealed a steady development of prehistoric material culture over many thousands of years. A series of periods could be distinguished within which broad similarities of prehistoric culture could be discerned, and the periods became developmental stages. This work was extended by Willey and Phillips in an important monograph in 1958,[19] in which they applied essentially the same techniques to the whole of the New World, devising a series of developmental stages for the entire continent. Their stages are defined on the basis of technology, economic data, settlement pattern, art traditions, and social factors, with chronology a less important consideration.

In the 1940s and 1950s, American archaeologists moved away from taxonomy toward the study of cultural processes in the past, viewing millennia of culture history against the complex and ever-changing environment.[20] This move had taken place earlier in the Old World, where prehistory was longer and climatic changes more obvious. The new emphasis on interpretation was based on carefully studied regional culture sequences from which emerge some broad trends in cultural development, showing some resemblance to the theoretical evolutionary stages of earlier archaeology. One conclusion is obvious—man's material culture and social organization have developed from the simple to the infinitely complex. So accounts of world prehistory or broad syntheses of large culture areas must allow for the general notion of progress in prehistory. Much recent archaeological writing has described the progress of man through various stages, in which he had progressively more effective mastery over

Fig. 11.1 An Inca settlement built high in the Peruvian Andes, Machu Picchu was forgotten for 400 years after the site's abandonment when the Spaniards arrived. It was rediscovered by the American explorer Hiram Bingham in 1912, and is a beautiful example of adaptation to a mountain environment.

his environment. Childe with his revolutions,[21] Robert J. Braidwood in the Near East,[22] and Gordon Willey in North America[23] have all attempted to look at culture history from the standpoint of human culture being in constant and dynamic relationship with its environment and other factors interacting with it. Mid-twentieth-century archaeology has come a long way from the taxonomy and classification of earlier decades.

ECOLOGICAL APPROACHES TO ARCHAEOLOGY

We have seen how Gordon Childe's approach to the European past lacked the lively appreciation of the importance of environmental change and cultural ecology that characterizes recent research. But he began, in his latest writings, to move closer to an ecological approach to prehistory.[24] Grahame Clark, who began his career in the study of Post Glacial hunter-gatherers and early farmers in Northern Europe, has long advocated an ecological approach in a series of important articles and books, the most famous of which are his *Prehistoric Europe: The Economic Basis* (1952) and his classic report on the Star Carr excavations.[25] Clark's ecological studies are about people and how they lived, not about things, and now that the chronological problem has to a large extent been solved by the advent of radiocarbon and potassium argon techniques, increasing attention has been paid in the Old World to cultural ecology. The move toward an ecological

303

approach was less self-conscious in Europe than in the New World, where only in the last few years have archaeologists moved away from the direct-historical approach and a major concern with stratigraphy, classification, chronology, and areal studies. American scholars were busy building up local sequences rather than wider syntheses—one detects here some Childean influence and a persistent concern with major evolutionary and mildly diffusionist schemes for the past. Although there had been some attempts at culturally ecological studies before 1950, only recently have such approaches had a real vogue, in part due to great expansion of research in the wake of increased funding for archaeological work, to more rescue campaigns, and to more professional workers in the field. American archaeologists have begun to analyze the processes of culture change that they have been observing for years and to compare them with others. This trend has been strongly stimulated by the training in the theory of cultural and social anthropology given to every American archaeologist.

In 1948, W. W. Taylor published *A Study of Archaeology*, a critique of American archaeology's overriding preoccupation with chronology.[26] Every issue of archaeological journals was crowded with reports of arid pottery chronologies, with little reference to their context or meaning in human terms. Taylor called for a "conjunctive approach" to archaeology, a shift of emphasis from chronological sequences and distributions to detailed studies of individual sites and their features, such as cultural layers, floors, or hearths. The "conjunctive approach" entailed bringing together all possible sources of evidence on a site—technology, style, ecological evidence, architecture, and information on social life—to study the people behind the site and the processes of culture change involved.

A Study of Archaeology was, for its time, a controversial statement and suffered from a lack of examples to support the theoretical polemic.[27] But a number of new departures in archaeology were stimulated by the monograph. Radiocarbon dating provided an opportunity for lesser emphasis on chronology, and settlement pattern archaeology came into vogue in the early 1950s. The potential of settlement archaeology for ecological and social inferences is obvious, but it is, as Gordon Willey has pointed out, a convenient point for the "conjunction" of inquiry into other aspects of prehistoric societies.[28] The last decade has seen the publication of many studies in which settlement patterns of individual structures and whole sites or distributions of settlements have been integrated with detailed analyses of pottery types and other artifacts to throw light on kinship and social organization.[29]

Julian Steward has attempted to develop a methodology for "determining regularities of form, function, and process which recur cross-culturally among societies found in different cultural areas."[30] In contrast to the unilinear evolutionists, who postulated that all societies passed through similar developmental stages, and the cultural relativists, Steward accepted multilinear evolution as a basic assumption—whereby "certain basic types of culture may develop in similar ways under similar conditions but that few concrete aspects of culture will appear among all groups of mankind in a regular sequence."[31] Tylor, Morgan, Childe, and White had all sought to think of cultural development in terms of universal stages, but Steward tried to look for causes of cultural change, developing a method for recognizing the ways in which culture change is caused by adaptation to environment. Steward called this process cultural ecology, arguing that similar adaptive processes occur in other cultures in similar environments—thus the cross-cultural regularities that result are functional. No culture has ever achieved a stable adaptation to its environment, and differences and changes during periods of cultural development in any area are not only more complex, but involve new cultural patterns. Cultural development should therefore be thought of as the emergence of successive levels of sociocultural integration. These, unlike the developmental taxonomies of Tylor, Morgan, and others, are simply regarded as a tool for studying cultures of different complexity.

Steward defined culture types on the basis of cultural features and characteristics represented by a particular developmental level. His cross-cultural regularities are identified on the basis of regular associations of basic cultural features, known as the *cultural core*. These have "similar functional interrelationships resulting from local ecological adaptations and similar levels of sociocultural integration."[32] The traits that make up his culture core have the advantage, from our point of view, in that they often consist of items identifiable in the archaeological record. The culture-core concept is a research device designed to isolate and define distinguishing characteristics of particular culture types abstracted from all data on hand. To Steward, a cultural type consists of core features "that, first, are determined by cross-cultural regularities of cultural ecological adaptation, and second represent a similar level of sociocultural integration."[33] For example, patrilineal bands among the Bushmen, Australians, and Fuegians are a cultural type because the ecological adaptation and level of integration are similar in each case. The environments of these groups differed greatly, ranging from desert to cold and rainy plains, but the practical requirements of the hunting and gathering techniques grouped the people into small patrilocal exogamous bands, each with its own territory. The structure and social function of the bands in each area were very similar, but their adaptations to their environments were similar in terms of function rather than in specific detail. Steward assumed that the existence of a culture trait at a given locality was due to diffusion. He argued that diffusion does not explain the occurrence of certain critical cultural features; one must look rather to the relationship between environment and culture to explain many features of a cultural system. In this sense Steward was carrying a form of functionalism in a direction counter to diffusionism; he was pushing American anthropology to a new view of culture, different from that of Boasian diffusionistic thought. Steward's approach represents a new historical theme that replaces the diffusionist one that dominated American anthropology during the early part of this century.

The acceptance of Steward's theories involves using cultural ecology as both a research problem and a method of interpretation. He asked whether the adjustments of human society to various environments require characteristic modes of behavior and chose those cultural features most closely related to subsistence activities and economic arrangements to answer the question, trying to isolate those aspects of the environment considered by the people themselves as having the greatest importance. Steward recognized as his central thesis that "cultural ecological adaptations constitute creative processes."[34]

Environment has been relegated to a secondary role by Boas and others who believed that the environment is passive and that man's culture has developed because of his selection of certain environmental possibilities while ignoring others. At the other extreme, the environmental determinist believes that forces in nature determine human culture, which is passive. Both approaches have had their advocates among archaeologists and need not detain us here.[35] Steward and the cultural ecologists reject the notion that either culture or the environment is passive, paying closer attention to constant and dynamic interactions between cultures and their environments. Some of the most sophisticated research in archaeology is taking place in this area, as archaeologists wrestle with developing a meeting ground between the necessity for a broad overview of cultural process and the need to look at each particular changing culture in the archaeological record and its micro-adaptation to a dynamic environment. We are as much concerned with the question of why in archaeology as we are with how, the direction in which much energy was expended by earlier scholars.

EXPLANATION AND VERIFICATION

Archaeologists generally agree that there are three basic objectives for their discipline: reconstructing culture history, reconstructing past lifeways, and the study of cultural process. Most of this book has

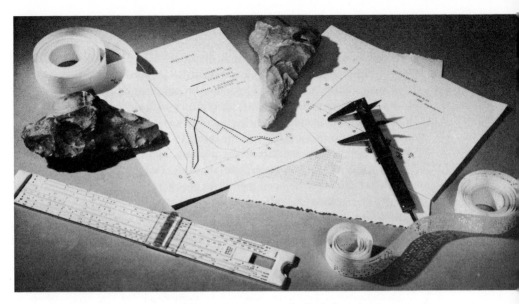

Fig. 11.2 "Still life with hand axes, 1968"—a pleasing group by D. A. Roe showing not only two hand axes, but also the tools of the modern typologist of Stone Age artifacts.

been taken up with a consideration of the first two aims, and we have shown how achieving the third has been regarded as unfeasible by some scholars and as a matter of despair by others. But although some scholars' curiosity about the past has been satisfied by the development of new chronologies and a whole battery of sophisticated aids for studying living floors and prehistoric artifacts, others have faced the challenge of explaining cultural process and are taking archaeology in new directions (Figure 11.2). It is safe to say that our discipline is on the threshold of a new era of discovery in which explanation of the past is as important, if not more significant, than description. The concern with explanation is a recent one, for in 1958 Willey and Phillips were able to say that "so little work has been done in American archaeology on the explanatory level that it's difficult to find a name for it." Although such studies as the Virú Valley project had been remarkably successful, many scholars were despairing, citing the limitations of archaeological evidence and its fragmentary nature as reasons for avoiding explanation.[36]

Several developments have moved us to new thresholds of investigation. The first has been the discovery by social scientists of Systems Theory, the second the advent of computers and quantitative methods for artifact classification, and the third a realization that cultural ecology—the study of dynamic relationship between culture and environment—was a promising approach to interpreting the past. Several archaeologists have been particularly active in developing new

307

methods of investigation, among them Lewis Binford, William Long-acre, Stuart Struever, and D. L. Clarke.[37] The 1960s saw a reevaluation of the scientific methods of archaeology, from which it became evident that much archaeological interpretation was unscientific and based on intuition and insufficiently rigorous data. In other words, we needed to develop a more scientific approach to the past that would employ normal scientific procedures in analysis of archaeological data with the objective of attempting explanation as well as description.

Lewis Binford has been the most vigorous advocate of more rigorous scientific testing in archaeology, arguing that statements about the historical, functional, or processual significance of the archaeological record have so far been evaluated on how far our knowledge of contemporary peoples can be projected back to prehistoric contexts and on our judgment of the professional competence and honesty of the archaeologists involved with interpreting the past.[38] Simple induction has been the basis of inferences about the archaeological record, based on guidance from ethnographic data and experimental archaeology. Binford argues that although induction and inferences are perfectly sound methods of understanding the past, independent methods of testing propositions about the past must be developed and be far more rigorous than the time-honored value judgments based on the assessment of professional competence.

Under the normal scientific method, a research problem is approached from a collection of observed data that enables one to pose research hypotheses about the reasons for the observations made from the data. The hypotheses may concern processes of change: Why did barbed harpoons develop larger bases during the occupation of a hunting camp? Why did the Magdalenian culture replace the Solu-trean in the Les Eyzies Caves of southwestern France? How and why did the hunter-gatherers of the Near East turn to agriculture and domestic animals for their livelihood? Alternatively, the hypotheses may touch on relationships: What is the relationship between two neighboring but contemporary sites with major differences in food residues and implements of tillage? A new pottery type suddenly appears in a Midwest cultural sequence: Is it the result of trade, population movement, or invention? The artistic style of the ornaments in one Iron Age La Tène cemetery in Central Europe is markedly similar to that of another burial ground hundreds of miles away: What was their stylistic relationship?

Working hypotheses are nothing new in science, and we have been using them unconsciously in archaeology for years. What is new, however, is the development of new research strategies based on verifying propositions through hypothesis testing. These propositions in turn raise others, also subject to proof or disproof. An accepted proposition is one that has been tested against archaeological data and against other alternatives that have been rejected. Once proved, it joins the body of reliable knowledge upon which further hypotheses can be erected which may, in their turn, require additional data or even entirely new approaches to the excavation and collection of archaeological information.

Although the use of scientific method in archaeology is only now gaining ground, the results from its use have been both productive and provocative. Scientific method implies the use of high probability statements rather than generalizations with little quantitative validity, and any proposition is calculated on the basis of the hypotheses and testing procedures used in its formulation. Binford and his colleagues also challenge the assumption that the incompleteness of the archaeological record precludes reliable interpretation of the nonmaterial and perishable components of prehistoric society and culture. All artifacts found in an archaeological site have functioned within a culture and society with reference to many perishable factors like fashion or decorative motifs, each of which has, in itself, a history of acceptance, use, and rejection within the society concerned. The artifacts found in the sites are far more than material items that functioned in the society without reference to the many, often intangible variables determining the form of the objects preserved. Binford argues that "data relevant to most, if not all, the components of past sociocultural systems *are* preserved in the archaeological record."[39] The archaeologist's task is to devise methods for extracting this information that deal with all determinants operating within the society or culture being studied. Accessible or inaccessible phenomena of the past on the basis of empirically tested propositions are the real criteria for recovering the prehistoric past rather than the archaeological record. Thus we lack the methodological sophistication and scientific method and must develop them before much progress in explanation in archaeology can be expected.

SYSTEMS THEORY

In recent years some archaeologists have become aware of systems theory and have introduced some of its ideas and concepts into the study of lifeways in the past. Systems theory involves complicated abstract ideas that are often hard to grasp without a scientific background. Information and games theory which follow on logically from the systems approach are even more mathematical, and although claimed to have some archaeological significance, these are still the province of specialist mathematicians turned archaeologist. Yet some understanding of what systems theory has to offer archaeology is important to any scholar of the past, even if he has no intention of using it. The basic principles of "general systems theory" were enumerated by 1950 and are readily accessible in lucid publications. A system is defined by A. D. Hall and R. E. Fagen as being "a series of objects together with relationships between the objects and their attributes."[40] The components of a machine are a system, as are the neurons forming the brain or the cells forming a living organism. Thus, a system is concerned not only with objects and their individual features but also with the relationships between them. Obviously, the items and relationships within the system that are important will change according to the problem under investigation. The type of rock used to make a stone hand axe is obviously irrelevant in studying the house design and layout of activity areas on a living floor. If all elements in a system interact with one another, then some are clearly more important than others, and the research problem, be it in archaeology, physics, or sociology, concerns only those items in the system that affect, are affected by, or change in response to the way in which the system behaves. "Open systems," those that are dynamic and tend toward growth and diversity, are probably the group to which human society belongs, and offer the best prospect for studying diverse human adaptations through time.

To mention some important concepts of systems theory, we can do no better than quote James Doran's recent able summary:

> Important concepts of system theory are those of *self-regulation* (or *homeostasis*), *positive* and *negative feedback*, *oscillation* and *dynamic equilibrium*. Perhaps the easiest way to convey the meaning of these terms is by an example. Consider a class of school children left by their teacher to work by themselves, and suppose that we are primarily interested in the overall noise level which the class generates. Initially the noise level will be low but it will soon start to climb as each child, hearing more noise around him, makes more noise himself. This tendency of the noise to amplify itself is an example of *positive feedback*. At length, however, we may assume that the noise level will reach such a pitch that the more responsible, or timid, members of the class will attempt to quieten their fellows. Now the greater the noise, the greater the dampening effect, and we have an example of *negative feedback*. The overall effect is that the class will settle to some particular noise level by a process of *self-regulation*. Of course, there will be a certain amount of *oscillation* in the noise level, both in the initial adjustment period, and even afterwards. When the teacher returns he will find that the class has found its way to a state of *dynamic equilibrium* in that although, of course, the individual components of the system (the children in the class) are far from motionless, the system

taken as a whole is unchanging. In fact, the equilibrium is also *stable,* in that any outside intervention which changes the noise level, for example a brief visit from another teacher, will, within limits, have only a temporary effect.

This example gives, of course, only a general impression of the meaning of these forms. It is possible to make them considerably more precise and to construct equivalent mathematical models. These latter, however, will be capable of productive use only in a few of the situations to which the original informal definitions apply.[41]

What relevance does systems theory have to archaeology? Very simply, the basic assumption is made that sociocultural systems are integral whole units. Under this notion, such parts of the system as material culture, social organization, settlement pattern, and economic life are merely subsystems that are arbitrarily abstracted by the research scholar for separate study *as part of the whole system.* The whole sociocultural system is "a unit system in which all the cultural information is a stabilized, but constantly changing network of intercommunicating attributes forming a complex whole—a dynamic system."[42] Clearly, then, material culture and, indeed, all archaeological finds should be studied with reference to their former linkage within a sociocultural system. Lewis Binford, perhaps the most eloquent advocate of explanation, roundly states that "culture is . . . the system of the total extrasomatic means of adaptation. Such a system involves complex sets of relationships among people, places, and things whose matrix may be understood in multivariate terms."[43]

This view of human culture is most useful when we are interpreting or explaining cultural process, settlement pattern, or ecological adaptation. The adaptation theme runs right through this book and through archaeology, the study of fossilized human behavior. Human society is a mechanism, like culture, oriented toward survival and, like the ecosystem of which it is part, will change in response to an alteration in another part of the system to which it belongs. Then, simplistic explanations of culture change in archaeology hardly accurately reflect the actual situation, and clearly no one element in any cultural system is a primary cause of change, since a complex range of different factors—for example, rainfall, vegetation, technology, social restrictions, and population density, interact with one another and react to a change in one element in the system. Human culture is, therefore, from the ecologist's viewpoint, merely one element in the ecosystem, a mechanism of behavior whereby man adapts to his environment.

Kent V. Flannery, who has worked in both the Near East and Mesoamerica, has turned to systems theory to explain culture change. He points out that most archaeologists look at culture as a set of shared beliefs and contends that this view of culture is inadequate to explain culture change; culture changes through time and through space, and therefore shared beliefs must also change. Flannery, along with other system-oriented archaeologists, views human behavior "as a point of overlap (or 'articulation') between a vast number of systems, each of which encompasses both cultural and noncultural phenomena—often much more of the latter."[44] Minor changes may occur in any one of the systems involved and will cause readjustments in the other systems until a new state of equilibrium is reached.

Flannery's systemic view is the point of departure for his discussion of the origins of agriculture in Mesoamerica between *ca.* 8000 B.C. and 200 B.C.—which certainly counts as a major cultural change. The adaptation of the preagricultural peoples of Mesoamerica who later became agriculturalists, Flannery maintains, was not to a given environment or even a microenvironment, but to a few plant and animal genera whose range cross-cut several environments. Using the palynological and faunal analyses of preagricultural sites, Flannery listed the different plants and animals upon which these people depended. The list included maguey (century plant) leaves, the fruits of various cacti, the pods of mesquite trees, white-tailed deer, cottontail rabbits, wild water fowl, and wild grasses including wild corn. Some foods were available the year round, such as the maguey leaves and the cottontails. Others—mesquite pods and deer—were exploited during the dry season, but the cactus fruit and other species were only eaten during the rainy season.

To obtain these foods, the people had to be in the right places at the right times, and the right time depended on the particular plants and animals rather than on the people. Flannery refers to the planning of a group's movements so that it will be in the right place at the right time as "scheduling." The entire food procurement system of a group will then depend both on the seasonality of the particular plant or animal and on the scheduling of the hunters and gatherers. A minor change in any one procurement system will be reflected in the group's scheduling and might preclude exploiting those foods whose seasonality conflicts with the new schedule.

Regulatory factors that prevent exhausting food supplies are obviously important in this connection, too. Genetic changes in two food plants, corn and beans, through time made these plants more important than they had been to the people who used them. Both plants became slightly more productive and this slight increase in productivity acted as positive feedback for their procurement systems. Gradually, more time was spent on corn and beans, and the groups had to reschedule their activities to accommodate this change. Because a group could not be in two places at once, those foods that were procured at times when corn and beans had to be planted or harvested would necessarily be neglected, and negative feedback might be said to have operated in their procurement systems. The role which systems theory plays in the study is rather limited and Flannery does not claim much for it beyond the avoidance of oversimplification in research design and hypothesis testing by attributing major cultural change to a single factor like the discovery that corn could be cultivated.

Another American archaeologist, James W. Judge, recently used a systems theory orientation to discuss the differences and similarities in two types of Paleo-Indian projectile points—Folsom and Midland— found in many sites in North America.[45] In some Southwest and Texan sites, the points have been found in association with an extinct form of bison; they date from about 10,000 B.C. to 7000 B.C., making them among the oldest distinct lithic types in America. Folsom and Midland points are quite similar in appearance and have been found together in a few sites. Both types of points are about 5.1 centimeters (2 inches) long, have concave bases and are beautifully pressure-flaked on both faces (Figure 7.13). Folsom points, unlike Midland ones, have a characteristic flute on each face, produced by the removal of a thin longitudinal flake from each face, and are also somewhat thicker than Midland points. There has been some dispute in the literature about whether Folsom and Midland points should be considered two different archaeological types or not. Judge maintains that in order to explain the differences in the two kinds of points, we must consider the production of each kind as part of a total system; in this way, we see that at each phase of production, constraints are built into the system that affect the form of the finished project.

Judge details the production process involved in making Folsom points, and derives his data from experiments in making points in laboratories as well as from the study of waste-flake material recovered from archaeological sites that contained Folsom points. The first step in Folsom point manufacture is the preparation of a large rectangular, bifacially flaked blank from a suitably large flake (Figure 7.13). One end of this blank is then bevelled by pressure flaking, and a nipple-shaped striking platform is prepared on the other end. The first flute is removed from this platform; the same shape of striking platform is then prepared for a second time and the second flute (on the other face) is removed. The unfluted tip of the point is then snapped off. The basal concavity on the finished point is the result of the platform preparation necessary for the fluting to be completed.

Midland points were produced from thin, unifacially flaked blanks. These were worked by careful pressure flaking until they reached the characteristic Midland shape. This shape includes a basal concavity, but this was not the result of preparing a striking platform for removing longitudinal flakes, since Midland points are not fluted. Judge sees the early step in the production process (preparation of a striking platform) as a constraint upon the eventual Folsom point shape. The basal concavity in the Midland points, however, is a final step in shaping the point. Judge offers two propositions that might explain the difference between Folsom and Midland points and could be tested against empirical data. The first proposition is that the makers of Folsom and Midland points could not control the width and thickness of the initial flake blanks. If they were wide and thick, Folsom points were made; if they were thin and narrow, however, Midland points were produced. This proposition could be tested through controlled experiments by examining the shape of the cores used to derive the initial flake and by tests on the kinds of stone used. His second proposition is that the producers of Folsom and Midland points could control the width and thickness of the original flake and that the two kinds of points produced served two different functions, or were just two different fashionable designs. The empirical data that would refute the first proposition would lend support to the second one.

While Judge's analysis of Folsom and Midland points is of great interest, and his propositions will undoubtedly be tested in the future, one wonders whether he might not have reached the same deductions and basic research design without using the terminology and ideas of the systems approach. As Hole and Heizer have recently pointed out,[46] systems theory is so new that its potential is largely unrealized in archaeology. David Clarke and James Doran have both approached the problem from complicated, mathematically based angles that daunt the nonscientist, and much basic theoretical inquiry will be needed before systems theory can replace what David Clarke called "the murky exhalation which passes for 'interpretative thinking' in archaeology."[47] Certainly archaeological thinking and research will benefit from such better organized and more objective conceptual frameworks as, theoretically, systems theory offers. Many elements of human cultural systems are not capable of being quantitatively tested, nor is it possible to measure with the necessarily rigorous degrees of mathematical activity the actual volumes of such concepts as positive feedback which archaeologists have begun to use in some field studies. The value of systems theory is that it allows us to put archaeological situations into a wider systems framework for research purposes, especially those concerned with behavior, organizations, and ecological adaptations. Preliminary results, which appear at intervals in these pages, are promising, and we can expect systems theory to take its place among other diverse research tools of the archaeologist, fenced around, as are other methods, with limitations and restrictions of usage and definition.

Although most archaeologists would agree with Binford and his colleagues that the reconstruction of culture history, ancient lifeways, and the delineation of culture process are central aims of archaeology, there is great disagreement on method and theory. "The major methodological and theoretical points of contrast," says Binford, "involve distinctions between cultural analogies and homologies, between culture viewed as a summation of traits and culture viewed as a system, between units of observation and units of analysis, between inductive and deductive approaches to the archaeological record."[48] What Binford is really arguing for is an elaboration of method and theory using the latest data collection and storage techniques and advanced quantitative analytical methods, which in themselves require a rigorous scientific method and new theoretical ground. "We assume that the past is knowable; that with enough methodological ingenuity, propositions about the past are testable; and that there are valid scientific criteria for judging the probability of a statement about the past,"[49] Binford adds.

The next decades will see the elaboration of a new theoretical structure for much of archaeology based on the systematic application of testable propositions to the archaeological record; the objective will be to study variability in the functioning of cultural systems in the past, with the ultimate aim of formulating some fundamental laws of cultural dynamics. It remains to be seen whether we are on the threshold of a major change in the evolution of archaeology. Certainly the quantitative armory now at the archaeologist's disposal will aid our search for explanations in archaeology.

Chapter 12

Conclusion

"The Professor ... declared that apes had hippopotamus majors in their brains just as men have. Which was a shocking thing to say."[1]*
Many archaeological sites have been dug since the Victorian public learned with shock of its primate origins. The emergence of archaeology as a serious and popular field of investigation has been a cultural phenomenon of this century. Sixty years ago, professional archaeologists were few and far between; now museums, archaeological surveys, and universities are staffed with trained graduates. A flood of monographs and learned journals devoted to antiquity has been accompanied by a spate of popular literature on the subject. Television specials and articles in the *National Geographic* and other periodicals have led to great public awareness of the prehistoric past. Reconstructions of the Australopithecines making their living in the African savannah are commonplace in popular literature and textbooks, and spectacular archaeological discoveries merit prominent headlines in many newspapers.

But why do we study archaeology? Why does it have such widespread popular appeal? The glamour and romance of discovery have often been cited as reasons for lay interest, but this notion of archaeology has become less fashionable as more and more students are exposed to its methods at their schools and universities. The urge to collect and to own is a strong human impulse, one that receives gratifying reward through archaeology. For centuries, the spectacular monuments of the Nile Valley have been raped for their riches, and

* See page 340 for notes to Chapter 12.

modern times have witnessed the systematic plundering of tombs and every type of site, even shell middens, both for valuable finds for the antique market and for "Indian arrowheads." This ruthless exploitation of archaeological sites may gratify profit-hungry dealers or the acquisitively curious, but the damage to human history is incalculable. Fortunately, some nations have implemented rigorous antiquities laws, which have slowed the export of valuable artifacts. But many countries have lagged in this respect, despite UNESCO declarations and the lobbying of professional archaeologists. As a result, much of man's earlier history is lost forever, even though some of his finer artistic achievements are displayed, out of archaeological context, in museums and private collections (Figure 12.1).

Our interest in the remote past stems from philosophical considerations, too. We live in a world of urban environments and crowded humanity, surrounded by sophisticated technology and constant pressure. Our society has yet to create social mechanisms that will allow us to live in harmony in a technological world, using machines for our benefit and that of our polluted and shrinking world. As population pressures increase, and the crisis in cities deepens, we find a nostalgia for the simpler days of the past. The songs of the 1930s are revived; *Time* and *Newsweek* run articles on the "good old days";

Fig. 12.1 Reindeer and salmon engraved on an Upper Paleolithic (Magdalenian) antler fragment from Lorthet, France.

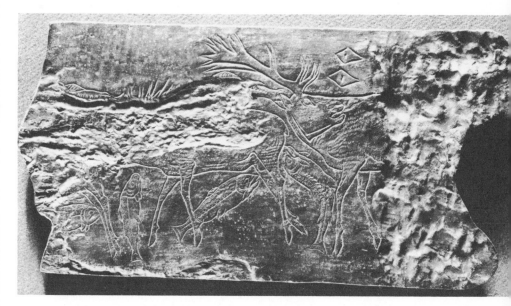

copies of the artifacts of fifty years ago fill boutiques and department stores. Perhaps we are seeking an outlet for our philosophical longings for a less complicated and slower world like that of prehistoric man, where life was determined by the seasons of vegetable food and the movements of game. Our ardent internationalism leads many to study anthropology and the great diversity of mankind—many then proceed to a study of archaeology, to insights into a less complicated world based on subsistence economies and controllable technology. Archaeology has achieved a relevance in many people's eyes simply because it enables them to gain a lengthier perspective on their experience than merely that of the 5,000 years of written history.

Archaeology has a more pressing relevance to many of the world's peoples for whom prehistoric times lasted until the twentieth century. In parts of Africa, Asia, and Latin America, many former colonies have received their independence and developed a fierce and proud nationalism. Like governments throughout history, they seek historical justification for their actions, but the precolonial history of such countries as Kenya or Tanzania has never been written down and can only be recorded through oral tradition or archaeological research. It is no coincidence that African governments are supporting excavations, the results of which sometimes appear in school publications before they do in learned journals.[2] Thus archaeology has a direct relevance to many new nations, and is fulfilling a vital educational role in writing national histories. A distinction should be made here between such activities, based on the latest methods of archaeological research, and attempts to use prehistory for political ends. A notorious example was the racist type of archaeology conducted by some European countries between the wars; more recently, the Zimbabwe Ruins in southern Africa have been the subject of political concern (Figure 12.2).[3] Fortunately, most such attempts are based on unsound reasoning or bad research, but their propaganda value is still regarded by their initiators as useful.

All over the world archaeologists are busy digging up the past and interpreting their findings for their colleagues. Many scholars pay lip service to the educational value of their discoveries, but do little to disseminate their results to schools or the public. Yet archaeologists have a responsibility to do this because research is often supported by public money and the findings may illuminate the history of an Indian community or African population and have a special relevance to their modern descendents. The prehistoric periods of American history may be remote to twentieth-century white Americans, but they are far from irrelevant to the American Indian who may still live in areas inhabited by his prehistoric forebears. Very often his historical education takes no account of the archaeological

Fig. 12.2 *The ruins at Zimbabwe, Rhodesia, which was a trading and religious center of the Karanga peoples of south-central Africa in the second millennium* A.D. *Most of the Great Enclosure, or Temple, was built later than 1400* A.D.

sites he sees every day. Archaeologists have so far failed to rise to this educational challenge, as urgent as that of writing the histories of new nations. We should not allow this vital objective of archaeology to be obscured in the morass of methods and techniques used for reconstructing and explaining the past.

Much of this book has dealt with objects of, and theoretical approaches to the past and with the basic workings of archaeology. The excitement of the subject is difficult to communicate: the pleasure of gaining a new perspective on our long history as human beings, or of handling the artifacts of our forebears, or of visiting the sites where they lived. Secure in our cushioned, twentieth-century world, we forget our awesome and long ancestry among the Australopithecines over five million years ago and, like the Victorians, ignore our primate origins and "primitive" past. Dr. Hastings Banda, the President of Malawi, caused a ripple some years ago by saying that he wished he could erect Stonehenge on the highlands of central Africa to show the world that the British also had a savage past.[4] His remark is apposite. If this book has given you an awareness of the prehistoric past, then it has succeeded in its task.

319

Notes

Chapter 1
INTRODUCTION

[1] For a discussion of the Classical writers' views of the origins of man, see J. H. Plumb, *The Death of the Past*, London, 1969, Chap. 1, and Glyn E. Daniel, *A Hundred Years of Archaeology*, London, 1950, pp. 14–16.

[2] The best accounts of the early antiquarians are in Daniel's *Hundred Years*, already referred to, pp. 16–24, and the same author's *The Origins and Growth of Archaeology*, London, 1967, pp. 33–56.

[3] William Camden is discussed at length by T. D. Kendrick, *British Antiquity*, London, 1950, pp. 134–168.

[4] William Stukeley has been the subject of a delightful biography by Stuart Piggott, *William Stukeley: An Eighteenth-Century Antiquary*, Oxford, 1950. The same author's *The Druids*, London and New York, 1968, is also informative on Druidic cults.

[5] John Aubrey, *An Essay towards the Description of the North Division of Wiltshire*, written between 1659 and 1670.

[6] Glyn E. Daniel's *The Idea of Prehistory*, London, 1962, pp. 1–61, is relevant here.

[7] Richard Colt-Hoare, *History of Ancient Wiltshire*, 1810–1821.

[8] For an illustration of some "thunderbolts," see Michael Mercati's *Metallotheca* (published in 1717—he died in 1593).

[9] The original publication is *Archaeologia*, 1800, p. 204; but there is a reprint in Daniel's *Origins and Growth*, pp. 58–59.

[10] This type of literature is perpetuated in more modern versions by some religious sects. For example, Watchtower Bible and Tract Society, *Did Man Get Here by Evolution or by Creation*, New York, 1967.

[11] These events have been described many times. One good account appears in Daniel's *Idea of Prehistory*, pp. 23–61.

[12] The *Oxford Dictionary* defines a uniformitarian as "One who attributes geological processes and phenomena to forces operating continuously and uniformly."

[13] Alan Morehead's *Darwin and the Beagle*, London, 1961, is "must" reading for everyone interested in Charles Darwin. Michael T. Ghiselin, *The Triumph of the Darwinian Method*, Berkeley, 1969, is an admirable critique of Darwin's published works.

[14] Boucher de Perthes, *De la Création: Essai sur l'origine et la progression des êtres*, Abbeville, 1838–1841; *Antiquités Celtiques et Antédiluviennes*, Abbeville, 1847. These accounts are only for those with a strong interest.

[15] John Evans, "On the Occurrence of Flint Implements in Undisturbed Beds of Gravel, Sand and Clay," *Archaeologia*, 1860, 38:280–308.

[16] T. H. Huxley, *Man's Place in Nature,* London, 1863. Huxley's prose style is justly famous and worth reading for its own sake. A good biography is Cyril Bibby, *T. H. Huxley: Scientist, Humanist and Educator,* London, 1959.

[17] The succinct summary by Gordon R. Willey, "One Hundred Years of American Archaeology," in J. O. Brew (ed.), *One Hundred Years of Anthropology,* Harvard, 1968, pp. 29–55, is probably the best account of the development of New World archaeology available, and it is drawn heavily upon here.

[18] J. L. Stephens, *Incidents of Travel in Central America: Chiapas and Yucatan,* New York, 1841.

[19] Thomas Jefferson, *Notes on the State of Virginia,* Philadelphia, 1801.

[20] Caleb Atwater, "Description of the Antiquities Discovered in the State of Ohio and other Western States," *Transactions and Collections of the American Antiquarian Society,* Worcester, 1820.

[21] *The American Antiquarian and Oriental Journal,* 1884, 6:96–97.

[22] F. H. Cushing, "Preliminary Notes on the Origin, Working Hypothesis and Primary Researches of the Hemenway Southwestern Archaeological Expedition." *Seventh International Congress of Americanists,* Berlin, 1890, pp. 151–152, 163, 167, 170–172.

[23] For a discussion see J. G. D. Clark, *Archaeology and Society,* Cambridge, 1939, pp. 17–37, and James Deetz, *Invitation to Archaeology,* New York, 1967, pp. 1–20.

[24] J. G. D. Clark's *Archaeology and Society* contains much discussion of this point, as does Stuart Piggott's *Approach to Archaeology,* London, 1959, Chaps. 1–2.

[25] For more information see Lewis R. and Sally R. Binford (eds.), *New Perspectives in Archeology,* Chicago, 1968. We return to this subject in Chapter 11.

[26] Bruce Trigger, "Aims in Prehistoric Archaeology," *Antiquity,* 1970, 44:26–37.

[27] Probably the most comprehensive study of theoretical problems in archaeology is D. L. Clarke, *Analytical Archaeology,* London, 1968, though it is not recommended for beginners.

[28] This point is well made by James Deetz in his *Invitation,* pp. 1–2, and by Gordon R. Willey and Philip Phillips, *Method and Theory in Archaeology,* Chicago, 1948, pp. 1–7.

[29] This point was made forcibly by Glyn Daniel in an editorial article in *Antiquity,* 1969, 43:86–87.

[30] J. G. D. Clark, *Archaeology and Society, Chap. 1.*

[31] John Dent, *The Quest for Nonsuch,* London, 1962, and Martin Biddle, "Nonsuch Palace 1959–60: An Interim Report," *Surrey Archaeological Collections,* 1961, 58:1–20.

[32] For two views on analogy, see the articles by Robert Ascher and Raymond H. Thompson reprinted in Brian M. Fagan (ed.), *Introductory Readings in Archaeology,* Boston, 1970, pp. 347–362.

[33] Jan Vansina, *Oral Tradition,* Chicago, 1961, is the standard reference on the methodology of oral history. The same author's *Kingdoms of the Savannah,* Wisconsin, 1966, shows the use of oral records in historical research.

Chapter 2
TIME

[1] Rasmus Nyerup, *Oversyn over Faedrelandets Mindesmaerker fra Oldtiden,* Copenhagen, 1806.

[2] C. J. Thomsen, *Ledestraad til Nordisk Oldkyndighed,* Copenhagen, 1836 (translated by Lord Ellesmere, *A Guide to Northern Archaeology,* London, 1848).

[3] J. J. A. Worsaae, *Danmarks Oldtid,* Copenhagen, 1843.

[4] Edouard Lartet and Henry Christy, *Reliquiae Aquitanicae,* London, 1874.

[5] The Swiss lake dwellings have been described in many publications. Stuart Piggott's *Ancient Europe,* Edinburgh and Chicago, 1965, pp. 57–59, has a short account and bibliography.

[6] For more on this subject, see Glyn E. Daniel's *A Hundred Years of Archaeology,* London, 1950, pp. 85–111, and *The Idea of Prehistory,* London, 1962, pp. 42–61.

[7] N. C. Nelson, *Pueblo Ruins of the Galisteo Basin, New Mexico,* New York, 1914. Manuel Gamio, a student of Franz Boas, carried out stratigraphic excavations in the Valley of Mexico as early as 1909.

[8] Alfred V. Kidder, "An Introduction to the Study of Southwestern Archaeology," *Papers of the Southwestern Expedition*, No. 1, New Haven, 1924.

[9] For some of the latest developments in this field, see Don R. Brothwell and Eric S. Higgs, *Science in Archaeology*, 2nd ed., London, 1969, Sec. 1.

[10] The general question "When was it made?" has been aired by V. Gordon Childe in *Piecing Together the Past*, London, 1956, Chap. 5.

[11] Sir Mortimer Wheeler, *Archaeology from the Earth*, Oxford, 1954, Chap. 4, is the best account of stratigraphy.

[12] Wheeler, *Archaeology*, p. 57 (1956 ed.).

[13] Childe's essay on the "Archaeological Record" in *Piecing Together the Past*, Chap. 3, defines this term.

[14] A good summary of Pleistocene geography and geology for the archaeologist may be found in Karl Butzer, *Environment and Archeology*, London, 1964. Two classic, but somewhat outdated, works are F. E. Zeuner's *Dating the Past*, London, 1946, and *The Pleistocene Period*, London, 1959. K. P. Oakley's *Frameworks for Dating Fossil Man*, London, 3rd ed., 1969, is also very useful. I. W. Cornwall, *Ice Ages*, London and New York, 1970, is a more popular account.

[15] Oakley, *Frameworks*, Chaps. 1–2.

[16] Loess has considerable importance to archaeology, especially to the chronology of the Middle and Upper Paleolithic cultures of Central Europe. Zeuner's *Pleistocene Period*, pp. 24–34, has a good account of periglacial geological phenomena which might serve as a basis for further study.

[17] Oakley, *Frameworks*, Chap. 6.

[18] Coastal shell midden sites are discussed in Chapter 5.

[19] For a summary see C. B. M. McBurney, *The Stone Age of Northern Africa*, Harmondsworth, 1960, pp. 114–121. A later summary of the evidence can be found in P. Biberson's article "Some Aspects of the Lower Palaeolithic of Northwest Africa" in W. W. Bishop and J. Desmond Clark (eds.), *Background to Evolution in Africa*, Chicago, 1967, pp. 447–476.

[20] C. B. M. McBurney and R. G. West, "The Quaternary Deposits at Hoxne, Suffolk, and Their Archaeology," *Proceedings of the Prehistoric Society*, 1954, 20:131–154.

[21] The literature is enormous—F. C. Howell, "Observations on the Earlier Phases of the European Paleolithic," *American Anthropologist*, 1966, 68 (2):88–201 summarizes much of the European material. African sites are covered in part by J. Desmond Clark, *The Prehistory of Africa*, London and New York, 1970.

[22] C. D. Ovey (ed.), "Swanscombe: A Survey of a Pleistocene Site," *Occasional Papers of the Royal Anthropological Institute*, No. 20, 1964.

[23] L. S. B. Leakey, *Olduvai Gorge*, Vol. 1, Cambridge, 1964.

[24] Oakley, *Frameworks*, Chap. 4. An essay on animal bones and the Pleistocene appears in J. M. Coles and E. S. Higgs, *The Archaeology of Early Man*, London, 1969, Chap. 2. For the fluorine dating method see the article by Oakley in Brothwell and Higgs, *Science in Archaeology*, Sec. 1.

[25] Jane Gray and Watson Smith, "Fossil Pollen and Archaeology," *Archaeology*, 1962, 15 (1):16–26.

[26] Oakley, *Frameworks*, Chaps. 3, 11.

[27] Sir Flinders Petrie, "Sequences in Prehistoric Remains," *Journal of the Royal Anthropological Institute*, 1899, 29:295–301. Other relevant literature includes: Childe, *Piecing Together the Past*, Chap. 5, and James Deetz, *Invitation to Archaeology*, New York, 1967, pp. 26–33.

[28] G. W. Brainerd, "The Place of Chronological Ordering in Archaeological Analysis," *American Antiquity*, 1951, 16:301–313.

[29] Owing to space limitations, a number of quite well known but still experimental dating methods have been omitted. See solar radiation in Zeuner, *Pleistocene Period*, pp. 173–207; fission track and obsidian dating, thermoluminescence, in Brothwell and Higgs, *Science in Archaeology*, Sec. 1.

[30] Childe, *Piecing Together the Past*, Chap. 6, contains a detailed account of cross-dating, and "synchronism" in prehistory.

[31] Brian M. Fagan, *Southern Africa during the Iron Age*, London and New York, 1965, contains an account of early trade and the Zimbabwe site.

[32] J. F. Schofield, "Southern African Beads," in Roger Summers, *Inyanga*, Cambridge, 1958, pp. 189–194—a technical article.

[33] J. G. D. Clark, *Prehistoric Europe: The Economic Basis*, London, 1952, pp. 266–269.

[34] B. Bannister, "Dendrochronology," in Brothwell and Higgs, *Science in Archaeology*, pp. 191–205. For an account of the potential of the Bristlecone pine, see G. W. Ferguson, "Bristlecone Pine: Science and Esthetics," *Science*, 1968, 159:839–846.

[35] The literature on thermoluminescence is scattered and mostly technical, but try two articles by D. W. Zimmerman: "Thermoluminescence Dating Using Fine Grains from Pottery," *Archaeometry*, 1971, 13:29–52; and "Thermoluminescent Dating of Upper Palaeolithic Fired Clay from Dolni Věstonice, *Archaeometry*, 1971, 13:53–58. For a brief general account, see E. T. Hall, "Dating Pottery by Thermoluminescence," in Brothwell and Higgs (eds.), *Science in Archaeology*, pp. 106–108.

[36] Discussion of all three techniques will be found in Brothwell and Higgs, *Science in Archaeology*, Chaps. 3–5.

[37] The literature on radiocarbon dating is huge. Try J. R. Arnold and W. F. Libby, "Age Determinations by Radiocarbon Content: Checks with Samples of Known Age," *Science*, 1949, 110:678–680, and also W. F. Libby, *Radiocarbon Dating*, Chicago, 1955, and E. H. Willis, "Radiocarbon Dating" in Brothwell and Higgs, *Science in Archaeology*, pp. 46–57.

[38] The half-life is at present accepted as 5,568 ± 30 by all laboratories, but is liable to correction.

[39] There is a growing literature on this subject. See Hans E. Suess, "Secular Variations of the Cosmic-Ray-Produced Carbon 14 in the Atmosphere and Their Interpretations," *Journal of Geophysical Research*, 1965, 70:23. It has been realized for some time that the radiocarbon dates for historical sites in Egypt were too old (W. F. Libby, "The Accuracy of Radiocarbon Dates," *Science*, 1963, 140:278–280), and the calibration of dendrochronology and radiocarbon dates offers a hopeful way out of the dilemma. The effects of the new research on Old World archaeology have been assessed by Colin Renfrew, "Tree-ring Calibration of Radiocarbon: An Archaeological Evaluation," *Proceedings of the Prehistoric Society*, 1970, 36:280–311. For a typical example of calibration in action, see C. W. Ferguson, B. Huber, and H. E. Suess, "Determination of the Age of Swiss Lake-dwellings as an Example of Dendrochronologically-Calibrated Radiocarbon Dating," *Zeitschrift für Naturforschung*, 1966, 21A, 1173–1177. See also E. K. Ralph and M. C. Han, "Potential of Thermoluminescence in Supplementing Radiocarbon Dating," *World Archaeology*, 1969, 1 (2):157–169.

[40] Potassium argon dating is well covered by W. Gentner, H. J. Lippolt, and J. A. Miller in Brothwell and Higgs, *Science in Archaeology*, Chaps. 6–7. Another useful source is G. Brent Dalrymple and Mason A. Lamphere, *Potassium Argon Dating: Principles, Techniques and Applications to Geochronology*, San Francisco, 1970.

[41] Potassium argon dates for early man are being released with increasing frequency. For a summary of the dates up to 1970, see J. Desmond Clark, *The Prehistory of Africa*, pp. 27–28. New dates are often released in articles in *Nature*. A recent case is *The New York Times* report (February 19, 1971) of a 5.5 million-year-old date for an Australopithecine find—no tools were discovered—from Lothagam, Lake Rudolf, in Kenya. For Old World chronology in general, see Robert W. Ehrich (ed.), *Chronologies in Old World Archaeology*, Chicago, 1965.

[42] R. E. F. Leakey, A. K. Behrensmeyer, F. J. Fitch, J. A. Miller, and M. D. Leakey, "New Hominid Remains and Early Artifacts from Northern Kenya," *Nature*, 1970, 226:223–230. K. P. Oakley, "Pliocene Man," *Antiquity*, 1970, 44 (176):307–308. R. E. F. Leakey, "Further Evidence of Lower Pleistocene Hominids from East Rudolf, Northern Kenya," *Nature*, 1971, 231:245–248. Also F. Vendra, *et al.*, "Preliminary Stratigraphical Studies of the East Rudolf Basin, Kenya," *Nature*, 1971, 231:248–249.

Chapter 3
PRESERVATION AND DISCOVERY

[1] Giovanni Belzoni must be one of the most remarkable characters ever to have turned his hand to archaeology. The quotation is from his *Narrative of the Operations*

and Recent Discoveries within the Pyramids, Temples, Tombs, and Excavations in Egypt and Nubia, London, 1820. A theatrical strong-man turned tomb-robber, Belzoni is well worth an afternoon's reading.

² Brian M. Fagan and F. Van Noten, *The Hunter-Gatherers of Gwisho,* Tervuren, Belgium, 1972.

³ J. Desmond Clark, *The Kalambo Falls Prehistoric Site,* Vol. 2 (in press, 1972).

⁴ P. V. Glob, *The Bog People,* London, 1969, is a popular and fascinating account of the Danish bog corpses.

⁵ Howard Carter, *et al., The Tomb of Tut-ankh-Amen,* London: Vol. 1, 1923; Vol. 2, 1927; Vol. 3, 1933.

⁶ An admirable account of Ancient Egyptian civilization is in Cyril Aldred, *The Egyptians,* London and New York, 1961.

⁷ Jesse D. Jennings, "Danger Cave," *University of Utah Anthropological Papers,* No. 27, 1953.

⁸ Earl H. Morris and Robert F. Burgh, "Basket Maker II Sites near Durango, Colorado." *Carnegie Institution of Washington Publications,* No. 604, Washington, 1954.

For details of the Southwest cultural sequence, see Gordon R. Willey, *Introduction to American Archaeology,* New York, 1966, Vol. 1: *North and Middle America,* Chap. 4, pp. 178–245.

⁹ G. H. S. Bushnell, *Peru,* London, 2nd ed., 1965, gives a succinct and well-illustrated description of Peruvian archaeology.

¹⁰ Herbert W. Dick, "Bat Cave," *School of American Research Monograph,* No. 27, Santa Fe, 1965.

¹¹ R. S. MacNeish, "Ancient Mesoamerican Civilization," *Science,* 1964, 143:531–537.

¹² Bassett Digby, *The Mammoth and Mammoth-hunting in North-East Siberia,* London, 1926.

¹³ The interested reader is referred to Rudenko's monograph for further details: S. I. Rudenko, *Frozen Tombs of Siberia: The Pazyryk Burials of Iron Age Horsemen,* Berkeley, 1970 (translated by M. W. Thompson).

¹⁴ H. B. Collins, *The Archaeology of St. Lawrence Island, Alaska,* Smithsonian Miscellaneous Collections, 96, 1, 1937.

¹⁵ Hedge Larsen and F. G. Rainey, *Ipiutak and the Arctic Whale Hunting Culture,* Anthropological Papers, Vol. 42, American Museum of Natural History, New York, 1948.

¹⁶ A good survey of a wide range of preservative situations is given in J. G. D. Clark's *Archaeology and Society,* Cambridge, 1939, Chap. 3. The examples in the preceding paragraphs are partly drawn from Clark's summary and also from S. J. de Laet, *Archaeology and Its Problems,* London, 1957.

¹⁷ Richard G. Klein, *Man and Culture in the Late Pleistocene,* San Francisco, 1969.

¹⁸ William Camden, *Britannia,* London, 1695 ed., p. 126.

¹⁹ O. G. S. Crawford, *Archaeology in the Field,* London and New York, 1953.

²⁰ O. G. S. Crawford and Alexander Keiller, *Wessex From the Air,* Oxford, 1928, is an early publication on this subject. John Bradford, *Ancient Landscapes: Studies in Field Archaeology,* London, 1957, deals with the Mediterranean area.

²¹ The basic principles of aerial photography in archaeology are enumerated by R. J. C. Atkinson, *Field Archaeology,* London, 1953, pp. 18–29. Infrared photography is still a new technique for archaeology. A sample reference is George J. Gumerman, "Infrared Scanning Images: An Archaeological Application," *Science,* 1969, 164:712–713.

²² Gordon R. Willey, "Prehistoric Settlement Patterns in the Virú Valley, Peru," *Smithsonian Institution, Bureau of American Ethnology, Bulletin* 155, 1953. The relevant passage on aerial photography is on pp. 3–6.

²³ Geoffrey Bibby, *The Testimony of the Spade,* London, 1957, pp. 349–359, has an attractive account of the Gallehus horns. This volume is an interesting introduction to European archaeology and well worth reading.

²⁴ Brian M. Fagan, D. W. Phillipson, and S. G. H. Daniels, *Iron Age Cultures in Zambia—II,* London, 1969, pp. 57–186.

²⁵ The literature is proliferating rapidly, but try Fred Wendorf, *et al., The Prehistory of Nubia,* Dallas, 1968.

[26] L. S. B. Leakey, *Olduvai Gorge, 1931–1951,* Cambridge, 1951, gives an account of early work at Olduvai.

[27] S. J. Laet, *Archaeology and Its Problems,* p. 28.

[28] F. Clark Howell, G. H. Cole, and M. R. Kleindienst, "Isimila. An Acheulian Occupation Site in the Iringa Highlands, Southern Highlands Province, Tanganyika," *Actes du IVe Congrès Panafricain de Préhistoire et de l'étude du Quaternaire, Leopoldville, 1959, Section III—pré- et protohistoire,* Tervuren, Belgium, 1962, pp. 43–80.

[29] Joe Ben Wheat, "A Paleo-Indian Bison Kill," *Scientific American,* January 1967, pp. 44–52.

[30] Brian M. Fagan, *Iron Age Cultures in Zambia—I,* London, 1957, contains a basic description of this area.

[31] The reader is referred to Crawford's *Archaeology in the Field* for further information on field survey. R. F. Heizer's reader, *The Archaeologist at Work,* New York, 1959, contains an important section of examples of site surveys, pp. 186–213.

For techniques of surface collection, see Charles L. Redman and Patti Jo Watson, "Systematic, Intensive Surface Collection," *American Antiquity,* 1970, 35 (3):279–291.

Chapter 4
EXCAVATION

[1] Thomas Wright, "Wanderings of an Antiquary: Part VII," *Gentleman's Magazine,* 1852, p. 569.

[2] Quoted from Glyn E. Daniel's *The Origins and Growth of Archaeology,* London, 1967, pp. 232–233. Some account of the work of Layard, Mariette, and Schliemann can be found in this volume, too.

[3] Carl W. Blegan and others, *Troy,* 4 Vols., Princeton, 1950–58.

[4] General Pitt Rivers, *Excavations in Cranborne Chase,* 1887–98, 4 Vols. Privately printed. His first volume describes his methods.

[5] See Gordon R. Willey's essay in J. O. Brew (ed.), *One Hundred Years of Anthropology,* Harvard, 1968, pp. 29–56.

[6] Sir Mortimer Wheeler's *Archaeology from the Earth,* Oxford, 1954, Chap. 2, contains an arresting account of the history of excavation.

[7] Chapters 4 and 5 are studded with names and examples. Although they all are not referenced, most sites mentioned briefly appear in major works of synthesis.

[8] Handbooks on archaeological excavation include: R. J. C. Atkinson, *Field Archaeology,* London, 1953; R. F. Heizer, *A Guide to Archaeological Field Methods,* Palo Alto, 1966 (3d ed.); and the latest, John Alexander, *The Directing of Archaeological Excavations,* London, 1970.

[9] The Evans family and their work in archaeology have been described by Joan Evans, *Time and Chance,* London, 1943—a fascinating story.

[10] The Minoan civilization is summarized in Sinclair Hood, *The Home of the Heroes: The Aegean before the Greeks,* London and New York, 1967; J. Pendlebury, *The Archaeology of Crete,* London, 1939; M. S. F. Hood, *The Minoans,* London and New York, 1971. Linear B was deciphered by Michael Ventris. See J. Chadwick, *The Decipherment of Linear B.,* Cambridge, 1958.

[11] Wheeler, *Archaeology from the Earth,* 1956 ed., p. 152.

[12] Not covered here are electronic methods of locating subsurface features. Try Alexander, *The Directing of Archaeological Excavations,* pp. 28–30.

[13] This remarkable excavation is mentioned in Chapter 1. See also John Dent, *The Quest for Nonsuch,* London, 1962.

[14] Sampling technique is a comparative newcomer to excavation, but any serious student should read Lewis R. Binford, "A Consideration of Archaeological Research Design," *American Antiquity,* 1964, 29:425–441.

[15] For tools see Atkinson, *Field Archaeology,* pp. 44–49; Alexander, *The Directing of Archaeological Excavations,* pp. 42–45; and Heizer, *A Guide to Archaeological Field Methods,* pp. 32–34.

[16] Recording is admirably covered by Wheeler, *Archaeology from the Earth,* pp. 68–69.

[17] A major controversy arose over Evans's field notes some years ago; see J. Boardman and L. R. Palmer, *On the Knossos Tablets,* Oxford, 1963.

[18] Archaeological surveying is covered in detail by Atkinson in *Field Archaeology,* Chap. 3. Also see Heizer's *Guide,* pp. 21–31.

[19] Wheeler, *Archaeology from the Earth,* pp. 22–37.

[20] Excavation organization on a large scale is covered by Wheeler in *ibid.,* pp. 153–177; on a small scale, by Alexander, *The Directing of Archaeological Excavations,* pp. 17–18.

Chapter 5
EXCAVATION PROBLEMS

[1] John Alexander, *The Directing of Archaeological Excavations,* London, 1970, Chap. 6, has published the only guide to living-floor excavation yet available.

[2] J. G. D. Clark, *Star Carr,* Cambridge, 1954.

[3] B. Klima, *Dolní Věstonice,* Prague, 1963. A more general account of Russian finds can be found in Richard G. Klein, *Man and Culture in the Late Pleistocene,* San Francisco, 1969.

[4] Joe Ben Wheat, "A Paleo-Indian Bison Kill," *Scientific American,* January 1967, pp. 44–52.

[5] A basic reference on hunter-gatherers of great interest to archaeologists is Richard Lee and Irven DeVore (eds.), *Man the Hunter,* Chicago, 1968.

[6] For example, the Gwisho settlements in Zambia. Brian M. Fagan and F. Van Noten, *The Hunter-Gatherers of Gwisho,* Tervuren, Belgium, 1972.

[7] L. S. B. Leakey, *Olduvai Gorge, 1931–1951,* Cambridge, 1951, and F. Clark Howell, *Early Man,* New York, 1965.

[8] L. S. B. Leakey, *Olduvai Gorge,* Vol. 1, Cambridge, 1965.

[9] For a more popular account of the Olduvai discoveries see John Pfeiffer, *The Emergence of Man,* New York, 1969, pp. 72–111.

[10] Glynn L. Isaac, "Studies of Early Culture in East Africa," *World Archaeology,* 1969, 1 (1):1–29.

[11] J. Desmond Clark, *The Kalambo Falls Prehistoric Site,* Cambridge, 1969 and later.

[12] J. Desmond Clark and C. V. Haynes, "An Elephant Butchery Site at Mwanganda's Village, Karonga, Malawi, and Its Relevance to Palaeolithic Archaeology," *World Archaeology,* 1:390–398.

[13] F. Clark Howell, G. H. Cole, and M. R. Kleindienst, "Isimila. An Acheulian Occupation Site in the Iringa Highlands, Southern Highlands Province, Tanganyika," *Actes du IVe Congrès Panafricain de préhistoire et de l'étude du Quaternaire, Leopoldville, 1959, Section III—pre- et protohistoire,* Tervuren, Belgium, 1962, pp. 43–80.

[14] J. Desmond Clark, "The Middle Acheulian Occupation Site at Latamne, Northern Syria," *Quaternaria,* 9, 1967, 10, 1969.

[15] Howell, *Early Man,* pp. 85–99.

[16] E. W. Haury, E. B. Sayles, and W. W. Wasley, "The Lehner Mammoth Site, South-eastern Arizona," *American Antiquity,* 1959, 25:2–30.

[17] For evidence of early hunting sites in the New World, see A. D. Krieger, "Early Man in the New World," in J. D. Jennings and E. Norbeck (eds.), *Prehistoric Man in the New World,* Chicago, 1964, pp. 23–84.

[18] Examples are found in Olduvai Gorge.

[19] The Acheulian floor at Kalambo Falls has evidence of these.

[20] Kalambo Falls, Isimila, Olduvai, Olorgesaillie are only a few examples.

[21] Brian M. Fagan and F. Van Noten, *The Hunter-Gatherers of Gwisho,* Tervuren, Belgium, 1972.

[22] J. Desmond Clark, *The Prehistory of Southern Africa,* Harmondsworth, 1959, Chaps. 8–10.

[23] John Yellen is in the process of reporting on this important project—he has kindly supplied me with some information in advance of publication.

[24] These are vividly illustrated in Howell's *Early Man,* pp. 145–167.

[25] D. A. E. Garrod and Dorothea Bate, *The Stone Age of Mt. Carmel,* Vol. 1, Cambridge, 1937.

[26] Jesse D. Jennings, "Danger Cave," *University of Utah Anthropological Papers No. 27,* 1957.

[27] Jesse D. Jennings, *Prehistory of North America,* New York, 1968, pp. 140–143.

[28] C. B. M. McBurney, *The Haua Fteah (Cyrenaica),* Cambridge, 1967.

[29] C. B. M. McBurney, "First Season's Fieldwork on British Upper Palaeolithic Cave Deposits," *Proceedings of the Prehistoric Society,* 1959, 25:260–269.

[30] This excavation is described in Howell, *Early Man,* pp. 164–165.

[31] For further examples see Chris Musson, "House-plans and Prehistory," *Current Archaeology,* 1970, 2:267–275.

[32] James Mellaart, *Çatal Hüyük,* London and New York, 1967, p. 62.

[33] For further discussion see John Alexander, *The Directing of Archaeological Excavations,* Chap. 7.

[34] A good example is illustrated in Sir Mortimer Wheeler, *Archaeology from the Earth,* Oxford, 1954, Pl. 5.

[35] For sheer complication, nothing rivals London's archaeology. See W. F. Grimes, *The Excavation of Roman and Medieval London,* London, 1968.

[36] Wheeler, *Archaeology from the Earth,* pp. 91–97.

[37] Stuart Piggott, *Ancient Europe,* Edinburgh and Chicago, 1965, p. 52.

[38] *Ibid.,* pp. 147–148.

[39] *Ibid.,* pp. 179–185.

[40] R. J. C. Atkinson, *Field Archaeology,* London, 1953, pp. 65–67.

[41] Ivor Noël Hume, *Historical Archaeology,* New York, 1968, pp. 140–141.

[42] For a discussion of urban archaeology, start with Alexander, Chap. 8, and then peruse *World Archaeology,* Vol. 2, No. 2, October 1970, which deals with a variety of urban problems.

[43] Robber trenches are discussed by Martin Biddle and Birthe Kjolbye-Biddle in "Metres, Areas and Robbing," *World Archaeology,* 1969, 1 (2):208–219.

[44] Andrew and Wendy Selkirk, "Winchester: The Brooks," *Current Archaeology,* 1970, 2:250–255.

[45] Sir Austin Henry Layard, *Nineveh and Its Remains,* London, 1848.

[46] James Mellaart, *The Earliest Civilizations of the Near East,* London and New York, 1965.

[47] Brian M. Fagan, *Iron Age Cultures in Zambia—I,* London, 1967.

[48] Philip Phillips, James A. Ford, and James B. Griffin, "Archaeological Survey in the Lower Mississippi Alluvial Valley," *Papers of the Peabody Museum of American Archaeology and Ethnology,* 1951, Vol. 25. Also see William H. Sears, "The Southeastern United States," in J. D. Jennings and E. Norbeck (eds.), *Prehistoric Man in the New World,* Chicago, 1964, pp. 259–287.

[49] R. J. Braidwood and B. Howe, "Prehistoric Investigations in Iraqi Kurdistan," *Studies in Ancient Oriental Civilization,* Oriental Institute, Chicago, 1960, 31:39.

[50] Mound excavations are common in many parts of the world. See Seton Lloyd, *Mounds of the Near East,* Edinburgh, 1963.

[51] Sir Mortimer Wheeler, *The Indus Civilization,* Cambridge, 1963, and *Early India and Pakistan,* London and New York, 1959.

[52] Paul Ashbee, *The Bronze Age Round Barrow in Britain,* London, 1960, is a standard work on burial mounds.

[53] Paul Ashbee, *The Earthen Long Barrow in Britain,* London, 1970, is a companion volume on these mounds.

[54] Glyn E. Daniel, *The Megalith Builders of Western Europe,* London, 1958, is a standard work.

[55] This system is described by Atkinson, *Field Archaeology,* pp. 65–68.

[56] M. W. Thompson and Paul Ashbee, "Excavation of a Barrow near the Hardy Monument, Black Down, Portesham, Dorset," *Proceedings of the Prehistoric Society,* 1957, 23:124–136.

[57] Population data is discussed by W. W. Howells and H. V. Vallois in two important papers in R. F. Heizer and S. F. Cook (eds.), "The Application of Quantitative Methods in Archaeology," *Viking Fund Publications in Anthropology,* 1960, 28:158–222.

[58] The excavation of cemeteries is discussed by Alexander, *The Directing of Archaeological Excavations,* pp. 215–20.

[59] A simple manual on skeletal excavation is D. R. Brothwell's *Digging Up Bones,* London, 1965.

[60] As an example, the Ingombe Ilede burials from Zambia; see D. W. Phillipson and Brian M. Fagan, "The Date of the Ingombe Ilede Burials," *Journal of African History,* 1969, 10, 2:199–204.

[61] For techniques of preservation in archaeology generally, see H. J. Plenderleith, *The Conservation of Antiquities and Works of Art,* London, 1956.

[62] For a summary of these cultures, see Jennings, *Prehistory of North America,* pp. 191–214.

[63] Sir Mortimer Wheeler, *Maiden Castle, Dorset,* London, 1943.

[64] W. Dehn and E. Sangmeister, "Die Heuneburg bei Tallhof," *Germania,* 1954, 32:22–59.

[65] Wheeler, *Maiden Castle,* pp. 61–68.

[66] Alexander, *The Directing of Archaeological Excavations,* pp. 224–261.

[67] *Ibid.,* pp. 232–233, 228–230.

[68] *Ibid.,* pp. 255–258. For some interesting experimental archaeology, see P. A. Jewell (ed.), *The Experimental Earthwork on Overton Down,* London, 1960.

[69] The literature is enormous. For the more quantitative aspects of shell midden digging, see S. F. Cook and A. E. Treganza, "The Quantitative Investigation of Indian Mounds," *University of California Publications in American Archaeology and Ethnology,* 1950, 40:223–261.

[70] E. W. Gifford, "Composition of California Shellmounds," *University of California Publications in American Archaeology and Ethnology,* 1916, 12:1–29.

[71] W. Shawcross, "Prehistoric Diet and Economy on a Coastal Site at Galatea Bay, New Zealand," *Proceedings of the Prehistoric Society,* 1967, 33 (7):125–130.

[72] Unfortunately this important excavation is still largely unpublished. Try R. R. Inskeep, "University of Capetown Excavations at Plettenberg Bay," *Scientific South Africa,* 1965, 2:12.

[73] Clement Meighan, "The Little Harbor Site, Catalina Island: An Example of Ecological Interpretation in Archaeology," *American Antiquity,* 1959, 24:383–405.

[74] For example, the Annual Reports of the California Archaeological Survey often contain collections of early records of Pacific Coast Indians.

Chapter 6
ENVIRONMENT AND SUBSISTENCE

[1] The basic principles of ecology are enumerated in Eugene P. Odum, *Ecology,* New York, 1963, and numerous other introductory texts.

[2] J. G. D. Clark's *Aspects of Prehistory,* Berkeley, 1970, is a provocative trilogy of essays on human culture as a product of evolution. It is worth reading in this context.

[3] C. B. M. McBurney's *The Haua Fteah (Cyrenaica),* Cambridge, 1967, is a massive report on this important site. The second chapter by E. S. Higgs (pp. 16–44) summarizes the environmental and mammalian evidence. It is a book for advanced students.

[4] See Jesse D. Jennings, *Prehistory of North America,* New York, 1968, for many examples.

[5] The vegetational changes resulting from agriculture are discussed more fully on pp. 170–171, but see Johannes Iversen, "Land Occupation in Denmark's Stone Age," *Danmarks Geologiske Undersøgelse,* II Raekke, 1941, 66:20–26.

[6] J. G. D. Clark, *Star Carr,* Cambridge, 1954, is the classic monograph. It is drawn on extensively in this book.

[7] J. Desmond Clark, *The Kalambo Falls Prehistoric Site,* Vol. 1, Cambridge, 1969.

[8] An early book was J. G. D. Clark, *Archaeology and Society,* London, 1939.

[9] Chronology and classification were primary concerns. See Chapter 11.

[10] J. G. D. Clark, *Archaeology and Society,* pp. 174–177.

[11] This point has been made by J. G. D. Clark in many publications, notably *Prehistoric Europe: The Economic Basis,* London, 1952—a standard work on economic archaeology.

[12] Rodents are not discussed in this book, but they are a fascinating field of research.

Basic references can be obtained from I. W. Cornwall, *Bones for the Archaeologist*, London, 1956.

[13] This important topic has been discussed by Patricia Daly, "Approaches to Faunal Analysis in Archaeology," *American Antiquity*, 1969, 34 (2):146–153.

[14] Cornwall's *Bones for the Archaeologist* is a classic. Less well known, but useful is M. L. Ryder, *Animal Bones in Archaeology*, Oxford, 1969.

[15] There is no substitute for the actual handling of bones to learn how to analyze them. Students seriously interested in such analysis should express this to an archaeologist who handles bones.

[16] Brian M. Fagan and F. Van Noten, *The Hunter-Gatherers of Gwisho*, Tervuren, Belgium, 1972.

[17] For drawings, see Cornwall, *Bones*, Chaps. 4–5.

[18] An excellent example of a Near Eastern faunal report appears in Frank Hole, Kent V. Flannery, and James A. Neely, "Prehistory and Human Ecology of the Deh Luran Plain," *Memoirs of the Museum of Anthropology, University of Michigan*, 1969, 1:262–330.

[19] Even measurements are inadequate, for numerous factors affect growth rates in cattle and buffalo, to say nothing of sexual dimorphism.

[20] The comment in footnote 19 applies.

[21] The reader is referred to the literature for a review of the question. See, for example, Daly, "Approaches to Faunal Analysis."

[22] Richard B. Lee, "The Subsistence Ecology of the !Kung Bushmen," unpublished Ph.D. thesis, University of California, Berkeley, 1965.

[23] Phillip Smith, *Le Solutréen en France*, Paris, 1966.

[24] J. G. D. Clark, *Star Carr*, Cambridge, 1954.

[25] Howard D. Winters, "The Riverton Culture," *Illinois Archaeological Survey Monograph*, No. 1, 1969.

[26] Gordon R. Willey, *An Introduction to American Archaeology*, Englewood, N.J., 1966, 1:26–77.

[27] For an account of Indian Bison hunting, see John C. Ewers, "The Last Bison Drives of the Blackfoot Indians," *Journal of the Washington Academy of Sciences*, 1949, 39 (11):355–360.

[28] F. E. Zeuner, *A History of the Domesticated Animals*, London, 1963, pp. 203–211.

[29] Lee, *Subsistence Ecology*, p. 116.

[30] Wolf Herre, "The Science and History of Domestic Animals," in Don R. Brothwell and Eric S. Higgs (eds.), *Science in Archaeology*, London, 1969, pp. 257–272.

[31] An important information source on research into domesticated animals is Peter J. Ucko and G. W. Dimbleby (eds.), *The Domestication and Exploitation of Plants and Animals*, London and Chicago, 1969. It has been drawn on extensively here.

[32] For a summary, see Charles A. Reed, "The Pattern of Animal Domestication in the Prehistoric Near East," in *ibid.*, pp. 361–380.

[33] Belt Cave—a much quoted example—is vividly described by Carleton Coon, *Seven Caves*, London, 1957, pp. 129–167.

[34] Herre, "The Science and History of Domestic Animals," p. 261.

[35] In practice, this is harder, for the vertebrae are often very fragmentary.

[36] N. de G. Davies, *The Rock Tombs of El Amarna—V*, Archaeological Survey of Egypt, London, 1908.

[37] P. Duxos, "Methodology and Results of the Study of the Earliest Domesticated Animals in the Near East (Palestine)," in Ucko and Dimbleby (eds.), *Domestication and Exploitation*, pp. 265–276, gives an insight into some of the methodology.

[38] Richard Lee makes this point about the !Kung Bushmen (personal communication to the author).

[39] Some vivid artists' reconstructions of early kills appear in F. Clark Howell, *Early Man*, New York, 1965, pp. 94–99.

[40] Theodore White, "Observations on the Butchering Techniques of Some Aboriginal Peoples," *American Antiquity*, 1953, 19 (2):160–164.

[41] Oswald Heer, "Die Pflanzen der Pfahlbauten," *Mittelungen Antiq. Ges.,* Zurich, 1866, 15:310–317.

[42] G. Caton-Thompson and E. W. Gardner, *The Desert Fayum,* London, 1934.

[43] Stuart Struever, "Flotation Techniques for the Recovery of Small Archaeological Remains," *American Antiquity,* 1968, 33:353–362. A general book on vegetal remains is Geoffrey Dimbleby's *Plants and Archaeology,* London, 1967.

[44] Hans Helbaek has written a series of important papers on grain impressions and food plants. A significant one is his Appendix to the Deh Luran monograph "Plant Collecting, Dry-farming, and Irrigation Agriculture in Prehistoric Deh Luran," Ann Arbor, Mich., 1969, pp. 383–427—a full bibliography is appended.

[45] Johannes Iversen, "Land Occupation in Denmark's Stone Age," *Danmarks Geologiske Undersøgelse,* Copenhagen, 1941, II Raekke, 66:20–26.

[46] See Helbaek, "Plant Collecting."

[47] Clark, *Star Carr,* p. 14.

[48] Fagan and Van Noten, *Gwisho.* Reprinted in Brian M. Fagan (ed.), *Introductory Readings in Archaeology,* Boston, 1970, pp. 168–174.

[49] Paul S. Martin, *et al.,* "Mogollon Cultural Continuity," *Fieldiana: Anthropology,* Chicago, 1952, Vol. 40.

[50] Herbert W. Dick, "Bat Cave," *School of American Research Monograph,* Sante Fe, 1965, No. 27.

[51] Jesse D. Jennings, "Danger Cave," *University of Utah Anthropological Papers,* Salt Lake City, 1957, No. 27.

[52] A general discussion occurs in Jennings, *Prehistory of North America,* pp. 139–150.

[53] The most accessible references are R. S. MacNeish, "Ancient Mesoamerican Civilization," *Science,* 1964, 143:531–537, and "The Origins of New World Civilization," *Scientific American,* 1964, 211 (5):29–37.

[54] Stuart Struever, "Woodland Subsistence-Settlement Systems in the Lower Illinois Valley," in Lewis R. and Sally R. Binford (eds.), *New Perspectives in Archeology,* Chicago, 1968, pp. 285–312.

[55] Hole, *et al., Deh Luran,* pp. 23–28.

[56] J. G. D. Clark, *Prehistoric Europe,* pp. 108–109.

[57] Patrick Munson, "Recent Archaeological Research in the Dhar Tichitt Region of South-Central Mauretania," *West African Archaeological Newsletter,* 1968, 10:6–13.

[58] W. C. Darrah, "Technical Contributions to the Study of Archaeological Materials," *American Antiquity,* 1938, 3:269–270.

[59] Iversen, "Land Occupation."

[60] R. L. Kendall, "An Ecological History of the Lake Victoria Basin," *Ecological Monographs,* 1969, 39:121–176.

[61] Richard B. Lee and Irven DeVore (eds.), *Man the Hunter,* Chicago, 1968. Bushmen diet figures are from Dr. Lee.

[62] Thayer Scudder, *The Ecology of the Gwembe Tonga,* Manchester, 1962, is an excellent study of subsistence agriculture, which is relevant here.

[63] Charles F. W. Higham, "Stock Rearing as a Cultural Factor in Prehistoric Europe," *Proceedings of the Prehistoric Society,* 1967, 33 (6):99–103.

[64] Hole, *et al., Deh Luran,* p. 367.

[65] Brian M. Fagan, *Iron Age Cultures in Zambia—I,* London, 1967.

[66] Brian M. Fagan, D. W. Phillipson and S. G. H. Daniels, *Iron Age Cultures in Zambia—II,* London, 1969, pp. 199–205, 254–255.

[67] For an interesting account of tsetse flies and human settlement, see Frank L. Lambrecht, "Aspects of the Evolution and Ecology of Tsetse Flies and Trypanosomiasis in the Prehistoric African Environment," *Journal of African History,* 1964, V (1):1–24.

[68] Published by Steenstrup in the *Proceedings of the Copenhagen Academy,* 1848–55, as part of a committee report on the middens.

[69] Lord John Avebury, *Prehistoric Times,* London, 1865.

[70] Hildegarde Howard, "The Avifauna of Emeryville Shellmound," *University of California Publications in Zoology,* Berkeley, 1929, 32, 378–383.

[71] Fagan, *Iron Age Cultures,* p. 75. For a review of birds in archaeology, see Elliot

W. Dawson, "Bird Remains in Archaeology" in Brothwell and Higgs (eds.), *Science in Archaeology*, pp. 359–375.

[72] J. G. D. Clark, *Prehistoric Europe*, p. 44.

[73] *Ibid.*, pp. 44–45.

[74] Jennings, *Prehistory of North America*, pp. 125–127.

[75] J. G. D. Clark, *Prehistoric Europe*, p. 47.

[76] For illustrations, see F. Bordes, *The Old Stone Age*, London and New York, 1968, Fig. 59.

[77] J. Scheffer, *The History of Lappland*, Oxford, 1674 (translation).

[78] Fagan and Van Noten, *Gwisho*.

[79] Chester King, Thomas Blackburn, and Ernest Chandonet, "The Archaeological Investigation of Three Sites on the Century Ranch, Western Los Angeles County, California," *California Archaeological Survey Annual Report*, 1968, 10:12–161.

[80] The site has been studied by the author; the report is not yet published.

[81] R. Raven-Hart, *Before Van Riebeeck*, Capetown, 1967, p. 100.

[82] See footnote 61.

[83] Robert M. Crabtree, *et al.*, "Archaeological Investigations at Batiquitos Lagoon, San Diego County," *California Archaeological Survey Annual Report, 1962–3*, Los Angeles, 1963, pp. 319–462.

[84] J. G. D. Clark, *Prehistoric Europe*, pp. 241–243.

[85] D. J. Mulvaney, *The Prehistory of Australia*, London and New York, 1969, Fig. 19.

[86] Brian M. Fagan, "Early Trade and Raw Materials in South Central Africa," *Journal of African History*, 1969, 10 (1):1–14.

[87] J. Desmond Clark, *The Prehistory of Southern Africa*, Harmondsworth, 1959, p. 217.

[88] P. Vinnecombe, "A Fishing Scene from the Tsoelike River, Southeastern Basutoland, *South African Archaeological Bulletin*, 1960, 15:15–19.

[89] J. Desmond Clark, "A Note on Early River-craft and Fishing Practices in South-east Africa," *South African Archaeological Bulletin*, 1960, 15:77–79.

[90] S. H. Warren, "On a Prehistoric Interment near Walton-on-Naze," *Essex Naturalist*, 1911, 16:198–208.

[91] P. V. Glob, *The Bog People*, London, 1969, is a fascinating account of bog corpses in Denmark.

[92] Jennings, "Danger Cave."

[93] R. F. Heizer, "Analysis of Human Coprolites from a Dry Nevada Cave," *Reports of the University of California Archaeological Survey*, 1967, 70:1–20. Also see his "The Archaeology of Prehistoric Great Basin Coprolites," in Brothwell and Higgs (eds.), *Science in Archaeology*, pp. 244–250.

[94] E. O. Callen, "Diet as Revealed by Coprolites," in Brothwell and Higgs (eds.), *Science in Archaeology*, pp. 235–243.

[95] R. F. Heizer, "Physical Analysis of Habitation Residues," in R. F. Heizer and S. F. Cook (eds.), "The Application of Quantitative Methods in Archaeology," *Viking Fund Publications in Anthropology*, 1960, 28:93–102.

[96] An account of early Australian stoneworking occurs in A. W. Howitt, *The Native Tribes of South-East Australia*, London, 1904, pp. 311–312, 340–341. Also see Mulvaney, *Prehistory of Australia*, pp. 170–171.

[97] J. G. D. Clark, *Prehistoric Europe*, pp. 244–251, summarizes research on this topic.

[98] A. C. Renfrew, J. E. Dixon, and J. R. Cann, "Obsidian and Early Cultural Contact in the Near East," *Proceedings of the Prehistoric Society*, 1966, 32, 1–29, and subsequent articles.

[99] Horace Beck and J. F. Schofield, "Beads," in Roger Summers, *Inyanga*, Cambridge, 1958, pp. 180–229.

[100] See Willey, *An Introduction to American Archaeology*, 1:261, for further references.

[101] J. G. D. Clark, *Prehistoric Europe*, pp. 261–266.

[102] Stuart Piggott, *Ancient Europe*, Edinburgh and Chicago, 1965, pp. 137–138.

[103] For this and further examples, see F. Hole and R. F. Heizer, *An Introduction to Prehistoric Archaeology*, New York, 1969, pp. 292–296.

Chapter 7
TECHNOLOGY AND ARTIFACTS

[1] J. G. D. Clark, *Prehistoric Europe*, London, 1952, p. 171.

[2] Parts of this chapter draw again on J. G. D. Clark's *Aspects of Prehistory*, Berkeley, 1970.

[3] The principles of stoneworking have been described in more detail in F. Clark Howell, *Early Man*, New York, 1965, pp. 101–108. Several excellent films on stoneworking have been released; among the best are two produced by the University of California, Berkeley.

[4] An interesting example of this type of natural fracture was described by J. Desmond Clark, "The Natural Fracture of Pebbles from the Batoka Gorge, Northern Rhodesia, and Its Bearing on the Kafuan Industries of Africa," *Proceedings of the Prehistoric Society*, 1958, 24:64–77.

[5] Perfect "pebble tools" have been made by throwing flint cobbles into a cement mixer!

[6] Dr. L. S. B. Leakey has often demonstrated the efficiency of Stone Age tools for dismembering game. See L. S. B. Leakey, "Exploring 1,750,000 Years into Man's Past," *National Geographic*, October 1961, pp. 586–587.

[7] A summary of the controversy occurs in M. C. Burkitt, *The Old Stone Age*, Cambridge, 1955, pp. 103–111.

[8] A. S. Barnes, "Les Outils de l'homme tertiaire en Angleterre. Etude critique," *L'Anthropologie*, 1938, 47.

[9] M. D. Leakey, *Olduvai Gorge*, Vol. 3, Cambridge, 1971.

[10] Four good summary articles deal with hand-axe industries: F. Clark Howell and J. Desmond Clark, "Acheulian Hunter-Gatherers of Sub-Saharan Africa," in F. Clark Howell and François Bourlière (eds.), "African Ecology and Human Evolution," *Viking Fund Publications in Anthropology*, 1963, 36:458–533; J. Desmond Clark, "Acheulian Occupation Sites in the Middle East and Africa: A Study in Cultural Variability," *American Anthropologist*, 1966, 68 (2):202–229; F. Clark Howell, "Observations on the Earlier Phases of the European Lower Paleolithic," *American Anthropologist*, 1966, 68 (2):88–201; D. A. Roe, "The British Lower and Middle Palaeolithic: Some Problems, Methods of Study and Preliminary Results," *Proceedings of the Prehistoric Society*, 1964, 30:245–267.

[11] For a description of this technique, see Howell, *Early Man*, p. 112.

[12] Indian blade- and pressure-flaking has been described by several observers, and a summary of the early literature is in W. H. Holmes, *Handbook of Aboriginal American Antiquities*, Pt. 1, Introductory: The Lithic Industry, Bureau of American Ethnology, Bulletin 60, 1919.

For a lighthearted look at stoneworking, see H. Mewhinney, *A Manual for Neanderthals*, Houston, 1957.

[13] J. G. D. Clark, *Aspects of Prehistory*, pp. 70–79.

[14] Howell, *Early Man*, pp. 114–115.

[15] For the microburin technique, see J. G. D. Clark, *The Mesolithic Age in Britain*, Cambridge, 1932, Appendix 1.

[16] William H. Townsend, "Stone and Steel Tool Use in a New Guinea Society," *Ethnology*, 1969, 8 (2):199–205.

[17] J. G. D. Clark, *World Prehistory*, Cambridge, 1969, Chap. 11.

[18] G. de Mortillet, *Le Préhistorique*, Paris, 1883.

[19] The Bushmen's stoneworking methods were vividly described by George Stow, *The Native Tribes of South Africa*, Capetown, 1905.

[20] The Brandon flintmakers fabricated gunflints for flintlock guns, and were still doing good business until recent years. Rainbird Clark, "The Flint-Knapping Industry at Brandon," *Antiquity*, 1935, 9:38–56.

Another account of gunflint-making is D. W. Phillipson's "Gunflint manufacture in North-western Zambia," *Antiquity*, 1969, 43:301–304.

[21] The films were released by the University of California, Berkeley.

[22] Quantitative methods for studying stone implements have a long history, and the literature is enormous. An early and much used method is that of François Bordes, "Principes d'une methode d'étude des techniques et de la typologie du Paléolithique ancien et moyen," *L'Anthropologie*, 1950, 54:19–34. A. C. Spaulding's essay "Statistical Techniques for the Study of Artifact Types," *American Antiquity*, 1953, 18 (4):305–313, is essential reading for those concerned with this aspect of archaeology. Multivariate analyses are now widely used, and the reader is advised to consult an archaeologist working in this area if he wants up-to-date information. Spaulding's "The Dimensions of Archaeology," in Gertrude E. Dole and Robert L. Carneiro (eds.), *Essays in the Science of Culture in Honor of Leslie A. White*, New York, 1960, pp. 437–456, is also relevant.

[23] S. A. Semenov, *Prehistoric Technology*, London, 1964 (trans. by M. W. Thompson).

[24] Charles M. Keller, "The Development of Edge Wear Patterns on Stone Tools," *Man*, 1966, 1 (4):501–511.

[25] See references in footnote 10.

[26] J. Desmond Clark, *The Kalambo Falls Prehistoric Site*, Vol. 2, Cambridge, 1972.

[27] Illustrated by J. G. D. Clark, *Aspects of Prehistory*, p. 66.

[28] J. Desmond Clark, *The Prehistory of Southern Africa*, Harmondsworth, 1959, pp. 86–89.

[29] Brian M. Fagan and F. Van Noten, *The Hunter-Gatherers of Gwisho*, Tervuren, Belgium, 1972.

[30] A summary occurs in J. D. Jennings, *Prehistory of North America*, New York, 1968, pp. 247–286.

[31] Gosta Montell, *Dress and Ornaments in Ancient Peru*, Goteborg, 1929.

[32] Sir Leonard Woolley's description of the Royal Tombs at Ur-of-the-Chaldees is rightly famous: *Ur Excavations, Publications of the Joint Expedition of the British Museum and of the Museum of the University of Pennsylvania to Mesopotamia*, London, 1934, Vol. 2, *The Royal Cemetery*, pp. 33–38, 41–42.

[33] An introduction to European Bronze Age typology can be obtained from Stuart Piggott, *Ancient Europe*, Edinburgh and Chicago, 1965—where numerous references will be found.

[34] R. A. Dart, *The Osteodontokeratic Culture of Australopithecus prometheus*, Pretoria, 1957.

[35] Donald L. Wolberg, "The Hypothesized Osteodontokeratic Culture of the Australopithecinae: A Look at the Evidence and the Opinions," *Current Anthropology*, 1970, 11 (1):23–38. Also, C. K. Brain, "Bone Weathering and the Problem of Bone Pseudotools," *South African Journal of Science*, 1967, 63 (3):97–99; and "Hottentot Food Remains and Their Bearing on the Interpretation of Fossil Bone Assemblages," *Scientific Papers of the Namib Desert Research Station, Pretoria, South Africa*, 1967, 32 (6):1–7.

[36] M. D. Leakey, "Preliminary Survey of the Cultural Material from Beds I and II, Olduvai Gorge, Tanzania," in W. W. Bishop and J. Desmond Clark (eds.), *Background to Evolution in Africa*, Chicago, 1967, pp. 417–446.

[37] F. Bordes, *The Old Stone Age*, New York, 1968.

[38] Gordon R. Willey, *An Introduction to American Archaeology*, New York, 1966, 1:42–43.

[39] P. Graziosi, *Palaeolithic Art*, London, 1960, contains illustrations of the most important pieces.

[40] J. G. D. Clark, *Star Carr*, Cambridge, 1954, pp. 115–119.

[41] H. B. Collins, "The Archaeology of St. Lawrence Island, Alaska," *Smithsonian Miscellaneous Collections*, 1937, 96:1.

[42] A recent summary is Gary A. Wright's "Origins of Food Production in Southwestern Asia: A Survey of Ideas," *Current Anthropology*, 1971, 12 (45):447–478.

[43] For Tehuacán, see R. S. MacNeish, "The Origins of New World Civilization," *Scientific American*, 1964, 211:29–37.

For the remarkable Japanese discoveries, see Richard E. Morlan, "The Perceramic Period of Hokkaido: An Outline," *Arctic Anthropology*, 1967, 4:164–220; Kensaku Hayashi, "The Fukui Microblade Technology and Its Relationships in Northeast Asia and North America," *Arctic Anthropology*, 1968, 5:128–190.

[44] Alfred V. Kidder, *An Introduction to the Study of Southwestern Archaeology with a Preliminary Account of the Excavations at Pecos*, New Haven, 1924.

[45] F. R. Matson, "Ceramics and Man," *Viking Fund Publications in Anthropology*, No. 41, 1965, is a recent corpus on the subject.

[46] Brian M. Fagan, *Iron Age Cultures in Zambia—I*, London, 1967.

[47] Anna O. Shepard, *Ceramics for the Archaeologist*, Washington, D.C., 1965, is a classic on pottery, but definitely a technical monograph.

[48] Nuclear fingerprinting of pottery is another promising method being developed in the United States.

[49] F. Asaro and I. Perlman, "Deduction of Provenience of Pottery from Trace Element Analysis," *Lawrence Radiation Laboratory*, Berkeley, 1967.

[50] Basic references on metallurgy include R. J. Forbes, *Studies in Ancient Technology*, London, 1955–58; R. F. Tylecote, *Metallurgy in Archaeology*, London, 1962.

[51] M. E. L. Mallowan, *Early Mesopotamia and Iran*, London and New York, 1965.

[52] For early metallurgy in Europe, see Piggott, *Ancient Europe*, pp. 71–112.

[53] J. G. D. Clark, *Prehistoric Europe*, pp. 183–204.

[54] Jan Vansina, *Kingdoms of the Savannah*, Madison and London, 1966.

[55] Willey, *An Introduction to American Archaeology*, 1:261.

[56] J. G. D. Clark, *Prehistoric Europe*, pp. 189–194.

[57] Roger Summers, *Ancient Mining in Rhodesia*, Salisbury, 1969.

[58] For the early history of ironworking in the Old World, Stuart Piggott's *Ancient Europe* is a fruitful source of references.

[59] Brian M. Fagan and Roland Oliver, "The Emergence of Bantu Africa," in *The Cambridge History of Africa*, Vol. 2 (to be published).

[60] Iron and copper smelting techniques have not received the attention that they should. Tylecote has summarized some smelting methods, and African metallurgy has been described by several authors. See J. H. Chaplin, "Notes on Traditional Smelting in Northern Rhodesia," *South African Archaeological Bulletin*, 1962, 16 (63):53–60.

[61] Piggott, *Ancient Europe*, pp. 185 ff.

[62] F. Hole and R. F. Heizer, *An Introduction to Prehistoric Archaeology*, New York, 1969, p. 167. V. Gordon Childe's *Piecing Together the Past*, London, 1956, Chap. 7, contains an excellent discussion of classification in archaeology.

[63] The concept of "type" has been the subject of lengthy controversy in New World archaeology, and to a lesser extent in European circles. The literature is bulky and sometimes acrimonious. A few references include Irving Rouse, "The Classification of Artifacts in Archaeology," *American Antiquity*, 1960, 25 (3):313–323; Albert C. Spaulding, "Statistical Techniques"; J. A. Ford, "A Comment on A. C. Spaulding, 'Statistical Techniques. . . ,'" *American Antiquity*, 1954, 19:390–391; J. A. Ford, "On the Concept of Types," *American Anthropologist*, 1954, 56:42–54; A. D. Krieger, "The Typological Concept," *American Antiquity*, 1944, 9:271–288.

[64] James Deetz, *Invitation to Archaeology*, New York, 1967, p. 51.

[65] *Ibid.*, pp. 45–49.

[66] A major discussion of advanced taxonomic methods is found in David Clarke's *Analytical Archaeology*, London, 1968, Chaps. 11–14.

[67] This example drawn from James Deetz's *Invitation to Archaeology*, pp. 45–48, is by far the most articulate discussion of this point so far published.

[68] To learn classification, there is no substitute for actually handling artifacts—interested readers should get involved in some analytical research in a nearby laboratory if possible.

Chapter 8
ORDERING AND INTERPRETATION

[1] John Evans, "On the Date of British Coins," *Numismatic Chronicle*, 1849–50, 12:127.

[2] Flinders Petrie, "Sequences in Prehistoric Remains," *Journal of the Royal Anthropological Institute*, 1899, 29:295–301.

[3] J. J. A. Worsaae, *The Primeval Antiquities of Denmark*, London, 1849 (translation of Danish edition, Copenhagen, 1843).

[4] John Rowe, "Worsaae's Law and the Use of Grave Lots for Archaeological Dating," *American Antiquity*, 1962, 28:129–137.

[5] Frank Roy Hodson, "The La Tène Cemetery at Munsingen-Rain: Catalogue and Relative Chronology," *Acta Bernensia,* V, Bern, 1968.

[6] James Deetz, *Invitation to Archaeology,* New York, 1967, pp. 26–33. Edwin Dethlefsen and James Deetz, "Death's Heads, Cherubs and Willow Trees: Experimental Archaeology in Colonial Cemeteries," *American Antiquity,* 1966, 31:502–510.

[7] See, for example, Robert C. Dunnell, "The Seriation Method and Its Evaluation," *American Antiquity,* 1970, 35 (3):305–319; F. Hole and M. Shaw, "Computer Analysis of Chronological Seriation," *Rice University Studies,* 1967, 53:3; and L. Johnson, "Item Seriation as an Aid for Elementary Scale and Cluster Analysis," *Bulletin of the Museum of Natural History, University of Oregon,* Eugene, 1968, No. 15.

[8] For sampling procedure, see F. Hole and R. F. Heizer, *An Introduction to Prehistoric Archaeology,* New York, 1969, pp. 139–140.

[9] A pungent description of the role of distribution maps in archaeology is in V. Gordon Childe, *Piecing Together the Past,* London, 1956, pp. 115–122.

[10] V. Gordon Childe, *Prehistoric Migrations in Europe,* Oslo, 1950, p. 2.

[11] Fundamental reading on archaeological units is contained in Gordon R. Willey and Philip Phillips, *Method and Theory in American Archaeology,* Chicago, 1958, pp. 11–43. This important book explores the subject in depth and should be read by all students seriously interested in archaeology.

[12] *Ibid.,* pp. 16–17.

[13] W. C. McKern, "The Midwestern Taxonomic Method as an Aid to Archaeological Culture Study," *American Antiquity,* 1939, 4:301–313.

[14] J. G. D. Clark, *Aspects of Prehistory,* Berkeley, 1970.

[15] Clyde Kluckhohn and William Kelly, "The Concept of Culture," in Ralph Linton (ed.), *The Science of Man in the World Crisis,* New York, 1945, pp. 78–106, quote, p. 97.

[16] V. Gordon Childe, "Neolithic House-types in Temperate Europe," *Proceedings of the Prehistoric Society,* 1949, 15:77–86. Quote, p. 81.

[17] This section draws extensively from two works: Childe's *Piecing Together the Past* and Bruce Trigger's *Beyond History: The Methods of Prehistory,* New York, 1968, pp. 26–47. The latter is abundantly referenced.

[18] K. P. Oakley, "Fire as a Palaeolithic Tool and Weapon," *Proceedings of the Prehistoric Society,* 1955, 21:36–48.

[19] Stuart Piggott, *Ancient Europe,* Edinburgh and Chicago, 1965, Chap. 5.

[20] J. G. D. Clark, *Prehistoric Europe,* London, 1952, pp. 266–269. There has been recent discussion about manufacture of British faience beads—some think they were made locally.

[21] Alfred L. Kroeber, *Anthropology,* New York, 1948, is a major corpus of this great anthropologist's work.

[22] Deetz, *Invitation to Archaeology,* pp. 55–59.

[23] Leslie Spier, "The Sun Dance of the Plains Indians," *Anthropological Papers of the American Museum of Natural History,* 1921, 16:7.

[24] Brian M. Fagan, *Southern Africa,* London and New York, 1965, pp. 100–135.

[25] The Indus Civilization made use of coolie labor. See Sir Mortimer Wheeler, *Early India and Pakistan,* London and New York, 1959, Chap. 5.

[26] Hole and Heizer's *An Introduction,* pp. 331–339, has been drawn on here.

[27] Lewis R. Binford, et al., "Archaeology at Hatchery West," *Memoirs of the Society for American Archaeology,* 1970, 24.

[28] *Ibid.,* p. 89.

[29] Another example is the Carter Ranch work by William Longacre, discussed in Chapter 9. See William A. Longacre, "Some Aspects of Prehistoric Society in East-Central Arizona," in Lewis R. and Sally Binford (eds.), *New Perspectives in Archeology,* Chicago, 1968, pp. 89–102.

[30] James Deetz, "The Inference of Residence and Descent Rules from Archeological Data," in Binford and Binford, *New Perspectives,* pp. 41–48.

[31] James Deetz, "The Dynamics of Stylistic Change in Arikara Ceramics," *Illinois Studies in Anthropology,* 1965, No. 4.

[32] The Shang Civilization (1766–1122 B.C.) is discussed by W. Watson, *China before the Han Dynasty*, London, 1961; and Chinese urban archaeology in general, by Paul Wheatley, "Archaeology and the Chinese City," *World Archaeology*, 1970, 2 (2):159–185.

[33] Lewis R. Binford, "Archaeology as Anthropology," *American Antiquity*, 1962, 28 (2):217–225. Brian M. Fagan, D. W. Phillipson, and S. G. H. Daniels, *Iron Age Cultures in Zambia—II*, London, 1969, contains an account of the Ingombe Ilede burials, some of which were adorned with rich grave goods.

[34] John Alexander has described some problems connected with the excavation of such sites. *The Directing of Archaeological Excavations*, London, 1970, Chap. 9.

[35] P. Graziosi, *Palaeolithic Art*, London, 1960.

[36] P. J. Ucko, "The Interpretation of Prehistoric Anthropomorphic Figurines," *Journal of the Royal Anthropological Institute*, 1962, 92:38–54.

[37] A. Leroi-Gourhan, *Treasures of Prehistoric Art*, New York, 1967.

[38] The most famous example of astronomical archaeology is undoubtedly Stonehenge. G. S. Hawkins, *Stonehenge Decoded*, New York, 1965, is a monograph that prompted a lively controversy: R. J. C. Atkinson, "Moonshine on Stonehenge," *Antiquity*, 1966, pp. 212–216.

[39] Clark suggested that some red deer antler frontlets from the site were akin to the headdresses worn by Mongolian shamans. J. G. D. Clark, *Star Carr*, Cambridge, 1954, pp. 168–172.

[40] W. J. Sollas, *Ancient Hunters*, London, 1911.

[41] S. I. Rudenko, "The Ancient Culture of the Bering Sea and the Eskimo Problem," *Arctic Institute of North America—Anthropology of the North: Translations from Russian Sources/No. 1*, University of Toronto Press, 1961, pp. 163–164.

[42] *Ibid.*, p. 165.

[43] M. A. Smith, "The Limitations of Inference in Archaeology," *Archaeological Newsletter*, 1955, 6:3–7.

[44] Among others, see K. C. Chang, "Major Aspects of the Interrelationship of Archeology and Ethnology," *Current Anthropology*, 1967, 8 (34):227–243; and Christopher Hawkes, "Suggestions from the Old World," *American Anthropologist*, 1954, 56:155–168.

[45] R. H. Thompson, "The Subjective Element in Archaeological Inference," *Southwestern Journal of Anthropology*, 1956, 12 (3):327–332. See also Robert Ascher, "Analogy in Archaeological Interpretation," *Southwestern Journal of Anthropology*, 1961, 17 (4):317–325.

[46] See Julian H. Steward, "The Direct Historical Approach to Archaeology," *American Antiquity*, 1942, 7:337–343; Christopher Hawkes, "Archaeological Theory" and W. D. Strong, "Historical Approach in Anthropology," in Alfred L. Kroeber (ed.), *Anthropology Today*, Chicago, 1953.

[47] J. C. Harrington, "Evidence of Manual Reckoning in the Cittie of Ralegh," *The North Carolina Historical Review*, 1956, 33:1.

[48] Hawkes, "Archaeological Theory."

[49] Sir Mortimer Wheeler, *Maiden Castle*, London, 1943, pp. 126–129.

[50] Jesse D. Jennings, "The Desert West," in J. D. Jennings and E. Norbeck (eds.), *Prehistoric Man in the New World*, Chicago, 1964, pp. 149–174.

[51] Lewis R. Binford, "Smudge Pits and Hide Smoking: The Role of Analogy in Archaeological Reasoning," *American Antiquity*, 1967, 32 (1):1–12.

[52] James N. Hill, "Broken K. Pueblo: Prehistoric Social Organization in the American Southwest," *Anthropological Papers, University of Arizona*, 1970, No. 18.

Chapter 9
SETTLEMENT ARCHAEOLOGY

[1] Sir Samuel Baker, *The Albert Nyanza*, London, 1866, 1:150.

[2] The recent volume *Settlement Archaeology*, edited by K. C. Chang (Palo Alto, 1968), has been drawn on extensively in writing this chapter. The book is strongly recommended both for further reading and references.

[3] Gordon R. Willey, "Prehistoric Settlement Patterns in the Virú Valley," *Bureau of American Ethnology, Bulletin No. 155*, Washington, D.C., 1953.

⁴ Bruce C. Trigger's important contribution to the Chang volume, "The Determinants of Settlement Patterns," in *Settlement Archaeology*, pp. 53–78, is used to a considerable extent in this chapter. Quote, p. 55.

⁵ Good descriptions of such dwellings are to be found in Richard G. Klein, *Man and Culture in the Late Pleistocene*, San Francisco, 1969.

⁶ Barrie Reynolds, *The Material Culture of the Gwembe Tonga*, Manchester, 1967.

⁷ George Silberbauer, *Bushman Survey Report*, Gaberones, 1965.

⁸ C. Daryll Forde, *Habitat, Economy, and Society*, London, 1934.

⁹ For discussion, see Trigger, "Determinants," pp. 55–60.

¹⁰ M. D. Coe, *The Maya*, New York, 1967.

¹¹ Brian M. Fagan, *Southern Africa*, London and New York, 1965, pp. 82–84, 121–122.

¹² James Mellaart, *The Earliest Civilizations of the Near East*, London and New York, 1965, p. 107.

¹³ Cyril Aldred, *The Egyptians*, London and New York, 1961, pp. 182–183.

¹⁴ G. P. Murdock, *Social Structure*, New York, 1949, p. 79.

¹⁵ M. E. L. Mallowan, *Early Mesopotamia and Iran*, London and New York, 1965.

¹⁶ Neville Chittick, "Kilwa and the Arab Settlement of the East African Coast," *Journal of African History*, 1963, 4 (2):179–190.

¹⁷ R. S. MacNeish, "Iroquois Pottery Types," *National Museum of Canada Bulletin*, 1952, No. 124.

¹⁸ Sir Mortimer Wheeler, *The Indus Valley Civilization*, Cambridge, 1960.

¹⁹ George L. Cowgill, "Computer Analysis of Archaeological Data from Teotihuacán, Mexico, in Lewis R. and Sally R. Binford (eds.), *New Perspectives in Archeology*, Chicago, 1968, pp. 143–150. Also see René Millon, "Teotihuacán: Completion of Map of Giant Ancient City in the Valley of Mexico," *Science*, 1970, 170:1077–1082.

²⁰ William A. Longacre, "Some Aspects of Prehistoric Society in East-Central Arizona," in Binford and Binford (eds.), *New Perspectives*, pp. 89–102.

²¹ *Ibid.*, p. 89.

²² *Ibid.*, p. 91.

²³ *Ibid.*

²⁴ *Ibid.* Final report: *Archaeology as Anthropology*, Tucson, 1970.

²⁵ For a distribution map of the tsetse fly in Africa, see J. Desmond Clark (ed.), *Atlas of African Prehistory*, Chicago, 1967.

²⁶ Audrey I. Richards, *Land, Labour and Diet among the Bemba of Northern Rhodesia*, Oxford, 1937, pp. 228–350.

²⁷ Mosheshwe was a fascinating character. See E. Casalis, *Les Bassoutos*, Paris, 1859, and Leonard Thompson and Monica Wilson (eds.), *Oxford History of South Africa*, Oxford, 1969, 1:398 ff.

Chapter 10
INTELLECTUAL FRAMEWORKS:
MERCATI TO DURKHEIM

¹ Julian H. Steward and Frank M. Setzler, "Function and Configuration in Archaeology," *American Antiquity*, 1938, 4 (1):4–10.

² Michael Mercati, *Metallotheca*, 1717.

³ A delightful account of the discovery of the South Seas and of the "Noble Savage" was written by Alan Moorehead, *The Fatal Impact*, London, 1966. Marvin Harris, *The Rise of Anthropological Theory*, New York, 1968, Chaps. 2–3, has been used extensively in writing this part of the text. His discussion of eighteenth-century thought is valuable.

⁴ See J. W. Burrow, *Evolution and Society*, New York, 1966.

⁵ Gustav Klemm, *Allgemeine Cultur-Geschichte der Manscheit*, Leipzig, 1843.

⁶ Loren Eiseley, *Darwin's Century*, New York, 1958, is an invaluable history of the roots of Darwinism.

⁷ See Chapter 1.

⁸ Charles Darwin, *The Origin of Species*, London, 1859.

⁹ *Ibid.*, p. 275. Many years later, Darwin wrote the *Descent of Man*, London, 1871, in which he explored human evolution.

[10] Herbert Spencer, *Social Statistics*, London, 1855, p. 27.

[11] Gabriel de Mortillet, *Promenades Préhistoriques á l'Exposition Universelle*, Paris, 1867.

[12] Henry A. Layard, *Nineveh and Its Remains*, London, 1849.

[13] J. L. Stephens, *Incidents of Travel in Central America: Chiapas and Yucatan*, New York, 1841.

[14] The most celebrated acceptance of the art was that Emil Cartailhac, "Les Cavernes ornées de dessins: La grotte d'Altamira. Mea culpa d'un sceptique," *L'Anthropologie*, 1901, 12:671.

[15] The descriptions of Tylor, Durkheim, and Boas in this book have been drawn extensively from Abram Kardiner and Edward Preble, *They Studied Man*, New York, 1961.

[16] Edward Tylor, *Anahuac*, London, 1861.

[17] Edward Tylor, *Anthropology*, London, 1881, p. 275 (pagination from Ann Arbor edition, 1960).

[18] Gordon R. Willey, "A Hundred Years of American Archaeology," in J. O. Brew (ed.), *One Hundred Years of Anthropology*, Cambridge, 1968, pp. 29–56.

[19] J. J. A. Worsaae, *The Primeval Antiquities of Denmark*, London, 1849.

[20] Edward Tylor, *Researches into the Early History of Mankind*, London, 1865. Chapter 6 contains a discussion of this point. Quote, p. 3.

[21] Ably discussed by Glyn E. Daniel, *The Idea of Prehistory*, London, 1962, Chap. 5.

[22] Kardiner and Preble, *They Studied Man*, pp. 95–116.

[23] Quoted from *ibid.*, p. 102.

[24] Malinowski was a remarkable character. See *ibid.*, pp. 140–162.

[25] *Ibid.*, p. 151. For an assessment of Malinowski's work, see Clyde Kluckhohn, "Bronislaw Malinowski, 1884–1942," *Journal of American Folklore*, 1943, 56:208–219. Also see Bronislaw Malinowski, *A Scientific Theory of Culture and Other Essays*, London, 1944.

[26] A. R. Radcliffe-Brown, *Structure and Function in Primitive Society*, New York, 1952.

Chapter 11

TOWARD EXPLANATION: 1900 TO THE 1970s

[1] Franz Boas, "The Central Eskimo," *Smithsonian Institution, Bureau of Ethnology, Annual Report No. 6, 1884–5*, 1888, pp. 399–669. Quote, p. 21.

[2] Boas's greatest book was the *Mind of Primitive Man*, New York, 1911. He published a series of his most important papers in *Race, Language and Culture*, New York, 1940. His descriptive work appears in, among other publications, *The Handbook of American Indians*, Washington, D.C. For a biography, see M. J. Herskovits, *Franz Boas: The Science of Man in the Making*, New York, 1953.

[3] Franz Boas, "Archaeological Investigations in the Valley of Mexico by the International School, 1911–12," *Proceedings of the Eighteenth International Congress of Americanists*, London, 1913, pp. 176–179.

[4] W. D. Strong, "An Introduction to Nebraska Archeology," *Smithsonian Miscellaneous Collections*, 1935, Vol. 93, No. 10.

[5] Alfred L. Kroeber was another great gatherer of basic information on the American Indian. One of his most magisterial works was his edited "Handbook of the Indians of California," *Bureau of American Ethnology*, Washington, D.C., Bulletin 78, 1925.

[6] This account of V. Gordon Childe has been drawn from his own "Retrospect," *Antiquity*, 1958, 32:69–74, and Stuart Piggott's "The Dawn and an Epilogue," *Antiquity*, 32:75–79.

[7] V. Gordon Childe, *The Dawn of European Civilization*, London, 1925, Preface.

[8] Childe, "Retrospect," p. 70.

[9] *Ibid.*

[10] J. H. Plumb, *The Death of the Past*, London, 1969, p. 136.

[11] J. G. D. Clark, *World Prehistory: A New Outline*, Cambridge, 1969, and Chester Chard, *Man in Prehistory*, New York, 1968.

[12] For Childe's own assessment of this episode in his life, see "Retrospect," pp. 71–72.

[13] Childe's own admission—see "Retrospect," p. 72.

[14] V. Gordon Childe, *Social Evolution,* London, 1951, p. 3.

[15] Leslie White's work is not discussed in this volume, but see Leslie White, *The Evolution of Culture,* New York, 1959.

[16] W. C. McKern, "The Midwestern Taxonomic Method as an Aid to Archaeological Culture Study," *American Antiquity,* 1939, 4 (4):301–313.

[17] See the essay by Gordon R. Willey, "Horizon Styles and Pottery Traditions in Peruvian Archaeology," *American Antiquity,* 1945, 11:49–56.

[18] J. A. Ford and Gordon R. Willey, "An Interpretation of the Prehistory of the Eastern United States," *American Anthropologist,* 1941, 43 (3):325–363; J. B. Griffin, "Culture Change and Continuity in Eastern United States," in F. Johnson (ed.), *Man in Northeastern North America,* Andover, 1946, pp. 37–95.

[19] Gordon R. Willey and Philip Phillips, *Method and Theory in American Archaeology,* Chicago, 1958.

[20] Again see Gordon R. Willey, "One Hundred Years of American Archaeology," in J. O. Brew (ed.), *One Hundred Years of Anthropology,* Cambridge, 1968, pp. 29–56.

[21] Childe's syntheses are still widely read. Apart from *The Dawn,* the most famous are: *The Most Ancient East,* London, 1928; *The Danube in Prehistory,* Oxford, 1929; *The Bronze Age,* Cambridge, 1930; *New Light on the Most Ancient East,* London, 1934; *Man Makes Himself,* London, 1936; *What Happened in History,* Harmondsworth, 1942; *Prehistoric Migrations in Europe,* Oslo, 1950; *Social Evolution,* London, 1951; *Piecing Together the Past,* London, 1956.

[22] Robert J. Braidwood and B. Howe, *Prehistoric Investigations in Iraqi Kurdistan,* Chicago, 1960. R. M. Adams, *The Evolution of Urban Society,* Chicago, 1966, is another important reference.

[23] Gordon R. Willey, *An Introduction to American Archaeology,* Vol. 1, New York, 1966.

[24] Childe, "Retrospect," p. 74.

[25] J. G. D. Clark, *Star Carr,* Cambridge, 1954.

[26] W. W. Taylor, *A Study of Archaeology,* Menasha, 1948.

[27] See the commentary by Willey in "One Hundred Years," pp. 51–52.

[28] Gordon R. Willey, "Settlement Archaeology: An Appraisal," in K. C. Chang (ed.), *Settlement Archaeology,* Palo Alto, 1968, pp. 208–226, is an important reference, as are the brief comments on p. 52 of "One Hundred Years."

[29] See Chapter 9.

[30] Julian H. Steward, *Theory of Culture Change,* Urbana, 1963, p. 3.

[31] *Ibid.,* p. 4.

[32] *Ibid.,* p. 7.

[33] *Ibid.*

[34] *Ibid.,* p. 34.

[35] One example of the determinist approach is that of Betty Meggers. For a synthesis, see her *Ecuador,* London and New York, 1965.

[36] Stuart Piggott, *Approach to Archaeology,* New York, 1965, pp. 4–5, contains a rather pessimistic statement.

[37] The results of some recent work were summarized in Lewis R. and Sally R. Binford (eds.), *New Perspectives in Archeology,* Chicago, 1968. See also David L. Clarke, *Analytical Archaeology,* London, 1968.

[38] Lewis R. Binford, "Archaeological Perspectives," in Binford and Binford, *New Perspectives,* pp. 5–32.

[39] *Ibid.,* p. 22. Another important reference is by the same author, "Archaeology as Anthropology," *American Antiquity,* 1962, 28 (2):217–225.

[40] A. D. Hall and R. E. Fagen, "Definition of System," *General Systems Yearbook,* 1956, 1:18.

[41] James Doran, "Systems Theory, Computer Simulations and Archaeology," *World Archaeology,* 1970, 1 (3):289–298, quotation from p. 290. This paper is a "must" for all archaeologists, and comes from the pen of a computer scientist concerned with archaeology.

[42] Clarke, *Analytical Archaeology,* p. 43.

[43] Lewis R. Binford, "Systematics and Cultural Process," *American Antiquity,* 1965, 31 (2):209.

[44] The relevant paper is Kent V. Flannery, "Archaeological Systems Theory and Early Mesoamerica," in Betty Meggers (ed.), *Anthropological Archaeology in the Americas,* Washington, D.C., 1968, pp. 67–87. Quote, p. 68.

[45] James W. Judge, "Systems Analysis and the Folsom-Midland Question," *Southwestern Journal of Anthropology,* 1970, 1:40–51.

[46] F. Hole and R. F. Heizer, *An Introduction to Prehistoric Archaeology,* New York, 2nd ed., 1970, p. 385.

[47] In addition to Clarke's book and Doran's paper, the following papers on systems theory may be of interest: Kenneth E. Boulding, "General Systems Theory—the Skeleton of Science," *Management Science,* 1966, 2:197–208. Ludwig von Bertalanffy, "General System Theory," *General Systems Yearbook,* 1956, 1:1–10.

An important paper on explanation in archaeology is Albert C. Spaulding's "Explanation in Archaeology," in Binford and Binford, *New Perspectives,* pp. 33–40.

[48] Binford, "Archaeological Perspectives," p. 26.

[49] *Ibid.*

Chapter 12
CONCLUSION

[1] Charles Kingsley, *The Water Babies,* London, 1863, p. 153 (pagination from 1910 ed.).

[2] *Tarikh,* a journal published in West Africa, is designed to acquaint schoolteachers with the latest results of archaeological and historical research in Africa.

[3] Brian M. Fagan "Review of A. J. Bruwer, *Zimbabwe: Rhodesia's Ancient Greatness,*" *Antiquity,* 1970, 3:320.

[4] This remark is attributed to President Banda and is a fitting note upon which to end this book.

Bibliography of Area Archaeologies

To give a comprehensive list of area archaeologies in the limited space available is impossible. In general, English language references predominate, on the assumption most readers of this text are English-speaking. The rate of archaeological publication is such that some works have inevitably been missed. The Ancient Peoples and Places Series (Thames and Hudson, London, and Praeger, New York) is recommended as a source of accurate and scientific information on area archaeology; the volumes are comparatively inexpensive.

WORLD ARCHAEOLOGIES

Chard, Chester. *Man in Prehistory.* New York, 1968.
Clark, Grahame (J. G. D.). *World Prehistory: A New Outline.* Cambridge, 1969.

AFRICA

Clark, J. Desmond. *The Prehistory of Africa.* London and New York, 1970.

ARCTIC

Bandi, M. G. *Eskimo Archaeology.* London, 1969 (originally published in German, 1964).
Giddings, J. L. *Ancient Men of the Arctic.* London and New York, 1967.
Mathiassen, T. *Archaeology of the Central Eskimos.* Copenhagen, 1927.

AUSTRALIA

Mulvaney, D. J. *The Prehistory of Australia.* London and New York, 1969.

CHINA

Chang, Kwang-Chih. *The Archaeology of Ancient China.* New Haven, 1963.
Watson, W. *China.* London and New York, 1959.

EGYPT

Aldred, Cyril. *The Egyptians.* London and New York, 1961.

EUROPE

General Surveys

Clark, J. G. D., and Stuart Piggott. *Prehistoric Societies.* London and New York, 1965.
Roe, Derek. *Prehistory.* London and Berkeley, Calif., 1970.
Thomas, Homer I. *Near Eastern, Mediterranean, and European Chronology.* Lund, 1967.
The archaeological literature of Europe is scattered in publications in many languages. The references given here are those most readily available to Americans. Information on more up-to-date literature should be obtained from archaeologists working in the field.

Stone Age

Bordes, F. *The Old Stone Age.* New York, 1968.
Coles, John, and E. S. Higgs. *The Archaeology of Early Man.* London, 1969.
Both volumes cover other areas of the world as well.

Neolithic and Later

Clark, J. G. D. *Prehistoric Europe: The Economic Basis.* London, 1952.
Piggott, Stuart. *Ancient Europe.* Edinburgh and Chicago, 1965.
Both volumes have some coverage of earlier archaeology.

INDIA AND PAKISTAN

Wheeler, Sir Mortimer. *Early India and Pakistan.* London and New York, 1959.

JAPAN

Kidder, J. E. *Japan.* London and New York, 1959.
The Kidder volume is somewhat outdated. Recent numbers of *Arctic Anthropology* are recommended for information on the pre-ceramic cultures of Japan. It is advisable to contact a specialist before starting a detailed study of Japanese archaeology.

NEAR EAST

Lloyd, S. *Early Highland Peoples of Anatolia.* London and New York, 1967.
Mallowan, M. E. L. *Early Mesopotamia and Iran.* London and New York, 1965.
Mellaart, James. *The Earliest Civilizations of the Near East.* London and New York, 1966.

NORTH AMERICA AND MESOAMERICA

Coe, M. D. *Mexico.* London and New York, 1962.
Coe, M. D. *The Maya.* London and New York, 1966.
Jennings, J. D. *Prehistory of North America.* New York, 1968.
Sanders, William T., and Barbara J. Price. *Mesoamerica: The Evolution of a Civilization.* New York, 1968.
Willey, Gordon R. *Introduction to American Archaeology.* Vol. I: *North and Mesoamerica.* Englewood Cliffs, N.J., 1966.
Wormington, H. M. *Ancient Man in North America.* Denver, 1957.

PACIFIC OCEAN AREA AND NEW ZEALAND

Freeman, J. D., and W. R. Geddes (eds.). *Anthropology in the South Seas.* New Plymouth, N.Z., 1959.
Golson, J., and P. Gathercole. "New Zealand Archaeology." *Antiquity,* 1962, 36:168–174, 271–278.
Sharp, A. *Ancient Voyages in the Pacific.* London, 1957.
Suggs, R. C. *The Island Civilization of Polynesia.* New York, 1960.

SIBERIA

Michael, Henry N. *The Archaeology and Geomorphology of Northern Asia.* Toronto, 1964.
Okladnikov, A. P. *The Ancient Peoples of Siberia and Its Cultures.* London, 1959.

Rudenko, Sergei I. *The Ancient Cultures of the Bering Sea and the Eskimo Problem*. Toronto, 1961.
Rudenko, Sergei I. *Frozen Tombs of Siberia: The Pazyryk Burials of Iron Age Horsemen* (trans. by M. W. Thompson). Berkeley, 1970.

SOUTH AMERICA

Bushnell, G. H. S. *Peru*. London and New York, 1963 (2nd ed.).
Griffin, J. B. "Handbook of South American Indians." *Bureau of American Ethnology Bulletin*, 1946, No. 143.
Lathrap, Donald W. *The Upper Amazon*. London and New York, 1970.
Meggers, Betty J. *Ecuador*. London and New York, 1965.
Willey, Gordon R. *Introduction to American Archaeology*, Vol. 2: *South America*. Englewood Cliffs, N.J., 1971.

SOUTHEAST ASIA

There are numerous articles about this area. See the bibliography in J. G. D. Clark, *World Prehistory*, p. 314.

UNION OF SOVIET SOCIALIST REPUBLICS

Klein, Richard. *Man and Culture in the Late Pleistocene*. San Francisco, 1969.
Mongait, A. *Archaeology in the U.S.S.R.* London, 1959.
Rice, T. T. *The Scythians*. London and New York, 1957.
Sulimirski, Tadeusz. *Prehistoric Russia: An Outline*. London, 1970.

UNITED STATES

General Surveys

Bushnell, G. H. S. *The First Americans*. London and New York, 1968.
Sanders, William T., and Joseph Marino. *New World Prehistory*. New York, 1970.

Glossary

(Those technical terms defined in the text are not included here.)

Absolutist: despotic.
Ake: a shrub (antique English).
Arroyo: a gully.
Articular end: the process at the end of a bone, which serves as the joint.
Artifact: any object manufactured or modified by man.
Assemblage: all the industries at one site.
Attribute: a well-defined feature found on an artifact.

Barrow: a burial mound.
Burin: a blade tool, flaked on either or both ends to form a small chisel or grooving tool.
Byre: a cow shed.

Cambium: a viscid substance lying under the bark of trees, in which the annual growth of wood and bark takes place.
Component: the manifestation of a given archaeological focus at a specific site (*focus* or *phase* in the Willey and Phillips sense—see *Phase*).
Conchologist: one who studies shells.
Coprolite: petrified excrement.
Core: in archaeology, a lump of stone from which humanly struck flakes have been removed.
Cultigen: a cultivable plant.
Cultural anthropology: those aspects of anthropology focusing on cultural facets of human societies—a term widely used in the United States.
Culture: similar assemblages found at several sites, defined in a context of time and space.

Culture trait: an item, element, or feature in an archaeological (or anthropological) culture.

Cusp: a projection on the crown of a tooth.

Datum point: a reference point on an archaeological site, normally surveyed onto a large-scale map, and used as a base point for all measurements on the site.

Dendrochronology: tree-ring chronology.

Detritus: debris or droppings.

Downcutting: erosion of a river channel by water action.

Epigrapher: one who studies inscriptions.

Epiphysis: articular end of a long bone, a process that fuses at adulthood.

Escarpment: a hill range or cliff (a geological term).

Ethnography: a descriptive study, normally an in-depth examination of a particular culture.

Ethnology: a cross-cultural study of particular aspects of various cultures, usually theoretically based.

Exogamy: a rule requiring marriage outside a social or cultural unit (*endogamy* means the opposite).

Extrasomatic: outside the body.

Faience: glazed terracotta.

Fibula: a brooch.

Fire setting: a technique for quarrying stone by using fire to shatter the outcrops of rock.

Focus: approximately equivalent to a phase.

Fuller: a clothmaker.

Functional type: an archaeological classification based on the supposed function of the artifact concerned.

Geochronology: geological dating.

Glacial eustasy: the adjustments made in sea levels and the earth's crust as a result of the expansion and contraction of Pleistocene ice sheets.

Heuristic: serving to find out; a means of discovery.

Historiography: the writing of history.

Hominid: a member of the family Hominidae, represented by a single genus *Homo sapiens.*

Homotaxial: strata or cultures that have the same relative position, but are not necessarily contemporaneous.

Horizon: "a primarily spatial continuity represented by cultural traits and assemblages whose nature and mode of occurrence permit the assumption of a broad and rapid spread."—Willey and Phillips, *Method and Theory in American Archaeology,* Chicago, 1958, p. 33.

Hydrology: the scientific study of water—its properties and laws.

Industry: all artifacts of one particular kind (viz., bone, stone, or wood) found at one site, made at the same time, by the same population.

Innominate bones: pelvis and scapula.

Knapper: a stoneworker.

Lactation: the secretion of milk from mammary glands.

Lense: a term used in stratigraphic interpretation to mean a thin line of deposit such as a "sand lense" which is often of minor significance relative to the major layers. On small sites, lenses can sometimes assume greater importance.

Loess: windblown glacial sand.

Matriarchal society: family authority rests with the woman's family.

Matrilocal society: married couples live with or near the wife's mother.

Mica: a mineral, occurring in a glittering scaly form, widely prized for ornamental purposes.

Midden: a deposit of occupation debris, rubbish, or other by-products of human activity.

Monotheistic: a religion recognizing one god.

Moraine: a deposit of debris left by an advancing or retreating glacier.

Obsidian: black volcanic glass.

Ossification: the fusion of a limb bone with its articular end. Also used to imply stagnation, or calcification of soft tissue into bone-like material.

Osteologist: one who studies bones.

Paleobotanist: one who studies prehistoric botany.

Paleoecology: the study of ecology in ancient times.

Paleontology: the study of fossil (or ancient) bones.

Palynology: pollen analysis.

Patrilocal society: married couples live with or near the husband's father.

Pedology: the scientific study of soil.

Periglacial: surrounding a glacial area.

Permafrost: permanently frozen subsoil.

Phase: "an archaeological unit possessing traits sufficiently characteristic to distinguish it from all other units similarly conceived, whether of the same or other cultures or civilizations, spatially limited to the order of magnitude of a locality or region and chronologically limited to a relatively brief interval of time."—Willey and Phillips, *Method and Theory,* p. 22.

Physical anthropology: basically biological anthropology, it includes the study of fossil man, genetics, primates, and blood groups, among other subjects.

Potsherd: a fragment of a clay vessel.

Quaternary era: the last great subdivision of geological time, of which the Pleistocene is a part.

Revetment: a retaining wall supporting an earthwork.

Seriation: ordering.

Social anthropology: the British equivalent for cultural anthropology, but with an emphasis on sociological factors.

Spore: pollen grain.

Stalagmite: a cement-like deposit formed over long periods of time in caves. Stalagmite often seals layers of occupation deposit, especially in limestone caves.

Stela or *stele:* a column or stone slab often with an inscribed or sculptured surface.

Strandlooper: a beachcomber, or shellfish eater.

Superposition: the deposition of one stratum on another.

Tectonic: a term referring to the earth's crust; tectonic movement is an earthquake.

Tell: a mound; a term used to refer to archaeological sites of this type in the Near East.

Tempering: a process for hardening iron blades, involving heating and rapid cooling.

Tradition: in archaeological terms, "a [primarily] temporal continuity represented by persistent configurations in single technologies or other systems of related forms."—Willey and Phillips, *Method and Theory,* p. 37.

Trypanosomiasis: sleeping sickness.

Tsetse: a fly that carries trypanosomiasis. Because of belts of tsetse fly country in Africa, inhabitants are prevented from raising cattle.

Tuff: volcanic lava.

Type fossil: a tool type characteristic of a particular "archaeological era," an outdated concept borrowed from geology.

Typology: classification of artifacts in archaeology.

Unaerated: not exposed to the open air.

Unilineal evolution: evolution in a single direction, without branching.

Unit: in archaeological terms, an artificial taxonomic grouping used for description of artifacts.

Votive: intended as an offering as a result of a vow.

Index

(Page numbers in italics indicate illustrations)